Contemporary Japanese

Contemporary Japanese

AN INTRODUCTORY TEXTBOOK
FOR COLLEGE STUDENTS

Volume 1

by Eriko Sato, Ph.D.

TUTTLE PUBLISHING
Boston • Rutland, Vermont • Tokyo

Published by Tuttle Publishing, an imprint of Periplus Editions (HK) Ltd.,
with editorial offices at 153 Milk Street, Boston, Massachusetts 02109 and
130 Joo Seng Road, #06-01/03, Singapore 368357.

ISBN 0-8048-3377-X
ISBN 4-8053-0799-4 (for sale in Japan only)

Distributed by:

North America, Latin America & Europe
Tuttle Publishing
364 Innovation Drive
North Clarendon, VT 05759-9436
Tel: (802) 773 8930; Fax (802) 773 6993
Email: info@tuttlepublishing.com
www.tuttlepublishing.com

Japan
Tuttle Publishing
Yaekari Building, 3rd Floor
5-4-12 Osaki, Shinagawa-ku
Tokyo 141-0032
Tel: (03) 5437 0171; Fax: (03) 5437 0755
Email: tuttle-sales@gol.com

Asia Pacific
Berkeley Books Pte. Ltd.
130 Joo Seng Road, #06-01/03
Singapore 368357
Tel: (65) 6280 1330; Fax: (65) 6280 6290
Email: inquiries@periplus.com.sg
www.periplus.com

08 07 06 05 6 5 4 3 2 1

Printed in Singapore

The following publisher has generously given permission to use their clickart images:
From Hataraku Jinbutsu Irasutoshu (Working People illustration Collection) by 株式会社 エム・ピー・シー (MPC, Inc).

Contents

About the Author vii

Preface viii

Structure of this Textbook x

Orthography xii

Introduction xiii

Chapter One
Basic Sounds, Words, Phrases and Kana 1

Lesson 1 : Familiar Japanese Words and Phrases for Gratitude 2
Lesson 2 : Words for Japanese Food and Phrases for Introduction 4
Lesson 3 : Numbers in Japanese and Phrases for Greeting 6
Lesson 4 : Classroom Expressions............................... 8
Lesson 5 : Words for Body Parts and Phrases for Apology 10
Lesson 6 : Words for Family Members and Phrases for Getting Attention 12
Lesson 7 : Names of Japanese Cities and Phrases for Small Talk 14

Chapter Two
Identifying Things and People 25

Lesson 8 : 私は日本人です Home Countries..26
Lesson 9 : せんこうは何ですか Academic Major..28
Lesson 10 : それはわえいじてんですか Things in the Classroom.............................30
Lesson 11 : あのたてものは何ですか Campus 32

Chapter Three
Describing Things and People 41

Lesson 12 : あの人は私の母です Family 42
Lesson 13 : 大学のえいごの先生です Attributes 44
Lesson 14 : あれはだれのですか Ownership 46

Chapter Four
Using Numbers and Katakana 51

Lesson 15 : でんわばんごう Telephone Numbers 52
Lesson 16 : 今、何年生ですか Age and Academic Year............................ 54
Lesson 17 : 今、何時ですか Time.. 56
Lesson 18 : それはいくらですか Shopping 58
Lesson 19 : カタカナ Katakana Characters................................ 60
Lesson 20 : がいらいご Loan Words 62

Chapter Five
Coming and Going 71

Lesson 21 : An Overview of Japanese Verb Conjugation 72
Lesson 22 : 今日はクラスに行きますか Today's Plan..74
Lesson 23 : デパートに行きませんか Weekend Plans 76
Lesson 24 : カラオケ・バーにはよく行きますか Nightlife.. 78

Chapter Six
Describing Daily-life Activities............................ 89

Lesson 25 : 大学には何で来ますか Daily Commute 90
Lesson 26 : みそしるは何で飲みますか Dining at a Restaurant...............................92
Lesson 27 : どこで朝ごはんを食べましたか Breakfast 94
Lesson 28 : ひまなときは何をしますか Pastime Activity 96

Chapter Seven
Location of People and Things......................... 105

Lesson 29 : 山田さんはどこにいますか Campus 106
Lesson 30 : 本やは近くにありますか Neighborhood... 108
Lesson 31 : ヒーターはどこにありますか Things in Your Room.................................. 110
Lesson 32 : ていきゅうびは金曜日です Days of the Week 112

Chapter Eight
Expressing What You Have 119
Lesson 33 : ノートが３冊あります
Things in Your Bag or Colors 120
Lesson 34 : へやにはつくえと本ばこがあります
Things in Your Room............................... 122
Lesson 35 : 私は兄が２人います
Family 124
Lesson 36 : 明日はしけんがあります
Daily Schedule... 126

Chapter Nine
Describing the Property of Things and People 133
Lesson 37 : どんなたてものですか
Describing Buildings 134
Lesson 38 : リーさんのへやはどうですか
Describing Rooms 136
Lesson 39 : 日本語はむずかしくありません
Foreign Languages.................................. 138

Chapter Ten
Requesting 145
Lesson 40 : Te-forms 146
Lesson 41 : テープをかして下さい
Request 148
Lesson 42 : もう少しきれいに書いて下さい
Manners... 150
Lesson 43 : この道をまっすぐ行って下さい
Giving Directions 152

Chapter Eleven
Expressing the Characteristics of People and Things 161
Lesson 44 : かのじょは目がきれいです
Appearance of People.............................. 162
Lesson 45 : おみやげは何がいいですか
Souvenir 164
Lesson 46 : 何がとくいですか
Skills and Preferences.............................. 166
Lesson 47 : カタカナで名前が書けますか
Abilities and Potentials 168
Lesson 48 : 何が一ばんほしいですか
Desire 170
Lesson 49 : しょうらいは何をしたいですか
Your Future.. 172

Chapter Twelve
Talking About the Past 183
Lesson 50 : 夏休みはどこかへ行きましたか
Vacation.. 184
Lesson 51 : 私のたんじょうびは１２月２４日です
Dates and Time 186
Lesson 52 : あのレストランはどうでしたか
Dining Experiences.................................. 188
Lesson 53 : 兄弟とけんかしたことがありますか
Experiences... 190

Chapter Thirteen
Relating States and Events 201
Lesson 54 : 難しくて、たいへんです
College Courses 202
Lesson 55 : 昨日はテレビを見て、ねました
Listing Activities 204
Lesson 56 : かぜをひいて、クラスを休みました
Causes and Results 206

Chapter Fourteen
Talking About Now 213
Lesson 57 : なおきくんがわらっていますよ
Ongoing Events 214
Lesson 58 : 父はびょういんでいしゃをしています
Occupation 216
Lesson 59 : うちの子供は遊んでばかりいます
Extreme Habit.. 218
Lesson 60 : おさけを飲んでいますね
Resulting State 220
Lesson 61 : ティーシャツを着ている人です
Clothing 222

Challenge
(Chapter One to Chapter Fourteen).................. 231

Appendix One
Hiragana and Katakana 234

Appendix Two
Verbs and Adjectives 238

Appendix Three
Counter List 241

Appendix Four
Vocabulary Collection 245

Appendix Five
Kanji List 253

Appendix Six
Basic Vocabulary List 255

Appendix Seven
Note List 266

About the Author

Professor Eriko Sato has been teaching Japanese over a decade at the State University of New York at Stony Brook, where she received her Ph.D. degree in linguistics in 1996. She is the Founding Director of the Pre-college Japanese Language Program, the Executive Director of the Japan Center, and a lecturer of the Department of Asian and Asian American Studies at the State University of New York at Stony Brook. Her linguistic study focuses on semantics, syntax, phonology and morphology, and her major interest is in developing new methods of teaching Japanese as a foreign language and as a heritage language. Her research interests also include comparative analyses of English and Japanese in terms of formal linguistics, pragmatics, psycholinguistics, sociolinguistics and principles of translation. She is the author of *Japanese for Dummies* (2002) and *Japanese Phrases for Dummies* (2004).

Preface

Contemporary Japanese: An Introductory Textbook for College Students is designed for beginning students of the Japanese language at the university level. It is a classroom text, but can be an effective self-study text if used with the accompanying audio CDs and Teacher's Guide. This textbook introduces about 1,000 basic vocabulary words that are essential for daily life and campus life, over 250 basic kanji characters, basic grammar including passive and causative constructions, and basic cultural information that is the key to the understanding of various speech styles and conversational interactions. It helps the students quickly build the foundation necessary for tackling various real-life Japanese-speaking situations in neutral and polite contexts, without overwhelming them with too advanced honorific speech styles, too colloquial potentially-offensive informal speech styles, or too advanced kanji characters. Yet, it provides useful tips and additional information including the modern trend of language use. After completing this textbook, the students are ready to pursue the specific area of their interest while improving their general proficiency in Japanese. This comprehensive textbook is characterized by a unique "multi-vitamin-style" organization and an innovative "Guess and Try" method of learning.

The text consists of 26 chapters, each of which has a distinct general objective. Each chapter has several lessons, and there are a total of 106 lessons in the entire textbook. Each lesson serves as a nucleus of the textbook, and includes a full course of learning processes (observation, analysis, practice and performance) and the four language skills (speaking, listening, reading and writing), focusing on a single communicative objective. All the materials of each lesson are compactly placed on two facing pages, and are designed to be completed in one (or two) class sessions. This one-lesson-in-one-class format makes the objective of each class clear, and gives the students the feeling of achievement at the end of each class. Furthermore, the students can apply a little bit of all of the four skills in a balanced way in every class, without losing the objective of the class and without being limited to one aspect of language learning. It is like taking a "multi-vitamin" tablet daily, rather than taking vitamin C on Monday and vitamin E on Wednesday. This makes each class period stimulating and multifaceted, and helps the students to stay curious, lively and assertive during the class. As they accumulate a number of completed lessons, they can feel a strong sense of progress. Important points found in the lessons are thoroughly and clearly explained in grammar, usage, culture and writing notes at the end of each chapter, and they are reinforced and integrated in review questions.

Another characteristic of this textbook is found in the innovative and effective way of teaching the rules and facts of the Japanese language. This textbook does not spoonfeed the rules and facts. Instead, it introduces them by a unique method, the "Guess and Try" method. In each lesson, the students first observe a real-life conversation. Translation is highly limited in this program. Then, they are asked to "guess" what was going on in the dialog, using logic and open-mindedness, and to try out what they have guessed. As they work on the "Guess and Try" section, the students become curious, and eventually discover interesting facts and important generalizations themselves, either naturally, or by being surprised at an unexpected fact or generalization. Compared with being spoonfed these rules and facts by hearing a lecture or reading a written explanation, discovering them through guessing and trying makes the learning process fun and extremely challenging, and effective for the students. When one is curious, new information can be absorbed easily, just as when one is hungry, food can be digested easily. As shown in psychological studies, the guessing and trying process minimizes the time needed both for the acquisition and retention of language rules and facts. After the students understand the new rules and facts through "Guess and Try," they proceed to practice them in drill sections, and then to make use of them through a number of interesting communicative tasks, which can be done in pairs, small groups, or as a whole class activity. By performing these tasks, the students can engage in real-life situations for different communicative purposes. At this stage, they can experience the joy of learning Japanese, since Japanese becomes their tool for communication, rather than their master. The advantage of this system is that they can apply their knowledge to real contexts, and experience the delight of using Japanese in every class, or every lesson. In addition, what they do in each class or lesson, namely, continuous observation, guessing, trying, and using what they discover, is what they will be doing when they learn Japanese by being in a Japanese-speaking situation, outside the classroom. The students are encouraged to continue studying Japanese with pleasure, as this book truly makes their learning experience an enjoyable one.

Acknowledgment

This book project started in 1993, when I was inspired to develop the "Guess and Try" methodology by the course "Structure of Japanese" that I taught with Richard Larson at the State University of New York (SUNY) at Stony Brook. I am very grateful to Richard for giving me this precious opportunity. Many special thanks to Shigeru Miyagawa of MIT for giving me valuable advice on how to pursue this project at its early stage. Since then, this project has been supported by many people at SUNY-Stony Brook. I thankfully acknowledge the warm encouragement from Sachiko Murata, S.N. Sridhar and Mark Aronoff, the insightful comments from the Japanese instructors, Eva Nagase, Hiroko Yamakido, Etsuko Maruoka-Ng and Naoko Takahashi, and the dedicated assistance and continuous support of Leslie Cloper and Pieter Van Volkenburgh. My sincere appreciation also goes to Kenji Higaki, Yuri Ichihara, Megan Roth-Ueno, Tomotaka Umemura and Hiroko Yamakido for assisting me in the creation of the accompanying audio CDs, to Susan Carter for the illustrations of this book, and to Jeff Brown, Ray Chen, Mike Falk, Russel Gulizia, Mimu Tsujimura, Anthony Pelosi and all of the other students and my teaching assistants for their valuable input.

Many people at Tuttle Publishing, especially the Acquisition Editor, Flavia Hodges and the Production Editor, Doreen Ng, also deserve my heartfelt appreciation for their professionalism in making this textbook a reality.

Last, but not least, I would like to thank my husband, Yimei, our daughter, Anna and my parents in Japan for their never ending support.

Eriko Sato, Ph.D.
State University of New York at Stony Brook
Fall 2004

Structure of this Textbook

This textbook has a total of 26 chapters in 2 volumes. Each chapter has sections called “Lessons”, “Grammar and Usage”, “Culture”, “Writing”, “Kanji List”, “Review” and “Tips and Additional Knowledge”, with a few exceptions.

Each lesson is presented on two facing pages as in the illustration, and contains the following:

- “Notes Relating to This Lesson” lists the note numbers and brief titles of all the grammar, usage, culture and writing explanations relevant to each lesson, in a little box located at the upper left corner of the left page.
- The “note-link”, in the form of individual note numbers, is specified for each relevant part in the lesson (for example, [2], Ⓐ) for the convenience of the students.
- “Basic Vocabulary and Kanji” introduces the required vocabulary and kanji. The required vocabulary are listed in a three-columned table, where the first column specifies the item in hiragana or katakana. An accent mark is provided for content words. The second column specifies how the item is written in kanji, what its conjugation category is if it is a verb (for example *k*-**u**, *i*-**ru**), and what its basic conjugation forms are if it is a verb or an adjective. The following is the list of verb conjugation category specifications:

e-**ru** : a **ru**-verb whose root ends in the vowel e
i-**ru** : a **ru**-verb whose root ends in the vowel i
r-**u** : an **u**-verb whose root ends in the consonant r
k-**u** : an **u**-verb whose root ends in the consonant k
g-**u** : an **u**-verb whose root ends in the consonant g
s-**u** : an **u**-verb whose root ends in the consonant s
m-**u** : an **u**-verb whose root ends in the consonant m
n-**u** : an **u**-verb whose root ends in the consonant n
b-**u** : an **u**-verb whose root ends in the consonant b
w-**u** : an **u**-verb whose root ends in the consonant w
t-**u** : an **u**-verb whose root ends in the consonant t
irr. : an irregular verb

The third column specifies the item’s grammatical category (for example, *n* and *vi*), its English translation, and possibly, example phrases. The following is the list of grammatical category specifications:

adj : adjective
adv : adverb
aux : auxiliary
c : counter
con : conjunction / connective word
cop : copula
interj : interjection
n : noun
pn : proper noun
pron : pronoun
prt : particle
q : question word
vi : intransitive verb
vt : transitive verb
no category mark : phrases, suffixes or prefixes

The kanji found in the second column are not always the required kanji. The required kanji are listed right below the three-columned table, and headed by “Newly Introduced Kanji”. If a particular kanji character is introduced for the very first time, its stroke order is also provided in this section as well as in “Kanji List,” but otherwise, its stroke order is found only in “Kanji List”.

- "Vocabulary Collection" lists a group of vocabulary relevant to one of the themes of the lesson for optional use.
- "Dialog" provides a short conversation that can be easily memorized and recited by the students. It can be used as a model for skit-creation. All dialogs are recorded in the accompanying audio CDs.
- "Guess and Try" asks the students to try out what they have discovered after listening to the dialog on the audio CD or after observing the dialog recited in the class.
- "Drill" provides simple sentence formation drills. It includes Reading, Repeating, Conjugation, Formation and Mini-Conversation.
- "Task" offers various tasks that train the students' communicative skills. It includes Pair Work, Small Group Work, Classroom Activity, Survey, Skit Performance and Role Play.
- "Short Reading" provides a short passage, often related to the theme of the lesson. It includes kanji characters not previously introduced, so that the students can see how the written forms actually appear in Japanese.
- In "Writing", the students start writing about the related topic using the passage they have seen in "Short Reading" as a model.

Sample Lesson:

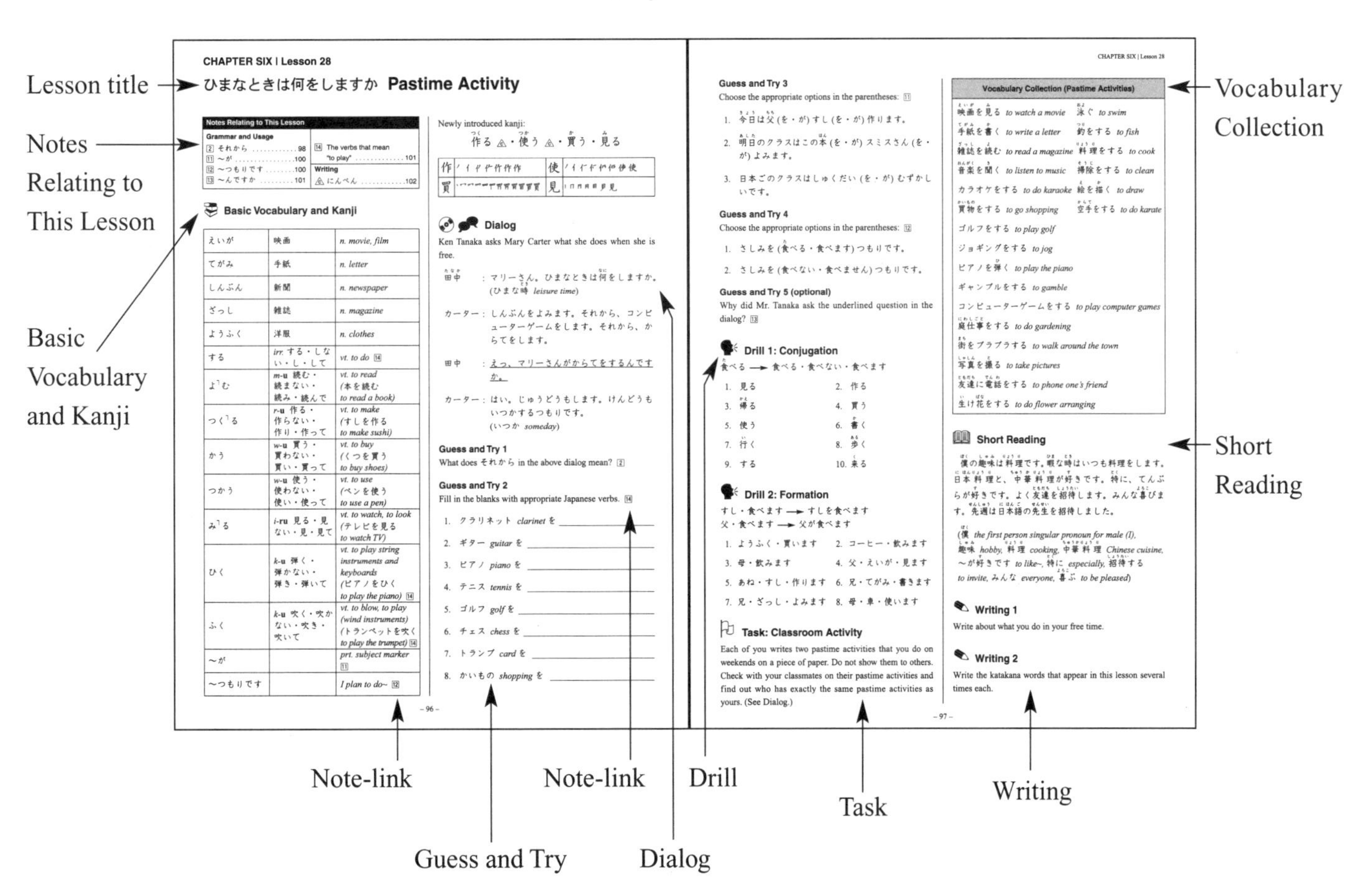

Orthography

A brief discussion on hiragana, katakana, romaji, and kanji characters is provided in "Introduction". In Chapter One, hiragana characters are gradually introduced, and the students are expected to be able to read them starting in Chapter Two. Katakana characters are introduced in Chapter Four.

A few new basic kanji words are introduced in each lesson, starting in Chapter Two. They appear in big font, with furigana (hiragana for pronunciation specification) in the "Basic Vocabulary and Kanji" section, and they appear without furigana in the rest of the parts in the same lesson. When they appear in the following lessons, furigana is sparingly provided, wherever it is thought to be helpful for the students, and its use is gradually reduced. In "Short Reading", kanji characters that have never been introduced will also appear, but their first instance will have furigana.

All the kanji words that are introduced in "Basic Vocabulary and Kanji" are listed in "Kanji List" at the end of each chapter. The kanji characters that are listed may be brand new characters for the students or may be previously introduced characters. Each character is provided with its stroke count, reading, meaning, usage example, and stroke order. The kunyomi-reading (Japanese-way of reading) is written in hiragana, and the onyomi-reading (Chinese-way of reading) is written in katakana. Where present, okurigana (the hiragana-written inflectional part that immediately follows a kanji character) is preceded by a dash.

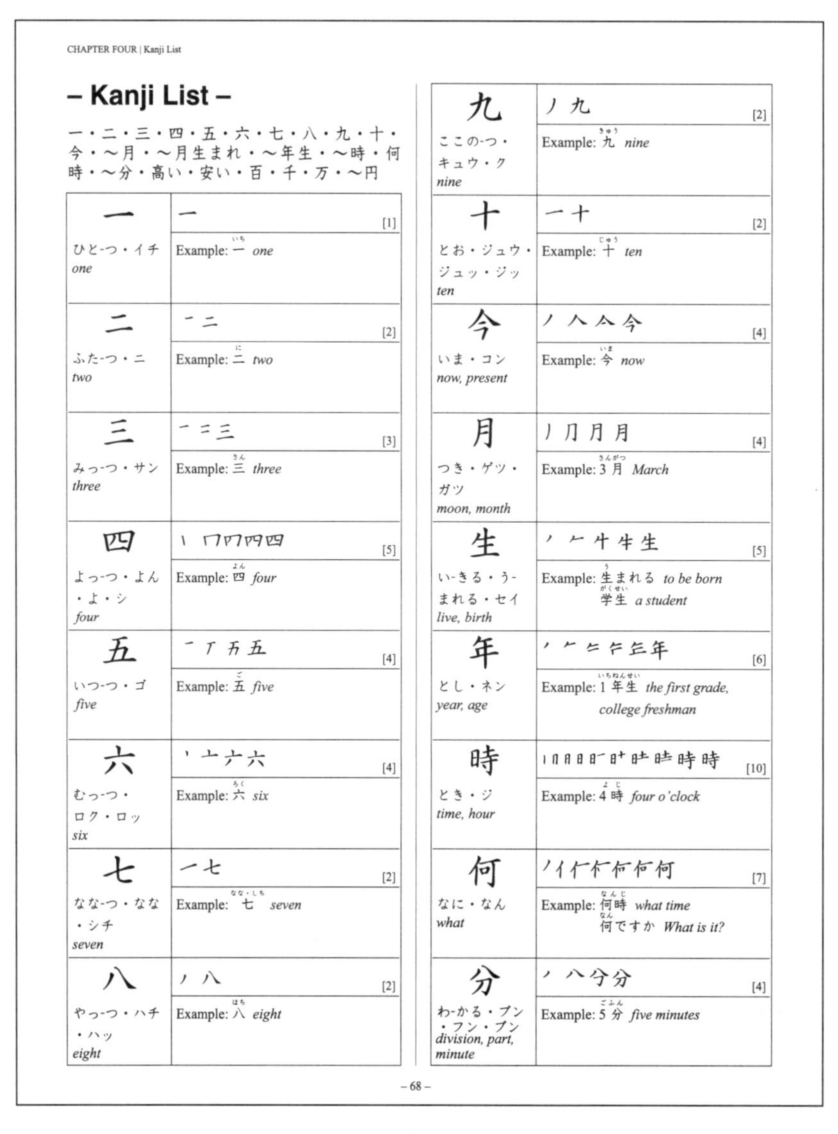

CHAPTER FOUR | Kanji List

– Kanji List –

一・二・三・四・五・六・七・八・九・十・今・～月・～月生まれ・～年生・～時・何時・～分・高い・安い・百・千・万・～円

Kanji	Reading / Meaning	Stroke order	Strokes	Example
一	ひと-つ・イチ *one*	一	[1]	Example: 一（いち） *one*
二	ふた-つ・ニ *two*	一 二	[2]	Example: 二（に） *two*
三	みっ-つ・サン *three*	一 二 三	[3]	Example: 三（さん） *three*
四	よっ-つ・よん・よ・シ *four*	丨 冂 刀 四 四	[5]	Example: 四（よん） *four*
五	いつ-つ・ゴ *five*	一 丅 五 五	[4]	Example: 五（ご） *five*
六	むっ-つ・ロク・ロッ *six*	丶 亠 六 六	[4]	Example: 六（ろく） *six*
七	なな-つ・なな・シチ *seven*	一 七	[2]	Example: 七（なな・しち） *seven*
八	やっ-つ・ハチ・ハッ *eight*	ノ 八	[2]	Example: 八（はち） *eight*
九	ここの-つ・キュウ・ク *nine*	ノ 九	[2]	Example: 九（きゅう） *nine*
十	とお・ジュウ・ジュッ・ジッ *ten*	一 十	[2]	Example: 十（じゅう） *ten*
今	いま・コン *now, present*	ノ 人 亼 今	[4]	Example: 今（いま） *now*
月	つき・ゲツ・ガツ *moon, month*	丿 冂 月 月	[4]	Example: 3月（さんがつ） *March*
生	い-きる・う-まれる・セイ *live, birth*	ノ 𠂉 十 牛 生	[5]	Example: 生（う）まれる *to be born* 学生（がくせい） *a student*
年	とし・ネン *year, age*	ノ 𠂉 ⺍ 午 㐄 年	[6]	Example: 1年生（いちねんせい） *the first grade, college freshman*
時	とき・ジ *time, hour*	丨 冂 日 日 日一 日十 旪 時 時 時	[10]	Example: 4時（よじ） *four o'clock*
何	なに・なん *what*	ノ イ 亻 仃 何 何 何	[7]	Example: 何時（なんじ） *what time* 何（なん）ですか *What is it?*
分	わ-かる・ブン・フン・プン *division, part, minute*	ノ 八 分 分	[4]	Example: 5分（ごふん） *five minutes*

– 68 –

Introduction

1. The Japanese Writing System

Modern Japanese is written horizontally or vertically, by combining the Chinese characters called **kanji** and two sets of syllabic alphabets called **kana** (hiragana and katakana). There is another writing system, called **romaji** (romanized Japanese), which was developed for the convenience of foreigners.

Kanji

Kanji characters were imported to Japan from China around the 5th century AD. Each kanji character represents a concrete meaning, and it usually has at least two readings. For example, the kanji character 車 represents a *car*, and is read as KURUMA or SHA depending on the context. Kanji characters are used for most nouns, verbs, adjectives and adverbs. Japanese students learn about 2,000 kanji characters by the time they graduate from high school.

車	食	高
car	*to eat*	*high, expensive*
KURUMA SHA	TA-BERU SHOKU	TAKA-I KŌ

Hiragana

Hiragana characters were created by women during the Heian period (794–1192) by modifying the kanji characters, mainly by deforming them so that they can be written by a few cursive lines with one continuous flow of a brush stroke. For example, the hiragana character か was created by deforming and simplifying the kanji character 加, and was assigned the sound of 加, which is **ka**. Unlike kanji characters, each hiragana character does not represent any meaning, but represents a syllable sound. So, the hiragana character か just represents the sound **ka**. There are 46 basic hiragana characters and a few diacritic marks that may be added to some of them. Hiragana is used for grammatical items such as particles, suffixes, and inflectional endings and the native Japanese words not covered by kanji.

ん **n**	わ **wa**	ら **ra**	や **ya**	ま **ma**	は **ha**	な **na**	た **ta**	さ **sa**	か **ka**	あ **a**
		り **ri**		み **mi**	ひ **hi**	に **ni**	ち **chi**	し **shi**	き **ki**	い **i**
		る **ru**	ゆ **yu**	む **mu**	ふ **fu**	ぬ **nu**	つ **tsu**	す **su**	く **ku**	う **u**
		れ **re**		め **me**	へ **he**	ね **ne**	て **te**	せ **se**	け **ke**	え **e**
	を **o**	ろ **ro**	よ **yo**	も **mo**	ほ **ho**	の **no**	と **to**	そ **so**	こ **ko**	お **o**

Katakana

Katakana characters were also created in the Heian period (794–1192) by modifying the kanji characters. Some of their creators were Buddhist monks. Unlike hiragana characters, each katakana character was made by taking a portion of a kanji character, rather than by deforming it. As a result, they are mainly composed of straight lines and sharp angles. For example, the katakana character カ was created by taking a part of the kanji character 加, and it inherited the sound of 加, which is **ka**. Like hiragana characters, each katakana character represents a syllable sound. Katakana is used for non-Chinese foreign names, loan words from the West, and most of onomatopoetic (imitative) expressions. (Chinese names and loan words can be written in either kanji or katakana.)

ン **n**	ワ **wa**	ラ **ra**	ヤ **ya**	マ **ma**	ハ **ha**	ナ **na**	タ **ta**	サ **sa**	カ **ka**	ア **a**
		リ **ri**		ミ **mi**	ヒ **hi**	ニ **ni**	チ **chi**	シ **shi**	キ **ki**	イ **i**
		ル **ru**	ユ **yu**	ム **mu**	フ **fu**	ヌ **nu**	ツ **tsu**	ス **su**	ク **ku**	ウ **u**
		レ **re**		メ **me**	ヘ **he**	ネ **ne**	テ **te**	セ **se**	ケ **ke**	エ **e**
	ヲ **o**	ロ **ro**	ヨ **yo**	モ **mo**	ホ **ho**	ノ **no**	ト **to**	ソ **so**	コ **ko**	オ **o**

For example, the sentence *I will eat kimchee, steak and vegetables* will appear as below when written horizontally:

私はキムチと、ステーキと、野菜を食べます。
Watashi wa kimuchi to, sutēki to, yasai o tabemasu.
I TOP kimchee and steak and vegetable D.O. eat polite
(TOP = topic marker, D.O. = direct object marker)

In the above sentence, non-Chinese loan words (*kimchee* and *steak*) are written in katakana, other content words (*I, vegetables* and *to eat*) are written in kanji, and grammatical items are written in hiragana.

Romaji

Romaji (Rōmaji) is used in many public places in Japan for the convenience of traveling foreigners. It is very easy for you to read. You just have to know that the diacritic mark " ¯ " or " ˆ " represents long vowels. Japanese has five basic vowels, which are **a**, **e**, **i**, **o** and **u**, and their longer counterparts, which are represented by placing a diacritic mark " ¯ " or " ˆ ", or by doubling the vowel. For example, the long o is represented as **ō**, **ô** or **oo**. In this textbook, long vowels are usually represented by placing the diacritic mark " ¯ ", and occasionally by doubling the vowel.

Guess and Try

1. Can you identify the kanji, katakana, hiragana, romaji and English words in the following pictures?

2. Match the kanji characters and pictures: (1. 月 2. 田 3. 山 4. 川 5. 木 6. 日 7. 火)

tree ( ) river ( ) mountain ( ) rice field ( ) moon ( ) sun ( ) fire ( )

3. Each of the following characters is made by combining two or three characters and it means one of the following (woods, a forest, a cultivated field, bright). Guess which character means what.

a. 明 ( ) b. 林 ( ) c. 森 ( ) d. 畑 ( )

2. Sentence Structures in Japanese

Free Word Order and Particles

The verb must occur at the end of a sentence, but the order of the rest of the phrases is very flexible in Japanese. For example, the English sentence in (a) is equivalent to any one of the Japanese sentences in (b), (c), (d), (e), (f) and (g).

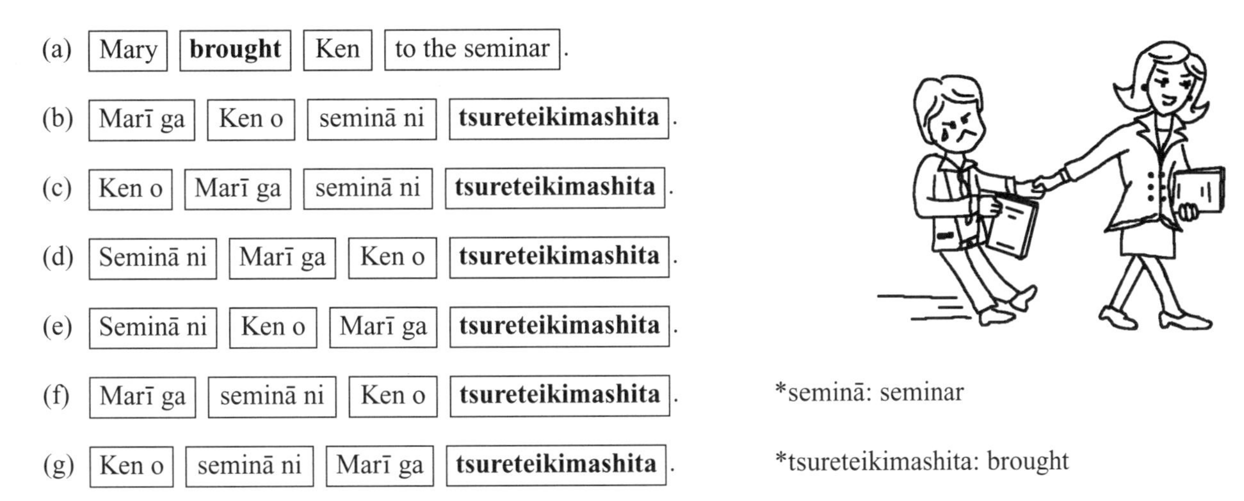

(a) [Mary] [**brought**] [Ken] [to the seminar].

(b) [Marī ga] [Ken o] [seminā ni] [**tsureteikimashita**].

(c) [Ken o] [Marī ga] [seminā ni] [**tsureteikimashita**].

(d) [Seminā ni] [Marī ga] [Ken o] [**tsureteikimashita**].

(e) [Seminā ni] [Ken o] [Marī ga] [**tsureteikimashita**].

(f) [Marī ga] [seminā ni] [Ken o] [**tsureteikimashita**].

(g) [Ken o] [seminā ni] [Marī ga] [**tsureteikimashita**].

*seminā: seminar

*tsureteikimashita: brought

The reason why the Japanese know *who* brought *whom* to *where* is because each phrase is followed by a particle such as **ga**, **o** and **ni**. The particles **ga**, **o** and **ni** specify the subject, direct object and destination, respectively. English has a marker for destination, namely, the preposition *to*, but doesn't have markers for the subject and the object. As a result, the word order in English is not very flexible. Note that English markers (prepositions such as *to*, *with*, *on*, *by*, *in* and *at*) precede the noun, but Japanese markers (particles) follow it.

English:		**Japanese:**	
to	the seminar	seminā	**ni**

Omission of Contextually Understood Phrases

In Japanese, contextually understood phrases in a sentence tend to be unpronounced rather than expressed by pronouns. So, don't be surprised if you hear a sentence without the subject noun.

Topic-comment Constructions

Japanese sentences typically start with a noun phrase marked by **wa**, which specifies the topic of the sentence.

(a) Ano hi wa Ben ga kimashita. — *As for that day, Ben came.*
(that day Ben came)

(b) Watashi wa sushi desu. — *As for myself, (it is) sushi. / I will have sushi.*
(I sushi is)

(c) Kore wa omoshiroi desu. — *As for this, (it is) interesting. / It is interesting.*
(this interesting is)

No Articles Before a Noun

Japanese nouns do not have to be preceded by articles that correspond to *the* and *a* in English. In addition, nouns do not have to change their forms depending on the number. **Hon** (book) can be just one book or multiple books.

3. Speech Styles

There are three basic speech styles in Japanese: plain / informal style, polite / neutral style, and formal style. For example, we can ask a question like *Did you buy it?* in three different ways:

(a) Katta no. (plain / informal)
(b) Kaimashita ka. (polite / neutral)
(c) O-kai ni narimashita ka. (formal)

It is extremely important for the Japanese to use the appropriate speech style since an inappropriate speech style may insult others or create an unnecessary distance from others. There are two major criteria for determining the appropriate speech style.

One is the "social grouping", where one can be either an insider or outsider of a group such as a family, a team, a school, a company, or an institution. For example, you would use (a) above with the insider of your family, but (b) or (c) with most outsiders.

The other criterion for determining the speech style is the "social superiority", which is based on the combination of age, experience, status, position and rank. There are three basic social levels: "subordinates", "equals" and "superiors". With your social subordinates such as your assistants, employees and students, you would use (a) or (b). With your social equals such as your colleagues and classmates, you would use (b), or possibly (a) or (c), depending on how close you are to them. With your superiors such as your teachers and employers, you would use (c).

In addition to social grouping and social superiority, the personality of the speaker, location of the conversation and closeness between the speaker and listener are important key factors that determine the speech style. Beginners of the Japanese languages are advised to start from the polite / neutral speech styles and gradually master the plain / informal and formal speech styles.

Social Grouping

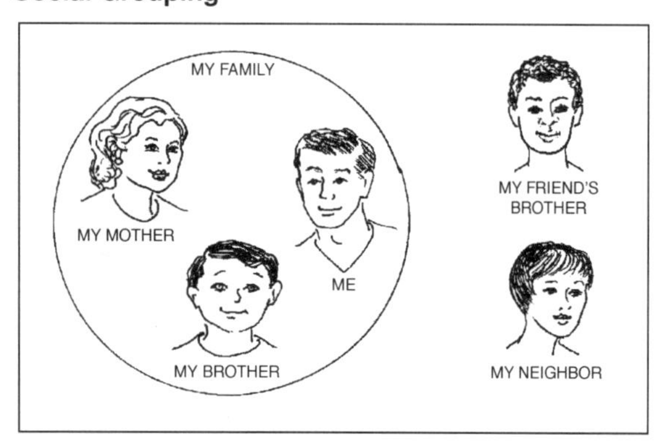

Social Superiority

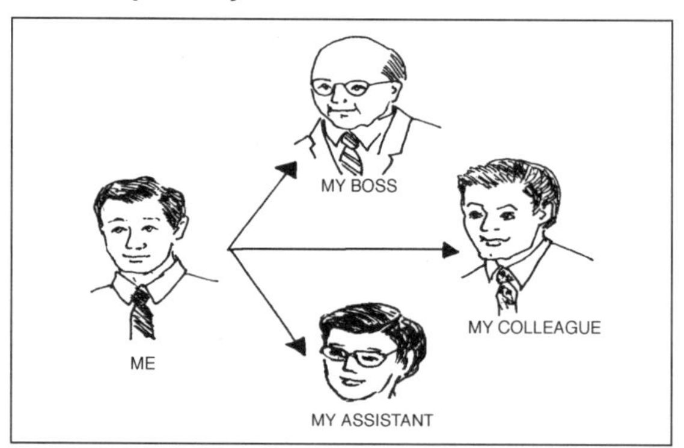

Guess and Try

Guess which one of the above three speech forms (a) to (c), the Japanese would use with the following people, then ask the opinion of the Japanese around you. There may be individual variations.

1. Their business customer
2. Their teacher
3. Their father
4. Their close friends
5. Their friend's father
6. Their employee who happen to be much older than they are
7. Strangers

4. Pitch-accent

Unlike English words, Japanese words do not have any stress accent and Japanese speech sounds very flat for English speakers. But that does not mean that Japanese words do not have any accent. In fact, most Japanese words do have an accent. It is just that the accent in Japanese is realized by pitch-shift, not by stress. Pitch-accent in Japanese can affect the meaning of a word. For example, the Japanese word HASHI means *chopsticks* if the pitch goes down from high to low (HL), but it means *bridge* if the pitch goes up from low to high (LH). It is a good idea to remember the position of pitch-accent when learning a new word.

The pitch-accent may fall on any syllable, or mora more precisely, in a word, or it may be absent. A mora is a syllable-like unit that corresponds to one hiragana or katakana character. In the following words, the accented mora, if any, is marked by " ⌉ " on its right upper corner:

te ki su to	ta te mo no	hi ra ga na	i mo o to	su ki ya ki
テ⌉キスト	たて⌉もの	ひらが⌉な	いもうと⌉	すきやき
text	*building*	*hiragana*	*younger sister*	*sukiyaki*

Note: もう in いもうと is pronounced as a long o, which is specified by **ō** or by **oo** in the romaji system adopted in this textbook.

You can find out the entire pitch pattern of a word by taking the following three steps:

Step 1: Make all the moras high pitched.

te ki su to	ta te mo no	hi ra ga na	i mo o to	su ki ya ki
テ⌉キスト	たて⌉もの	ひらが⌉な	いもうと⌉	すきやき
H HH H	H H H H	H H H H	H H H H	H H H H

Step 2: Make all the moras after the accented mora low pitched.

te ki su to	ta te mo no	hi ra ga na	i mo o to	su ki ya ki
テ⌉キスト	たて⌉もの	ひらが⌉な	いもうと⌉	すきやき
H L L L	H H L L	H H H L	H H H H	H H H H

Step 3: Make the initial mora low pitched if it does not bear an accent.

te ki su to	ta te mo no	hi ra ga na	i mo o to	su ki ya ki
テ⌉キスト	たて⌉もの	ひらが⌉な	いもうと⌉	すきやき
H L L L	L H L L	L H H L	L HH H	L H H H

They are diagrammed as:

いもうと⌉ and すきやき have exactly the same pitch pattern (LHHH), but when a particle such as が (subject marker) follows them, their pitch patterns become different:

i mo o to ga	su ki ya ki ga
いもうと⌉が	すきやきが
L H H H L	L H H H H

Guess and Try

Pronounce each of the following words:

1. かんじ (ka n ji) *kanji character*
2. かたか⌉な (ka ta ka na) *katakana character*
3. すし⌉ (su shi) *sushi*
4. にほ⌉ん (ni ho n) *Japan*
5. にほんご (ni ho n go) *Japanese language*
6. にほんじ⌉ん (ni ho n ji n) *Japanese people*
7. みそし⌉る (mi so shi ru) *miso soup*

CHAPTER ONE

Basic Sounds, Words, Phrases and Kana

Lesson 1
Familiar Japanese Words and Phrases for Gratitude 2

Lesson 2
Words for Japanese Food and Phrases for Introduction 4

Lesson 3
Numbers in Japanese and Phrases for Greeting 6

Lesson 4
Classroom Expressions 8

Lesson 5
Words for Body Parts and Phrases for Apology 10

Lesson 6
Words for Family Members and Phrases for Getting Attention 12

Lesson 7
Names of Japanese Cities and Phrases for Small Talk 14

Grammar and Usage 16

1 Basic Japanese sounds 16
2 どうぞ: Go ahead (and do～), please (do～) [Offering] 16
3 Gratitude (ありがとうございます, etc) 16
4 どうも: Indeed [Gratitude / apology-intensifier] 17
5 Introduction (はじめまして, よろしく, etc) 17
6 Respectful titles (～さん, ～くん, etc) 17
7 Greetings (こんにちは, おはようございます, etc) . 17
8 Parting (さようなら, etc) 18
9 ～ください: Please do～ [Requesting] 18
10 おねがいします: Please～ [Favor] 18
11 あっ: Oops! / oh! [Shock] 18
12 すみません: Excuse me / I am sorry [Apology / attention catching] 18
13 あのう: Ahhh, ... [Initiating talk] 19
14 ちょっと: A little bit [Expression softener] 19
15 おげんきですか: How are you? 19
16 Polite prefix (お～ and ご～) 19

Culture 20

A Traditional martial arts 20
B Bowing 20
C Japanese food 20
D Japanese names 20
E Japanese islands 21
F Modesty 21

Writing 21

a Hiragana 21
b Punctuation and format 22

Review 23

Tips and Additional Knowledge: Must-know Set Phrases 24

Familiar Japanese Words and Phrases for Gratitude

Notes Relating to This Lesson

Grammar and Usage	Culture
[1] Basic Japanese sounds . . 16	Ⓐ Traditional martial arts . . . 20
[2] どうぞ 16	Ⓑ Bowing 20
[3] Gratitude 16	**Writing**
[4] どうも 17	(a) Hiragana 21

Basic Vocabulary and Hiragana [1] (a)

にほ˥ん	nihon 日本	*n. Japan*
にほんご	nihongo 日本語	*n. Japanese language*
きもの	kimono 着物	*n. kimono*
おり˥がみ	origami 折り紙	*n. origami*
からて	karate 空手	*n. karate* Ⓐ
じゅ˥うどう	jūdō 柔道	*n. judo* Ⓐ *(Japanese wrestling)*
け˥んどう	kendō 剣道	*n. kendo* Ⓐ *(Japanese fencing)*

Note: どう in じゅうどう and けんどう is pronounced as **dō**, and not **dou**. [1] (a)

Guess and Try 1

Make a list of the Japanese words that you know.

Guess and Try 2

Do you know any Japanese martial arts? Ⓐ

Guess and Try 3

1. Which hiragana character does each of the following strokes belong to?

A. B. C.

D. お E.

	Kaisho style	Mincho style	Hand-writing	Stroke order	Example
a	あ	あ	あ	あ	あし ashi *leg*
i	い	い	い	い	いぬ inu *dog*
u	う	う	う	う	うえ ue *top*
e	え	え	え	え	え e *drawing*
o	お	お	お	お	おりがみ origami *origami*
ka	か	か	か	か	からて karate *karate*
ki	き	き	き	き	きもの kimono *kimono*
ku	く	く	く	く	くるま kuruma *car*
ke	け	け	け	け	けむり kemuri *smoke*
ko	こ	こ	こ	こ	こども kodomo *child*

2. Are there any two hiragana characters that look alike in the above table?

3. Read the following words aloud.

うえ *top*   え *drawing / picture*

くうき *air*   くき *stem*

おおきい *big*

Drill: Reading

Read the following nonsensical phrases several times, then, do it again backwards.

1. あいあうい　　いういえうえう　　えおえおあ
2. あおあおい　　うえうええうえ　　いうえあお
3. かきかくき　　くけくけこけく　　こかけきく
4. あかいきく　　くけえおこおあ　　いこけうお

Dialog 1

Ms. Suzuki gives her neighbor a box of cookies she has baked.

Suzuki　:　どうぞ。
　　　　　Dōzo.

Neighbor :　どうもありがとうございます。
　　　　　Dōmo arigatō gozaimasu.

Suzuki　:　いいえ。
　　　　　Īe.

Note: どう in どうも and どうぞ is pronounced as dō. The last vowel in ありがとうございます (arigatō gozaimasu) is often whispered. 1 A

Dialog 2

Ms. Tanaka serves a cup of tea to Yoko Yamada.

Tanaka　:　どうぞ。
　　　　　Dōzo.

Yamada　:　どうも。
　　　　　Dōmo.

Tanaka　:　いいえ。
　　　　　Īe.

Guess and Try 4 2 3 4 B

1. Is there any body gesture necessary for giving and receiving?
2. いいえ (Īe) literally means *no*. What does it actually mean in the dialogs?
3. Pretend that you have one hundred dollars in an envelope. Give it to your partner as a gift.
4. Pretend that your partner forget to bring a pen. Loan yours to him / her.

Task: Classroom Activity

Your teacher gives several items (for example, a pen, an eraser, tissue paper, a cup, a ring and a gift certificate) to a group of students. These students are required to pass them on to other students in the room, using appropriate expressions and gestures when giving or receiving the items.

Writing

Write the hiragana characters introduced in this lesson several times each.

a	あ	あ	あ	あ	あ	あ
i	い	い	い	い	い	い
u	う	う	う	う	う	う
e	え	え	え	え	え	え
o	お	お	お	お	お	お
ka	か	か	か	か	か	か
ki	き	き	き	き	き	き
ku	く	く	く	く	く	く
ke	け	け	け	け	け	け
ko	こ	こ	こ	こ	こ	こ

Words for Japanese Food and Phrases for Introduction

Notes Relating to This Lesson

Grammar and Usage	Culture
1 Basic Japanese sounds . . 16	C Japanese food 20
5 Introduction 17	D Japanese names 20
6 Respectful titles 17	**Writing**
	a Hiragana 21

 Basic Vocabulary and Hiragana 1 a

さしみ⌉	sashimi 刺身	*n. sliced raw fish* C
すし⌉	sushi 鮨・寿司	*n. sushi* C
てんぷら	tempura 天麩羅	*n. tempura* C
うなぎ	unagi 鰻	*n. eel* C
すきやき	sukiyaki すき焼き	*n. sukiyaki* C

Note: ん is represented by **n** or **m** depending on the following sound. 1 a

	Kaisho style	Mincho style	Hand-writing	Stroke order	Example
sa	さ	さ	さ	さ	さしみ sashimi *sashimi*
shi	し	し	し	し	しろ shiro *white*
su	す	す	す	す	すし sushi *sushi*
se	せ	せ	せ	せ	せかい sekai *world*
so	そ	そ	そ	そ	そら sora *sky*
ta	た	た	た	た	たこ tako *octopus*
chi	ち	ち	ち	ち	ちかてつ chikatetsu *subway*
tsu	つ	つ	つ	つ	つくえ tsukue *desk*
te	て	て	て	て	て te *hand*
to	と	と	と	と	と to *door*

Guess and Try 1

List the names of the Japanese dishes that you know. C

Guess and Try 2

1. Which hiragana character does each of the following strokes belong to?

   A. ˘ B. ら C. く

   D. ℈ E. し

2. Identify the differences and similarities between the two hiragana characters in each set.

   A. き・さ B. た・こ C. う・つ

   D. そ・て

3. Read the following words aloud.

   たこ *octopus* つくえ *desk*

   せかい *world* いす *chair*

   おと *sound*

Drill: Reading

Read the following nonsensical phrases several times, then, do it again backwards.

1. さしさしす　　すせすそすせそ　　せそさすし
2. たちたちつ　　つてとつてとつ　　たてとつち
3. さたしてつ　　つそとてせすそ　　とそせちつ
4. あさしせこ　　せそおけすえく　　きいすうと

Dialog

Sara Brown and Yoko Yamada introduce themselves to each other.

Brown　: はじめまして。ブラウンです。よろしく。
Hajimemashite. Buraun desu. Yoroshiku.
(～です desu / *to be* ～)

Yamada　: ブラウンさんですか。
Buraunsan desuka?
(～か ka / *question particle*)

Brown　: はい。
Hai.
(はい hai / *yes*)

Yamada　: はじめまして。やまだです。こちらこそよろしく。
Hajimemashite. Yamada desu. Kochirakoso yoroshiku.

Guess and Try 3

1. はじめまして (Hajimemashite) and よろしく (yoroshiku) literally mean *for the first time* and *appropriately*, respectively. What do they actually mean in the dialog? What should you say when someone tells you よろしく (yoroshiku)? [5]
2. When do you use ～さん (san) after proper names? [6]
3. List the names of Japanese people that you know. Are there any tendencies? (D)

Task 1: Pair Work

Introduce yourself to your partner. Do not forget to bow.

Task 2: Classroom Activity

Name-search competition: Introduce yourself to each of your classmates and find out everyone's name as quickly as possible.

Writing

Write the hiragana characters introduced in this lesson several times each.

sa	さ	さ	さ	さ	さ	さ
shi	し	し	し	し	し	し
su	す	す	す	す	す	す
se	せ	せ	せ	せ	せ	せ
so	そ	そ	そ	そ	そ	そ
ta	た	た	た	た	た	た
chi	ち	ち	ち	ち	ち	ち
tsu	つ	つ	つ	つ	つ	つ
te	て	て	て	て	て	て
to	と	と	と	と	と	と

Numbers in Japanese and Phrases for Greeting

Notes Relating to This Lesson	
Grammar and Usage	**Writing**
1 Basic Japanese sounds . . 16	a Hiragana 21
7 Greetings 17	
8 Parting 18	

 Basic Vocabulary and Hiragana 1 a

いち˥	ichi 一	*n. one*
に˥	ni 二	*n. two*
さん	san 三	*n. three*
よ˥ん / し˥	yon / shi 四	*n. four*
ご˥	go 五	*n. five*
ろく˥	roku 六	*n. six*
な˥な / しち˥	nana / shichi 七	*n. seven*
はち˥	hachi 八	*n. eight*
きゅ˥う / く˥	kyū / ku 九	*n. nine*
じゅ˥う	jū 十	*n. ten*

Guess and Try 1

Count up to ten in your native language, using fingers. Depending on the country, how the fingers are used for counting may be different.

1

2

3

4

5

Guess and Try 2

1. Identify the differences and similarities between the two hiragana characters in each set.

   A. は・ほ　　B. に・け　　C. な・た

   D. ぬ・ね　　E. の・あ

2. Read the following words aloud.

   ねこ *cat*　　ふね *ship*

   くに *country*　　いなか *countryside*

   にく *meat*　　ほし *star*

	Kaisho style	Mincho style	Hand-writing	Stroke order	Example
na	な	な	な	な	なまえ namae *name*
ni	に	に	に	に	に ni *two*
nu	ぬ	ぬ	ぬ	ぬ	いぬ inu *dog*
ne	ね	ね	ね	ね	ねこ neko *cat*
no	の	の	の	の	のり nori *seaweed*
ha / wa	は	は	は	は	は ha *tooth*
hi	ひ	ひ	ひ	ひ	ひ hi *fire*
fu	ふ	ふ	ふ	ふ	ふね fune *boat*
he / e	へ	へ	へ	へ	へや heya *room*
ho	ほ	ほ	ほ	ほ	ほし hoshi *star*

Drill: Reading

Read the following nonsensical phrases several times, then, do it again backwards.

1. なにになにぬ　　ぬねのぬねのぬ　　になぬのね
2. はひはひふ　　ふへふほへほふ　　はひほふへ
3. はなほのへ　　ふぬひにはほね　　ねぬのへは
4. さかなにの　　ふうほおきにひ　　ほおへえぬ

Dialog 1

John Smith sees his classmate, Yoko (Yōko) Yamada, at the library at 9 a.m. They are going to meet again in class later.

Smith	:	ようこさん。おはよう。 Yōko san. Ohayō.
Yamada	:	ああ、ジョンさん。おはよう。 Ā, Jon san. Ohayō.
Smith (smile)	:	じゃあ、また。 Jā, mata.
Yamada	:	ええ。じゃあ、また。 Ē. Jā, mata.

Guess and Try 3

Pretend that it is 9 a.m., greet one of your classmates and say goodbye. Address him / her appropriately. 7 8

Dialog 2

John Smith sees his Japanese teacher, Kanako Tanaka, at the library at 9 a.m. They are going to meet again in class later.

Smith	:	たなか せんせい。おはようございます。 Tanaka sensē. Ohayō gozaimasu.
Tanaka	:	ああ、スミスさん。おはよう。 Ā, Sumisu san. Ohayō.
Smith (smile)	:	じゃあ、しつれいします。 Jā, shitsurē shimasu.
Tanaka	:	はい。じゃあ、また。 Hai. Jā, mata.

Guess and Try 4

Pretend that it is 9 a.m., greet your teacher and say goodbye. 7 8

Dialog 3

John Smith sees his teacher, Emiko Yoshikawa, at the library at 3 p.m.

Smith	:	よしかわ せんせい。こんにちは。 Yoshikawa sensē. Konnichiwa.
Yoshikawa	:	ああ、ジョンさん。こんにちは。 Ā, Jon san. Konnichiwa.
Smith (smile)	:	じゃあ、しつれいします。さようなら。 Jā, shitsurē shimasu. Sayōnara.
Yoshikawa	:	はい。さようなら。 Hai. Sayōnara.

Guess and Try 5 7 8

1. Pretend that it is 3 p.m., and greet your classmates and teacher.
2. Ask a few Japanese when they say さようなら (Sayōnara).

Note: よう in ようこ, おはよう and さようなら is pronounced as **yō**, は in こんにちは is pronounced as **wa**, せい in せんせい is pronounced as **sē**, and れい in しつれいします is pronounced as **rē**. a

Writing

Write the hiragana characters introduced in this lesson.

na	な	な	な	な	な	な
ni	に	に	に	に	に	に
nu	ぬ	ぬ	ぬ	ぬ	ぬ	ぬ
ne	ね	ね	ね	ね	ね	ね
no	の	の	の	の	の	の
ha / wa	は	は	は	は	は	は
hi	ひ	ひ	ひ	ひ	ひ	ひ
fu	ふ	ふ	ふ	ふ	ふ	ふ
he / e	へ	へ	へ	へ	へ	へ
ho	ほ	ほ	ほ	ほ	ほ	ほ

Classroom Expressions

Notes Relating to This Lesson	
Grammar and Usage	**Writing**
1 Basic Japanese sounds . . 16	ⓐ Hiragana 21
9 ～ください 18	
10 おねがいします 18	

Basic Vocabulary and Hiragana 1 ⓐ

もういちど	mōichido もう一度	*once more*
ゆっく˥り	yukkuri	*adv. slowly*
いっしょに	isshoni 一緒に	*adv. together*
しつもん	shitsumon 質問	*n. question*
なまえ・おなまえ	namae 名前・お名前	*n. name*
せんせ˥い	sensē 先生	*n. teacher*
しゅくだい	shukudai 宿題	*n. homework*
がっこう	gakkō 学校	*n. school*
がくせい	gakusē 学生	*n. student*
いってくださ˥い	ittekudasai 言って下さい	*Please say (it).*

Note: せい in がくせい is pronounced as **sē**. 1 ⓐ

Guess and Try

1. Pronounce the two hiragana characters in each set. Identify the differences and similarities between them.

   A. む・な　　B. よ・ま

   C. も・ま　　D. あ・め

2. Read the following words aloud, then, try writing them as your teacher pronounces them.

   やま *mountain*　　ゆめ *dream*

   むすめ *daughter*　　むすこ *son*

   まいにち *every day*

	Kaisho style	Mincho style	Hand-writing	Stroke order	Example
ma	ま	ま	ま	ま	まめ mame *beans*
mi	み	み	み	み	みみ mimi *ear*
mu	む	む	む	む	むし mushi *insect*
me	め	め	め	め	め me *eye*
mo	も	も	も	も	もも momo *peach*
ya	や	や	や	や	やま yama *mountain*
yu	ゆ	ゆ	ゆ	ゆ	ゆめ yume *dream*
yo	よ	よ	よ	よ	よる yoru *night*

Drill: Reading

Read the following nonsensical phrases several times, then, do it again backwards.

1. まみまみむ　　むめむもめもむ　　まめみもむ
2. やゆやゆよ　　よまよまやまや　　よもやむゆ
3. はまやむく　　よもよぬめぬめ　　ひゆふけよ
4. あまかやの　　いきしちひみに　　おむけよぬ

Useful Classroom Phrases

Requesting doing something: 9

1. いってください。
   Ittekudasai.
   (Please) say (it).

2. みてください。
   Mitekudasai.
   (Please) look at (it).

3. かいてください。
   Kaitekudasai.
   (Please) write (it).

4. よんでください。
   Yondekudasai.
   (Please) read (it).

5. たってください。
   Tattekudasai.
   (Please) stand up.

6. すわってください。
   Suwattekudasai.
   (Please) sit down.

Requesting some manners of doing something: 10

1. もういちど(おねがいします)。
   Mōichido (onegaishimasu).
   One more time, please.

2. ゆっくり(おねがいします)。
   Yukkuri (onegaishimasu).
   Slowly, please.

3. いっしょに(おねがいします)。
   Isshoni (onegaishimasu).
   Together, please.

Others:

1. しつもんは。 — いいえ。
   Shitsumonwa. — Īe.
   Any question? — No.

2. いいですか。 — はい。
   Ii desuka? — Hai.
   Are you all right? / Is it fine? — Yes.

Dialog

In the classroom.

Students : かきくけこ。
Kakikukeko.

Teacher : もういちどいってください。
Mōichido ittekudasai.

Students : かきくけこ。
Kakikukeko.

Teacher : ゆっくりいってください。
Yukkuri ittekudasai.

Students : か　き　く　け　こ。
Ka　ki　ku　ke　ko.

Teacher : いいですか。
Ii desuka.

Students : はい。
Hai.

Writing

Write the hiragana characters introduced in this lesson several times each.

ma	ま	ま	ま	ま	ま	ま
mi	み	み	み	み	み	み
mu	む	む	む	む	む	む
me	め	め	め	め	め	め
mo	も	も	も	も	も	も
ya	や	や	や	や	や	や
yu	ゆ	ゆ	ゆ	ゆ	ゆ	ゆ
yo	よ	よ	よ	よ	よ	よ

Words for Body Parts and Phrases for Apology

Notes Relating to This Lesson	
Grammar and Usage	**Writing**
1 Basic Japanese sounds . . 16	a Hiragana 21
11 あっ 18	
12 すみません 18	

 Basic Vocabulary and Hiragana 1 a

みみ˥	mimi 耳	*n. ear*
め˥	me 目	*n. eye*
て˥	te 手	*n. hand, arm*
あし˥	ashi 足	*n. foot, leg*
はな	hana 鼻	*n. nose*
くち	kuchi 口	*n. mouth*

Guess and Try 1

Pronounce the two hiragana characters in each set and identify the difference between them.

1. ろ・る 2. わ・ね 3. れ・わ

4. い・り 5. ら・ち

Note: を is used only as the direct object marking particle. a

Drill 1: Reading

Read the following nonsensical phrases several times, then, do it again backwards.

1. らりらりる るれるれろるろ るろれらり
2. れわらんれ るわろんるれら れわれんろ
3. けんれみよ そらにくむめぬ のりらるも

	Kaisho style	Mincho style	Hand-writing	Stroke order	Example
ra	ら	ら	ら	ら	らくだ rakuda *camel*
ri	り	り	り	り	りんご ringo *apple*
ru	る	る	る	る	くるま kuruma *car*
re	れ	れ	れ	れ	れきし rekishi *history*
ro	ろ	ろ	ろ	ろ	ろく roku *six*
wa	わ	わ	わ	わ	わたし watashi *I / me*
o	を	を	を	を	～を o *Particle*
n	ん	ん	ん	ん	さん san *three*

Drill 2: Reading

Read each column from the top to the bottom, starting at the right side (for example, あいうえお、かきくけこ…), then, read each row from the right to the left (for example, あかさたな…、いきしちに…).

	わ	ら	や	ま	は	な	た	さ	か	あ
		り		み	ひ	に	ち	し	き	い
		る	ゆ	む	ふ	ぬ	つ	す	く	う
		れ		め	へ	ね	て	せ	け	え
ん	を	ろ	よ	も	ほ	の	と	そ	こ	お

Dialog 1

John Smith accidentally stepped on the foot of the man behind him in a train.

Smith : あっ、すみません
Ah, sumimasen.

Man : いいえ。
Īe.

Smith : だいじょうぶですか。
Daijōbu desuka?
Are you all right?

Man : はい、だいじょうぶです。
Hai, daijōbu desu.

Guess and Try 2 11 12

1. Why did John say あっ (Ah)? What would be the equivalent interjection in your native language?
2. What is the function of すみません (sumimasen) in Dialog 1?
3. Pretend that your partner looks very sick, ask him / her whether he / she is all right.

Dialog 2

John Smith forgot to do his homework.

Smith : せんせい。どうもすみません。
Sensē. Dōmo sumimasen.

Teacher : はい。きをつけてください。
Hai. Kiotsukete kudasai.
Be careful.

Smith : はい
Hai.

Guess and Try 3

Why did the teacher say はい (hai) rather than いいえ (Īe) in Dialog 2? 12

Task: Classroom Activity

Your teacher gives a folder (or a sheet of paper) to half of the class and each student who receives one gives it to a student who does not receive any, pretending that he / she is giving his / her homework late to his / her teacher. Try it with different people several times. You must look serious. Use Dialog 2 as a model.

Writing 1

Write the hiragana characters introduced in this lesson several times each.

ra	ら	ら	ら	ら	ら	ら
ri	り	り	り	り	り	り
ru	る	る	る	る	る	る
re	れ	れ	れ	れ	れ	れ
ro	ろ	ろ	ろ	ろ	ろ	ろ
wa	わ	わ	わ	わ	わ	わ
o	を	を	を	を	を	を
n	ん	ん	ん	ん	ん	ん

Writing 2

Make a table like the one below and complete the hiragana characters in the appropriate order. (See Drill 2 in this lesson.)

	わ	ら	や	ま	は	な	さ	た	か	あ
		り		み	ひ	に	し	ち	き	い
		る	ゆ	む	ふ	ぬ	す	つ	く	う
		れ		め	へ	ね	せ	て	け	え
ん	を	ろ	よ	も	ほ	の	そ	と	こ	お

Words for Family Members and Phrases for Getting Attention

Notes Relating to This Lesson	
Grammar and Usage	**Writing**
1 Basic Japanese sounds . . 16	ⓐ Hiragana 21
12 すみません 18	
13 あのう 19	
14 ちょっと 19	

Basic Vocabulary and Hiragana 1 ⓐ

おか⌉あさん	okāsan お母さん	*n. mother*
おと⌉うさん	otōsan お父さん	*n. father*
おに⌉いさん	onīsan お兄さん	*n. older brother*
おね⌉えさん	onēsan お姉さん	*n. older sister*

おかあさん

おとうさん

おにいさん

おねえさん

Long Vowels	Double Consonants	Voicing Markers and Plosive Markers				
ああ ā / aa	pp, tt, kk, ss っ (small size)	ぱ pa	ば ba	だ da	ざ za	が ga
いい ī / ii		ぴ pi	び bi	ぢ ji	じ ji	ぎ gi
うう ū / uu		ぷ pu	ぶ bu	づ zu	ず zu	ぐ gu
えい（ええ） ē / ee		ぺ pe	べ be	で de	ぜ ze	げ ge
おう（おお） ō / oo		ぽ po	ぼ bo	ど do	ぞ zo	ご go

Guess and Try 1

1. Pronounce the two words in each set, paying attention to the differences in their sounds.

A. おばさん *aunt* おばあさん *grandmother*

B. おじさん *uncle* おじいさん *grandfather*

C. ふけい *parents* ふうけい *scenery*

D. みつ *honey* みっつ *three pieces*

E. おと *sound* おっと *husband*

F. かき *persimmon* かっき *liveliness*

2. Read the following words and phrases.

てんぷら

うなぎ

おりがみ

はじめまして。

せんせい

がっこう

ゆっくり いってください。

3. Find an orthographic mistake in each of the following items and circle it.

A. せんせえ (✕)
teacher

B. ありがとお。 (✕)
Thanks.

C. おねいさん (✕)
older sister

D. おとおさん (✕)
father

Dialog 1

John Smith picks up a wallet on the seat where a man had been sitting.

Smith : あのう、すみません。
Anō, sumimasen.

Man : (Turns around.)

Smith : どうぞ。
Dōzo.

Man : あっ、どうも。
Ah, dōmo.

Guess and Try 2

あのう (Anō) is an interjection and does not have any literal meaning. Guess what its function is in this context. What would be the equivalent interjection in your native language? 13

Guess and Try 3

What is the function of すみません (Sumimasen) in Dialog 1? 12

Dialog 2

John Smith wants to walk through in front of a man, who is sitting next to him, in an airplane.

Smith : あのう、ちょっと すみません。
Anō, chotto sumimasen.

Man : どうぞ。
Dōzo.

Smith : どうも。
Dōmo.

Guess and Try 4

ちょっと literary means *a little*. What does it mean in Dialog 2? 14

Task: Classroom Activity

Half of the students in your class each draws a picture of a pen on a small sheet of paper. Your teacher collects them and randomly places them under the textbooks of the rest of the students. Those of you who have drawn the pens are then required to look for your own drawings. When you check under someone's textbook, you must tell him / her すみません nicely.

Writing

Write the following words several times each.

おかあさん	おとうさん
おかあさん	おとうさん
おかあさん	おとうさん
おかあさん	おとうさん
おかあさん	おとうさん
おかあさん	おとうさん
おにいさん	おねえさん
おにいさん	おねえさん
おにいさん	おねえさん
おにいさん	おねえさん
おにいさん	おねえさん
おにいさん	おねえさん

Names of Japanese Cities and Phrases for Small Talk

Notes Relating to This Lesson

Grammar and Usage	Culture
1 Basic Japanese sounds . . 16	E Japanese islands 21
15 おげんきですか 19	F Modesty 21
16 Polite prefix 19	**Writing**
	a Hiragana 21
	b Punctuation and format . . . 22

Basic Vocabulary and Hiragana 1 a

とうきょう	Tōkyō 東京	*pn. Tokyo (name of a place)*
きょ⌉うと	Kyōto 京都	*pn. Kyoto (name of a place)*
おおさか	Ōsaka 大阪	*pn. Osaka (name of a place)*
な⌉りた	Narita 成田	*pn. Narita (name of a place)*

りゃ	みゃ	ぴゃ	びゃ	ひゃ	にゃ	ちゃ	じゃ ぢゃ	しゃ	ぎゃ	きゃ
rya	**mya**	**pya**	**bya**	**hya**	**nya**	**cha**	**ja**	**sha**	**gya**	**kya**
りゅ	みゅ	ぴゅ	びゅ	ひゅ	にゅ	ちゅ	じゅ ぢゅ	しゅ	ぎゅ	きゅ
ryu	**myu**	**pyu**	**byu**	**hyu**	**nyu**	**chu**	**ju**	**shu**	**gyu**	**kyu**
りょ	みょ	ぴょ	びょ	ひょ	にょ	ちょ	じょ ぢょ	しょ	ぎょ	きょ
ryo	**myo**	**pyo**	**byo**	**hyo**	**nyo**	**cho**	**jo**	**sho**	**gyo**	**kyo**

Guess and Try 1

Read the names of the cities and islands in the map. E

Guess and Try 2

List the names of the Japanese cities that you know.

Guess and Try 3

Read the following words and phrases.

1. しゅくだい
2. だいじょうぶです。
3. ちょっと。
4. じゃあ、また。

Guess and Try 4

The following are very informal memos from Ben Lee to Yoko Yamada. The one on the left is written horizontally and the one on the right is written vertically. Read and see how the Japanese punctuation and small sized characters っ, ゃ, ゅ and ょ look. Note that ー in リー (りい) represents a long vowel in katakana system. a b

ようこさん きょう、いっしょにえいがをみませんか。でんわをください。 リー	ようこさん きょう、いっしょにえいがをみませんか。でんわをください。 リー

Drill: Reading

Pronounce the following syllables.

1. A. しゃ　　きゃ　　じゃ
   B. しゅ　　きゅ　　じゅ
   C. しょ　　きょ　　じょ

2. A. にゃ　　みゃ　　びゃ
   B. にゅ　　みゅ　　びゅ
   C. にょ　　みょ　　びょ

3. A. ら　　りゃ　　る
   B. りゅ　　ろ　　りょ
   C. りゃあ　　りゅう　　りょう

Dialog 1

Sara Brown greets Yoko (Yōko) Yamada.

Brown : ああ、ようこさん。こんにちは。
Ā, Yōko san. Konnichiwa.

Yamada : ああ、こんにちは。
Ā, konnichiwa.

Brown : さむいですね。
Samuidesune.

Yamada : ええ、そうですね。
Ē, sōdesune.

Vocabulary Collection (Weather)	
さむいですね。 Samuidesune.	*It is cold, isn't it?*
あついですね。 Atsui desune.	*It is hot, isn't it?*
あたたかいですね。 Atatakai desune.	*It is warm, isn't it?*
すずしいですね。 Suzushii desune.	*It is cool, isn't it?*
いいてんきですね。 Iitenki desune.	*It is nice weather, isn't it?*

Task 1: Group Work

Greet three of your classmates, mentioning today's weather.

Dialog 2

Mike Falk sees Yoko (Yōko) Yamada, after one year of absence.

Falk : ああ、ようこさん。おげんきですか。
Ā, Yōko san. Ogenkidesuka?

Yamada : ええ、げんきです。マイクさんは。
Ē, genkidesu. Maikusanwa?

Falk : ええ、おかげさまで。
Ē, okagesamade.

Guess and Try 5 15 16 F

1. おげんきですか (ogenkidesuka) is often translated as *How are you?* in English. Investigate the difference between the two. How often do you ask these questions?

2. Why didn't Mike answer with おげんきです (ogenkidesu), but with げんきです (genkidesu), in Dialog 2?

3. おかげさまで (okagesamade) literally means *Thanks to you*, and なんとか (nantoka) literally means *(I am) barely (managing things)*. Why are the replies to おげんきですか (Ogenkidesuka?) in Japanese very negative in general? Compare them with the typical replies to *How are you?* in English.

Task 2: Pair Work

Pretend that you have not seen your partner for three months. Greet him / her.

Writing 1

Write the following numbers in hiragana a few times each.

いち	いち	いち	いち
に	に	に	に
さん	さん	さん	さん
よん	よん	よん	よん
ご	ご	ご	ご
ろく	ろく	ろく	ろく
なな	なな	なな	なな
はち	はち	はち	はち
きゅう	きゅう	きゅう	きゅう
じゅう	じゅう	じゅう	じゅう

Writing 2

Write all the words introduced in Basic Vocabulary in this chapter, three times each, and copy the dialogs in this lesson, paying attention to the punctuation.

– Grammar and Usage –

1 Basic Japanese sounds

Japanese has only five basic vowels **a**, **i**, **u**, **e** and **o**, and their longer counterparts **ā**, **ī**, **ū**, **ē** and **ō** (**aa**, **ii**, **uu**, **ee** and **oo**). Long vowels are pronounced by holding the basic vowels a moment longer.

Basic Vowels		
a	as in the vowel in "Aha"	ashi *leg*
i	as in the initial part of the vowel in "eat"	inu *dog*
u	as in the initial part of the vowel in "boot", but without lip rounding	ue *top*
e	as in the initial part of the vowel in "eight"	e *drawing*
o	as in the initial part of the vowel in "oat"	origami *origami*

Long Vowels		
ā / aa	okāsan / okaasan	*mother*
ī / ii	onīsan / oniisan	*elder brother*
ū / uu	kūki / kuuki	*air*
ē / ee	onēsan / oneesan	*elder sister*
ō / oo	otōsan / otoosan	*father*

The vowels **i** and **u** are whispered or devoiced when they are between two voiceless consonants such as **p**, **t**, **k**, **s**, **sh**, **ch**, **ts** and **h**, or when they are at the end of the word preceded by a voiceless consonant (for example, **kushi** *comb*, **sukiyaki** *sukiyaki*).

Most of the Japanese consonants are similar to English consonants, except the following:

- The sound **r** is made by tapping the tip of the tongue behind the upper teeth. It is similar to the brief flap sound in "lettuce" or "letter" in American English.
- The sound **f** occurs only before the vowel **u** and is pronounced by bringing the upper and lower lips close to each other, and blowing air between them gently. Lips are not rounded very much.
- The sound **w** occurs only before the vowel **a** and is pronounced without rounding lips too much.
- The sound **y** occurs only before the vowels **a**, **u** and **o**.
- The sound **ts** occurs only before the vowel **u**.
- The sound **g** is often nasalized when it occurs between vowels.
- The sound **n** at the end of a syllable (ん) sounds like **m**, **n** or **ng**, depending on the sound following it. ん sounds like **m** when followed by **p**, **b** and **m**. It sounds like **ng** when followed by **k** and **g**. In other contexts, it sounds like **n**.

Complex consonants are limited to palatalized sounds such as **ky**, **gy**, **sy (=sh)**, **zy (=j)**, **ty (=ch)**, **ny**, **hy**, **by**, **py**, **my**, and **ry**. The complex sound **ry** is particularly difficult to pronounce for non-Japanese speakers. When you make the **ry** sound, try to make the **y** sound and tap the tip of your tongue behind the upper teeth at the same time. Or, you can say **ri** and **yu**, one after the other, repeatedly, as **ri yu ri yu ri yu ri yu ....** Then, gradually increase the speed until you can pronounce **ri** and **yu** as one syllable.

2 どうぞ: Go ahead (and do～), please (do～) [Offering]

The adverb どうぞ (dōzo) means *go ahead* or *please*. It is used when offering someone an item (for example, food, present, tool) or opportunity (for example, entering, seating, eating, speaking, receiving, using things).

(a) どうぞすわってください。
Dōzo suwattekudasai.
Please have a seat.

(b) どうぞうけとってください。
Dōzo uketottekudasai.
Please take it.

(c) どうぞつかってください。
Dōzo tsukattekudasai.
Go ahead and use (it.)

When the expected action is contextually clear, just saying どうぞ (dōzo) along with a hand or body gesture is sufficient and preferred.

3 Gratitude (ありがとうございます, etc)

ありがとう(arigatō) or ありがとうございます (arigatōgozaimasu) expresses one's gratitude most straightforwardly. ありがとう (arigatō) can be used only in an informal context and may not be used in a neutral / polite or formal context. In the latter case, ありがとうございます (arigatōgozaimasu) must be used. Either form can be preceded by どうも (dōmo), which emphasizes the feeling of gratefulness. Just by saying どうも, you can express your gratitude without sounding rude in most contexts.

The common reply to these expressions is いいえ (īe). This literally means *no*, but what it actually means in such a context is *not a big deal, no need to mention it* or *no problem*. It is short, but can be safely used in any context. どういたしまして (dōitashimashite) is another well-known reply to the expressions of gratitude, but it is not as frequently used as いいえ (īe).

4 どうも: Indeed [Gratitude / apology-intensifier]

The adverb どうも is used with the expressions of gratitude and apology, and makes them sound serious.

(a) どうもありがとうございます。
Dōmo arigatōgozaimasu.
Thank you very much.

(b) どうもすみません。
Dōmo sumimasen.
I am very sorry.

For expressing appreciation briefly, you can just say どうも (dōmo) with a slight bow. Although it is short, it never sounds impolite. In fact, saying どうも (dōmo) with a slight bow is more polite than saying just ありがとう (arigatō). どうも (dōmo) can also be used for a brief greeting. The spirit behind it is that the speaker always appreciates everything that the person does.

5 Introduction (はじめまして, よろしく, etc)

When you meet someone for the very first time, say はじめまして (hajimemashite), which means *This is the very first time (to see you)*. Then tell your name and say (どうぞ) よろしく (dōzo) yoroshiku. よろしく (yoroshiku) literally means *appropriately* or *as needed*, but it actually means *(Please) be nice and friendly (to me).* or *Pleased to meet you.*, in this context. It expresses the speaker's modest and friendly attitude toward the newly acquainted person. The typical reply to よろしく (yoroshiku) is こちらこそ (Kochirakoso), which means *That is I, (who should say that).*

When the Japanese introduce themselves, they often bow and exchange めいし (mēshi) *name cards* or *business cards*. For information on bowing, see Culture in this chapter. For information on めいし (mēshi), see Culture in Chapter Four.

6 Respectful titles (〜さん, 〜くん, etc)

〜さん ~san	Used for men and women in general.
〜さま ~sama	Used for business customers and for those to whom respect is due.
〜くん ~kun	Used for boys and one's subordinates.
〜ちゃん ~chan	Used for children and close childhood friends.

〜さん (~san) is one of the respectful titles that you can add at the end of other people's first or last names. 〜さん (~san) is gender neutral and appropriate for both polite / neutral and formal contexts. Other respectful titles like 〜さま (~sama), 〜くん (~kun) and 〜ちゃん (~chan) must be used carefully since they may sound too polite or too informal.

If available, occupational titles such as 〜せんせい (~sensē) *Professor~* are preferred to respectful titles since the former can indicate the social relationship between the speaker and listener more clearly than the latter. Remember that no respectful title is used for the speaker's own name in any situation.

For addressing close friends and family members, their first names alone without any respectful title may be used. The last names alone without any respectful title are used only in athletic clubs, among male friends and in a context with traditional hierarchical human relationships like superiors and subordinates.

7 Greetings (こんにちは, おはようございます, etc)

The following are phrases of あいさつ (aisatsu) *greetings*.

(a) おはようございます。
Ohayōgozaimasu.
Good morning.

(b) こんにちは。
Konnichiwa.
Good afternoon.

(c) こんばんは。
Konbanwa.
Good evening.

(a) is used in the (early) morning, (b) is used around noon and in the afternoon, and (c) is used in the late evening, after the sunset. When greeting your close friends, ございます (gozaimasu) in おはようございます (ohayōgozaimasu) can be omitted. The Japanese often just say どうも (dōmo) for brief greeting, regardless of the time of the day and the relative social status of the person you are greeting. Note that the last character of こんにちは (konnichiwa) and こんばんは (konbanwa) is は (ha), but its pronunciation is **wa**.

8 Parting (さようなら, etc)

The following are expressions used before parting from someone.

(a) じゃあ、また。
Jā, mata.
Okay, see you later. (lit.: Then, again.)

(b) じゃあ、また。さようなら。
Jā, mata. Sayōnara.
Okay, see you next time. Goodbye.
(lit.: Then, again. Goodbye.)

(c) しつれいします。
Shitsurēshimasu.
I will get going. (lit.: I will be rude.)

(d) いってきます。
Ittekimasu.
I am leaving. (lit.: I will go (there) and return.)

For your social equals and subordinates, (a) or (b) is appropriate. If you are going to see the person again on the same day, (a) is appropriate, but (b) is not. For your social superiors, (c) is the best choice. (d) is appropriate only for your family members because it implies that the person leaves his / her home but will return. さようなら (Sayōnara) is not usually used with one's own family members.

9 〜ください: Please do〜 [Requesting]

ください (kudasai) literally means *give (it) to me*, and when it follows a verb (in the "te-form"), it expresses a request.

(a) いってください。
Itte kudasai.
Please say (it).

(b) たべてください。
Tabete kudasai.
Please eat (it).

10 おねがいします: Please〜 [Favor]

おねがいします (onegaishimasu) literally means *I will beg you* and is used for politely requesting some action understood in the context.

(a) おねがいします。
Onegaishimasu.
Please. / Please do (it).

(b) ゆっくりおねがいします。
Yukkuri onegaishimasu.
Slowly, please. / Please do (it) slowly.

(c) もういちどおねがいします。
Mōichido onegaishimasu.
One more time, please. / Please do (it) one more time.

11 あっ: Oops! / oh! [Shock]

The interjection あっ (ah) is used when the speaker noticed or realized something all of a sudden, with surprise.

(a) あっ、すみません。だいじょうぶですか。
Ah, sumimasen. Daijōbudesu ka?
Oops, ... Excuse me, are you all right?

(b) あっ、さいふをわすれました。
Ah, saifu o wasuremashita.
Oh, I forgot my wallet.

12 すみません: Excuse me / I am sorry [Apology / attention catching]

すみません (sumimasen) can be used for apologizing. Its typical reply is いいえ (Īe: *Don't mention it. It's okay.*), but if the person thinks the mistake is serious, he / she will say はい (hai).

(a) あっ、すみません。
Ah, sumimasen.
Oops, ... Sorry.
— いいえ。だいじょうぶです。
— Īe. Daijōbudesu.
— *Not (to worry). I'm fine.*

(b) どうもすみません。
Dōmo sumimasen.
I am really sorry.
— はい。
— Hai.
— *Okay, (apology accepted).*

すみません (sumimasen) can be used with the phrase of gratitude, implying that the speaker feels sorry for receiving overwhelming kindness from others.

(c) どうも すみません。ありがとうございます。
Dōmo sumimasen. Arigatōgozaimasu.
I feel bad, but thank you very much.
— いいえ。
— Iie.
— *Not (to worry).*

すみません (sumimasen) can be also used for catching someone's attention:

(d) あのう、ちょっとすみません。
Anō, chotto sumimasen.
Ahhh... Excuse me, a little bit.
(e) あのう、すみません。
Anō, sumimasen.
Ahh... Excuse me.
(f) ちょっとすみません。
Chotto sumimasen.
Excuse me, a little bit.

13 あのう: Ahhh, ... [Initiating talk]

The interjection あのう (anō) is used when the speaker is about to talk about a new subject or topic.

(a) あのう、…
Anō, ...
Ahhh, ...

It may be used for attracting someone's attention in public.

(b) あのう、すみません。
Anō, sumimasen.
Ahhh, ... Excuse me.

14 ちょっと: A little bit [Expression softener]

The adverb ちょっと (chotto) literally means *a little*, but it has many conversational functions. One of them is to soften the utterance and show the speaker's friendly attitude.

(a) あのう、ちょっとすみません。
Anō, chotto sumimasen.
Ahhh, ... Excuse me, a little bit.

15 おげんきですか: How are you?

おげんきですか (Ogenkidesu ka?) is often translated as *How are you?* in English; however; there are two differences between them. First, *How are you?* in English can be used with someone you see every day, but おげんきですか (Ogenkidesu ka?) may not, as the latter literally asks about other people's physical or mental health. Second, the common replies to *How are you?* in English are positive ones, for example, *I am fine.* and *Great!*. By contrast, the common replies to おげんきですか (Ogenkidesu ka?) in Japanese are neutral, modest, or negative. The following are typical replies to おげんきですか (Ogenkidesu ka?):

(a) げんきです。
Genkidesu.
(I am) fine.
(b) まあまあです。
Māmā desu.
So so.
(c) おかげさまで。
Okagesamade.
Luckily, (I am fine). /
Thanks to (you and other people), I am fine.
(d) なんとか。
Nantoka.
(I am) barely (managing things around myself).

16 Polite prefix (お～ and ご～)

The polite prefix お (o) is used optionally to show respect to others and the things that belong to them. For example, you can say to someone げんきですか (Genkidesu ka?) *How are you?* or more politely, おげんきですか (Ogenkidesu ka?). On the other hand, when you talk about yourself or things that belong to you, you should not use お. For example, わたしはおげんきです (Watashiwa ogenkidesu) *I am fine.* or わたしのおなまえはやまだです (Watashino onamaewa Yamada desu) *My name is Yamada.* is inappropriate.

However, the use of お (o) is almost obligatory for some words such as おなか (onaka) *belly / abdomen*, regardless of whether you are talking about yourself or about others. There is another polite prefix in Japanese, which is ご (go), as in ごきょうだい (gokyōdai) *siblings*. The basic rule is to use the prefix お for a native Japanese word and to use the prefix ご for a word borrowed from Chinese, but this also has numerous exceptions.

– Culture –

Ⓐ Traditional martial arts

すもう (Sumō) *sumo wrestling* is the national sport, with a long history in Japan. It was referred to in the "Kojiki" (Legendary Stories of Old Japan) and "Nihon Shoki" (Chronicles of Japan). "Sumo" was originally practiced during festivals and on holy days at "Shinto" shrines. "Sumo" wrestlers are not limited to Japanese citizens. In 1993, a foreign sumo wrestler called "Akebono", who was from Hawaii, became the first non-Japanese "Yokozuna" grand champion.

からて (karate) *karate* was originally developed in China as a way of unarmed self-defense. It was then further developed in "Okinawa" in Japan. It involves techniques such as thrusting, striking and kicking. A "karate" expert can break through a thick stack of bricks or wood with a single stroke.

じゅうどう (jūdō) *judo* originated in Japan and has attained global recognition. In 1964, it became an official event at the Tokyo Olympics.

けんどう (kendō) *kendo* is the Japanese fencing, developed from the swordsmanship of the "samurai". Practitioners use bamboo swords and wear heavy cotton padding and lacquered armor.

Ⓑ Bowing

Bowing plays an important role for communication in Japan. Phrases for gratitude, apology and greeting are almost always accompanied by bowing. People sometimes bow without saying anything. The deeper the bow, the deeper the respect for the person to whom you are bowing. The deep bow, using the upper half of the body, will be needed if you make a horrible mistake, receive overwhelming kindness or associate with people to whom you must show your respect seriously.

Otherwise, you do not have to bow very deeply. You can lower your head and shoulders slightly or just tilt your head forward for a moment or two in casual situations. At the time of introduction, the Japanese do not shake hands, hug or kiss, but just bow and smile. However, Westerners do not have to bow if they are not used to it and they can just shake hands at the time of introduction.

Ⓒ Japanese food

- さしみ (sashimi) is the thinly sliced raw seafood arranged beautifully on a plate.
- すし (sushi) is vinegared rice dishes such as にぎりずし (nigirizushi), which is raw seafood arranged on vinegared rice balls, and ちらしずし (chirashizushi), which is raw seafood arranged on a bowl of vinegared rice. They are served with soy sauce and the Japanese horseradish called わさび (wasabi).

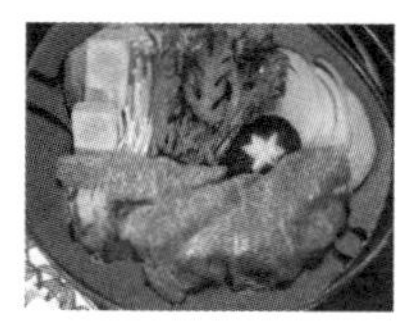

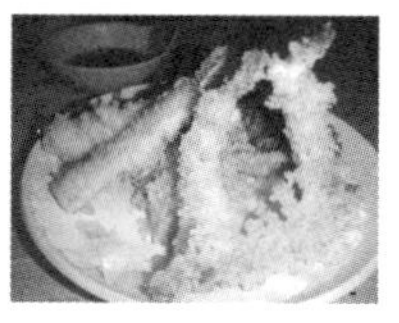

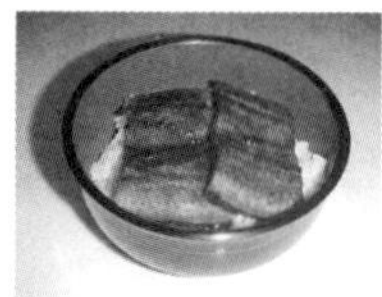

- すきやき (sukiyaki) is a thinly-sliced beef stew cooked in a soy-based sauce in a shallow pot. The ingredients are beef, bean curd, arum root gelatin noodles, mushrooms and vegetables. It is served with raw egg.
- てんぷら (tempura) is deep-fried vegetables and / or seafood in batter.
- うなぎ (unagi) is eel. It is grilled, brushed with a special sauce similar to teriyaki sauce and typically placed on rice in a big bowl.

Ⓓ Japanese names

The Japanese say or write their family names first, then their first names next. They apply the same convention to Chinese names and Korean names. However, Westerners' names do not have to follow this convention.

Most Japanese family names consist of two or three Chinese characters. The most common family names in Japan include 鈴木 *Suzuki* (すずき Suzuki), 佐藤 *Sato* (さとう Satō), 田中 *Tanaka* (たなか Tanaka), 山本 *Yamamoto* (やまもと Yamamoto), 渡辺 *Watanabe* (わたなべ Watanabe), 高橋 *Takahashi* (たかはし Takahashi), 小林 *Kobayashi* (こばやし Kobayashi), 中村 *Nakamura* (なかむら Nakamura), 伊藤 *Ito* (いとう Itō) and 斎藤 *Saito* (さいとう Saitō).

Most men's first names consist of one, two or three Kanji characters, for example, 正 (ただし Tadashi), 真 (まこと Makoto), 望 *Nozomu* (のぞむ Nozomu), 良夫 *Yoshio* (よしお Yoshio), 健一 *Kenichi* (けんいち Kenichi), 太郎 *Taro*

(たろう Tarō), 昌太郎 *Shotaro* (しょうたろう Shōtarō), and 喜一郎 *Kiichiro* (きいちろう Kiichirō).

Many women's first names end in 子 (こ ko), especially for post-WWII generations, for example, 洋子 *Yoko* (ようこ Yōko), 幸子 *Sachiko* (さちこ Sachiko), 良子 *Yoshiko* (よしこ Yoshiko), and 真理子 *Mariko* (まりこ Mariko). Other names have two or three syllables, for example, 俊江 *Toshie* (としえ Toshie), ゆかり *Yukari* (Yukari), 友恵 *Tomoe* (ともえ Tomoe), 由里 *Yuri* (ゆり Yuri), and まり *Mari* (Mari). Some names are written only in Hiragana.

E Japanese islands

Japan consists of four major islands, which are ほんしゅう (Honshū) *Honshu*, ほっかいどう (Hokkaidō) *Hokkaido*, きゅうしゅう (Kyūshū) *Kyushu* and しこく (Shikoku) *Shikoku*, and about 7,000 small islands, which are in a chain from northeast to southwest. The length of Japan is about 3,000 km and its north end, えとろふとう (Etorofutō) is located near 45º N. L., which is the same latitude as Montreal, Canada and its south end, おきのとりしま (Okinotorishima), is located near 20º N. L., which is the same latitude as the southern part of Florida. The total area of Japan is 380,000 km^2, which is only 1/25 of the total area of the United States (9,370,000 km^2). The following are the largest seven islands in Japan:

ほんしゅう	Honshū 本州	*Honshu*	227,414 km^2
ほっかいどう	Hokkaidō 北海道	*Hokkaido*	78,073 km^2
きゅうしゅう	Kyūshū 九州	*Kyushu*	36,554 km^2
しこく	Shikoku 四国	*Shikoku*	18,256 km^2
えとろふとう	Etorofutō 択捉島	*Etorofu Island*	3,139 km^2
くなしりとう	Kunashiritō 国後島	*Kunashiri Island*	1,500 km^2
おきなわとう	Okinawatō 沖縄島	*Okinawa Island*	1,185 km^2

F Modesty

The Japanese respect modesty. Modesty can be seen in many Japanese set phrases. For example, when the Japanese introduce themselves to others, they often say よろしくおねがいします (Yoroshiku onegaishimasu), which literally means *Please be nice to me*. As a reply to おげんきですか (Ogenkidesu ka?) *How are you?*, they often say おかげさまで (Okagesamade), which means *(I am fine) thanks to you*. When Japanese give a gift to others, they often say つまらないものですが (Tsumaranaimono desu ga), which literally means *It is not a great gift, but (please accept it)*.

Modesty can be also seen in how the Japanese react when they (or their family members) receive a compliment from others. For example, if you say that their mother is pretty, they usually deny it. If you say that their jacket is pretty, they usually mention all the negative aspects of it (for example, old, cheap). However, it does not mean that you should not give a compliment to Japanese people. In fact, they do give a lot of compliments to other people. It is just that they tend to negate the compliments when they receive them.

– Writing –

A Hiragana

Hiragana characters were created by women during the Heian period (794 - 1192) by modifying the kanji characters. If you follow the correct stroke order, you will see that all the strokes in each hiragana character form one imaginary line. Each hiragana character represents a syllable sound and is mainly used for specifying grammatical particles, suffixes, inflections and native Japanese words not covered by kanji.

Basic hiragana

ん n	わ wa	ら ra	や ya	ま ma	は ha	な na	た ta	さ sa	か ka	あ a
		り ri		み mi	ひ hi	に ni	ち chi	し shi	き ki	い i
		る ru	ゆ yu	む mu	ふ fu	ぬ nu	つ tsu	す su	く ku	う u
		れ re		め me	へ he	ね ne	て te	せ se	け ke	え e
	を o	ろ ro	よ yo	も mo	ほ ho	の no	と to	そ so	こ ko	お o

- は represents the sound **ha**, but it exceptionally represents the sound **wa** if used for the topic marking particle or an item that was historically a topic marking particle, for example, おなまえは (Onamae wa?) *Your name?*, こんにちは (Konnichiwa) *Good afternoon.*
- へ represents the sound **he**, but it exceptionally represents the sound **e** if used for the direction marking particle.
- を is exclusively used for the direct object marking particle (accusative case marking particle).

- ん represents the syllable-ending **n / m** sound, but does not represent a syllable-initial **n** sound.

Voicing markers and plosive markers

Voiced sounds are specified by the voicing marker " ゛ " as in うなぎ (unagi) *eel*. Voiceless plosive sounds are specified by the plosive marker " ゜ " as in てんぷら (tempura) *tempura*. The sound **ji** is usually represented as じ, but as ぢ in some limited cases, for example, にほんじん (nihonjin) *Japanese person*, はなぢ (hanaji) *nose-bleeding*. Similarly, the sound **zu** is usually represented as ず, but as づ in some limited cases, for example, かず (kazu) *number*, つづく (tsuzuku) *to continue*.

ぱ pa	ば ba	だ da	ざ za	が ga
ぴ pi	び bi	ぢ ji	じ ji	ぎ gi
ぷ pu	ぶ bu	づ zu	ず zu	ぐ gu
ぺ pe	べ be	で de	ぜ ze	げ ge
ぽ po	ぼ bo	ど do	ぞ zo	ご go

Double consonants

The first consonant of double consonants is represented by a small っ, for example, きっぷ (kippu) *tickets*, きって (kitte) *stamps*, けっこん (kekkon) *marriage*, まっすぐ (massugu) *straight*. The small っ is realized as a brief pause.

pp, tt, kk, ss	っ

Long vowels

In hiragana, long vowels are represented by adding a hiragana character, あ, い, う, え or お to another hiragana character. For example, the long vowel **ā** is represented by adding あ to a hiragana character with a vowel **a**, as in かあ (**kā**), さあ (**sā**) and ああ (**ā**). The same logic applies to the long vowels **ī** and **ū**. The long vowel **ī** is represented by adding い and the long vowel **ū** is represented by adding う, to another hiragana character, as in きい (**kī**) and くう (**kū**). However, the long vowel **ē** is usually represented by adding い (for example, せんせい (sensē) *teacher*) and only occasionally by adding え (for example, おねえさん (onēsan) *older sister*) and the long vowel **ō** is usually represented by adding う (for example, おとうさん (otōsan) *father*) and only occasionally by adding お (for example, おおきい (ōkii) *big* and とおり (tōri) *street*).

ā / aa	ああ
ī / ii	いい
ū / uu	うう
ē / ee	えい (ええ)
ō / oo	おう (おお)

Complex sounds (Palatalized sounds)

Japanese syllables may begin with a palatalized sound, which is a combination of a consonant and the semi-vowel **y** (for example, **kya**, **gyu** and **nyo**). Palatalized sounds are found only before **a**, **u** or **o**. Syllables with palatalized sounds are represented by combining two hiragana characters. The first character is the one that represents the initial consonant plus the vowel **i** and the second character is small-sized ゃ, ゅ or ょ, depending on whether the following vowel is **a**, **u** or **o**, respectively. For example, the syllables **kya**, **gyu** and **nyo** are represented as きゃ, ぎゅ and にょ respectively.

りゃ rya	みゃ mya	ぴゃ pya	びゃ bya	ひゃ hya	にゃ nya	ちゃ cha	じゃ ぢゃ ja	しゃ sha	ぎゃ gya	きゃ kya
りゅ ryu	みゅ myu	ぴゅ pyu	びゅ byu	ひゅ hyu	にゅ nyu	ちゅ chu	じゅ ぢゅ ju	しゅ shu	ぎゅ gyu	きゅ kyu
りょ ryo	みょ myo	ぴょ pyo	びょ byo	ひょ hyo	にょ nyo	ちょ cho	じょ ぢょ jo	しょ sho	ぎょ gyo	きょ kyo

Ⓑ Punctuation and format

The marker " 。 " is placed at the end of each sentence, just like a period in English. The marker " 、 " is placed at the end of a phrase, just like a comma in English, but the Japanese do not follow strict rules on when and where they place " 、 ".

Example 1: すみません。
Sumimasen.
I'm sorry.

Example 2: いいえ、ちがいます。
Iie, chigaimasu.
No, it's wrong.

A quotation is specified by quotation markers 「　」.

Example: やまださんは「こんにちは」と、いいました。
Yamadasan wa Konnichiwa to iimashita.
Ms. Yamada said, "Good morning".

Japanese does not have a question mark, although you often see? in memos and personal letters.

Example: おげんきですか。
Ogenkidesu ka.
How are you?

The marker "・" is used between listed items, and between the first name and the last name of Western people.

Example 1: ジョン・スミス
Jon Sumisu
John Smith

Example 2: すし・すきやき・さしみ・てんぷら
sushi, sukiyaki, sashimi, tempura
sushi, sukiyaki, sashimi and tempura

Japanese paragraphs are written either horizontally from left to right, as in English, or vertically from top to down, from right to left on a page. Academic papers, research documents, business contracts, business letters and instruction manuals are conventionally written horizontally. Novels and essays are formally written vertically. Personal letters, diaries, memos and informal essays can be written either vertically or horizontally, but most young Japanese write them horizontally.

寒くなりましたが、山田さんはお元気ですか。・・・花子は今高校三年生で、「早く大学に入学したい」と言っています。
・・・ →

Horizontal

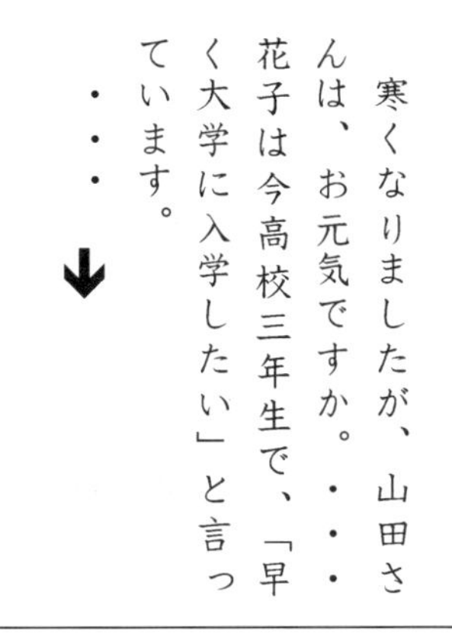

Vertical

When written horizontally, the small-size characters (つ・や・ゆ・よ) will occupy the lower half (or the lower left part) of the space between the two neighboring characters, but when written vertically, they will occupy the right half (or the upper right part) of the space.

– Review –

Q1. Read the hiragana characters in each set, paying attention to the differences and similarities among them. Different typefaces are purposely used.

1. つ・し・も・つ
2. お・あ・の・ぬ・め・ぬ
3. き・き・さ・ち・さ
4. ね・わ・れ・ね
5. ら・ろ・る・さ・ち
6. よ・ま・は・ほ・な
7. こ・り・り・こ・り・い
8. そ・て・そ・て

Q2. Complete the following hiragana table appropriately. Follow the regular あいうえお order.

	わ	ら	や	ま	は	な	た	さ	か	あ
		り		み	ひ	に	ち	し	き	い
		る	ゆ	む	ふ	ぬ	つ	す	く	う
		れ		め	へ	ね	て	せ	け	え
ん	を	ろ	よ	も	ほ	の	と	そ	こ	お

Q3. Read the following words and phrases.

1. にほん
2. どうもありがとうございます。
3. はじめまして。
4. おはようございます。
5. こんにちは。
6. もういちどいってください。

Q4. What would you say in the following situations?

1. Your friend has just served you a cup of tea.
2. You accidentally stepped on someone's foot in the train.
3. You met someone for the first time and you want to tell him / her your name.

4. You run into your Japanese language teacher in the library in the morning.
5. You want to ask your teacher to speak slowly.
6. You want to ask your teacher to repeat what he / she said.
7. You are going to leave the teacher's office.

Q5. Respond to the following phrases.

1. ありがとうございます。
2. じゃあ、また。
3. いいですか。
4. よろしく。

Q6. Say the entire sequence of the following ten numbers until you know it by heart.

いち	に	さん	よん	ご	ろく	なな	はち	きゅう	じゅう
1	2	3	4	5	6	7	8	9	10

Q7. Fill in the blanks.

1. *Homework* しゅ く だ い
2. *School* がっ こ う
3. *Student* が く せ い
4. *Mother* お か あ さん
5. *Older sister* お ね え さん

Q8. Fill in the blanks and complete the following short dialogs.

1. Dialog A

Tanaka : はじめまして。たなかです。よろしく。

Yamada : はじめまして。やまだ です。どうぞ よろしく。

2. Dialog B

Tanaka : どうぞ。

Yamada : どうも ありがとう ございます。

Tanaka : いいえ。

Tips and Additional Knowledge: Must-know Set Phrases

Any language has a number of set-phrases that have to be used for specific situations. The following Japanese set phrases may not have the exact English equivalents, but they are necessary once you go to Japan and live there. Understanding in what context you need them is the key to success.

Set Phrases and Meaning	Context
1. いただきます。 *I will receive the meal.*	Right before you start eating.
2. ごちそうさま。 *It was a feast.*	Right after you finish your meal.
3. いってきます。 *I'm leaving and will be back.*	When you leave your home for work or school.
4. いってらっしゃい。 *You go and come back.*	When you send your family members off to work or schools.
5. ただいま。 *I'm home.*	When you return home.
6. おかえりなさい。 *You are home.*	When your family member returns home.

CHAPTER TWO

Identifying Things and People

Lesson 8
私は日本人です **Home Countries** 26

Lesson 9
せんこうは何ですか **Academic Major** 28

Lesson 10
それはわえいじてんですか **Things in the Classroom** 30

Lesson 11
あのたてものは何ですか **Campus** 32

Grammar and Usage 34

1 こちら: This person 34
2 Personal pronouns (私, あなた, etc) 34
3 はい, いいえ: Yes / no [Agreement / disagreement] 34
4 ～じん [Nationality / citizenship / ethnic background of people] 34
5 ～は: As for～, speaking of～ [Topic marker] 35
6 ～です (だ): To be [Copula] 35
7 ～か [Sentence final question particle] 36
8 なに, なん: What [Question word for non-human items] 36
9 ちょっと, まあまあ: Slightly, more or less 36
10 ～よ: I tell you [Sentence final emphasis particle] . . 37
11 Demonstratives (あれ, あの～, etc) 37
12 じゃあ: Then, in that case [Transition] 37
13 ～も: Too, also [Addition] 37
14 だれ, どなた: Who [Question word for people] 38

Culture 38

A Acknowledging and responding 38

Writing 38

a Kanji strokes 38
b Reading kanji 38

Kanji List 39

Review 39

Tips and Additional Knowledge: Paper Crane 40

CHAPTER TWO | Lesson 8

私は日本人です Home Countries

Notes Relating to This Lesson	
Grammar and Usage	
1 こちら 34	6 ～です(だ) 35
2 Personal pronouns 34	7 ～か 36
3 はい, いいえ 34	**Writing**
4 ～じん 34	ⓐ Kanji strokes 38
5 ～は 35	

Basic Vocabulary and Kanji

にほんじꜜん	日本人	*n. Japanese people*
アメリカ(あめりか)	アメリカ	*n. the United States of America*
ちゅꜜうごく	中国	*n. China*
かꜜんこく	韓国	*n. Korea*
こちら		*pron. this way, this side, this person* 1
どꜜちら		*q. which way, which direction*
わたし	私	*pron. I, me (1st person pronoun)* 2
あなꜜた	貴方	*pron. you (2nd person pronoun)* 2
はꜜい		*yes, right* 3
いいえ		*no, wrong* 3
～じん	～人	*~person (nationality) (日本人 Japanese people)* 4
～は (wa)		*prt. as for~ (topic marker) Exceptional pronunciation (wa)* 5
～です		*cop. to be (polite / neutral present affirmative form of ～だ)* 6
～じゃありません / ～ではありません		*cop. not to be (polite / neutral present negative form of ～だ)* 6
～か		*prt. sentence final question particle* 7
～から		*prt. from~*

Newly introduced kanji:

私(わたし) ⓐ・～人(じん)・日本人(にほんじん)

私	ˊ 二 千 禾 禾 私 私	人	ノ 人
日	｜ 冂 冃 日	本	一 十 才 木 本

Dialog

Yoko Yamada introduces John Smith to Ben Lee.

やまだ　：リー(りい)さん、こちらはスミス(すみす)さんです。

スミス(すみす)　：はじめまして。スミス(すみす)です。よろしく。

リー(りい)　：はじめまして。リー(りい)です。こちらこそよろしく。

スミス(すみす)　：リー(りい)さんは日本人(にほんじん)ですか。

リー(りい)　：いいえ、私(わたし)は日本人じゃありません。ちゅうごく人(じん)です。

スミス(すみす)　：ああ、そうですか。

リー(りい)　：スミス(すみす)さんはどちらからですか。

スミス(すみす)　：私はアメリカ(あめりか)からです。

リー(りい)　：ああ、そうですか。

Guess and Try 1 2 3 4 5 6 7

1. What does こちら mean in the above dialog?
2. In こちらはスミス(すみす)さんです, how is "は" pronounced?
3. Did you find "あなた *you*" in the above dialog?
4. Ask your partner whether he / she is a Japanese, and let him / her answer in Japanese.

Drill 1: Formation

日本 ⟶ 日本人

1. ちゅうごく　2. かんこく　3. アメリカ(あめりか)
4. インド(いんど)　5. フランス(ふらんす)　6. フィリピン(ふぃりぴん)
7. カナダ(かなだ)　8. オーストラリア(おーすとらりあ)

Drill 2: Formation

Variation 1:

たなかさん・日本人 ⟶ たなかさんは日本人です

Variation 2:

たなかさん・日本人 ⟶ たなかさんは日本人じゃありません (たなかさんは日本人ではありません)

1. スミス(すみす)さん・アメリカ(あめりか)人
2. チェン(ちぇん)さん・ちゅうごく人
3. キム(きむ)さん・かんこく人
4. シェボレー(しぇぼれえ)さん・フランス(ふらんす)人
5. ミトラ(みとら)さん・インド(いんど)人

Task: Classroom Activity

Ask your classmates where they are from.

A : Bさん、Bさんはどちらからですか。

B : 私はかんこくからです。

A : ああ、そうですか。

B : Aさんはどちらからですか。

A : 私はとうきょうからです。

Vocabulary Collection (Countries)	
日本(にほん) *Japan*	中国(ちゅうごく) *China*
韓国(かんこく) *Korea*	アメリカ(あめりか) *U.S.A.*
台湾(たいわん) *Taiwan*	ホンコン(ほんこん) *Hong Kong*
インド(いんど) *India*	タイ(たい) *Thailand*
フランス(ふらんす) *France*	スペイン(すぺいん) *Spain*
イギリス(いぎりす) *England*	ドイツ(どいつ) *Germany*
イタリア(いたりあ) *Italy*	ポーランド(ぽうらんど) *Poland*
カナダ(かなだ) *Canada*	フィリピン(ふぃりぴん) *Philippines*
オーストラリア(おうすとらりあ) *Australia*	マレーシア(まれえしあ) *Malaysia*
ペルー(ぺるう) *Peru*	メキシコ(めきしこ) *Mexico*
ロシア(ろしあ) *Russia*	
ニュージーランド(にゅうじいらんど) *New Zealand*	

Writing 1

Write the Japanese words introduced in Basic Vocabulary and Kanji in this lesson, several times each.

にほんじん	にほんじん	アメリカ	アメリカ
ちゅうごく	ちゅうごく	かんこく	かんこく
こちら	こちら	どちら	どちら
わたし	わたし	あなた	あなた
はい	はい	いいえ	いいえ
～じん	～じん	～は	～は
～です	～です	じゃありません	じゃありません
～か	～か	～から	～から
私	私	人	人
日	日	本	本

Writing 2

Write the kanji characters learned in this lesson, paying attention to how each stroke is drawn. ⓐ

私	私	私	私
人	人	人	人
日	日	日	日
本	本	本	本
日本人	日本人	日本人	日本人
私	私	私	私

せんこうは何ですか Academic Major

Notes Relating to This Lesson	
Grammar and Usage	**Culture**
8 なに, なん 36	A Acknowledging and responding 38
9 ちょっと, まあまあ 36	
10 〜よ 37	

Basic Vocabulary and Kanji

せんこう	専攻	*n. academic major*
せんもん	専門	*n. specialty (cf.* 専攻(せんこう)*)*
えいご	英語	*n. English language*
ぶ˥んがく	文学	*n. literature*
すうがく	数学	*n. mathematics*
な˥ん / な˥に	何	*q. what* 8
まあま˥あ		*adv. more or less* 9
とても		*adv. very much* 9
ちょ˥っと		*adv. slightly, a little* 9
むずかし˥い	難しい・難しくない	*adj. difficult*
かんたん(な)	簡単だ・簡単じゃない	*adj. easy*
〜ご	〜語	*~language (*日本語(にほんご) *Japanese language)*
〜よ		*prt. sentence-final emphasis marker* 10
そうですか		*Oh, I see. / Really?* A

Newly introduced kanji:

何(なん・なに)・ぶん学(がく)(文学(ぶんがく))・すう学(がく)(数学(すうがく))

何	ノイ仁仃何何何	学	、""⺍⺍⺍学学

Dialog

John Smith asks Ben Lee about his academic major.

スミス(すみす)：リー(りい)さん、せんこうは何ですか。

リー(りい)：せんこうはすう学です。

スミス：①ああ、そうですか。
すう学は むずかしいですか。

リー：いいえ、とても かんたんです。

スミス：②そうですか。
③すう学はちょっとむずかしいですよ。

リー：スミスさん、せんこうは。

スミス：まだきめていません。

(まだ決(き)めていません *I have not decided (it) yet.*)

Guess and Try 1

Ask your partner about his / her major. 8

Guess and Try 2

What is the difference between そうですか with a falling intonation in ① and そうですか with a falling-rising intonation in ②? If necessary, listen to the above dialog again. A

そうですか。(↘) : ____________________

そうですか。(↘↗) : ____________________

Guess and Try 3

Choose the appropriate options in the parentheses. 9

1. (まあまあ・ちょっと) かんたんです。
2. (まあまあ・ちょっと) むずかしいです。

Guess and Try 4

What is the function of よ in sentence ③ in Dialog? 10

Drill: Substitution

せんこうは<u>コンピューター・サイエンス</u>(こんぴゅうたあ・さいえんす)です。

1. 日本(にほん)ご
2. かんこくご
3. ぶん学
4. すう学
5. えいご

Task: Survey

Ask five of your classmates what their majors are and whether they are difficult.

私(わたし)		
さん		
さん		
さん		
さん		
さん		

Vocabulary Collection (Academic Subjects)	
日本語(にほんご) *Japanese language*	英語(えいご) *English language*
中国語(ちゅうごくご) *Chinese language*	韓国語(かんこくご) *Korean language*
文学(ぶんがく) *literature*	数学(すうがく) *mathematics*
社会学(しゃかいがく) *sociology*	化学(かがく) *chemistry*
生物学(せいぶつがく) *biology*	経済学(けいざいがく) *economics*
心理学(しんりがく) *psychology*	工学(こうがく) *engineering*
言語学(げんごがく) *linguistics*	歴史(れきし) *history*
物理(ぶつり) *physics*	人類学(じんるいがく) *anthropology*
政治学(せいじがく) *political science*	美術(びじゅつ) *fine art*
音楽(おんがく) *music*	教育学(きょういくがく) *education*
経営学(けいえいがく) *business administration*	
コンピューター・サイエンス(こんぴゅうたあ・さいえんす) *computer science*	

Short Reading

私(わたし)はエミリー(えみりい)・チェン(ちぇん)です。アメリカ人(あめりかじん)です。出身(しゅっしん)はロサンゼルス(ろさんぜるす)です。趣味(しゅみ)はテニス(てにす)です。専攻(せんこう)は経済学(けいざいがく)です。経済学(けいざいがく)はちょっと難(むずか)しいです。

(出身(しゅっしん) *birth place,* ロサンゼルス(ろさんぜるす) *Los Angeles,* 趣味(しゅみ) *hobby,* テニス(てにす) *tennis,* 経済学(けいざいがく) *economics*)

Writing 1

Write about yourself in Japanese. (For now, use hiragana or English for the words to be written in katakana.)

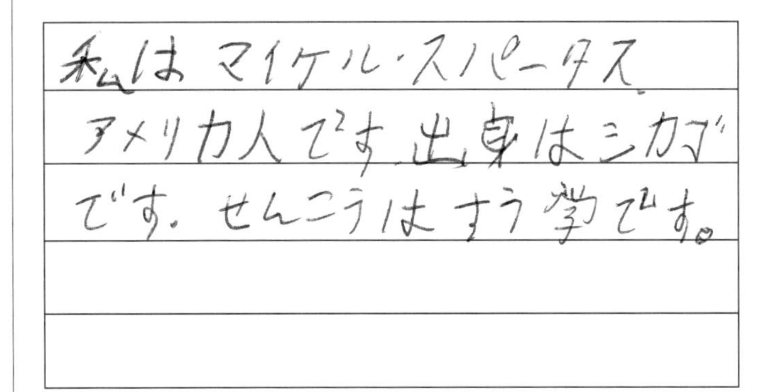

私はマイケル・スパータス
アメリカ人です。出身はシカゴ
です。せんこうはすう学です。

Writing 2

Write the Japanese words introduced in Basic Vocabulary and Kanji in this lesson, several times each.

せんこう	せんこう	せんもん	せんもん
えいご	えいご	ぶん学	ぶん学
すう学	すう学	何	何
まあまあ	まあまあ	とても	とても
ちょっと	ちょっと	むずかしい	むずかしい
かんたん	かんたん		

それはわえいじてんですか Things in the Classroom

Notes Relating to This Lesson	
Grammar and Usage	
[11] Demonstratives 37	
[12] じゃあ 37	
[13] 〜も 37	

Basic Vocabulary and Kanji

ほ⌉ん	本	*n. book*
ま⌉ど	窓	*n. window*
かばん	鞄	*n. bag*
くつ⌉	靴	*n. shoes*
つくえ	机	*n. desk*
いす	椅子	*n. chair*
ぼうし	帽子	*n. cap, hat*
とけい	時計	*n. watch, clock*
えんぴつ	鉛筆	*n. pencil*
わえいじ⌉てん	和英辞典	*n. Japanese-English dictionary*
えいわじ⌉てん	英和辞典	*n. English-Japanese dictionary*
これ		*pron. this one* [11]
それ		*pron. that one (near you)* [11]
あれ		*pron. that one (over there)* [11]
ど⌉れ		*q. which one* [11]
じゃ⌉あ		*interj. then* [12]
〜も		*prt. also* [13]

Newly introduced kanji:

本(ほん)・山田(やまだ) (surname)・川口(かわぐち) (surname)

山	丨 山 山	田	丨 冂 ⽥ 田 田
川	丿 川 川	口	丨 冂 口

Dialog

Yoko Yamada wants to use a Japanese-English dictionary. She wishes to borrow from Ken Kawaguchi who is holding a dictionary.

山田　：川口さん、それはわえいじてんですか。

川口　：いいえ。これはえいわじてんです。

山田　：ああ、そうですか。
(Pointing at the dictionary that is placed on the desk far away from them.)
じゃあ、あれはわえいじてんですか。

川口　：いいえ、あれもえいわじてんです。

山田　：ああ、そうですか。

Guess and Try 1

What is the function of the underlined interjection (じゃあ) in the above dialog? [12]

Guess and Try 2

Fill in the blanks with これ, それ, あれ or どれ. [11]

1. ________ ですよ。

2. ________ ですよ。

3. ________ ですよ。

4. ________ ですか。

Guess and Try 3

Choose the appropriate options in the parentheses. 13

1. これはペンです。あれ（は・も）ペンです。

2. これはペンです。あれ（は・も）えんぴつです。

Drill 1: Mini-Conversation

これです ⟶ ああ、それですか (with pointing gesture)

1. それです　　2. あれです　　3. これです

Repeat several times.

Drill 2: Mini-Conversation

これはいすですか ⟶ はい、それはいすです。

1. これは本ですか　　2. これはまどですか

3. それはかばんですか　　4. それはぼうしですか

5. あれはとけいですか　　6. あれはいすですか

Task 1: Pair Work

Point at an item in the classroom and ask your partner what that is. Use これ, それ and あれ appropriately. Make sure to say じゃあ before asking the next question.

For example:

A ： あれは何（なん）ですか。

B ： あれは本です。

A ： じゃあ、それは何ですか。

B ： これも本です。

Vocabulary Collection (Items in a Classroom)	
ドア *door*	黒板 *blackboard*
チョーク *chalk*	ペン *pen*
けしゴム *eraser*	教科書 / テキスト *textbook*
辞書 *dictionary*	ノート *notebook*
電気 *light, electricity*	ごみ箱 *trash can*

Task 2: Group Work (7 to 8 members)

Memory game: Each member in your group, except you, holds a small item such as えんぴつ, ぼうし, チョーク, さいふ *wallet*, ペン and けしゴム *eraser*. You are shown all the items at the same time for just 10 seconds, afterwhich the member holding the item will hide it behind his / her back. What you need to do is to recall what item each member is holding. Take turns to play the game. Find out who has the best memory.

For example:

A ： (Pointing at B.) それはとけいですね。

B ： いいえ、これは本です。(Showing the item.)

A ： (Pointing at C.) それはえんぴつですね。

B ： はい、これはえんぴつです。(Showing the item.)

Writing

Write the Japanese words introduced in Basic Vocabulary and Kanji in this lesson, several times each.

本	本	まど	まど
かばん	かばん	くつ	くつ
つくえ	つくえ	いす	いす
ぼうし	ぼし	とけい	とけい
えんぴつ	えんぴつ	かえいじてん	かえいじてん
えいかじてん	えいかじてん	これ	これ
それ	それ	あれ	あれ
どれ	どれ	じゃあ	じゃあ
山田	山田	川口	川口

あのたてものは何ですか Campus

Notes Relating to This Lesson	
Grammar and Usage 5 〜は .... 35 11 Demonstratives .... 37 14 だれ, どなた 38	**Writing** ⓑ Reading kanji 38

Basic Vocabulary and Kanji

たて⌉もの	建物	*n. building*
としょ⌉かん	図書館	*n. library*
たいいく⌉かん	体育館	*n. gym*
カフェテリア(かふぇてりあ)		*n. cafeteria*
りょ⌉う	寮	*n. dormitory*
どうぶつ	動物	*n. animal*
ね⌉こ	猫	*n. cat*
いぬ⌉	犬	*n. dog*
ひと	人	*n. person (cf. 〜かた)*
くるま	車	*n. car*
だ⌉れ	誰	*q. who* 14
ど⌉なた		*q. who (polite) (cf. だれ)* 14
この〜		*this~* 11
その〜		*that~ near you* 11
あの〜		*that~ over there* 11
どの〜		*which~* 11
〜かた⌉	〜方	*n. person (polite) (cf. 人(ひと))*

Newly introduced kanji:

人(ひと)ⓑ・犬(いぬ)・学生(がくせい)・先生(せんせい)・車(くるま)

犬	一ナ大犬	生	ノ𠂉十牛生
先	ノ𠂉⺧生𠂒先	車	一厂冂百百亘車

Dialog

Yoko Yamada is showing Ben Lee around the campus.

リー(りい): (Pointing at a building in the distance.) ①あのたてものは何(なん)ですか。

山田(やまだ): ②あれはカフェテリア(かふぇてりあ)です。

リー: ああ、そうですか。じゃあ、たいいくかんはどれですか。

山田: たいいくかんはこのたてものです。(Pointing at the building near them.)

リー: ああ、そうですか。あの人(ひと)はだれですか。(Ben Lee sees someone waving to Yoko Yamada from far away.)

山田: あの人は川口(かわぐち)さんです。

Guess and Try 1

Considering the difference between ① and ② in the above dialog, choose the appropriate options in the parentheses. 11

1. (あの・あれ) 車はBMW です。
2. (あれ・あの) はBMW です。
3. (これ・この) 車はBMW です。
4. (それ・その) 車はベンツ(べんつ)です。
5. ベンツ(べんつ)は(この・これ) です。
6. カフェテリア(かふぇてりあ)は(どの・どれ) たてものですか。

Guess and Try 2

What is the difference between the following sentences? 5

1. これはたいいくかんです。
2. たいいくかんはこれです。

Guess and Try 3

Choose the appropriate options in the parentheses. [14]

1. あの車は(何(なん)・だれ)ですか。
2. あのどうぶつは(何・だれ)ですか。
3. あの学生は(何・だれ)ですか。
4. あの先生は(だれ・どなた)ですか。
5. あのかたは(だれ・どなた)ですか。

Note:

1. Do not use a question word as a topic.
   どれはとしょかんですか。 (✕)
   (Ungrammatical) [5]

2. あれ, これ, それ and どれ are not used for people.
   これは川口(かわぐち)さんです。 (✕)
   (Ungrammatical) [11]

Drill: Formation

たてもの・カフェテリア(かふぇてりあ) → あのたてものはカフェテリア(かふぇてりあ)です

1. たてもの・たいいくかん
2. 車・BMW
3. どうぶつ・いぬ
4. 人・山田(やまだ)さん
5. 人・スミス(すみす)さん
6. 学生・川口(かわぐち)さん
7. 先生・山田先生

Task 1: Pair Work

Point at someone in the classroom and ask your partner who he / she is.

For example:

A ： あの人はだれですか。

B ： えっ?

A ： あの人です。

B ： ちょっと、わかりません。*I do not know.* / あの人はジョン(じょん)さんです。

Task 2: Pair Work

Ask your partner to identify the buildings overlooked from the window.

Vocabulary Collection (Campus)	
学生会館(がくせいかいかん) *student union*	本屋(ほんや) *bookstore*
レクチャー・ホール(れくちゃあ・ほうる) *lecture hall*	
駐車場(ちゅうしゃじょう) *garage / parking lot*	
文学部(ぶんがくぶ)の建物(たてもの) *the department of literature building*	

Writing 1

Write the Japanese words introduced in Basic Vocabulary and Kanji in this lesson, several times each.

たてもの	たてもの	としょかん	としょかん
たいいくかん	たいいくかん	りょう	りょう
どうぶつ	どうぶつ	ねこ	ねこ
犬	犬	人	人
車	車	だれ	だれ
どなと	どなた		

Writing 2

Write the kanji characters learned in this lesson, paying attention to how each is pronounced. [b]

犬	犬	犬	犬
人	人	人	人
学生	学生	学生	学生
先生	先生	先生	先生
車	車	車	車

– Grammar and Usage –

1 こちら: This person

こちら literally means *this way* or *this side*, but it also means *this person*. You can use こちら for politely introducing someone near yourself to others. For example, こちらは山田さんです means *This (person) is Mr. Yamada*.

2 Personal pronouns (私, あなた, etc)

Japanese has personal pronouns that correspond to English pronouns such as "I", "you" and "he" in English, but in actual conversational contexts, only the first person pronoun is used, and the second and third person pronouns are usually avoided.

The first person pronoun has many variations, including わたし, わたくし, わし, ぼく, おら and おれ. The choice among them depends on the speaker's gender, age, occupation, position, personality, geographic area and mood. Beginners of Japanese are advised to use わたし. わたくし sounds very formal. Men can use ぼく in an informal or neutral / polite context. おれ sounds rough and may be used only in an informal context. おら is appropriate only in some rural areas in Japan.

When you need to refer to your conversational partner, do not use the pronoun あなた *you*, as it will make you sound snobbish or arrogant. Instead, use the person's name, even though it will give the impression that your conversational partner is somewhere else. Another strategy to avoid using あなた is by simply not saying the pronoun. This is possible because any nouns in a Japanese sentence can be unpronounced if contextually understood.

	Singular	Plural
1st person	わたし *I*	わたしたち *we*
2nd person	あなた *you*	あなたたち *you*
3rd person (masculine)	かれ *he*	かれら *them*
3rd person (feminine)	かのじょ *she*	かのじょら *them*
3rd person (masculine and feminine)	—	かれら *them*

3 はい, いいえ: Yes / no [Agreement / disagreement]

はい and いいえ in Japanese correspond to *yes* and *no* in English in most cases, but not always. はい and いいえ specify *agreement* and *disagreement* respectively, whereas *yes* and *no* in English specify *affirmation* and *negation* respectively. So, depending on whether the question is negative or affirmative, はい may correspond to *no* in English, and いいえ may correspond to *yes* in English.

(a) これは本ですか。
Is this a book?
— はい、それは本です。
— *Yes, it is.*

(b) これは本ですか。
Is this a book?
— いいえ、それは本じゃありません。
— *No, it isn't.*

(c) これは本じゃありませんね。
This isn't a book, is it?
— はい、それは本じゃありません。
— *No, it isn't.*

(d) これは本じゃありませんね。
This isn't a book, is it?
— いいえ、それは本です。
— *Yes, it is.*

4 ～じん [Nationality / citizenship / ethnic background of people]

The dependent noun ～人 follows a country name or geographic location name and expresses the nationality, citizenship or ethnic background of people. For example, 日本 means *Japan* and 日本人 means *a Japanese*. Similarly, アジア means *Asia* and アジア人 means *an Asian*. More complex cases include 日系アメリカ人 *Japanese Americans* and 中国系アメリカ人 *Chinese Americans*. For referring to your nationality, you can use ～人, but for referring to someone else's nationality, it is better to replace ～人 with ～の人 or ～の方. Instead of saying that someone is アメリカ人, you can say he / she is アメリカの人 or アメリカの方. When you want to ask someone his / her nationality, do not say 何人ですか. It sounds rude. Instead ask questions like below:

(a) リーさんはどちらの国の方ですか。
As for you, Mr. Lee, which country's person are you?

(b) リーさんはどちらからですか。
As for you, Mr. Lee, where are you from?

(c) リーさん、お国(くに)はどちらですか。
Mr. Lee, as for your home country, where is it?

(d) リーさん、お国は。
Mr. Lee, how about your home country?

5 ～は: As for～, speaking of～ [Topic marker]

Before providing a new piece of information, the Japanese first say the topic, mentioning what the up-coming new piece of information is about. This introductory phrase is called the "topic phrase". The topic phrase sets the scene, bring the listener's attention to what both the speaker and listener are already familiar with and help the listener to get ready for the new information. For this reason, the topic phrase itself cannot be a new piece of information for the listener. The topic must be old shared information—something that is already familiar to both the speaker and listener. The topic phrase is marked by the particle は (wa). (The topic marker は is pronounced as **wa**, not as **ha**.)

(a) 山田(やまだ)さんは日本人(にほんじん)です。
As for Ms. Yamada, she is a Japanese.

(b) あの本(ほん)はたかいです。
As for that book, (it) is expensive.

(c) ねこはかわいいです。
Cats are cute.

In the above sentences, the listener is already familiar with 山田(やまだ)さん, あの本(ほん) and ねこ, and the new pieces of information that the speaker wants to convey regarding them are *being Japanese*, *being expensive* and *being cute*, respectively.

Students often think that topic phrases are subjects, but they are not always subjects. Any phrase (subject, direct object, indirect object, time phrase, etc) can be a topic phrase.

(d) あの本(ほん)は山田(やまだ)さんが昨日(きのう)読(よ)みました。
As for that book, Ms. Yamada read (it) yesterday.

(e) 山田(やまだ)さんはあの本(ほん)を昨日(きのう)読(よ)みました。
As for Ms. Yamada, (she) read that book yesterday.

(f) 昨日(きのう)は山田(やまだ)さんがあの本(ほん)を読(よ)みました。
As for yesterday, Ms. Yamada read that book.

(The subject-marking particle が and the direct object-marking particle を are discussed in Chapter Six.)

What the sentence implies differs depending on what is the topic. For example, sentence (g) is appropriate when the speaker wants to identify the building in front of him, but sentence (h) is appropriate when the speaker wants to say which one is the library.

(g) これは図書館(としょかん)です。
As for this, it is a library. (This is a library.)

(h) 図書館(としょかん)はこれです。
As for the library, it is this one.
(The library is this (one).)

Question words (for example, 何(なん) *what*, だれ *who*, どれ *which one*) cannot be the topic because they cannot represent old shared information. So, (i) is grammatical, but (j) is not:

(i) 図書館(としょかん)はどれですか (✓)
As for the library, which one is it?

(j) どれは図書館(としょかん)ですか。 (✕)
(Ungrammatical)

6 ～です (だ): To be [Copula]

X は Y です or X が Y です (see Chapter Six for the subject particle が) means *X* is *Y*. です is used for expressing the identity and properties of things and people. In an informal context, です is replaced by its plain / informal counterpart, だ.

(a) 私(わたし)は日本人(にほんじん)です。
I am a Japanese. (polite / neutral context)

(b) 私(わたし)は日本人(にほんじん)だ。
I am a Japanese. (plain / informal context)

The negative version of ～です is ～では (wa) ありません, or its contracted form, ～じゃありません. The latter is more frequently used than the former in conversations.

(c) リー(りい)さんは韓国人(かんこくじん)ではありません。
Mr. Lee is not a Korean.

(d) リーさんは韓国人(かんこくじん)じゃありません。
Mr. Lee is not a Korean.

The plain / informal counterparts of ～ではありません and ～じゃありません are ～ではない and ～じゃない, respectively.

(e) 私(わたし)は日本人(にほんじん)ではない。
I'm not a Japanese.

(f) 私は日本人じゃない。
I'm not a Japanese.

Noun + Copula Verb		
	Affirmative	**Negative**
Polite / neutral context	日本人(にほんじん)です	日本人ではありません 日本人じゃありません
Plain / informal context	日本人だ	日本人ではない 日本人じゃない

です may also follow an adjective, but then its conjugation pattern is slightly different from noun-plus-です cases. For the detail of adjective-plus-です cases, see Chapter Nine.

7 ～か [Sentence final question particle]

For asking whether your statement is true or not, you can simply place the question particle ～か at the end of your statement and pronounce the entire sentence with a rising intonation. For example, (a) is a statement but (b) is a question:

(a) これはいすです。
As for this, it is a chair.

(b) これはいすですか。↗
As for this, is it a chair?

In conversations, a sentence without the particle か can be understood as a question if pronounced with a rising intonation. On the other hand, a sentence with the particle か can be understood as an acknowledgement if pronounced with a falling intonation, as in the following context.

A ：あれはとしょかんです。
That is a library.

B ：ああ、あれはとしょかんですか。↘
Oh, that is a library.

8 なに, なん: What [Question word for non-human items]

何(なに・なん) is a question word that means *what*. It is used for asking the identity of things and animals. Unlike in English, a question word in Japanese does not have to be placed at the beginning of a sentence. It appears in the position where the answer would be placed in the sentence. And it must be used with the sentence final question particle ～か.

A ：せんこうは何(なん)ですか。
What is (your) academic major?

B ：せんこうはえいごです。
(My) academic major is English.

The pronunciation of 何 is なに when it is by itself. However, it is なん when followed by the copula verb です, a counter such as ～時(じ) (Chapter Four) and some particles such as の. The following tables list some phrases with 何.

なん	
何(なん)ですか	(what + copula + question marker)
何(なん)の	(what + of / *of what*)
何時(なんじ)	(what + o'clock / *what time*)

なに	
何(なに)が	(what + subject marker)
何(なに)を	(what + object marker)
何(なに)から	(what + from / *from what*)
何語(なにご)	(what + language / *what language*)

9 ちょっと, まあまあ: Slightly, more or less

ちょっと and まあまあ are degree adverbs, which mean *slightly* and *more or less*, respectively.

(a) 日本(にほん)ごはちょっとむずかしいです。
Japanese is slightly difficult.

(b) 日本ごはまあまあかんたんです。
Japanese is more or less easy.

ちょっと is used only for unfavorable properties, whereas まあまあ is used only for favorable properties. So, the following sentences are both inappropriate, assuming that "difficult" is an unfavorable property and "easy" is a favorable property for the speaker:

(c) 日本(にほん)ごはまあまあむずかしいです。 (✕)
(Inappropriate)

(d) 日本ごはちょっとかんたんです。 (✕)
(Inappropriate)

10 ～よ: I tell you [Sentence final emphasis particle]

The sentence final particle ～よ shows the speaker's confident attitude about the fact he / she is stating. It shows the speaker's strong, assertive and imposing attitude in some cases, but helpful and informative attitude in other cases.

(a) コンピューター・サイエンスはかんたんです。
Computer science is easy.
— いいえ、むずかしいですよ。
— *No, it is difficult, (I tell you although you may not think so).*

(b) コンピューター・サイエンスはむずかしいですよ。
Computer science is difficult, (I tell you since I do not think you know it).
— ああ、そうですか。
— *Oh, is that so?*

11 Demonstratives (あれ, あの～, etc)

Demonstratives can specify the item that the speaker is referring to, in terms of it is physical location relative to the speaker "1st person" and the listener "2nd person" in their visible domain. They are often accompanied by a pointing gesture, specifying where they are.

この, その and あの are "demonstrative adjectives". They must be followed by a common noun that denotes the referent. For example, この本 *this book* refers to a book close to the speaker, その本 *that book near you* refers to a book close to the listener but far from the speaker and あの本 *that book over there* refers to a book far from both the speaker and listener.

If a common noun doesn't have to be mentioned, you can use a demonstrative pronoun. Demonstrative pronouns for non-human items are これ *this one*, それ *that one near you* and あれ *that one over there*. The demonstrative pronouns for locations are ここ *here*, そこ *there near you* and あそこ *over there*. And those for directions are こちら *this way*, そちら *that way near you* and あちら *that way*. There is no demonstrative pronoun for people. So, for referring to people, demonstrative adjectives must be used along with a common noun (for example, この人 *this person*, この男の人 *this man*, このこども *this child* and この学生 *this student*). In a polite context, この方 or こちら is used (for example, この方はスミスさんです。*This person is Mr. Smith.* or こちらはスミスさんです。*This is Mr. Smith.*).

Their corresponding question words are どの～ *which~*, どれ *which one*, どこ *which place* and どちら *which direction*. These terms are summarized in the following table:

	Demonstrative Adjective	Demonstrative Pronoun		
		Things and Animals	Location	Direction
The speaker's domain (Close to the speaker)	この～	これ	ここ	こちら
The listener's domain (Close to the listener but far from the speaker)	その～	それ	そこ	そちら
Beyond the speaker and the listener's domain (Far from both the speaker and listener)	あの～	あれ	あそこ	あちら
Question words	どの～	どれ	どこ	どちら

12 じゃあ: Then, in that case [Transition]

じゃあ is one of the most frequently used interjections in Japanese. It is the contracted form of では (dewa). It is function is to mark the transition from one stage to another in logic (a), idea (b) or timing (c) during a conversation.

(a) 私は中国人です。
I am a Chinese.
— じゃあ、中国ごをはなしますか。
— *Then, do you speak Chinese?*

(b) 私はスーパーマーケットに行きます。
I will go to the supermarket.
— じゃあ、私も行きます。
— *In that case, I will go there, too.*

(c) じゃあ、私はそろそろ行きます。
Well, I get going.

13 ～も: Too, also [Addition]

You can use the particle も when you mention an additional item. For example, in the following context, the fact "being a student" holds with Ms. Yamada in addition to Mr. Tanaka, so Ms. Yamada is marked by も rather than by は:

(a) 田中(たなか)さんは学生(がくせい)です。山田(やまだ)さんも学生です。
Mr. Tanaka is a student. Ms. Yamada, too, is a student.

The particle ～も can occur more than once in a sentence.

(b) 田中(たなか)さんもスミス(すみす)さんも学生(がくせい)です。
Mr. Tanaka and Mr. Smith are both students.

(c) 田中(たなか)さんもスミス(すみす)さんもリー(りい)さんも学生です。
Mr. Tanaka, Mr. Smith and Mr. Lee are all students.

The noun phrase marked by も may not be simultaneously marked by particles such as ～は, ～が and ～を. (For more information on ～が and ～を, see Chapter Six.)

14 だれ, どなた: Who [Question word for people]

The question word だれ *who*, is used for asking the identity of people. In a formal context, use the polite counterpart, どなた *who*.

(a) あの人(ひと)はだれですか。
Who is that person over there?

(b) あの方(かた)はどなたですか。
Who is that person over there?

– Culture –

A Acknowledging and responding

In a Japanese conversation, the speaker often pauses briefly and the listener nods with a short interjection such as ああ, ええ and はい or a short sentence such as そうですか and そうですね. To carry a Japanese conversation smoothly, it is very important to frequently respond to or acknowledge what you hear. To acknowledge the given information, you can say そうですか *Is that so?* with a falling intonation. To show your disagreement or surprise, you can say そうですか with a falling-rising intonation. To show your agreement, you can say そうですね *That's right*. To strongly show your agreement, you can say そうですよ *absolutely!*. Intonation plays an important role in conveying your feelings.

– Writing –

a Kanji strokes

In general, horizontal strokes go from left to right, vertical strokes go from top to bottom and angled strokes go from left to right, then down, or go down, then left to right.

Horizontal Stroke	Vertical Stroke	Angled Stroke		

Each stroke ends with a hook, stop, flow or stop-flow.

Hook	Stop	Flow		Stop-flow

b Reading kanji

Most kanji characters are pronounced in two ways. One is 音読(おんよ)み, which is the Chinese-style reading, and the other is 訓読(くんよ)み, which is the native Japanese-style reading. For example, the character 人 is read as にん or じん in 音読(おんよ)み, but as ひと in 訓読(くんよ)み. In general 音読(おんよ)み is used when the character is a part of a compound kanji-word and 訓読(くんよ)み is used when it occurs independently.

For example: あの人(ひと)は日本人(にほんじん)です。
That person is a Japanese.

– Kanji List –

私・～人・日本人・何・ぶん学・すう学・本・山田・川口・人・犬・学生・先生・車

Kanji	Readings / Meaning	Stroke order	Strokes	Examples
私	わたし・わたくし・シ *private*	ノ 二 千 千 禾 私 私	[7]	Example: 私(わたし) *I, me*
人	ひと・ジン・ニン *person*	ノ 人	[2]	Example: あの人(ひと) *that person* 日本人(にほんじん) *Japanese people*
日	ひ・び・ニチ・ニ・ジツ *sun, day*	丨 冂 月 日	[4]	Example: 日本(にほん) *Japan* 日本人(にほんじん) *Japanese people*
本	もと・ホン *root, origin, true, main*	一 十 才 木 本	[5]	Example: 本(ほん) *book* 日本(にほん) *Japan*
何	なに・なん *what*	ノ イ 仁 仃 何 何 何	[7]	Example: 何(なん)ですか *What is it?*
学	まな-ぶ・ガク・ガッ *study*	丶 丷 ⺍ ⺍ ⺍ 学 学 学	[8]	Example: 学生(がくせい) *student* 大学(だいがく) *university* ぶん学(がく) *literature*
山	やま・サン *mountain*	丨 山 山	[3]	Example: 山田(やまだ) *surname* 山(やま) *mountain*
田	た・だ・デン *rice field*	丨 冂 冂 田 田	[5]	Example: 山田(やまだ) *surname*
川	かわ・がわ・セン *river*	ノ 川 川	[3]	Example: 川口(かわぐち) *surname* 川(かわ) *river*
口	くち・ぐち・コウ *mouth*	丨 冂 口	[3]	Example: 川口(かわぐち) *surname*
犬	いぬ・ケン *dog*	一 ナ 大 犬	[4]	Example: 犬(いぬ) *dog*
生	い-きる・う-まれる・セイ *live, birth*	ノ 𠂉 仁 牛 生	[5]	Example: 学生(がくせい) *student* 先生(せんせい) *teacher*
先	さき・セン *previous, foregoing*	ノ 𠂉 ⺧ 生 先 先	[6]	Example: 先生(せんせい) *teacher*
車	くるま・シャ *car*	一 丆 百 百 百 亘 車	[7]	Example: 車(くるま) *car*

– Review –

Q1. Write the pronounciation of the kanji characters in the following sentences in hiragana.

1. 川口さんは学生です。私も学生です。山田さんは先生です。
2. 日本ごはかんたんです。すう学はむずかしいです。
3. これは本です。あれは車です。あの人は日本人です。

Q2. Rearrange the items in each set to make a correct sentence.

1. 私・です・学生・は

2. じゃありません・私・ちゅうごく人・は
3. あの・です・人・は・日本人
4. 山田さん・学生・か・です・は
5. たてもの・何・は・あの・か・です

Q3. Fill in the blanks with appropriate question words.

1. せんこうは ___何___ ですか。
   — ぶん学です。

2. これは ___何___ ですか。
   — 本です。

3. あの人は ___だれ___ ですか。
   — スミス(すみす)さんです。

4. あの先生は ___どなた___ ですか。
   — 山田先生です。

Q4. Fill in the blanks with この or これ.

1. ___これ___ はむずかしいです。
2. ___この___ 本は むずかしいです。
3. BMW は ___これ___ です。
4. BMW は ___この___ 車です。

Q5. Fill in the blanks with これ, それ, あれ or どれ.

1. それは わえいじてんですか。
   — はい、___これ___ はわえいじてんです。

2. あれはとしょかんですか。
   — はい、___あれ___ はとしょかんです。

3. えいわじてんは ___それ___ ですか。
   — はい、えいわじてんはこれです。

4. わえいじてんは ___あれ___ ですか。
   — わえいじてんはあれです。

Q6. What would you say in the following situations?

1. You meet someone for the first time.
2. You want to ask someone where he is from.
3. You want to ask someone about his academic major.
4. You see a big building in the distance and you would like to know what it is.

Tips and Additional Knowledge: Paper Crane

Origami (paper folding) is one of the traditional Japanese arts. You can create hundreds of different paper creations such as animals, plants, pieces of furniture, and clothing, without using glue or scissors. The most popular, but not the easiest origami creation is 鶴(つる) *the crane.* 千羽鶴(せんばづる) *threaded one-thousand cranes* is well known as one of the most beautiful, warm and encouraging gift. Try creating a crane!

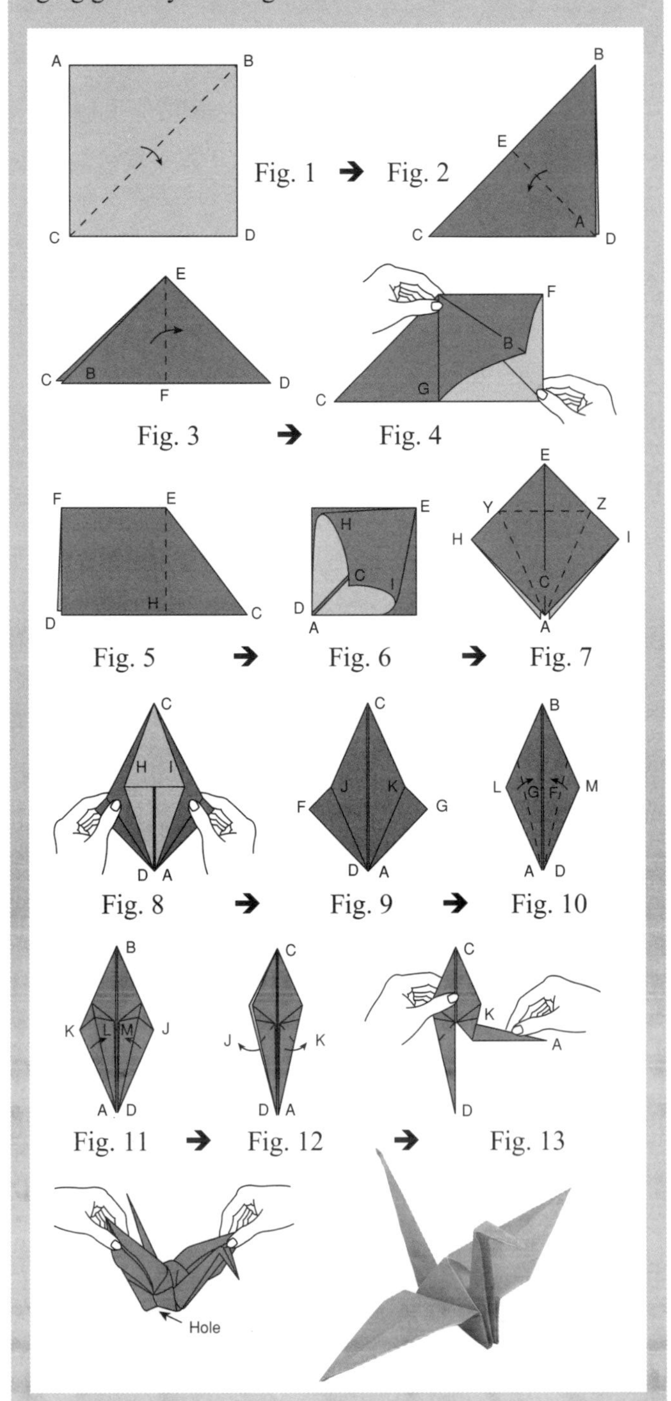

CHAPTER THREE

Describing Things and People

Lesson 12
あの人は私の母です **Family** **42**

Lesson 13
大学のえいごの先生です **Attributes** **44**

Lesson 14
あれはだれのですか **Ownership** **46**

Grammar and Usage **47**

1. Family members (母, お母さん, etc) 47
2. きれい (な): Beautiful, pretty, clean and neat 47
3. ～ね: ～, isn't it [Sentence final confirmation marker] 47
4. ～の: ～'s [Modifier marker] 47
5. Genders (男の人, 女の人, etc) 48

Culture **48**

A. Describing family members 48

Writing **48**

a. Kanji components 48
b. ひとあし 49
c. ちから 49

Kanji List **49**

Review **49**

Tips and Additional Knowledge:
Hey, Dad! Hey, Mom! **50**

あの人は私の母です Family

Notes Relating to This Lesson	
Grammar and Usage	**Culture**
1 Family members 47	Ⓐ Describing family members 48
2 きれい(な) 47	**Writing**
3 〜ね 47	ⓐ Kanji components 48
4 〜の 47	ⓑ ひとあし 49

Basic Vocabulary and Kanji

は˥は・おか˥あさん	母・お母さん	*n. mother* 1
ちち˥・おと˥うさん	父・お父さん	*n. father* 1
あ˥に・おに˥いさん	兄・お兄さん	*n. older brother* 1
あね・おね˥えさん	姉・お姉さん	*n. older sister* 1
いもうと˥・いもうとさん	妹・妹さん	*n. younger sister* 1
おとうと˥・おとうとさん	弟・弟さん	*n. younger brother* 1
こども・こどもさん / おこさん	子供・子供さん / お子さん	*n. child* 1
ともだち	友達	*n. friend*
ハ˥ンサム(な) (はんさむ)	ハンサムだ・ハンサムじゃない	*adj. handsome*
き˥れい(な)	綺麗だ・綺麗じゃない	*adj. pretty, beautiful* 2
かわい˥い	可愛い・可愛くない	*adj. cute*
〜ね		*prt. 〜, isn't it?* 3 (きれいですね *It's beautiful, isn't it?*)
〜の		*prt. 〜's, of〜* 4 (私の兄 *my brother*)

Newly introduced kanji:

母(はは)・お母(かあ)さん・
父(ちち)・お父(とう)さん・
兄(あに)・お兄(にい)さん ⓐ ⓑ

母	ㄴ 𠃊 母 母 母	父	ノ ハ ク 父
兄	ヽ ロ ロ 尸 兄		

Dialog

At an informal party with friends and family.

リー(りい)　：あの人(ひと)はだれですか。

山田(やまだ)　：私(わたし)の兄です。

リー　：ああ、山田さんのお兄さんですか。
　　　　じゃあ、あの人はだれですか。

山田　：私のいもうとです。

リー　：ああ、山田さんのいもうとさんですか。
　　　　<u>きれいですね</u>。

山田　：いいえ。

Guess and Try 1

Is the underlined part in the above dialog a question? 3

Guess and Try 2

Why did Ms. Yamada say いいえ in the above dialog? Ⓐ

Guess and Try 3

How do you say the following? 4

1. Mr. Kawaguchi's father:
   ____

2. Mr. Kawaguchi's father's older brother:
   ____

3. Mr. Kawaguchi's father's older brother's friend:
   ____

Guess and Try 4

Choose the appropriate options in the parentheses: 1

1. あの人(ひと)は私の(母・お母さん)です。

2. あの(人・かた)は私の父です。

3. あのかたは川口さんの(母・お母さん)です。

Guess and Try 5

Ask a few Japanese people how they address their family members at home. [1]

Drill 1: Formation

おとうとさん ⟶ おとうと

(Point at the picture as you form a phrase.)

1. お兄さん　　2. おねえさん
3. お父さん　　4. お母さん
5. いもうとさん

Drill 2: Formation

おとうと ⟶ おとうとさん

1. 父　　2. 兄
3. あね　　4. おとうと
5. いもうと　　6. 母

Drill 3: Mini-Conversation

おとうとです ⟶ ああ、おとうとさんですか

1. 父です　　2. あねです
3. 兄です　　4. 母です
5. 父のあねです

Task 1: Pair Work

Pretend that the people in the following photograph are your partner's family members. Point at each of them and ask for their identities.

For example:

A ：この人(ひと)はだれですか。

B ：私のいもうとです。

A ：ああ、Bさんのいもうとさんですか。
　　きれいですね。じゃあ、この人はだれですか。

B ：…

Variation: Use このかたはどなたですか instead of この人はだれですか.

Task 2: Pair Work

Show the picture of your family, relatives, friends or pet (ペット(ぺっと)) to your partner and talk about them.

Vocabulary Collection (People and Their Appearances)	
従兄弟(いとこ) *cousin*	ルームメート(るうむめえと) *roommate*
親友(しんゆう) *best friend*	知人(ちじん) *acquaintance*
きれいです *pretty*	若(わか)いです *young*
ガールフレンド(があるふれんど)・彼女(かのじょ) *girl friend*	
ボーイフレンド(ぼういふれんど)・彼氏(かれし) *boy friend*	
やさしそうです *to look kind*	
かっこいいです *good-looking for male*	
頭(あたま)がよさそうです *to look smart*	

Writing

Write the Japanese words introduced in Basic Vocabulary and Kanji in this lesson.

母	母	お母さん	お母さん
父	父	お父さん	お父さん
兄	兄	お兄さん	お兄さん
いもうと	いもうと	いもうとさん	いもうとさん
おとうと	おとうと	おとうとさん	おとうとさん
こども	こども	おこさん	おこさん
ともだち	ともだち	きれいな	きれいな

 かわいい ＊かわいい

CHAPTER THREE | Lesson 13

大学のえいごの先生です Attributes

Notes Relating to This Lesson	
Grammar and Usage	**Writing**
4 ～の 47	ⓒ ちから 49
5 Genders 48	

Basic Vocabulary and Kanji

だいがく	大学	*n. university*
だいがく⌉いん	大学院	*n. graduate school*
こうこう	高校	*n. high school*
おとこのひと	男の人	*n. man* 5
おんなのひと	女の人	*n. woman* 5

Newly introduced kanji:

大学(だいがく)・大学(だいがく)いん (大学院(だいがくいん))・
男(おとこ)の人(ひと) ⓒ・女(おんな)の人(ひと)

大	一ナ大	男	丶 口 口 田 田 男 男
女	く 女 女		

Dialog

Ben Lee and Mary Carter are chatting at a foreign student party.

リー(りい)　：あの人はだれですか。

カーター(かあたあ)：どの人ですか。

リー　：あの男の人ですよ。

カーター：ああ、あの人はジョン(じょん)さんです。
　　ジョン(じょん)さんは大学いんの学生(がくせい)です。

リー　：ああ。じゃあ、あの女の人はだれですか。

カーター：こうこうのえいごの先生(せんせい)です。

リー　：ああ、そうですか。

Guess and Try 1

Interpret the following sentences: 4

1. 日本(にほん)ごの先生(せんせい)はきれいです。
   ______________________ is beautiful.
2. 先生の日本ごはきれいです。
   ______________________ is beautiful.

Guess and Try 2

Fill in the blanks: 4

1. Mr. Yamada is a student, who is a Japanese (a Japanese student).

   山田さんは ________ の ________ です。

2. Mr. Smith is a student of the Japanese language.

   スミス(すみす)さんは ________ の ________ です。

3. Mr. Smith is a student of the Japanese language, at a university.

   スミス(すみす)さんは ________ の ________ の ________ です。

4. Mr. Smith is a student of the Japanese language, at a university in Tokyo.

   スミス(すみす)さんは ________ の ________ の ________ の________ です。

Drill: Formation

山田さん・お兄さん・車(くるま) ⟶ 山田さんのお兄さんの車です

1. 日本・車
2. えいご・本
3. 兄・えいご・本
4. 大学・学生
5. 日本ご・学生
6. 大学・日本ご・学生

7. とうきょう・大学・学生

8. とうきょう・大学・日本ご・学生

Task 1: Classroom Activity

Describe yourself in Japanese. Use as many words as you can.

私は ＿＿＿＿＿＿＿＿ の ＿＿＿＿＿＿＿＿ の
＿＿＿＿＿＿＿ ・・・の ＿＿＿＿＿＿＿ です。

Task 2: Pair Work

Pretend that your partner does not know anyone in the class. Point at each student in the class and tell your partner who he / she is. Take turns.

For example:

A ：あの女の人はすう学の学生です。

B ：ああ、そうですか。

Task 3: Classroom Activity

Talk about one of your family members or friends.

For example:

A ：私の兄はボストンの大学の（すう学の）学生です。

B ：ああ、そうですか。

A ：私のボーイフレンドはマクドナルドのてんいんです。

B ：ああ、そうですか。

Vocabulary Collection (Occupation)	
医者 *medical doctor*	弁護士 *lawyer*
主婦 *housewife*	店員 *salesclerk*
会社員 *company employee*	
～の社員 *the employee of ~company*	

Short Reading

私はアメリカの大学の社会学の学生です。日本人です。私の父は会社員です。母は主婦です。兄は日本の高校の英語の先生です。

(社会学 *sociology,* 会社員 *company employee,* 主婦 *housewife*)

Writing

Write a short passage describing your family members. (For now, use hiragana or English for the words to be written in katakana.)

大学 大学 だいがくいん
こうこう 男の人 男の人 女の人 女の人

あれはだれのですか Ownership

Notes Relating to This Lesson	
Grammar and Usage 4 〜の 47	

Basic Vocabulary and Kanji

かぎ˥	鍵	*n. key*
さいふ	財布	*n. wallet*
か˥さ	傘	*n. umbrella*
けいたいで˥んわ	携帯電話	*n. cellular phone*

Dialog

Ben Lee and Yoko Yamada are waiting at the driveway.

リー(りい) : (Pointing at the car in the distance.)
あれはだれの車(くるま)ですか。

山田(やまだ) : あれは先生の車です。

リー : (Pointing at another car in the distance.)
じゃあ、あれはだれのですか。

山田 : あれは川口(かわぐち)さんのです。

リー : じゃあ、山田さんの車はどれですか。

山田 : 私のはあれです。

Guess and Try 1

Point at an item in the classroom and ask your partner who the item belongs to. 4

Guess and Try 2

Interpret the following sentences and then omit some nouns in the second sentence in each context. 4

1. これは川口(かわぐち)さんの車(くるま)です。あれは私の車です。
2. これは川口さんのともだちのかばんです。あれは川口さんのお兄(にい)さんのかばんです。
3. これは日本(にほん)ごの本(ほん)です。あれはえいごの本です。

Drill: Formation

私の車です ⟶ 私のです

1. 山田さんのさいふです
2. あの女の人のかぎです
3. 私の兄の車です
4. 山田さんのともだちの本です
5. 兄のともだちのお父さんのかばんです

Task 1: Classroom Activity

Who is the owner?: Your teacher picks up some items (for example, hat, cap, glove, etc) from the class. He / She then asks the class who the owner is for each item. Repeat this activity several times.

For example:

Teacher : これはだれのですか。

Student : マイク(まいく)さんのです。

Task 2: Classroom Activity

Find the owner: Each student in your class is required to draw a picture of some items (for example, a watch, a pen, a key and a wallet) on a sheet of paper. Your teacher then collects these drawings and redistributes them randomly to each of you. You are required to find out the owner of the drawing you receive.

B : すみません。これはAさんのですか。

A : はい、私のです。 (Excitedly.) どうもありがとうございます。	A : いいえ。
B : いいえ。	B : ああ、そうですか。 (With a slight disappointment.) すみません。
	A : いいえ。

Writing

Write the Japanese words introduced in Basic Vocabulary and Kanji in this lesson.

– Grammar and Usage –

1 Family members (母, お母さん, etc)

When referring to your family members in front of outsiders in a formal or polite / neutral context, use humble forms such as 父(ちち), 母(はは), 兄(あに) and 姉(あね). However, when referring to someone else's family members, use the polite forms such as お父(とう)さん, お母(かあ)さん, お兄(にい)さん and お姉(ねえ)さん. The Japanese address their younger family members by their first names, but they address their older family members by polite forms such as お父(とう)さん, お母(かあ)さん, お兄(にい)さん and お姉(ねえ)さん. One interesting fact is that a wife sometimes addresses her husband by the pronoun あなた, which literally means *you*.

	*Humble form	**Polite form	***Addressing form
Grandfather	祖父(そふ)	お祖父(じい)さん	
Grandmother	祖母(そぼ)	お祖母(ばあ)さん	
Uncle	叔父(おじ)・伯父(おじ)	叔父(おじ)さん・伯父(おじ)さん	
Aunt	叔母(おば)・伯母(おば)	叔母(おば)さん・伯母(おば)さん	
Father	父(ちち)	お父(とう)さん	
Mother	母(はは)	お母(かあ)さん	
Older brother	兄(あに)	お兄(にい)さん	
Older sister	姉(あね)	お姉(ねえ)さん	
Younger brother	弟(おとうと)	弟(おとうと)さん	(first name)
Younger sister	妹(いもうと)	妹(いもうと)さん	(first name)
Parents	両親(りょうしん)	ご両親(りょうしん)	—
Siblings	兄弟(きょうだい)	ご兄弟(きょうだい)	—
Husband	主人(しゅじん)・夫(おっと)	ご主人(しゅじん)	あなた
Wife	家内(かない)・妻(つま)	奥(おく)さん	(first name)
Cousin	従兄弟(いとこ)	従兄弟(いとこ)(の方(かた))	(first name)
Son	息子(むすこ)	息子(むすこ)さん お坊(ぼっ)ちゃん	(first name)
Daughter	娘(むすめ)	娘(むすめ)さん お嬢(じょう)さん	(first name)
Child	子供(こども)	子供(こども)さん お子(こ)さん	(first name)

* Referring to one's own family members in front of others.

** Referring to someone else's family members.

*** Addressing one's own family members at home.

2 きれい(な): Beautiful, pretty, clean and neat

The adjective きれい(な) means *beautiful, pretty, clean* or *neat*, depending on the context.

(a) スミスさんのお母(かあ)さんはきれいです。
Mr. Smith's mother is pretty.

(b) あのドレスはきれいですね。
That dress is beautiful, isn't it?

(c) 私の手(て)はきれいです。
My hands are clean.

(d) 私の部屋(へや)はきれいです。
My room is neat.

3 〜ね: 〜, isn't it? [Sentence final confirmation marker]

By adding the particle 〜ね at the end of a sentence with a prolonged falling intonation, you can invite the listener's agreement:

(a) 山田(やまだ)さんは、きれいですね。↘
Ms. Yamada is pretty, isn't she?
— ええ、そうですね。
— *Yes, she is, isn't she?*

If ね is used along with a rising intonation, the sentence is understood as a confirmation question, demanding a reply from the listener.

(b) これは図書館(としょかん)ですね。↗
This is a library, right?
— はい、そうです。
— *Yes, it is.*

4 〜の: 〜's [Modifier marker]

The particle 〜の follows a noun, creating a modifier that describes ownership, affiliation and other properties of things and people.

(a) 山田(やまだ)さんの車(くるま)
Ms. Yamada's car

(b) 高校(こうこう)の先生(せんせい)
A high school teacher

(c) 日本語(にほんご)の先生(せんせい)
A Japanese language teacher

In English, a modifier may occur before or after the modified noun, but in Japanese, a modifier always precedes the modified noun. So, 日本語の先生 is referring to a teacher (a teacher who teaches Japanese), while 先生の日本語 is referring to the Japanese language (spoken by the teacher). There may be multiple modifiers for one item. For example, 大学の日本語の先生 means *A Japanese language teacher at a college*. The last noun in the sequence expresses what the entire phrase refers to and serves as the core noun. The core noun can be omitted if contextually understood.

(d) これは私の本です。あれは母の(本)です。
This is my book. That is my mother's (book).

(e) これは日本語の本です。あれは英語の(本)です。
This is a Japanese book. That is an English one (book).

Remember to avoid ending a phrase with の if the core noun denotes a human. (f) is grammatical, but (g) is not:

(f) あの車は山田さんの車です。あの車は田中さんのです。
That car is Ms. Yamada's car. That car is Mr. Tanaka's.

(g) あの人は山田さんの友達です。あの人は田中さんのです。(✕)
(Ungrammatical) Intended meaning: *That person is Ms. Yamada's friend. That person is Mr. Tanaka's.*

5 Genders (男の人, 女の人, etc)

男 and 女 mean *a man* and *a woman*, respectively, but it sounds very disrespectful if you refer to a man and a woman as 男 and 女. Remember to use them with a common noun such as 人, as in 男の人 and 女の人.

– Culture –

Ⓐ Describing family members

The Japanese are modest and they often deny compliments they receive from others on their appearances, clothing, talents and achievements. This extends to their family members. They also deny the compliments they receive on their family members. For example, if you tell your Japanese friend that his / her mother is pretty, he / she is very likely to respond to you, saying "No, my mother is not pretty at all."

– Writing –

ⓐ Kanji components

Most kanji characters are formed from two or more components. They have a semantic contribution, a sound contribution or just a shape contribution. There are about 300 kanji components and depending on the position in a kanji character, they are classified into seven categories, as shown in the following table.

1. かんむり *Top*	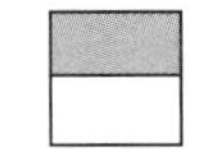	Example: 宀(うかんむり *roof*): 安・宿・家・字・空 亠(なべぶた *lid*): 高・夜・京・六・交・卒
2. あし *Bottom*		Example: 儿(ひとあし *human legs*): 見・兄・先 心(こころ *heart, mind*): 思・息・悲・意・志
3. へん *Left*	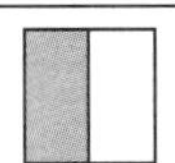	Example: イ(にんべん *person*): 休・体・住・何・作 シ(さんずいへん *water*): 海・湖・酒・泳・泣
4. つくり *Right*	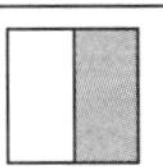	Example: 斤(おのづくり *axe, chop, cut*): 近・新・所・折 隹(ふるとり *bird*): 雑・難
5. かまえ *Enclosure*	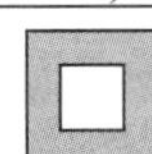	Example: 囗(くにがまえ *border*): 国・困・囚・囲
	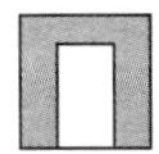	Example: 門(もんがまえ *gate*): 問・聞・間・閉・開 冂(どうがまえ *same*): 同・内・円・岡
	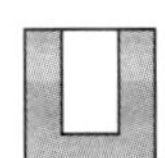	Example: 凵(うけばこ *container, vessel*): 画・凶・函
	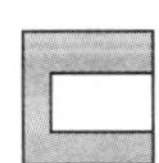	Example: 匚(かくしがまえ *conceal*): 匹・区・医
		Example: 气(きがまえ *air, spirit*): 気・汽 弋(しきがまえ *measure*): 式・弐

6. たれ *Upper left*
Example: 广 (まだれ *roof*): 店・床・庫・広・度 厂 (がんだれ *building*): 原・厚・厘
7. にょう *Lower left*
Example: 廴 (えんにょう *movement*): 延・建・廸 走 (そうにょう *run*): 越・起・赴・超

ⓑ ひとあし

儿	ひとあし *human legs*
	Example: 先生(せんせい) *teacher,* 兄(あに) *elder brother,* 見(み)る *to watch,* 売(う)る *to sell*

ⓒ ちから

力	ちから *power, strength*
	Example: 男(おとこ) *man,* 動(うご)く *to move,* 働(はたら)く *to work,* 助(たす)ける *to save or help*

– Kanji List –

母・お母さん・父・お父さん・兄・お兄さん・大学・大学いん・男の人・女の人

母 はは・ボ(ぼ) *mother*	㇄ 𠃊 母 母 母 [5] Example: 母(はは) *one's mother* お母(かあ)さん *mother*
父 ちち・フ(ふ) *father*	ノ ハ 父 父 [4] Example: 父(ちち) *one's father* お父(とう)さん *father*
兄 あに・ケイ(けい)・キョウ(きょう) *elder brother*	丶 口 口 尸 兄 [5] Example: 兄(あに) *one's elder brother* お兄(にい)さん *elder brother*
大 おお-きい・ダイ(だい)・タイ(たい) *big, great*	一 ナ 大 [3] Example: 大学(だいがく) *university*
学 まな-ぶ・ガク(がく)・ガッ(がっ) *study*	丶 丷 ⺍ ⺍ 𭕄 𭕄 学 学 [8] Example: 学生(がくせい) *student* 大学(だいがく) *university* ぶん学(がく) *literature*
男 おとこ・ダン(だん)・ナン(なん) *man, male*	丶 口 田 田 田 男 男 [7] Example: 男(おとこ)の人(ひと) *man*
女 おんな・ジョ(じょ) *woman, female*	く 女 女 [3] Example: 女(おんな)の人(ひと) *woman*
人 ひと・ジン(じん)・ニン(にん) *person*	ノ 人 [2] Example: 女(おんな)の人(ひと) *woman* 日本人(にほんじん) *Japanese people*

About 40 kanji components are introduced in this textbook.

– Review –

Q1. Write what they are in hiragana.

1. : かぎ
2. : かさ
3. : けいたいでんわ
4. : さいふ

Q2. Write the pronunciation of the kanji characters in the following sentences in hiragana.

1. 母は日本人です。父も日本人です。
2. 山田さんのお母さんは大学のぶん学の先生です。
3. あの男の人は日本人です。あの女の人はちゅうごく人です。

Q3. In each of the following, omit a noun while maintaing the intended meaning.

1. これは私の車です。
2. これはぶん学の本です。
3. 日本の車はきれいです。

Q4. Fill in the blanks with の or は. There may be more than one possibility.

1. 私 ____ 母 ____ 日本人です。
2. 山田さん ____ 大学 ____ 先生です。
3. 兄 ____ ともだち ____ お父さん ____ 先生です。
4. 私 ____ おとうと ____ ともだち ____ 日本ご ____ 学生です。

Q5. What would you say in the following situations?

1. You want to know who is the woman you see in the distance.
2. You want to know the owner of the car in front of you.
3. You want to say that your mother is a college English teacher.
4. You want to say that the car in front of you belongs to Ms. Yamada's mother's friend.

Tips and Additional Knowledge: Hey, Dad! Hey, Mom!

Not all the Japanese call their parents お父(とう)さん and お母(かあ)さん at home. The table below shows a set of variations for these phrases. However, if you are calling your host parents, it is always safe to call お父(とう)さん and お母(かあ)さん.

Hey, Dad!	Hey, Mom!
おとうさん!	おかあさん!
パパ(ぱぱ)!	ママ(まま)!
とうさん!	かあさん!
おとうちゃん!	おかあちゃん!
とうちゃん!	かあちゃん!

CHAPTER FOUR

Using Numbers and Katakana

Lesson 15
でんわばんごう Telephone Numbers 52

Lesson 16
今、何年生ですか Age and Academic Year 54

Lesson 17
今、何時ですか Time 56

Lesson 18
それはいくらですか Shopping 58

Lesson 19
カタカナ Katakana Characters 60

Lesson 20
がいらいご Loan Words 62

Grammar and Usage 64

1 Numbers 64
2 Counters 64
3 ごぜん, ごご: a.m., p.m. 65
4 いくら: How much? [Question word for price] 65
5 ～と: And [Listing marker for nouns] 65
6 ～をください: Please give me～ [Purchasing] 65
7 Syllable structure in Japanese 65

Culture 66

A Lucky and unlucky numbers 66
B Asking others their age 66
C Salesclerks and customers 66
D Japanese currency 66
E めいし: Name cards (Business cards) 66

Writing 67

a おくりがな 67
b ひとがしら 67
c なべぶた 67
d うかんむり 67
e カタカナ 67

Kanji List 68

Review 69

Tips and Additional Knowledge: At the Airport 70

でんわばんごう Telephone Numbers

Notes Relating to This Lesson	
Grammar and Usage	**Culture**
1 Numbers 64	A Lucky and unlucky numbers 66

 Basic Vocabulary and Kanji

れ˥い / ゼ˥ロ	零・ゼロ・0	*n. zero*
でんわ	電話	*n. telephone*
でんわば˥んごう	電話番号	*n. telephone number*
い˥い	*irr.* いい・よくない	*adj. fine, good*

Newly introduced kanji:

一(いち)・二(に)・三(さん)・四(よん・よ・し)・五(ご)・
六(ろく)・七(なな・しち)・八(はち)・九(きゅう・く)・十(じゅう)

一	一	六	丶 亠 六 六
二	一 二	七	一 七
三	一 二 三	八	ノ 八
四	丨 冂 冂 四 四	九	ノ 九
五	一 丆 五 五	十	一 十

  Dialog

Ken Kawaguchi asks Yoko Yamada for her telephone number.

川口(かわぐち) : 山田(やまだ)さん、ちょっとすみません。山田さんのでんわばんごうは何(なん)ですか。

山田(やまだ) : 私(わたし)のでんわばんごうは531－4428(ごさんいち よんよんにはち)です。

川口 : 531－4421(ごさんいち よんよんにいち)ですね。

山田 : いいえ。531－4428(ごさんいち よんよんにはち)です。

川口 : 531－4428(ごさんいち よんよんにはち)ですね。

山田 : はい、そうです。

川口 : じゃあ、マリー(まりい)さんのでんわばんごうはわかりますか。
(～はわかりますか *Do you know~?*)

山田 : ああ、すみません。ちょっとわかりません。
(わかりません *(I) do not know (it).*)

川口 : ああ、そうですか。じゃあ、いいです。

Guess and Try 1

Read the following telephone numbers aloud. 1

1. 212 – 304 – 6678
2. 03 – 3355 – 3476

Guess and Try 2

Ask your partner whether he knows the telephone number of the library.

Guess and Try 3

Discuss whether there are any lucky numbers or unlucky numbers in your country. A

 Drill 1: Reading

Read the following numbers several times each.

1. 1234 4321
2. 5678 8765
3. 7890 0987
4. 13579 97531
5. 2468 8642

Drill 2: Reading

Read the following numbers several times each.

1. 474 – 1123
2. 733 – 1213
3. 631 – 345 – 3435
4. 212 – 890 – 8980

Task 1: Dictation

As your teacher reads out a few telephone numbers, listen carefully and write them down.

Task 2: Classroom Activity

Your teacher has the telephone numbers of four different places (for example, a bookstore, restaurant, travel agency and grocery store). A few students are told each of these numbers secretly. All of you are required to find out the four telephone numbers from those who know by asking relevant questions. The first student to find out all the telephone numbers is the winner.

1. ____________________ ____-____-____
2. ____________________ ____-____-____
3. ____________________ ____-____-____
4. ____________________ ____-____-____

For example:

A：ちょっとすみません。
ピザハット(ぴざはっと)のでんわばんごうはわかりますか。

B：ピザハット(ぴざはっと)ですか。
A：はい。

B：すみません。ちょっとわかりません。
A：ああ、そうですか。じゃあ、いいです。

B：xxxx の xxxx の xxxx です。

A：xxxx の xxxx の xxxx ですね。

B：はい、そうです。

A：どうも。

B：いいえ。

Writing

Write the following kanji characters several times each.

一					
二					
三					
四					
五					
六					
七					
八					
九					
十					

今、何年生ですか Age and Academic Year

Notes Relating to This Lesson	
Grammar and Usage	**Culture**
1 Numbers 64	B Asking others their age . . .66
2 Counters 64	**Writing**
	b ひとがしら 67

Basic Vocabulary and Kanji

い⌉ま	今	*n. now*
～さい	～才・～歳	*c. a counter for age, ~years old*
～がつ	～月	*c. months of the year (一月(いちがつ) January)*
～がつうまれ	～月生まれ	*a person born in the month of~*
～ねんせい	～年生	*c. a counter for an academic year or grade (一年生(いちねんせい) first grade, freshman)*

Newly introduced kanji:

今(いま) b・～月(がつ)・～月生(がつう)まれ・～年生(ねんせい)

今	ノ 人 𠆢 今	月	ノ 几 月 月
年	ノ 𠂉 ⺧ 𠂒 𠃛 年		

  Dialog

Yoko Yamada and John Smith are chatting.

山田(やまだ)　：スミス(すみす)さんは今何(なん)年生ですか。

スミス(すみす)　：今1年生です。

山田　：ああ、そうですか。今何(なん)さいですか。

スミス　：22(にじゅうに)さいです。

山田　：ああ、そうですか。私も22さいです。
何月(なんがつ)生まれですか。

スミス　：12月生まれです。

山田　：えっ、私も12月生まれです。

Guess and Try 1

Discuss whether it is polite to ask others their age in your country. B

Guess and Try 2

Underline the ones that are not read as you would predict.
2

1. いちねんせい(1年生)
   にねんせい(2年生)
   さんねんせい(3年生)
   よねんせい(4年生)
   ごねんせい(5年生)
   ろくねんせい(6年生)
   なんねんせい(何年生)

2. いっさい(1歳)
   にさい(2歳)
   さんさい(3歳)
   よんさい(4歳)
   ごさい(5歳)
   ろくさい(6歳)
   ななさい(7歳)
   はっさい(8歳)
   きゅうさい(9歳)
   じゅっさい(10歳)
   なんさい(何歳)

3. いちがつ(1月)
   にがつ(2月)
   さんがつ(3月)
   しがつ(4月)
   ごがつ(5月)
   ろくがつ(6月)
   しちがつ(7月)
   はちがつ(8月)
   くがつ(9月)
   じゅうがつ(10月)
   じゅういちがつ(11月)
   じゅうにがつ(12月)
   なんがつ(何月)

今, 今, 月, 月, 年, 年
一年生です

Guess and Try 3

Fill in the blanks. [1]

0 :	れい(ゼロ(ぜろ))	23 :	にじゅうさん
1 :	いち	24 :	にじゅうよん
2 :	に	25 :	にじゅうご
3 :	さん	26 :	にじゅうろく
4 :	よん(し)	27 :	にじゅうなな
5 :	ご	28 :	にじゅうはち
6 :	ろく	29 :	にじゅうきゅう
7 :	なな(しち)	30 :	さんじゅう
8 :	はち	31 :	さんじゅういち
9 :	きゅう	32 :	さんじゅうに
10 :	じゅう	33 :	さんじゅうさん
11 :	じゅういち	34 :	さんじゅうよん
12 :	じゅうに	35 :	さんじゅうご
13 :	じゅうさん	36 :	さんじゅうろく
14 :	じゅうよん	37 :	さんじゅうなな
15 :	じゅうご	38 :	さんじゅうはち
16 :	じゅうろく	39 :	さんじゅうきゅう
17 :	じゅうなな	40 :	よんじゅう
18 :	じゅうはち	41 :	よんじゅういち
19 :	じゅうきゅう	42 :	よんじゅうに
20 :	にじゅう	53 :	ごじゅうさん
21 :	にじゅういち	87 :	はちじゅうなな
22 :	にじゅうに	99 :	きゅうじゅうきゅう

Drill: Reading

Read the following several times each.

1. 1 年生　　2 年生
   3 年生　　4 年生

2. 1 さい　　2 さい
   3 さい　　4 さい
   5 さい　　6 さい
   7 さい　　8 さい
   9 さい　　10 さい

3. 1 月　　2 月
   3 月　　4 月
   5 月　　6 月
   7 月　　8 月
   9 月　　10 月
   11 月　　12 月

Task 1: Pair Work

Ask your partner how old his / her grandmother is.

For example:

A : B さんのおばあさんはおいくつですか。

B : 母(はは)の方(ほう)のそぼは 89 さいです。父(ちち)の方(ほう)のそぼはなくなりました。

(おばあさん *someone else's grandmother*,
そぼ *one's own grandmother*,
母(はは)の方(ほう)の～ *~on one's mother's side*,
父(ちち)の方(ほう)の～ *~on one's father's side*,
おいくつですか *polite way of asking people's age*,
なくなりました *passed away*)

Task 2: Survey

Ask five of your classmates their academic year.

For example:

A : B さんは今(いま)何年生ですか。

B : 私は今 4 年生です。A さんは。

A : 私も 4 年生です。(私は 3 年生です。)

私		
さん		
さん		
さん		
さん		
さん		

Task 3: Classroom Activity

Look for your classmates who were born in the same month as you.

今、何時ですか Time

Notes Relating to This Lesson	
Grammar and Usage 2 Counters ....64 3 ごぜん, ごご..........65	

Basic Vocabulary and Kanji

ご˥ぜん	午前	*n. a.m.* 3
ご˥ご	午後	*n. p.m., afternoon* 3
〜じ	〜時	*c. ~o'clock*
〜ふん / ぷん	〜分	*c. minutes*
〜はん	〜半	*n. half*

Newly introduced kanji:

〜時(じ)・何時(なんじ)・〜分(ふん・ぷん)

時	丨 日 日 日 日一 日+ 日土 日士 時 時	分	ノ 八 分 分

Dialog

Yoko Yamada asks a man on the street what time it is.

山田(やまだ)　：すみません。今(いま)、何時ですか。

男の人(おとこのひと)：今(いま)、2時15分です。

山田　：ああ、そうですか。どうも。

Guess and Try 1

Underline the ones that are not read as you would predict. 2

1. いちじ (1時)
   にじ (2時)
   さんじ (3時)
   よじ (4時)
   ごじ (5時)
   ろくじ (6時)
   しちじ (7時)
   はちじ (8時)
   くじ (9時)
   じゅうじ (10時)
   じゅういちじ (11時)
   じゅうにじ (12時)
   なんじ (何時)

2. いっぷん (1分)
   にふん (2分)
   さんぷん (3分)
   よんふん / よんぷん (4分)
   ごふん (5分)
   ろくふん / ろっぷん (6分)
   ななふん (7分)
   はちふん / はっぷん (8分)
   きゅうふん (9分)
   じゅっぷん (10分)
   なんぷん (何分)

Guess and Try 2

Fill in the blanks. 3

For example:

3:30 p.m. : ごご3時30分 or ごご3時はん

1. 6 p.m. : ごご6時
2. 8:12 a.m. : ごぜん8時12分
3. 6:45 a.m. : ごぜん6時45分
4. 7:30 a.m. : ごぜん7時はん
5. 10:30 p.m. : ごご10時はん

Guess and Try 3

Ask your partner what time it is.

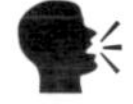

Drill 1: Reading

Read each of the following several times.

1. 1時　2時
   3時　4時
   5時　6時
   7時　8時
   9時　10時

2. 1 時はん　　2 時はん
   3 時はん　　4 時はん
   5 時はん　　6 時はん
   7 時はん　　8 時はん
   9 時はん　　10 時はん

Drill 2: Formation

3 p.m. ⟶ ごご 3 時です

1. 3 a.m.
2. 6:30 a.m.
3. 10 p.m.
4. 12:30 p.m.
5. 12:45 p.m.

Task 1: Classroom Activity

As your teacher reads out simple time phrases such as 3 時 and 9 時, show the time with your fingers, right after you hear each phrase.

For example:　3 時

Task 2: Dictation

As your teacher reads out several complex time phrases like ごご 6 時 38 分, listen to each phrase carefully and write it down.

Task 3: Classroom Activity

Every student takes turn to say what time he or she usually wakes up in the morning. Listen carefully and find out who wakes up the earliest in the class.

Task 4: Survey

Ask three of your classmates what time it is and find out whether their watches have the same time as yours.

さん		
さん		
さん		

Vocabulary Collection (Time Expressions)

3 時(さんじ)です *It is 3 o'clock.*

丁度(ちょうど) 3 時(さんじ)です *It is just 3 o'clock.*

もうすぐ 3 時(さんじ) です *It will be 3 soon.*

午前(ごぜん) 3 時(さんじ) です *It is 3 a.m.*

午後(ごご) 3 時(さんじ) です *It is 3 p.m.*

午後(ごご) 3 時(さんじ) 半(はん)です *It is 3:30 p.m.*

3 時(さんじ) 5 分(ごふん)前(まえ)です *It is five minutes before 3.*

3 時(さんじ) 5 分(ごふん)すぎです *It is five minutes after 3.*

ごぜん, ごご
一時五分

それはいくらですか Shopping

Notes Relating to This Lesson

Grammar and Usage

1 Numbers 64
2 Counters 64
4 いくら 65
5 〜と 65
6 〜をください 65

Culture

Ⓒ Salesclerks and customers 66
Ⓓ Japanese currency 66

Writing

ⓐ おくりがな 67
ⓒ なべぶた 67
ⓓ うかんむり 67

Basic Vocabulary and Kanji

てんいん	店員	*n. salesclerk*
きゃく	客	*n. customer, guest*
カ⌉メラ (かめら)		*n. camera*
ラ⌉ジオ (らじお)		*n. radio*
テ⌉レビ (てれび)		*n. television*
やす⌉い	安い・安くない	*adj. cheap, inexpensive*
たか⌉い	高い・高くない	*adj. expensive, tall, high*
ぜ⌉んぶで	全部で	*all together*
い⌉くら		*q. how much* 4
〜えん	〜円	*c. ~yen (¥)* Ⓓ
〜ドル (どる)	〜ドル	*c. ~dollars ($)*
〜まん	〜万	*n. ten thousand*
〜せん / ぜん	〜千	*n. one thousand*
〜ひゃく / びゃく / ぴゃく	〜百	*n. one hundred*
〜と		*prt. and* 5
くださ⌉い	下さい	*give me~ (〜を下さい give me~)* 6

Newly introduced kanji:

高い(たかい) ⓐ ⓒ・安い(やすい) ⓓ・百(ひゃく)・千(せん)・万(まん)・〜円(えん)

高	丶 亠 亡 亣 亯 亯 高 高 高 高	安	丶 丷 宀 安 安 安
百	一 丆 了 百 百 百	千	ノ 二 千
万	一 ア 万	円	丨 冂 円 円

Dialog

At the electronics store.

きゃく　：すみません。このカメラ(かめら)はいくらですか。

てんいん：それは 10,000 円です。

きゃく　：安いですね。じゃあ、このカメラ(かめら)と、あのラジオ(らじお)をください。

てんいん：はい。ぜんぶで 20,000 円です。

きゃく　：(Gives 20,000 yen to the salesclerk.)

てんいん：どうもありがとうございます。(Gives a camera and radio to the customer.) どうぞ。

きゃく　：どうも。

Guess and Try 1

Do salesclerks greet their customers when they enter the store in your country? Are they polite? Ⓒ

Guess and Try 2

Ask the price of the radio in front of you. 4

Guess and Try 3

Say that you want to buy the radio in front of you. 6

Guess and Try 4

Say that you want to buy the radio, camera and watch in front of you. [5] [6]

Guess and Try 5

The following table shows how the basic numbers above 10 are read. Underline the numbers that are not read as you would predict. [1]

10	: じゅう	1,000	: せん
20	: にじゅう	2,000	: にせん
30	: さんじゅう	3,000	: さんぜん
40	: よんじゅう	4,000	: よんせん
50	: ごじゅう	5,000	: ごせん
60	: ろくじゅう	6,000	: ろくせん
70	: ななじゅう	7,000	: ななせん
80	: はちじゅう	8,000	: はっせん
90	: きゅうじゅう	9,000	: きゅうせん
100	: ひゃく	10,000	: いちまん
200	: にひゃく	20,000	: にまん
300	: さんびゃく	30,000	: さんまん
400	: よんひゃく	40,000	: よんまん
500	: ごひゃく	50,000	: ごまん
600	: ろっぴゃく	60,000	: ろくまん
700	: ななひゃく	70,000	: ななまん
800	: はっぴゃく	80,000	: はちまん
900	: きゅうひゃく	90,000	: きゅうまん

Guess and Try 6

Write the following prices in hiragana. (¥: 円) [1] [2]

For example:

¥550 : ごひゃく ごじゅう えん

1. ¥459 : ______________________
2. ¥3,900 : ______________________
3. ¥100 : ______________________
4. ¥1,500 : ______________________
5. ¥56,900 : ______________________

Drill: Reading

Read the following several times each.

1. 10 円 20 円
   30 円 40 円
   50 円 60 円
   70 円 80 円
   90 円

2. 100 円 200 円
   300 円 400 円
   500 円 600 円
   700 円 800 円
   900 円

3. 1,000 円 2,000 円
   3,000 円 4,000 円
   5,000 円 6,000 円
   7,000 円 8,000 円
   9,000 円

4. 10,000 円 20,000 円
   30,000 円 40,000 円
   50,000 円 60,000 円
   70,000 円 80,000 円
   90,000 円

Task: Pair Work

Your partner is having a garage sale and the following are some of the items on sale. Ask the price of each item and buy one of them.

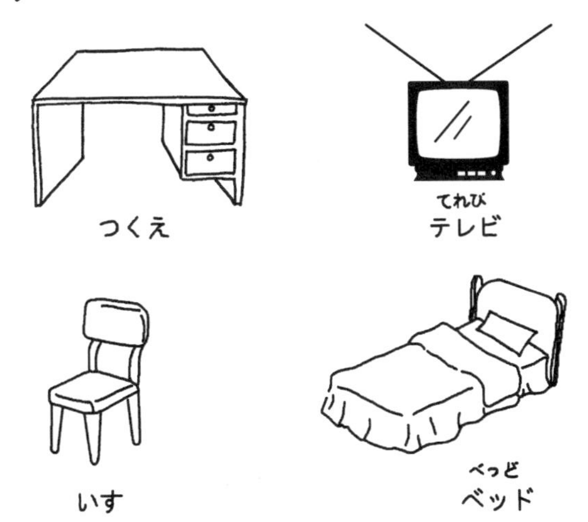

カタカナ Katakana Characters

Notes Relating to This Lesson

Writing

ⓔ カタカナ 67

あ	ア	ア	ア
い	イ	イ	イ
う	ウ	ウ	ウ
え	エ	エ	エ
お	オ	オ	オ
か	カ	カ	カ
き	キ	キ	キ
く	ク	ク	ク
け	ケ	ケ	ケ
こ	コ	コ	コ
さ	サ	サ	サ
し	シ	シ	シ
す	ス	ス	ス
せ	セ	セ	セ
そ	ソ	ソ	ソ
た	タ	タ	タ
ち	チ	チ	チ
つ	ツ	ツ	ツ
て	テ	テ	テ
と	ト	ト	ト

な	ナ	ナ	ナ
に	ニ	ニ	ニ
ぬ	ヌ	ヌ	ヌ
ね	ネ	ネ	ネ
の	ノ	ノ	ノ
は	ハ	ハ	ハ
ひ	ヒ	ヒ	ヒ
ふ	フ	フ	フ
へ	ヘ	ヘ	ヘ
ほ	ホ	ホ	ホ
ま	マ	マ	マ
み	ミ	ミ	ミ
む	ム	ム	ム
め	メ	メ	メ
も	モ	モ	モ
や	ヤ	ヤ	ヤ
ゆ	ユ	ユ	ユ
よ	ヨ	ヨ	ヨ
ら	ラ	ラ	ラ
り	リ	リ	リ
る	ル	ル	ル
れ	レ	レ	レ

ろ	ロ	ロ	ロ (stroke order)
わ	ワ	ワ	ワ (stroke order)
を	ヲ	ヲ	ヲ (stroke order)
ん	ン	ン	ン (stroke order)

Guess and Try 1

Write the katakana characters in the blank spaces provided in the table. Follow the correct stroke order, then, circle the katakana characters that resemble their hiragana counterparts.

Guess and Try 2

Circle the katakana character in each set.

1. り・リ
2. ウ・う
3. か・カ
4. き・キ
5. に・ニ
6. へ・ヘ
7. ヤ・や
8. も・モ
9. ら・ラ

Guess and Try 3

Read the katakana characters in each set and state their similarities and differences. Try writing them.

1. ク・タ
2. ク・ワ
3. ケ・ク
4. メ・ナ
5. ル・レ
6. ソ・ン
7. ツ・シ
8. ワ・ウ
9. ヌ・ス
10. コ・ユ
11. テ・チ

Guess and Try 4

Read each katakana word several times. Note that katakana characters are used in a parallel way with hiragana characters, except that long vowels are represented by a short horizontal line "ー" in katakana (for example, ガールフレンド *girlfriend*).

1. カメラ *camera*
2. ラジオ *radio*
3. ペン *pen*
4. チョーク *chalk*
5. アメリカ *America*
6. フランス *France*
7. スミス *Smith*
8. テニス *tennis*
9. ガールフレンド *girlfriend*
10. ボーイフレンド *boyfriend*

Task 1: Classroom Activity

Your teacher divides the class into small groups. He / she prepares two sets of katakana cards and reshuffles them. Each time, two groups are asked to rearrange the cards in the correct order (for example, ア・イ… ン). The group that takes the shortest time to reorder the cards sucessfully is the winner.

Task 2: Classroom Activity

Using two sets of (the first half of) katakana cards, play the memory game 神経衰弱(しんけいすいじゃく).

Writing

Write all the katakana characters, then, write the words listed in Guess and Try 4 several times each.

がいらいご Loan Words

Notes Relating to This Lesson	
Grammar and Usage	**Culture**
7 Syllable structure in Japanese 65	E めいし 66

When the Japanese borrow English words, they tend to insert the vowel **u** or the vowel **o** after any consonant that is not followed by a vowel. The only exceptions are the nasal sounds (**m** and **n**) and consonants followed by **y**.

Guess and Try 1

As your teacher reads the following words, listen carefully and take note where the vowels are added. 7

English Spelling	Pronunciation in Japanese (Rōmaji)
beer	bīru
necktie	nekutai
hint	hinto
tank	tanku
milk	miruku
strike	sutoraiku

Guess and Try 2

Listen carefully to the following English proper names as your teacher reads them and repeat after him / her.

1. ブライアン・ホフマン
   Buraian Hofuman
   Brian Hoffman

2. ロバート・ウエブスター
   Robāto Uebusutā
   Robert Webster

3. スーザン・ブラウン
   Sūzan Buraun
   Susan Brown

4. ジェニー・ジョンソン
   Jenī Jonson
   Jenny Johnson

Guess and Try 3

As your teacher reads the following Chinese and Korean proper names, listen carefully and repeat after him / her.

1. Chinese name:
   オウ ビリン or ワン メイリン
   Ō Bi Rin or Wan Mē Rin
   王 美林 or 王 美林

2. Korean name:
   パク ミュンスク
   Paku Myun Suku
   朴 明淑

Note: The pronunciation of proper names can vary.

Guess and Try 4

As your teacher reads the following words, listen carefully and guess what they mean, then practice pronouncing them.

1. ジュース
   jūsu ________________

2. ハンバーガー
   hambāgā ________________

3. サンドイッチ
   sandoicchi ________________

4. ピザ
   piza ________________

5. アイスクリーム
   aisukurīmu ________________

6. ワイン
   wain ________________

7. コーヒー
   kōhī ________________

8. クイズ
   kuizu ________________

9. テスト
   tesuto ________________

10. クラス
kurasu ________________

11. レストラン
resutoran ________________

12. サンフランシスコ
Sanfuranshisuko ________________

13. ロサンゼルス
Rosanzerusu ________________

14. シドニー
Shidonī ________________

15. トロント
Toronto ________________

16. ソウル
Souru ________________

17. ペキン
Pekin ________________

18. タイペイ
Taipei ________________

19. インターネット
intānetto ________________

20. ハリー・ポッター
Harī Pottā ________________

Task 1: Classroom Activity

Pronounce the name of your town in Japanese.

Task 2: Classroom Activity

Pronounce your name in Japanese and write it down in katakana, then make a simple めいし *business card.* Ⓔ

XXX 大学経済学部　研究生

ブライアン・ホフマン

TEL and FAX: (xxxx) xx-xxxx
E-mail: xxx@xxxx.xx.xx

XXX 大学文学部　学部生

王(オウ) 美(ビ) 林(リン)

TEL and FAX: (xxxx) xx-xxxx
E-mail: xxx@xxxx.xx.xx

XXX 大学文学部教授

山田あき子

TEL and FAX: (xxxx) xx-xxxx
E-mail: xxx@xxxx.xx.xx

(… 大学(だいがく) *... University,* … 学部(がくぶ) *Department of ...,* 経済学部(けいざいがくぶ) *Department of economics,* 文学部(ぶんがくぶ) *Department of literature,* 教授(きょうじゅ) *professor,* 研究生(けんきゅうせい) *graduate student,* 学部生(がくぶせい) *undergraduate student*)

Task 3: Classroom Activity

Your teacher writes everyone's first name in katakana on the board. Identify each name.

Writing 1

Write the words listed in Guess and Try 4 several times each.

Writing 2

Write your name in katakana several times.

ジュース

マイケル・スパータス

– Grammar and Usage –

1 Numbers

The following table shows how the basic numbers are read in Japanese.

0	: れい (ゼロ)	100	: ひゃく
1	: いち	200	: にひゃく
2	: に	300	: さんびゃく
3	: さん	400	: よんひゃく
4	: よん (し)	500	: ごひゃく
5	: ご	600	: ろっぴゃく
6	: ろく	700	: ななひゃく
7	: なな (しち)	800	: はっぴゃく
8	: はち	900	: きゅうひゃく
9	: きゅう	1,000	: せん
10	: じゅう	2,000	: にせん
11	: じゅういち	3,000	: さんぜん
12	: じゅうに	4,000	: よんせん
13	: じゅうさん	5,000	: ごせん
14	: じゅうよん	6,000	: ろくせん
15	: じゅうご	7,000	: ななせん
16	: じゅうろく	8,000	: はっせん
17	: じゅうなな	9,000	: きゅうせん
18	: じゅうはち	10,000	: いちまん
19	: じゅうきゅう	20,000	: にまん
20	: にじゅう	30,000	: さんまん
30	: さんじゅう	40,000	: よんまん
40	: よんじゅう	50,000	: ごまん
50	: ごじゅう	60,000	: ろくまん
60	: ろくじゅう	70,000	: ななまん
70	: ななじゅう	80,000	: はちまん
80	: はちじゅう	90,000	: きゅうまん
90	: きゅうじゅう		

In daily life, numbers are represented by Arabic numerals or by kanji numerals. The general rule is to use Arabic numerals when writing horizontally and to use kanji numerals when writing vertically, but there are many exceptions, arbitrariness and preferences over one to the other depending on the context. Numbers are read from left to right, using digit words such as 十(じゅう) *ten*, 百(ひゃく) *hundred*, 千(せん) *thousand*, 万(まん) *ten thousand* and 億(おく) *one hundred million*. In some cases, the pronunciation of the digit word 百(ひゃく) *hundred* becomes びゃく or ぴゃく, and that of 千(せん) *thousand* becomes ぜん.

The following are some examples:

(a)	12	:	じゅうに
(b)	24	:	にじゅうよん
(c)	120	:	ひゃくにじゅう
(d)	245	:	にひゃくよんじゅうご
(e)	1,800	:	せんはっぴゃく
(f)	2,345	:	にせんさんびゃくよんじゅうご
(g)	13,000	:	いちまんさんぜん
(h)	23,459	:	にまんさんぜんよんひゃくごじゅうきゅう
(i)	123,556	:	じゅうにまんさんぜんごひゃくごじゅうろく
(j)	1,000,000	:	ひゃくまん
(k)	10,000,000	:	いっせんまん
(l)	100,000,000	:	いちおく

Note that 10,000 is not じゅうせん (十千), but いちまん (一万).

Numbers can be followed by a counter (classifier) such as ～時(じ), ～分(ふん), ～円(えん) and ～ドル(どる). Some of the numbers are pronounced differently depending on the counter that follows them. For example, the number "4" is pronounced as よん, よ or し, the number "7" is pronounced as しち or なな and the number "9" is pronounced as きゅう or く.

2 Counters

The quantity or the amount of things is expressed by a numeral and a suffix called a "counter" in Japanese. Different counters are used depending on the type, shape, and size of the item you are counting or measuring. For example, ～人(にん) is the counter for people, ～台(だい) is the counter for machines, and ～円(えん) or ～ドル(どる) is the counter for money.

Some counters also specify the place in an order, for example, ～時(じ) *~o'clock*, ～分(ふん) *~minute*, ～番(ばん) *the number~*, ～年生(ねんせい) *~th grade*. They are called "ordinal counters".

When a counter is added to a number, it often creates an unsystematic change in pronounciation, especially when the counter starts with a consonant such as **k**, **s**, **t**, **f** and **h** (a voiceless consonant). For example, the counter ～分(ふん) is pronounced as ふん or ぷん depending on the numeral that precedes it and it also affects the reading of the preceding numerals, as in 1分(いっぷん)・2分(にふん)・3分(さんぷん) (see Appendix Three).

We can create a question word by combining 何(なん・なに) and a counter.

(a) 今(いま)、何時(なんじ)ですか。
What time is it now?
— 今、2時(じ) 25分(ふん)です。
— It is 2:25 now.

(b) 山田さんは何年生(なんねんせい)ですか。
Ms. Yamada, what grade are you in?

(c) 山田さんは何才(なんさい)ですか。
Ms. Yamada, how old are you?

3 ごぜん, ごご: a.m., p.m.

ごぜん *a.m.* and ごご *p.m.* are placed right before time phrases:

(a) ごぜん7時(じ)15分(ふん)
7:15 a.m.

(b) ごご7時15分
7:15 p.m.

4 いくら: How much? [Question word for price]

The question word いくら is used for asking the price of merchandise.

(a) あれは いくらですか。
How much is that?

A unit for money like ～円(えん) and ～ドル(どる) may be used with 何(なん) for asking the price, too.

(b) あれは何円(なんえん)ですか。

(c) あれは何ドル(なんどる)ですか。

Note that the pronunciation of 円 is "**en**", not "yen".

5 ～と: And [Listing marker for nouns]

～と occurs after each of the noun phrases that are listed, except that ～と is usually dropped at the end of the last item in the list.

(a) カメラ(かめら)と、ラジオ(らじお)と、時計(とけい)を下(くだ)さい。
Please give me a camera, a radio and a watch.

(b) 私はニューヨーク(にゅうようく)と、サンフランシスコ(さんふらんしすこ)と、ボストン(ぼすとん)に行(い)きました。
I went to New York, San Francisco and Boston.

(c) ニューヨーク(にゅうようく)はボストン(ぼすとん)と、ワシントン(わしんとん) DC(でぃいしい)の間(あいだ)にあります。
New York is between Boston and Washington D.C.

6 ～をください: Please give me～ [Purchasing]

When you want to buy something, you can either say ～をください or ～をおねがいします.

(a) すみません。このラジオ(らじお)を下(くだ)さい。
Excuse me. I will have this radio.

(b) すみません。このラジオをお願(ねが)いします。
Excuse me. I will have this radio.

7 Syllable structure in Japanese

A Japanese syllable has one (short or long) vowel, which may be preceded by a single consonant (C) or a palatalized consonant (Cy):

a-ki	ka-mi-na-ri	kya-ku
autumn	*thunder*	*guest*

The final consonants of a syllable is limited to a part of geminate consonants (for example, pp, tt, kk, ss) or nasal consonants (m, n).

ki**p**-pu	ki**t**-te	ke**k**-kon
ticket	*stamp*	*marriage*
ma**s**-su-gu	ki-ri**n**	ri**n**-go
straight	*giraffe*	*apple*
ki**n**-en	shi**m**-bun	
no smoking	*newspaper*	

When the final nasal consonant of a syllable is followed by a vowel as in "kin-en", it is separated by a brief pause.

When a loan word has a sequence of consonants that does not fit into the above Japanese syllable structures, a vowel **u** or **o** is inserted right after the problematic consonant—the vowel **o** is inserted if the problematic consonant is either **t** or **d** and the vowel **u** is inserted in other cases.

– Culture –

Ⓐ Lucky and unlucky numbers

The number "4" is a bad luck number in Japan because it can be pronounced as し, which is homophonous with 死 *death*. For this reason, the number "4" is usually pronounced as よん or よ, and it is pronounced as し only in counting (for example, 一、二、三、四、五 at a karate dojo) or for an established heavily used phrase such as 4 月 *April*. Besides the number "4", the number "9" is also considered as a bad luck number since it can be pronounced as く, which is homophonous with 苦 *suffering*.

By contrast, the Japanese consider "3", "5" and "7" to be lucky numbers. For example, when they give cakes to their friends or neighbors, they usually give 3, 5 or 7 cakes, but never 4 or 9 of them.

Ⓑ Asking others their age

The Japanese often ask others their age, but non-Japanese would often find this very rude. The Japanese ask others their age partly because age is one of the most important factors that determine the style of speech used in a Japanese conversation.

Ⓒ Salesclerks and customers

Customers are generally regarded as "gods" in Japan and salesclerks are trained to treat them very politely. When customers enter a store, the salesclerks welcome them with a bow, saying いらっしゃいませ *Welcome!*. They use a polite speech style and formal expressions specific to the business contexts. This is most obvious in prestigious department stores, but is less obvious in stores that sell inexpensive daily-life items (for example, fish market and vegetable market).

Ⓓ Japanese currency

The commonly-used Japanese banknotes are 10,000-yen-bills, 5,000-yen-bills and 1,000-yen-bills, and the commonly-used Japanese coins are 500-yen-coins, 100-yen-coins, 50-yen-coins, 10-yen-coins, 5-yen-coins and 1-yen-coins. The person who appears on the 10,000-yen-bill is 福沢諭吉 (1834–1901), a famous educator who founded Keio Gijuku University, the current Keio University. The person who appears on the 5,000-yen-bill is 新渡戸稲造 (1862–1933), who was a great educator and an internationally recognized government official, served as Vice-Secretary-General of the League of Nations in Geneva. The person who appears on the 1,000-yen-bill is the famous Japanese writer, 夏目漱石 (1867–1916). His publications include 坊ちゃん *Bottchan*, 我輩は猫である *I Am a Cat*, 三四郎 *Sainshiro*, 心 *Kokoro* and 道草 *Michikusa*.

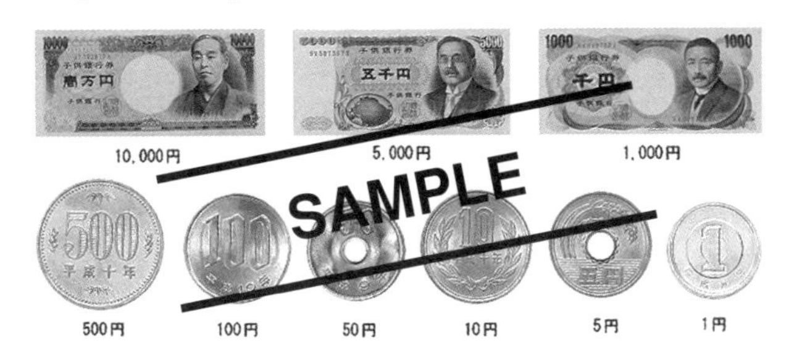

Ⓔ めいし: Name cards (Business cards)

Japanese business people and professionals almost always exchange their 名刺 *name cards* or *business cards* when they introduce themselves. A 名刺 is designed in the "landscape" or "portrait" orientation and includes one's affiliated company or institution with its address and telephone / fax number, his / her rank or title, and his / her name and e-mail address. It is very important to handle 名刺 with respect when you exchange them. When presenting your 名刺 to someone, hand it over so that it faces him / her. When receiving a 名刺, use both hands to accept it, bowing slightly. Spend a few moments reading it carefully. Once you read it, place it in front of you on the table if you are sitting at a table. If you are standing, it is best to put it in your business cardholder or in your purse. Do not put it in your back pocket.

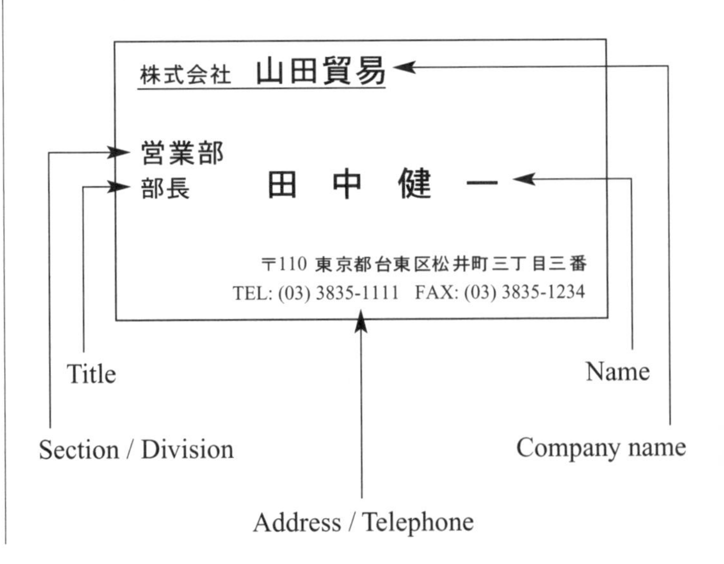

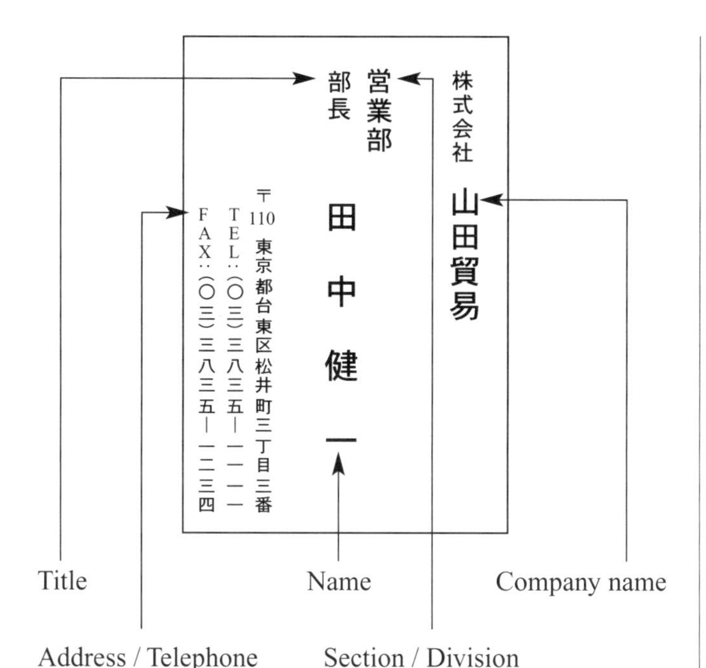

– Writing –

ⓐ おくりがな

おくりがな is the hiragana that follows a kanji character that represents a verb or an adjective, expressing its inflectional ending. For example, う in 買(か)う *to buy* and い in 高(たか)い *expensive* are おくりがな. The underlined parts in the following phrases are all おくりがな.

買<u>う</u> *to buy*	買<u>わない</u> *not to buy*
高<u>い</u> *expensive*	高<u>くない</u> *not expensive*

ⓑ ひとがしら

人	ひとがしら *person* Example: 今(いま) *now,* 会(あ)う *to meet,* 食(た)べる *to eat,* 命(いのち) *life,* 全部(ぜんぶ) *all together*

ⓒ なべぶた

亠	なべぶた *lid* Example: 高(たか)い *expensive,* 夜(よる) *night,* 京都(きょうと) *Kyoto*

ⓓ うかんむり

宀	うかんむり *roof* Example: 安(やす)い *cheap,* 字(じ) *characters,* 空(そら) *sky,* 家(いえ) *house,* 寝(ね)る *to sleep,* 客(きゃく) *guest,* 宿(やど) *inn*

ⓔ カタカナ

Katakana characters were made by simplifying the kanji characters. Katakana is used for writing the names of foreign people and places (for example, スミスさん *Mr. Smith* and サンフランシスコ *San Francisco*), items and concepts from foreign countries except China (for example, テニス *tennis* and プライド *pride*), and most onomatopoeic words (imitating or psychological impression words) like ツルツル *shiny / smooth*. Katakana characters are used parallel with hiragana characters, except that long vowels are represented by a short horizontal line "ー" in katakana (for example, ガールフレンド *girlfriend*). When the passage is written vertically, this bar also becomes vertical. However, to make the pronunciation of loan words closer to their original sound, the usage of katakana characters often violates basic Kana system: for example, ヴァ (ヴァイオリン / バイオリン *violin*), ティ (パーティー *party*), フィ (フィリピン *Philippines*), フォ (フォーク *fork*), ウォ (ウォークマン *walkman*) and ジェ (ジェシカ *Jessica*).

ン **n**	ワ **wa**	ラ **ra**	ヤ **ya**	マ **ma**	ハ **ha**	ナ **na**	タ **ta**	サ **sa**	カ **ka**	ア **a**
		リ **ri**		ミ **mi**	ヒ **hi**	ニ **ni**	チ **chi**	シ **shi**	キ **ki**	イ **i**
		ル **ru**	ユ **yu**	ム **mu**	フ **fu**	ヌ **nu**	ツ **tsu**	ス **su**	ク **ku**	ウ **u**
		レ **re**		メ **me**	ヘ **he**	ネ **ne**	テ **te**	セ **se**	ケ **ke**	エ **e**
	ヲ **o**	ロ **ro**	ヨ **yo**	モ **mo**	ホ **ho**	ノ **no**	ト **to**	ソ **so**	コ **ko**	オ **o**

– Kanji List –

一・二・三・四・五・六・七・八・九・十・今・～月・～月生まれ・～年生・～時・何時・～分・高い・安い・百・千・万・～円

Kanji	Readings / Meaning	Stroke order	Strokes	Example
一	ひと-つ・イチ *one*	一	[1]	Example: 一(いち) *one*
二	ふた-つ・ニ *two*	一 二	[2]	Example: 二(に) *two*
三	みっ-つ・サン *three*	一 二 三	[3]	Example: 三(さん) *three*
四	よっ-つ・よん・よ・シ *four*	丨 冂 冂 四 四	[5]	Example: 四(よん) *four*
五	いつ-つ・ゴ *five*	一 丆 五 五	[4]	Example: 五(ご) *five*
六	むっ-つ・ロク・ロッ *six*	丶 亠 六 六	[4]	Example: 六(ろく) *six*
七	なな-つ・なな・シチ *seven*	一 七	[2]	Example: 七(なな・しち) *seven*
八	やっ-つ・ハチ・ハッ *eight*	ノ 八	[2]	Example: 八(はち) *eight*
九	ここの-つ・キュウ・ク *nine*	ノ 九	[2]	Example: 九(きゅう) *nine*
十	とお・ジュウ・ジュッ・ジッ *ten*	一 十	[2]	Example: 十(じゅう) *ten*
今	いま・コン *now, present*	ノ 人 へ 今	[4]	Example: 今(いま) *now*
月	つき・ゲツ・ガツ *moon, month*	丿 刀 月 月	[4]	Example: 3月(さんがつ) *March*
生	い-きる・う-まれる・セイ *live, birth*	ノ 𠂉 牛 牛 生	[5]	Example: 生(う)まれる *to be born* 学生(がくせい) *a student*
年	とし・ネン *year, age*	ノ 𠂉 𠂉 午 左 年	[6]	Example: 1年生(いちねんせい) *the first grade, college freshman*
時	とき・ジ *time, hour*	丨 冂 日 日 日一 日十 日土 旪 時 時	[10]	Example: 4時(よじ) *four o'clock*
何	なに・なん *what*	ノ 亻 亻 仃 何 何 何	[7]	Example: 何時(なんじ) *what time* 何(なん)ですか *What is it?*
分	わ-かる・ブン・フン・プン *division, part, minute*	ノ 八 分 分	[4]	Example: 5分(ごふん) *five minutes*

高 たか-い・コウ *high, expensive*	丶 亠 亠 亠 亠 亠 高 高 高 高 [10] Example: 高(たか)い *expensive*
安 やす-い・アン *safe, cheap*	丶 丶 宀 宀 安 安 [6] Example: 安(やす)い *cheap*
百 ヒャク・ピャク・ビャク *hundred*	一 丆 了 百 百 百 [6] Example: 百(ひゃく) *100* 三百(さんびゃく) *300* 八百(はっぴゃく) *800*
千 セン・ゼン・ち *thousand*	丿 二 千 [3] Example: 千(せん) *1,000* 三千(さんぜん) *3,000*
万 まん *ten thousand, all*	一 丆 万 [3] Example: 一万(いちまん) *10,000* 二万(にまん) *20,000*
円 エン *circle, ~yen*	丨 冂 円 円 [4] Example: 10 円(えん) *10 yen*

– Review –

Q1. Read the following sentences.

1. 日本の車は高いですか。安いですか。
2. すみません。今、何時ですか。
   — 今、7 時 25 分です。
3. テレビと、カメラと、ラジオをください。

Q2. Write the pronounciation of the following numbers in hiragana.

1. 24 : にじゅうし
2. 105 : ひゃくご
3. 395 : さんびゃくきゅうじゅうご
4. 1,998 : せんきゅうひゃくきゅうじゅうはち
5. 12,000 : いちまんにせん

Q3. Write the pronounciation of the following phrases in hiragana.

1. 10 円 : じゅうえん
2. 4 月 : しがつ
3. 7 時 : しちじ
4. 9 時 : くじ
5. 30 分 : さんじゅうぷん

Q4. Fill in the blanks with appropriate question words.

1. すみません。これは いくら ですか。
   — 200 円です。
2. スミスさんのでんわばんごうは ~~なん~~ 何 ですか。
   — 852-8765 です。
3. 今、何時 ですか。
   — 2 時です。
4. 山田さんは 何年生 ですか。
   — 4 年生です。

Q5. What would you say in the following situations?

1. You want to ask the price of the hat you are holding.
2. You want to buy a radio, a camera and a watch.
3. You want to ask someone what time it is now.

Tips and Additional Knowledge: At the Airport

If you are flying to Japan from other countries, you will probably be arriving at the Narita International Airport near Tokyo or at Kansai International Airport near Osaka. Be ready for the typical questions asked at the immigration booth. They are found in the following dialog.

At the airport immigration desk

Officer : パスポート、お願(ねが)いします。
Passport, please.

Sean : どうぞ。
Here you are.

Officer : お名前(なまえ)は？
Your name?

Sean : ショーン・コーエンです。
Sean Cohen.

Officer : 生年月日(せいねんがっぴ)は？
Your date of birth?

Sean : 1980年5月11日(せんきゅうひゃくはちじゅうねんごがつじゅういちにち)です。
May 11th, 1980.

Officer : どちらから？
From where?

Sean : アメリカです。
The U.S.

Officer : 観光(かんこう)ですか？
Sightseeing?

Sean : はい。
Yes.

Officer : どこに泊(と)まりますか。
Where are you staying?

Sean : 東京(とうきょう)インです。
Tokyo Inn.

Officer : (The officer returns his passport.)
はい。じゃあ、どうぞ。
Okay. You can go now.

Sean : どうも。
Thank you.

CHAPTER FIVE

Coming and Going

Lesson 21
An Overview of Japanese Verb Conjugation 72

Lesson 22
今日はクラスに行きますか **Today's Plan** 74

Lesson 23
デパートに行きませんか **Weekend Plans** 76

Lesson 24
カラオケ・バーにはよく行きますか **Nightlife** 78

Grammar and Usage 80

1. An overview of verb conjugation 80
2. Plain forms of verbs (食べる, 食べない, etc) 82
3. ～ます, ～ません [Polite suffixes in the present tense] 82
4. Present tense 83
5. Relative time (明日, 昨日, etc) 83
6. Verbs of going and coming (行く, 来る and 帰る) . . . 83
7. わかる: To understand / to know 83
8. ～に: To ～ [Target, destination] 84
9. ～や (屋): ～store / ～shop 84
10. Demonstrative pronouns for location 84
11. ～ませんか: How about ～ing? [Suggesting] 84
12. ～ましょう: Let's do～ 84
13. ちょっと: It's a little ... [Declination] 84
14. Frequency (よく, ときどき, etc) 85
15. Negative adverbs (あまり, ぜんぜん, etc) 85
16. でも: But [Conflict / contrast] 85
17. Particle combination (～には, ～にも, etc) 85

Culture 86

- A デパート: Department store 86
- B Repeating 86
- C Rejecting 86
- D カラオケ: Karaoke 87
- E いざかや: Izakaya bar 87

Writing 87

- a ひへん 87

Kanji List 87

Review 88

Tips and Additional Knowledge: Skipping Particles and the Copula in an Informal Context 88

An Overview of Japanese Verb Conjugation

Notes Relating to This Lesson	
Grammar and Usage 1 An overview of verb conjugation 80	

Japanese verbs conjugate based on **tense** (present / past), whether they are affirmative or negative, and what suffixes and words follow them.

Guess and Try 1

Pay attention to the different forms of verbs in the following verb table and complete the passages that follow. 1

		Root Form	Plain Present Affirmative Form	Plain Present Negative Form	Stem Form
Regular Verbs	Ru-verbs	たべ *eat* tabe	たべる tabe-ru	たべない tabe-nai	たべ tabe
		き *wear* ki	きる ki-ru	きない ki-nai	き ki
		かり *borrow* kari	かりる kari-ru	かりない kari-nai	かり kari
	U-verbs	かk *write* kak	かく kak-u	かかない kak-anai	かき kak-i
		およg *swim* oyog	およぐ oyog-u	およがない oyog-anai	およぎ oyog-i
		とb *jump* tob	とぶ tob-u	とばない tob-anai	とび tob-i
		はなs *talk* hanas	はなす hanas-u	はなさない hanas-anai	はなし hanash-i
		よm *read* yom	よむ yom-u	よまない yom-anai	よみ yom-i
		しn *die* shin	しぬ shin-u	しなない shin-anai	しに shin-i
		かw *buy* kaw	かう ka-u	かわない kaw-anai	かい ka-i
		まt *wait* mat	まつ mats-u	またない mat-anai	まち mach-i
		きr *cut* kir	きる kir-u	きらない kir-anai	きり kir-i
		かr *trim* kar	かる kar-u	からない kar-anai	かり kar-i
Major Irregular Verbs		k? *come*	くる kuru	こない konai	き ki
		s? *do*	する suru	しない shinai	し shi

1. There are only two major "irregular" verbs in Japanese and other verbs are all "regular" verbs. (There are several regular verbs that have a slight sound change in one or two of their forms, but they are not considersed as major irregular verbs.)

2. The root is the common part found in all the pronounceable forms of a verb, but the root itself is unpronounceable for Japanese. The root always ends in one of the following 11 sounds: **e**, **i**, **k**, **g**, (b), (s), (m), (n), (w), (t) and (r). The dictionary form or the plain present affirmative form is the most basic pronounceable form. The verb whose root ends in a vowel and its dictionary form is its root plus ru is called a **ru**-verb. On the other hand, the verb whose root ends in a consonant and its dictionary form is its root plus (u) is called an **u**-verb.

3. In informal conversations, "plain" forms can be used.

   The plain present affirmative form (dictionary form) consists of the root and either **ru** or **u**: the root plus **ru** for a **ru**-verb; the root plus (u) for an **u**-verb. A minor sound change occurs when the root ends in **w** or (t) in this case.

   The plain present negative form consists of the root and either **nai** or **anai**: the root plus **nai** for a **ru**-verb; the root plus **anai** for an (u)-verb.

4. In a polite / neutral context, you need to add the polite suffix ます after the verb. The verb must be in the stem form when followed by ます. For **ru**-verbs, the stem form is identical to the (root) form. For **u**-verbs, the stem form consists of the root and the vowel (i). A minor sound change occurs when the root ends in **s**, **w**, or (t) in this case.

Guess and Try 2

For each of the following verbs in the dictionary forms, state whether it is a **ru**-verb or an **u**-verb. In some cases, it is ambiguous. Explain why.

1. かく
   kaku
2. およぐ
   oyogu

3. はなす
hanasu

4. のむ
nomu

5. しぬ
shinu

6. あそぶ
asobu

7. かう
kau

8. かつ
katsu

9. とる
toru

10. きる
kiru

11. かえる
kaeru

12. うる
uru

Guess and Try 3

Complete the following conjugation table. You need to first drop **ru** and **u** at the end of the dictionary form of a **ru**-verb and an **u**-verb, respectively, so you can reveal the root. Then you can add a suffix such as **anai**, **nai** and **i** to the root appropriately. Are there any two verbs that have the same dictionary form? Are there any two verbs that have the same stem form?

Plain Present Affirmative Form (Dictionary Form)	Plain Present Negative Form: root + (a) nai	Stem Form: root (+ i)
Example: のむ *drink*	のまない	のみ
Example: かす *loan*	かさない	かし
Example: かえる *return* (**u**-verb)	かえらない	かえり
Example: かえる *change* (**ru**-verb)	かえない	かえ
Example: つかう *use*	つかわない	つかい
1. とぶ *fly*	とばない	とび
2. はなす *speak*	はなさない	はなし
3. まつ *wait*	またない	まち
4. かく *write*	かがない	がき
5. およぐ *swim*	およがない	およぎ
6. よむ *read*	よまない	よみ
7. しぬ *die*	しなない	しに
8. かう *buy*	がわない	がい
9. かる *trim*	からない	かり
10. たべる *eat* (**ru**-verb)	たべない	たべ
11. きる *wear* (**ru**-verb)	きない	き
12. きる *cut* (**u**-verb)	きらない	きり
13. かりる *borrow* (**ru**-verb)	かりない	かり

Drill: Reading / Repeating

Read each of the following several times.

1. とぶ・とばない・とび(ます)
2. はなす・はなさない・はなし(ます)
3. まつ・またない・まち(ます)
4. かく・かかない・かき(ます)
5. およぐ・およがない・およぎ(ます)
6. よむ・よまない・よみ(ます)
7. しぬ・しなない・しに(ます)
8. かう・かわない・かい(ます)
9. かる・からない・かり(ます)
10. きる・きらない・きり(ます)
11. きる・きない・き(ます)
12. たべる・たべない・たべ(ます)
13. くる・こない・き(ます)
14. する・しない・し(ます)

今日はクラスに行きますか Today's Plan

Notes Relating to This Lesson	
Grammar and Usage	7 わかる 83
2 Plain forms of verbs 82	8 ～に 84
3 ～ます, ～ません 82	**Writing**
4 Present tense 83	ⓐ ひへん 87
5 Relative time 83	
6 Verbs of going and coming 83	

Basic Vocabulary and Kanji

きょ˥う	今日	*n. today* 5
あした˥	明日	*n. tomorrow* 5
ゆうがた	夕方	*n. early evening, dusk*
うち	家	*n. house, home*
ぎんこう	銀行	*n. bank*
ゆうび˥んきょく	郵便局	*n. post office*
びょういん	病院	*n. hospital*
ク˥ラス (くらす)		*n. class*
いく	*k-u* 行く・行かない・行き・行って	*vi. to go* 6
く˥る	*irr.* 来(く)る・来(こ)ない・来(き)・来(き)て	*vi. to come* 6
か˥える	*r-u* 帰る・帰らない・帰り・帰って	*vi. to return to one's home, country or base* 6
わか˥る	*r-u* 分かる・分からない・分かり・分かって	*vi. to know, to understand* 7
～に		*prt. to* 8
～ます		*polite present affirmative suffix for verbs* 3
～ません		*polite present negative suffix for verbs* 3

Newly introduced kanji:

今日(きょう)・明日(あした) ⓐ・行(い)く・来(く)る・来(き)ます・来(こ)ない・帰(かえ)る

明	丨 冂 日 日 町 明 明 明	行	ノ 彳 彳 行 行 行
来	一 一 丆 立 平 来 来	帰	丨 刂 刂 帰 帰 帰 帰 帰 帰 帰

Dialog 1

Early one morning, Yukiko is talking with her sister, Akiko, at home.

ゆきこ　：今日はクラス(くらす)に行く？

あきこ　：うんんん、行かない。ゆきこは？

ゆきこ　：私は行く。

あきこ　：ゆうがたはうちに帰る？

ゆきこ　：ちょっとわからない。

Dialog 2

In the morning, Mary Carter is talking with her classmate, Yoko Yamada.

カーター(かあたあ)：今日はとしょかんに<u>行きますか</u>。

山田(やまだ)　：いいえ、<u>行きません</u>。マリー(まりい)さんは。

カーター：私は<u>行きます</u>。

Guess and Try 1

Compare Dialog 1 and 2, and state the difference. 2 3

Guess and Try 2

Interpret the underlined parts in Dialog 2. 2 3 4

Guess and Try 3

Fill in the blanks with the appropriate particles. 6 8

1. 私は今日ぎんこう ____ 行きます。
2. ゆうがたうち ____ 帰ります。
3. 山田さんは明日うち ____ 来ます。

Drill 1: Reading / Repeating

1. 行く・行かない・行きます
2. 帰る・帰らない・帰ります
3. 来る・来ない・来ます
4. わかる・わからない・わかります

Drill 2: Conjugation

行く ⟶ 行く・行かない・行きます

1. 帰る
2. 来る
3. わかる
4. 行く

Repeat several times.

Drill 3: Substitution

<u>ぎんこう</u>に行きますか。

1. びょういん
2. クラス（くらす）
3. 大学（だいがく）
4. 大学のとしょかん
5. ともだちのうち

Task: Classroom Activity

Each of you is assigned to go to one of the listed locations today. You are required to find out the location assigned to each of your classmates by asking him / her a question in Japanese.

1. としょかん
2. L・L（える・える）教室（きょうしつ） *language lab*
3. 先生（せんせい）の研究室（けんきゅうしつ） *the professor's office*
4. ぎんこう
5. スーパーマーケット（すうぱあまあけっと） *supermarket*
6. レストラン（れすとらん） *restaurant*
7. ゆうびんきょく

For example:

A：今日はとしょかんに行きますか。

B：いいえ、行きません。/ はい、行きます。

A：ああ、そうですか。

Writing

Write the following Katakana characters several times each.

アイウエオ	カキクケコ	サシスセソ
アイウエオ	カキクケコ	サシスセソ
アイウエオ	カキクケコ	サシスセソ
アイウエオ	カキクケコ	サシスセソ
今日	今日	今日
明日	明日	ゆうがた
ゆうびんきょく	クラス	行く
行く	行く	行く
来る	来る	帰る
帰る	帰る	分かる
分かる		

デパートに行きませんか Weekend Plans

Notes Relating to This Lesson	
Grammar and Usage	**Culture**
9 〜や(屋) 84	Ⓐ デパート 86
10 Demonstrative pronouns for location 84	Ⓑ Repeating 86
11 〜ませんか 84	Ⓒ Rejecting 86
12 〜ましょう 84	
13 ちょっと 84	

Basic Vocabulary and Kanji

しゅうまつ	週末	*n. weekend*
えいが˥かん	映画館	*n. movie theater*
デパ˥ート (でぱーと)		*n. department store* Ⓐ
う˥み	海	*n. sea, ocean*
やま˥	山	*n. mountain*
こうえん	公園	*n. park*
どうぶつ˥えん	動物園	*n. zoo*
ほ˥んや	本屋	*n. bookstore* 9
ここ		*pron. here* 10
そこ		*pron. there (near you)* 10
あそこ		*pron. over there* 10
ど˥こ		*q. where*

Newly introduced kanji:

山(やま)・安田(やすだ) (surname)

Dialog

Robert White talks with his classmate, Akiko Yasuda, about the coming weekend.

ホワイト(ほわいと)：あきこさん。しゅうまつ、うみに行(い)きませんか。

安田　：うみですか。<u>うみはちょっと…</u>

ホワイト：ああ、そうですか。じゃあ、山に行きませんか。

安田　：山ですか。んん、<u>ちょっと…</u>

ホワイト：ああ、そうですか。じゃあ、デパート(でぱーと)に行きませんか。

安田　：いいですよ。行きましょう。

Guess and Try 1

Why does Akiko repeat the locations that Robert mentioned? Ⓑ

Guess and Try 2

Interpret the underlined part in the above dialog. 13 Ⓒ

Guess and Try 3

Suggest to your partner that he / she go to the bookstore, and let him / her reply to you. 11 12

You　: ________________________

Your patner　: ________________________

Drill: Substitution

<u>山</u>に行きませんか

1. えいがかん
2. デパート(でぱーと)
3. 本や
4. 山田さんのうち
5. うみ
6. あそこ

Task 1: Pair Work

Make a plan for the coming weekend with your partner.

Task 2: Classroom Activity

Your teacher assigns each student where to go on weekend (for example, 本や・うみ). At least two students receive the same assignment. Find the people who are assigned to go to the same place as you on weekend and ask them to go with you.

A：しゅうまつはどこに行(い)きますか。

B：本(ほん)やに行きます。	B：としょかんに行きます。
A：ああ、そうですか。私もです*。(Excitedly)	A：ああ、そうですか。(Disappointedly)
B：じゃあ、いっしょに行きませんか。	B：Aさんは。
A：ええ、いいですよ。いっしょに行きましょう。	A：私は本やに行きます。
	B：ああ、そうですか。じゃあ、また。
	A：ええ、じゃあ、また。

(* 私もです *me, too*)

Vocabulary Collection (Weekend Entertainment)

映画館(えいがかん) *movie theater*　博物館(はくぶつかん) *museum*
美術館(びじゅつかん) *art museum*　劇場(げきじょう) *theater*
おもちゃ屋(や) *toy store*　ゲームセンター(げーむせんたー) *arcade*
海(うみ) *sea, ocean*　山(やま) *mountain*
球場(きゅうじょう) *baseball stadium*　公園(こうえん) *park*
パチンコ屋(ぱちんこや) *Pachinko (Japanese pinball game) parlor*
地下街(ちかがい) *underground shopping mall*
遊園地(ゆうえんち) *amusement park*
ボーリング場(ぼーりんぐじょう) *bowling alley*

Short Reading: E-mail message

明子(あきこ)さん

明日大阪(あしたおおさか)から僕(ぼく)の従兄弟(いとこ)が来(き)ます。彼(かれ)の趣味(しゅみ)はサーフィン(さーふぃん)です。とても上手(じょうず)です。明子(あきこ)さんもサーフィン(さーふぃん)が好(す)きですよね。今週(こんしゅう)の週末(しゅうまつ)いっしょに湘南(しょうなん)に行(い)きませんか。いっしょにサーフィンをしましょう。

大介(だいすけ)

(大阪(おおさか)から *from Osaka,* 僕(ぼく) *me (for male),* 従兄弟(いとこ) *cousin,* 彼(かれ) *he / him,* 趣味(しゅみ) *hobby,* サーフィン(さあふぃん) *surfing,* 上手(じょうず)です *to be good at~,* ～が好(す)きです *to like~,* 今週(こんしゅう) *this week,* 湘南(しょうなん) *Shonan coast (name of a place),* ～をしましょう *Let's do~*)

Writing

Write the following Katakana characters several times each.

タチツテト	ナニヌネノ	ハヒフヘホ
タチツテト	ナニヌネノ	ハヒフヘホ
タチツテト	ナニヌネノ	ハヒフヘホ
しゅうまつ	しゅうまつ	えいがかん
えいがかん	うみ	うみ
やま	やま	こうえん
こうえん	どうぶつえん	どうぶつえん
ほんや	ほんや	安田
安田	安田	

カラオケ・バーにはよく行きますか Nightlife

Notes Relating to This Lesson	
Grammar and Usage	**Culture**
[14] Frequency 85	Ⓓ カラオケ 87
[15] Negative adverbs 85	Ⓔ いざかや 87
[16] でも 85	
[17] Particle combination 85	

Basic Vocabulary and Kanji

こ˥んばん	今晩	*n. this evening, tonight*
レ˥ストラン		*n. restaurant*
カラオケ		*n. karaoke* Ⓓ
いざかや	居酒屋	*n. izakaya bar (casual Japanese-style bar)* Ⓔ
よ˥く		*adv. often, well* [14]
ときどき	時々	*adv. sometimes* [14]
あまり (〜ない)		*adv. (not) often, (not) much* [15]
ぜんぜん (〜ない)	全然	*adv. (not) at all* [14] [15]
ひま(な)	暇だ・暇じゃない	*adj. not busy, free*
うたう	*w-u* 歌う・歌わない・歌い・歌って	*vt. to sing*
で˥も		*con. but, however* [16]

Newly introduced kanji:

田中 (surname)

中	丶 ロ 口 中

Dialog

Mary Carter asks Daisuke Tanaka whether he often goes to bars.

カーター：田中さんはよくいざかやに行きますか。

田中　　：いいえ、あまり行きません。でも、カラオケ・バーにはよく行きます。

カーター：ああ、そうですか。じゃあ、カラオケ・ボックスは。

田中　　：カラオケ・ボックスにもよく行きます。マリーさんは。

カーター：私もよく行きます。こんばんはひまですか。

田中　　：ええ。

カーター：いっしょに、うたいませんか。

田中　　：いいですね。

Guess and Try 1

Do you know カラオケ? How about いざかや? Ⓓ Ⓔ

Guess and Try 2

Fill in the blank. [17]

本やにはよく行きます。としょかん ________ よく行きます。

Guess and Try 3

Choose the appropriate options in the parentheses: [14] [15]

1. よく(行きます・行きません)
2. ときどき(行きます・行きません)
3. あまり(行きます・行きません)
4. ぜんぜん(行きます・行きません)

Guess and Try 4

Choose the appropriate options in the parentheses: [16]

兄の車は高いです。でも、私の車は(安いです・高いです)。

Guess and Try 5 (optional)

Guess what the following sentences mean. [14]

1. 1週間に3回行きます。(〜週間 *~week(s)*)
2. 2週間に1回行きます。(〜回 *~time(s)*)

Drill 1: Formation

あまり・行く ⟶ あまり行きません
よく・行く ⟶ よく行きます

1. ときどき・行く
2. ぜんぜん・行く
3. あまり・行く
4. あまり・帰る
5. ぜんぜん・帰る
6. ときどき・来る

Drill 2: Formation

本や・あまり・行く ⟶ 本やにはあまり行きません
本や・よく・行く ⟶ 本やにはよく行きます

1. レストラン・ときどき・行く
2. バー・ぜんぜん・行く
3. えいがかん・よく・行く
4. ともだちのうち・あまり・行く
5. ゲームセンター *arcade*・よく・行く

Task 1: Survey

Ask three of your classmates how often they go to the fun places listed in the table. Make sure to add one location of your choice.

	私	さん	さん	さん
えいがかん *movie theater*				
カラオケ・バー *karaoke bar*				
ゲームセンター *arcade*				
?				

For example:

A ：えいがかん (に) はよく行きますか。

B ：ときどき行きます。

A ：ああ、そうですか。

Task 2: Classroom Activity

Find some people with whom you can go to your favorite fun place tonight. Use the dialog as a guide.

Short Reading

日本の会社員はよく居酒屋に行きます。居酒屋は日本のバーです。居酒屋の食べ物は安いです。でも、おいしいです。男の人は週に3回ぐらい行きます。女の人は月に2回ぐらい行きます。私はよく居酒屋に行きます。金曜日は必ず行きます。

(会社員 *company employee,* バー *bar; pub,* 食べ物 *food,* おいしいです *delicious,* 週 *week,* ～回 *~times,* ～ぐらい *approximately~,* 月 *month,* 金曜日 *Friday,* 必ず *without fail*)

Writing 1

Write how often each of your family members eat out.

Writing 2

Write the following katakana characters several times each.

マミムメモ	ヤユヨ	ラリルレロ	ワヲン
マミムメモ	ヤユヨ	ラリルロ	ワヲン
こんばん	こんばん	こんばん	レストラん
レストラン	カラオケ	いざかや	よく
時々	時々	あまり	あまり
ぜんぜん	ひまな	うたう	でも
田中	田中		

– Grammar and Usage –

1 An overview of verb conjugation

Verb conjugation in Japanese is not very parallel to that of any European languages. Japanese verbs do not conjugate based on number, person or gender, but they conjugate based on tense (present / past) and polarity (affirmative / negative). In addition, Japanese verbs conjugate based on what follows them. Japanese verbs are often followed by "post-verbal elements", which are suffixes, particles, words or phrases that add grammatical or pragmatic information to the verb.

Hosting forms

A verb must take the "root" form (V^{Root}), "plain" form (V^{Plain}), "stem" form (V^{Stem}) or "te-" form (V^{Te}), depending on what post-verbal element is following. Let's call these "hosting" forms as they host post-verbal elements. All the hosting forms and some post-verbal elements are shown in the following table. (In this chapter, you are learning only the root forms, some of the plain forms and stem forms.)

Root Form (V^{Root})

For example: かk
kak
write

The root form is the most basic verb form, from which all other verb forms are created. It is unpronounceable by itself for native Japanese speakers.

1. かける
kak-eru
(I) can write.

2. かこう
kak-ō
Let's write.

3. かかれる
kak-areru
(It) is written.

4. かかせる
kak-aseru
(I) will make (someone) write.

5. かけば
kak-eba
if (I) write ...

6. かけ
kak-e
Write. (command)

Plain Form (V^{Plain})

For example:

Present		Past	
Affirmative	Negative	Affirmative	Negative
かく kaku *write*	かかない kakanai *don't write*	かいた kaita *wrote*	かかなかった kakanakatta *didn't write*

Plain forms typically host a post-verbal element with a noun-like character. Plain forms can be used without any post-verbal elements in informal conversations or in written reports.

1. かくつもりです
kaku-tsumoridesu
(I) plan to write.

2. かかないつもりです
kakanai-tsumoridesu
(I) plan not to write.

3. かくんです
kaku-ndesu
It is the case that (I) write.

4. かくかもしれません
kaku-kamoshiremasen
(I) may write.

5. かくでしょう
kaku-deshō
(I) will probably write.

6. かく
kaku
(I) will write.
(informal context)

Stem Form (V^{Stem})

For example: かき
kaki
write / to write / writing

Stem forms host a variety of post-verbal elements, creating one phrase. The stem form is also known as "pre-masu" form since it's the host of the polite suffix **masu**.

1. かきます
kaki-masu
(I) will write. (polite)

2. かきません
kaki-masen
(I) won't write. (polite)

3. かきたい
kaki-tai
to want to write

4. かきすぎる
kaki-sugiru
to write too much

5. かきにくい
kaki-nikui
to be difficult to write

6. かきながら
kaki-nagara
while writing

Te-Form (V^Te)

For example:

Affirmative	Negative		
かいて kaite *write / writing*	かかなくて kakanakute	or	かかないで kakanaide
	not write / not writing		

Te-forms typically host a post-verbal element with a verb-like character.

1. かいてください
   kaite-kudasai
   Please write.
2. かいている
   kaite-iru
   to be writing
3. かいてある
   kaite-aru
   to have been written

Verb classes

There are only two major "irregular" verbs (する *to do* and くる *to come*). Other verbs are all "regular" verbs, except that several regular verbs such as いく *to go*, ある *to exist*, いらっしゃる *to exist (honorific)* and くださる *to give (honorific)* are slightly irregular for one or two of their forms. (See Appendix Two).

Regular verbs are divided into two groups: (1) the verbs whose roots end in a vowel, which can only be **e** or **i**, and their dictionary forms are their roots plus **ru**; (2) the verbs whose roots end in a consonant, which can only be **k**, **g**, **s**, **m**, **n**, **b**, **t**, **w** or **r**, and their dictionary forms are their roots plus **u**. The former class of verbs are called **ru**-verbs, and the latter class of verbs are called **u**-verbs. In this textbook, wherever a verb is introduced in the Basic Vocabulary and Kanji section, the verb is listed in its dictionary form, with the specification of its root ending sound and either **ru** or **u**. For example, たべる is specified as *e*-**ru** because its root ending sound is **e** and it is a **ru**-verb, and かく is specified as *k*-**u** because its root ending sound is **k** and it is an **u**-verb.

In this chapter, you learn three verb forms beside the root form: "plain present affirmative" (dictionary) forms, "plain present negative" forms, and "stem" forms. They all contain the root. The plain present affirmative (dictionary) form is the root plus **ru** for **ru**-verbs, but it is the root plus **u** for **u**-verbs. The plain present negative form is the root plus **nai** for **ru**-verbs, but it is the root plus **anai** for **u**-verbs. And the stem form is identical to the root for **ru**-verbs, but it is the root plus **i** for **u**-verbs. Note that the root final **w** is deleted when followed by any vowels except **a** (for example, **kaw** + **u** → **kau**, **kaw** + **i** → **kai**). The root final **t** becomes **ts** and **ch** when followed by **u** and **i**, respectively (for example, **ut** + **u** → **utsu**, **ut** + **i** → **uchi**), and the root final **s** becomes **sh** when followed by **i** (for example, **hanas** + **i** → **hanashi**). Major irregular verbs do not follow any conjugation rules. They are all illustrated with examples in the following table.

		Root Form	Plain Present Affirmative Form Root + (r)u	Plain Present Negative Form Root + (a)nai	Stem Form Root + (i)
Regular Verbs	Ru-verbs	たべ *eat* tabe	たべる tabe-ru	たべない tabe-nai	たべ tabe
		き *wear* ki	きる ki-ru	きない ki-nai	き ki
	U-verbs	かk *write* kak	かく kak-u	かかない kak-anai	かき kak-i
		およg *swim* oyog	およぐ oyog-u	およがない oyog-anai	およぎ oyog-i
		とb *jump* tob	とぶ tob-u	とばない tob-anai	とび tob-i
		はなs *talk* hanas	はなす hanas-u	はなさない hanas-anai	はなし hanash-i*
		よm *read* yom	よむ yom-u	よまない yom-anai	よみ yom-i
		しn *die* shin	しぬ shin-u	しなない shin-anai	しに shin-i
		かw *buy* kaw	かう ka-u**	かわない kaw-anai	かい ka-i***
		まt *wait* mat	まつ mats-u****	またない mat-anai	まち mach-i*****
		きr *cut* kir	きる kir-u	きらない kir-anai	きり kir-i
Major Irregular Verbs		? *come*	くる kuru	こない konai	き ki
		? *do*	する suru	しない shinai	し shi

* s → sh
** w → deleted
*** w → deleted
**** t → ts
***** t → ch

Identifying ru-verbs and u-verbs

For conjugating verbs, you need to know whether they are **ru**-verbs or **u**-verbs. The question is how you can tell whether a verb is a **ru**-verb or an **u**-verb just by looking at its dictionary form.

If the dictionary form of a verb ends in く, ぐ, む, ぬ, ぶ, す, う or つ, it is definitely an **u**-verb. For example, かく (kaku) is definitely an **u**-verb. If the dictionary form of a verb ends in る and the preceding vowel is **a**, **o** or **e**, it is also an **u**-verb. For example, とる (toru) is definitely an **u**-verb because the preceding vowel is **o**. Recall that と (to) is not a possible root form as all the vowel ending roots end in either **e** or **i**. By contrast, if a verb ends in る and the preceding vowel is either **e** or **i**, it can be either a **ru**-verb or an **u**-verb. For example, きる (kiru) can be a **ru**-verb or an **u**-verb because either き (ki) or きr (kir) is a possible root form. Each time you learn a new verb with **e る** (**eru**) or **i る** (**iru**) ending, remember whether it is a **ru**-verb or an **u**-verb.

You can find out whether a verb is a **ru**-verb or an **u**-verb by comparing its dictionary form and its stem form: if the stem form is identical with the dictionary form minus る, it is a **ru**-verb. Otherwise, it is an **u**-verb. Try the two cases in the following table. In Case 1, the dictionary form minus る is き, and the stem form is also き. As they are identical, it is a **ru**-verb, whose root is き (ki). In Case 2, the dictionary form minus る is き, but the stem is きり. Since they are not identical, it is an **u**-verb, whose root is きr (kir).

	Case 1	Case 2
Dictionary Form	き る	き る
Stem Form	き	きり
Root Form	き	きr

2 Plain forms of verbs (食べる, 食べない, etc)

Plain forms have four variations depending on tense (present / past) and whether they are affirmative or negative (for example, 食べる present affirmative, 食べない present negative, 食べた past affirmative and 食べなかった past negative).

Plain forms host various post-verbal elements, most of which are historically derived from nouns:

(a) 食べる-つもりです。
(I) intend to eat.

(b) 食べる-んです。
It is the case that (I) will eat.

(c) 食べない-つもりです。
(I) intend not to eat.

(d) 食べる-はずです。
(He) is supposed eat.

(e) 食べる-べきです。
(He) should eat.

(f) 食べる-でしょう。
(He) will probably eat.

(g) 食べる-かもしれません。
(He) may eat.

(h) 食べた-かもしれません。
(He) may have eaten.

Plain forms can be used independently in informal conversations such as at home, with young children and with very close friends. In the following conversation, the verbs are all in the plain form and the question particle か is omitted.

Mother : 明日、大学に行く。
Will you go to the university tomorrow?

Daughter : 行かない。
I'm not going.

Mother : ああ、そう。
Oh, is it so.

Plain forms are also used in written forms such as academic papers, newspaper articles and some type of essays.

3 ～ます, ～ません [Polite suffixes in the present tense]

The polite suffix ます is added at the end of the verb in the "stem" form and expresses the speaker's polite attitude. It is necessary in formal or neutral contexts such as at offices, schools and stores, where politeness is required. It has four variations depending on tense (present / past) and polarity (affirmative / negative): ます (present affirmative), ません (present negative), ました (past affirmative) and ませんでした (past negative).

(a) 日本(にほん)に行(い)きますか。
Will you go to Japan?
— いいえ、行きません。
— No, I will not.

(b) 日本に行きましたか。
Did you go to Japan?
— いいえ、行きませんでした。
— No, I didn't.

4 Present tense

Verbs in the present tense, regardless of whether they are in the plain form or in the polite form, express either "future" events or "habitual" events. They are also called non-past tense.

(a) 明日(あした)食べます。
(I) will eat (it) tomorrow.

(b) よく食べます。
(I) eat (it) very often.

(c) あまり食べません。
(I) do not eat (it) very much.

(d) 明日食べる。
(I) will eat (it) tomorrow.

(e) よく食べる。
(I) eat (it) very often.

(f) あまり食べない。
(I) do not eat (it) very much.

5 Relative time (明日, 昨日, etc)

Relative time expressions specify the time relative to the time of the speech (for example, 明日(あした) *tomorrow*), as opposed to the absolute time expressions that specify the time that you can point at on a calendar or on a clock (for example, げつようび *Monday*). The following are typical relative time expressions:

Relative Time Expressions

Past ← ● → Future

-2	-1	0	+1	+2
一昨日(おととい) *the day before yesterday*	昨日(きのう) *yesterday*	今日(きょう) *today*	明日(あした) *tomorrow*	明後日(あさって) *the day after tomorrow*
先先週(せんせんしゅう) *the week before last*	先週(せんしゅう) *last week*	今週(こんしゅう) *this week*	来週(らいしゅう) *next week*	再来週(さらいしゅう) *the week after next*
先先月(せんせんげつ) *the month before last*	先月(せんげつ) *last month*	今月(こんげつ) *this month*	来月(らいげつ) *next month*	再来月(さらいげつ) *the month after next*
一昨年(おととし) *the year before last*	去年(きょねん) *last year*	今年(ことし) *this year*	来年(らいねん) *next year*	再後年(さらいねん) *the year after next*

6 Verbs of going and coming (行く, 来る and 帰る)

The Japanese verbs 行(い)く and 来(く)る correspond to the English verbs *to go* and *to come*, respectively. The only exceptional case is when the speaker is about to rush to the listener's position. In such a context, the English verb *to come* can be used, but the Japanese verb 来る cannot, and the verb 行く is used:

(a) いそいで下(くだ)さい。
Hurry!
— はい、すぐ来(き)ます。 (✕)
— (Inappropriate) Intended meaning: *I am coming.*

(b) いそいで下さい。
Hurry!
— はい、すぐ行(い)きます。 (✓)
— (Appropriate) *I am coming. (Lit. I will go (to you) right away.)*

7 わかる: To understand / to know

わかる has two meanings. One is *to understand*. The following are typical interactions between a teacher and a student in a classroom:

(a) わかりましたか。
Did you understand?
— はい、わかりました。/
いいえ、わかりません。
— Yes, I understood. / No, I do not understand.

(b) わかりますか。
Do you understand?
— はい、わかります。/ いいえ、わかりません。
— Yes, I understand. / No, I do not understand.

Another meaning is *to know*.

(c) 山田さんの電話番号はわかりますか。
Do you know Mr. Yamada's telephone number?
— いいえ、わかりません。
— No, I do not know it.

(d) 明日のパーティーに行きますか。
Will you go to the party tomorrow?
— わかりません。
— I don't know.

8 ～に: To～ [Target, destination]

The basic function of the particle ～に is to mark the target of an action. The typical example is the destination. For example, in the following sentence, the target of going (destination) is ニューヨーク *New York* and it is marked by the particle に.

(a) 私はニューヨークに行きます。
I will go to New York.

You can use the particle に with other verbs that express movement.

(b) スミスさんはうちに来ます。
Mr. Smith will come to my home.

(c) 私はうちに帰ります。
I will return home.

(d) 私はへやに入ります。
I will enter the room.

9 ～や (屋): ～store / ～shop

The kanji character 屋 creates a general friendly term for stores and professions such as 本屋 *bookstore*. For example, 本屋 and 書店 both mean *bookstores*, but the former sounds less formal than the latter. The following are some examples: 花屋 *flower shop*, 魚屋 *fish market*, 八百屋 *green market*, 肉屋 *meat store*, 酒屋 *liquor store*, 米屋 *rice store*, 靴屋 *shoe store*, おもちゃ屋 *toy store*, 床屋 *barbershop*, 居酒屋 *casual Japanese-style bar*, クリーニング屋 *dry-cleaner* and 不動産屋 *realtor*.

10 Demonstrative pronouns for location

ここ *here*, そこ *there near you*, あそこ *over there* and どこ *where / which place* are demonstrative pronouns that exclusively refer to locations.

(a) どこに行きますか。
Where will / do you go?

(b) あそこに行きます。
I'll go over there.

11 ～ませんか: How about ～ing? [Suggesting]

～ませんか is used for politely suggesting that someone do something. It is added at the end of a verb in the stem form. Most of the time, the speaker intends to be involved in the suggested activity:

(a) レストランに行きませんか。
Would you like to go to a restaurant (with me)?
— いいですよ。
— OK.

(b) うちに来ませんか。
How about coming to my house?

12 ～ましょう: Let's do～

～ましょう is used when the speaker wants to invite the listener to some activity enthusiastically. It is used for politely suggesting that someone do something:

(a) マンハッタンに行きましょう。
Let's go to Manhattan.

In this case, the speaker necessarily intends to be involved in the same activity. If the question particle か is added to ～ましょう, as in ～ましょうか, the invitation sounds less assertive:

(b) マンハッタンに行きましょうか。
Shall we go to Manhattan?

If ～ましょう is used along with the first person pronoun, it expresses the speaker's volition:

(c) 私が行きましょう。
I will go there.

13 ちょっと: It's a little ... [Declination]

When the Japanese want to decline another person's suggestion or offer, they tend to avoid direct and clear expressions and use phrases, words or interjections that signal their reluctance. For example, (a) is just a fragment of a sentence, but it is understood as a declination if used with a hesitant intonation and facial expression.

(それは) ちょっと…
(That is) a little ...

14 Frequency (よく, ときどき, etc)

Frequency of events is expressed by an adverb like よく *often*, ときどき *sometimes*, あまり *rarely* and ぜんぜん *never*. The adverbs あまり and ぜんぜん only occur with a verb in the negative form (〜ない・〜ません).

Frequency Adverbs		
よく	often	✓--✓---✓--✓✓--✓--✓✓--✓
ときどき	sometimes	---✓---------✓-----------✓---
あまり…(ない)	rarely, not very often	-------------- (✓) --------------
ぜんぜん…(ない)	never, not at all	-----------------------------------

To express frequency more precisely, specify the number of events in a certain period, using the construction "〜に…回", as in the following examples:

(a) 1時間に3回
Three times in an hour

(b) 2週間に3回
Three times in two weeks

15 Negative adverbs (あまり, ぜんぜん, etc)

あまり and ぜんぜん must occur with a verb in the negative form like 〜ません, 〜じゃありません and 〜ない, regardless of whether the verb expresses a favorable action or an unfavorable action.

(a) 私はぜんぜんデパートに行きません。
I do not go to department stores at all.

(b) 私はぜんぜんデパートに行きます。 (✕)
(Ungrammatical)

(c) 私はあまりデパートに行きません。
I do not go to department stores very much.

(d) 私はあまりデパートに行きます。 (✕)
(Ungrammatical)

(e) すう学はあまりかんたんじゃありません。
Mathematics is not very easy.

16 でも: But [Conflict / contrast]

The sentence connective word でも connects two conflicting or contrasting sentences. It is placed at the beginning of the second sentence.

(a) 兄のせんもんはすう学です。でも、私のせんもんはぶん学です。
My brother's major is mathematics. But my major is literature.

(b) 兄の車は高いです。でも、私の車は安いです。
My brother's car is expensive. But my car is cheap.

(c) 兄の車は高いです。でも、よくこわれます。
My brother's car is expensive. But it often breaks down.

17 Particle combination (〜には, 〜にも, etc)

Some particles such as に are called "grammatical particles" and they clarify the functions and roles of the items denoted by the nouns in the given sentence. On the other hand, particles such as は and も are called "pragmatic particles" and they clarify the status of the items denoted by the nouns with respect to the background contextual information outside of the given sentence. As a result, it is possible to have a grammatical particle such as に and a pragmatic particle such as は and も, next to each other, as in 〜には and 〜にも in the following sentences:

(a) カラオケ・バーにはよく行きます。
As for to karaoke bars, I go (there) very often.

(b) カラオケ・ボックスにもよく行きます。
I often go to karaoke boxes, too.

The only exception is that the grammatical particles が (subject marker) and を (direct object marker), cannot occur with a pragmatic particle (see Chapter Six), so combinations like 〜がは, 〜がも, 〜をは and 〜をも are not allowed, while が and を must be deleted if followed by は or も.

(c) 山田さんがはスミスさんに手紙を書きます。(✕)
(Ungrammatical) Intended meaning: *As for Ms. Yamada, she will write a letter to Mr. Smith.*

(d) 山田さんはスミスさんに手紙を書きます。
As for Ms. Yamada, she will write a letter to Mr. smith.

(e) 山田さんがもスミスさんに手紙を書きます。(✕)
(Ungrammatical) Intended meaning: *Ms. Yamada, too, will write a letter to Mr. Smith.*

(f) 山田さんもスミスさんに手紙を書きます。
Ms. Yamada, too, will write a letter to Mr. Smith.

– Culture –

Ⓐ デパート: Department store

There are many department stores in Japan and they serve as highly dependable stores but also as the centers of culture and family entertainment. Among them, Matsuzakaya, Mitsukoshi and Takashimaya are very old and well known. Typical department stores have deli, food and bakery departments in the basement, fashion goods and cosmetics on the first floor, a restaurant complex on the highest floor, and a children's amusement area on the roof. On other floors, they sell items such as outfits, books, electronics, furniture, futons, kitchen goods and sporting goods. Some department stores even have a small museum.

In many Japanese department stores, you can see female employees in their beautiful uniforms at the entrance, inside the elevator, at the escalator areas and at the information booth, greeting and bowing to you, and giving store information to you. They are trained to bow and smile elegantly and to speak extremely politely in a high pitched voice.

The following is the typical floor directory of a department store.

屋上	*Roof*	: ゆうえんち *amusement park*
10階	*10th floor*	: レストラン *restaurants,* ゲームセンター *game center / arcade*
9階	*9th floor*	: ペット *pets,* おもちゃ *toys,* スポーツようひん *sport goods,* じてんしゃ *bicycles*
8階	*8th floor*	: 本 *books, CD,* ぶんぼうぐ *stationary*
7階	*7th floor*	: きもの *kimono,* ふとん *futon*
6階	*6th floor*	: かぐ *furniture,* しょっき *china*
5階	*5th floor*	: でんかせいひん *electronic appliances,* だいどころようひん *kitchen goods*
4階	*4th floor*	: こどもふく *children's clothing*
3階	*3rd floor*	: しんしふく *men's clothing*
2階	*2nd floor*	: ふじんふく *women's clothing*
1階	*1st floor*	: けしょうひん *cosmetics,* くつ *shoes,* かばん *bags,* アクセサリー *accessories*
地下	*Basement*	: しょくひん *food*

Matsuzakaya department store in Ginza.

Ⓑ Repeating

In conversation, Japanese often repeat the phrase they heard and say 〜ですか or 〜ですね. This has a few implicit functions. One is, of course, to confirm the information:

(a) 3時に行きましょう。
Let's leave at three.
—3時ですね。
—*At three, right?*

The second function is to express politeness. By repeating the phrase you heard, you are showing your attentive attitude, acknowledging every new piece of information.

(b) 私は中国人です。
I am a Chinese.
—ああ、中国の方ですか。
—*Oh, you are a Chinese.*

The third function is to fill in the silence. When you need a few seconds in answering or responding, you can repeat the keyword you have just heard.

(c) デパートに行きませんか。
Shall we go to a department store?
—デパートですか。… いいですよ。
—*Department store? ... Okay.*

Ⓒ Rejecting

When the Japanese must reject other people's ideas and suggestions, they try to avoid direct, clear and firm rejection as much as possible. They often indicate their reluctant feelings just by using facial expressions, by making hissing sound while sucking air through their teeth or by saying incomplete sentences such as それは… *That is ...* and ちょっと… *a little ...*, which are understood to be a part of a full sentence like それはちょっとよくありません *That is not very good.*

Ⓓ カラオケ: Karaoke

カラオケ is an abbreviation of カラッポ・オーケストラ, which means *empty orchestra*. カラオケ started in Japan in the late 1970's, and has spread to other countries including China, Korea, Taiwan and the United States. At a karaoke bar, people sing one by one, as they drink. Those who want to focus on singing more than drinking go to a カラオケ・ボックス with their friends. カラオケ・ボックス is an insulated room that can be rented by the hours to a group of people. It is equipped with a karaoke set including a monitor, speakers, microphones, tables and chairs. They can order food and beverages there.

Ⓔ いざかや: Izakaya bar

居酒屋 is a casual Japanese-style bar. They serve inexpensive home-style dishes and alcoholic beverages. Chefs, waiters and waitresses are very friendly. If you sit at the counter, you can watch the chefs cook your food. Many office and factory workers in Japan go to 居酒屋 after their work very often. Japanese college students also enjoy having an informal party with their friends in 居酒屋. In Japan, one must be over 20 years old to be able to drink legally.

– Writing –

ⓐ ひへん

日	ひへん *sun, day*
	Example: 明日 *tomorrow,* 明るい *bright,* 暗い *dark,* 晩 *evening*

– Kanji List –

今日・明日・行く・来る・来ます・来ない・帰る・山・安田・田中

今	ノ 𠆢 𠆢 今 [4]
いま・コン *now, present*	Example: 今 *now* 今日 *today*

日	丨 冂 日 日 [4]
ひ・び・に・ニチ・ジツ *sun, day*	Example: 明日 *tomorrow* 日本 *Japan*

明	丨 冂 日 日 日丿 明 明 明 [8]
あか-るい・あ-ける・メイ *bright, light*	Example: 明日 *tomorrow*

行	ノ 彳 彳 彳 行 行 [6]
い-く・おこな-う・コウ・ギョウ *go, conduct, line*	Example: 行く *to go*

来	一 丆 丆 平 来 来 来 [7]
く-る・こ-ない・き-ます・ライ *come, next*	Example: 来る *to come* 来ます *to come* 来ない *not to come*

帰	丨 刂 リ 归 归 帰 帰 帰 帰 帰 [10]
かえ-る・キ *return*	Example: 帰る *to return*

山	丨 山 山 [3]
やま・サン *mountain*	Example: 山 *mountain* 山田 *surname*

安	' 丶 宀 安 安 安 [6]
やす-い・アン *safe, cheap*	Example: 安田 *surname* 安い *cheap*

田	丨 冂 冂 田 田 [5]
た・だ・デン *rice field*	Example: 安田 *surname* 山田 *surname*

中	丨 冂 口 中 [4]
なか・チュウ・ジュウ *middle, inside*	Example: 田中 *surname* 中 *inside*

– Review –

Q1. Write the reading of the following phrases in hiragana.

1. 行く・来る・帰る
2. 来る・来ない・来ます
3. 明日・今日・日本
4. 田中・山田・安田・川口

Q2. Choose the appropriate options in the parentheses.

1. 私はうちに(帰ります・行きます)。
2. ゆうびんきょくに(帰ります・行きます)。
3. 山田さんは明日私のうちに(来ます・行きます)。
4. 私はあまり本やに(行きます・行きません)。
5. 私のともだちはよくうちに(来ます・来ません)。
6. 明日デパートに(行く・行き)ましょう。
7. うちに(来る・来)ませんか。

Q3. Fill in the blanks.

For example:

帰る・(帰らない)・(帰ります)・(帰りません)

1. 来る・(　　　　)・(　　　　)・(来ません)
2. 行く・(　　　　)・(行きます)・(　　　　)
3. うたう・(　　　　)・(　　　　)・(うたいません)
4. わかる・(わからない)・(　　　　)・(　　　　)

Q4. What would you say in the following situations?

1. You are with Mr. Lee and you have just thought of going to a restaurant with him tonight.
2. John has invited you to his house, but you do not feel like going to his house.
3. You are talking with Ms. Yamada. You want to find out whether she often goes to a karaoke bar.

Tips and Additional Knowledge: Skipping Particles and the Copula in an Informal Context

The polite / neutral speech style is always the safest choice for beginners of Japanese, but when you are with your close friends or when you watch a Japanese home drama, you will hear the plain / informal speech style very often. Compare the following two versions of a conversation at a restaurant. In the plain / informal speech, particles such as は, the question particle か and the copula です tend to be omitted. はい *yes* is replaced by うん.

Plain / Neutral Style:

ジョン：それは何ですか。

たけし：これはすしです。

ジョン：ああ、すしですか。

たけし：それはすきやきですか。

ジョン：はい。

Plain / Informal Style:

ジョン：それ何。

たけし：すし。

ジョン：ああ、すしか。

たけし：それすきやき。

ジョン：うん。

CHAPTER SIX

Describing Daily-life Activities

Lesson 25
大学には何で来ますか **Daily Commute** 90

Lesson 26
みそしるは何で飲みますか **Dining at a Restaurant** 92

Lesson 27
どこで朝ごはんを食べましたか **Breakfast** 94

Lesson 28
ひまなときは何をしますか **Pastime Activity** 96

Grammar and Usage 98

1 Proportional frequency (たいてい, いつも, etc) 98
2 それから: And then / in addition [Multiple events] 98
3 ～かん [The duration of time] 98
4 ～ぐらい: Approximately～ 98
5 ～で: By, with, in, at [How the action takes place] 98
6 ～んです: It is the case that～ 98
7 Daily time frame (あさ, ばん, etc) 99
8 ～する [Verb formative] 99
9 ～を [Direct object marker] 100
10 ～ました, ～ませんでした [Polite suffixes in the past tense] 100
11 ～が [Subject marker] 100
12 ～つもりです: It is planned that～ [Plan] 100
13 ～んですか: Is it the case that～? [Confirming] . . 100
14 The verbs that mean "to play" 101

Culture 101

A Table manners 101
B Rice 101
C ファーストフード・レストラン 102

Writing 102

a もんがまえ 102
b しょくへん 102
c にんべん 102

Kanji List 102

Review 103

Tips and Additional Knowledge: Wax Food Models at a Restaurant 104

大学には何で来ますか Daily Commute

Notes Relating to This Lesson

Grammar and Usage	
1 Proportional frequency . . 98	5 ～で 98
2 それから 98	**Writing**
3 ～かん 98	ⓐ もんがまえ 102
4 ～ぐらい 98	

Basic Vocabulary and Kanji

でんしゃ	電車	*n. (electric) train*
じてんしゃ	自転車	*n. bicycle*
ひこ˥うき	飛行機	*n. airplane*
ちかてつ	地下鉄	*n. subway*
い˥つも		*adv. always, all the time* 1
たいてい		*adv. usually, in general* 1
たいへん(な)	大変だ・大変じゃない	*adj. a lot of trouble, difficult task*
かか˥る	***r*-u** かかる・かからない・かかり・かかって	*vi. to cost, to take*
ある˥く	***k*-u** 歩く・歩かない・歩き・歩いて	*vi. to walk*
ある˥いて	歩いて	*on foot, by walking*
それから		*con. and then, in addition* 2
どれぐらい		*approximately how long, how much, how many*
～じ˥かん	～時間	*c. ~hours* 3
～ふん(かん)/ぷん(かん)	～分(間)	*c. ~minutes (the duration of time)* 3
～ぐらい/～くらい		*approximately (10分ぐらいかかる It takes about 10 minutes.)* 4
～で		*prt. by~, in~, at~, with* 5

Newly introduced kanji:

でん車・じてん車・歩いて・～時間・～分(間) ⓐ

歩	丨 ⺊ 止 止 止 歨 歩 歩	間	丨 𠃍 𠃌 門 門 門 門 門 問 間 間 間

Dialog

Mr. Lee and Mr. Smith are chatting on campus.

リー　：大学には何で来ますか。

スミス：たいてい、バスとちかてつで来ます。

リー　：どれぐらいかかりますか。

スミス：バスで5分と、ちかてつで15分ぐらいです。それから、歩いて3分です。

リー　：たいへんですね。

スミス：リーさんは。

リー　：私はたいていじてん車で来ます。ときどき歩いて来ます。歩いて10分ぐらいです。

スミス：ああ、いいですね。

Guess and Try 1

Choose the appropriate options in the parentheses. 5

1. ひこうき(で・に)行きます。

2. 日本(で・に)行きます。

Guess and Try 2

What is the relationship between the following two sentences? 2

としょかんに行きます。
それから、クラスにきます。

Drill 1: Formation

車 → 車で行きます

1. ひこうき
2. でん車
3. じてん車
4. バス
5. ちかてつ

Drill 2: Formation

ちかてつ・大学・行きます → ちかてつで大学に行きます

1. ひこうき・日本・行きます
2. 日本・ひこうき・行きます
3. じてん車・大学・行きます
4. びょういん・バス・行きます
5. でん車・ここ・来ます
6. でん車・うち・帰ります

Task 1: Pair Work

Ask how would (or does) your partner go to スーパーマーケット.

For example:

A ：スーパーマーケットには何で行きますか。

B ：ともだちの車で行きます。

Task 2: Survey

Ask your classmates how they commute and how long it takes. Find out who is having the hardest time commuting in the class. Use the dialog as a model.

スーパーマーケット, スーパーマーケット
スクーター, スクーター, バイク, バイク
トラック, トラック, フェリー, フェリー

Vocabulary Collection (Transportation)	
車 *car*	自動車 *automobile*
電車 *train*	自転車 *bicycle*
地下鉄 *subway*	バイク *motorcycle*
スクーター *(motor) scooter*	トラック *truck*
バス *bus*	船 *ship*
フェリー *ferry*	飛行機 *airplane*
ヘリコプター *helicopter*	

Short Reading

私は毎日大学に行きます。まず、歩いて地下鉄の駅に行きます。それから、地下鉄で新宿に行きます。地下鉄は30分ぐらいです。それから、また歩きます。5分です。週に3回バイトに行きます。レストランです。自転車で行きます。父は毎日会社に行きます。いつも車で行きます。母は毎日パートに行きます。スーパーマーケットです。歩いて行きます。

(毎日 *every day,* まず *first of all,* 駅 *railway station,* 新宿 *Shinjuku (name of a place in Tokyo),* また *again,* 週に3回 *three times a week,* 会社 *company,* (アル)バイトに行く *to go to work part-time, to work part-time,* パートに行く *to go to work part-time, to work part-time*)

Writing 1

Write about the places where you and your family members go regularly, specifying the form of transportation used.

ヘリコプター, ヘリコプター

Writing 2

Write the katakana words that appear in this lesson several times each.

でん車 でん車 じてん車 じてん車
ひこうき, ひこうき, ちかてつ, ちかてつ, いつも,
たいてい, たいてい, たいへん, たいへん
かかる, かかる, 歩く, 歩く, 歩いて, 歩いて
時間, 時間, 何分, 何分, バス, バス,
リー, リー, スミス, スミス

みそしるは何で飲みますか Dining at a Restaurant

Notes Relating to This Lesson

Grammar and Usage	Culture
5 ～で 98	Ⓐ Table manners 101
6 ～んです 98	Ⓑ Rice 101
	Writing
	ⓑ しょくへん 102

Basic Vocabulary and Kanji

みそし⌉る	味噌汁	*n. miso soup*
は⌉し・おは⌉し	箸・お箸	*n. chopsticks*
ご⌉はん	ご飯	*n. cooked rice, meal* Ⓑ
スプ⌉ーン		*n. spoon*
ていしょく	定食	*n. set menu*
たべ⌉る	***e-ru*** 食べる・食べない・食べ・食べて	*vt. to eat*
の⌉む	***m-u*** 飲む・飲まない・飲み・飲んで	*vt. to drink*
か⌉く	***k-u*** 書く・書かない・書き・書いて	*vt. to write*
ひと⌉つ	一つ	*one (piece)*
ふたつ	二つ	*two (pieces)*
～んです		*it is the case that~* 6

Newly introduced kanji:

食(た)べる・飲(の)む ⓑ・書(か)く

食	ノ 入 𠆢 今 今 今 食 食 食	飲	ノ ﾉ𠂉 今 今 今 今 食 食 飲 飲 飲
書	フ ヲ ヨ ヨ 聿 聿 書 書 書 書		

メニュー，メニュー

フォーク，フォーク
ナイフ，ナイフ
グラス，グラス
コップ，コップ
コーヒーカップ，コーヒーカップ
ワイングラス，ワイングラス

 Dialog

George Baker tries a Japanese restaurant for the first time.

ウエートレス：ごちゅうもんは。
(ごちゅうもんは *Your order?*)

安田(やすだ)：私はさしみていしょくをおねがいします。

ベーカー：私はてんぷらていしょくをおねがいします。

ウエートレス：はい、さしみていしょくひとつと、てんぷらていしょくひとつですね。

安田：はい。
(The waitress brings the food.)

ウエートレス：おまたせしました。どうぞ。
(おまたせしました *Sorry to have kept you waiting.*)

ベーカー：みそしるのスプーンは?

安田：ジョージさん、みそしるはスプーンで<u>飲まないんです</u>。

ベーカー：ああ、そうですか。

Vocabulary Collection (Dining)

茶碗(ちゃわん) *rice bowl*	メニュー *menu*
スプーン *spoon*	フォーク *fork*
ナイフ *knife*	グラス / コップ *glass*
コーヒーカップ *coffee cup*	ワイングラス *wine glass*
皿(さら) *plate*	小皿(こざら) *small plate*
どんぶり *large bowl*	
お椀(わん) *Japanese lacquered soup bowl*	
湯呑(ゆの)み (湯飲(ゆの)み) *cups for Japanese tea*	

みそしる，みそしる，はし，はし，おはし，おはし
ごはん，ごはん，スプーン，スプーン，ていしょく
ていしょく，てい食，食べる，食べる
飲む，飲む，書く，書く，一つ，一つ，二つ

Guess and Try 1

Discuss the following: Ⓐ

1. What is used for eating rice and soup in Japan and in your country?
2. What is the proper way of eating rice, noodles, sushi and soup in Japan and in your home country?

Guess and Try 2

What do the items marked by で in the following sentences have in common? 5

1. ピザはてで食べます。
2. 大学は車で行きます。
3. しゅくだいはペンで書きます。
4. ステーキはナイフできります。(きります *cut*)

Guess and Try 3

In conversation, many statements end in ～んです as in the underlined part in Dialog. It helps conversational interaction flow well. Rephrase the following sentences by adding ～んです. 6

1. 今日はえいがかんに行きます。

____

2. 明日は大学に行きません。

____

Drill 1: Conjugation

食べる ⟶ 食べる・食べない・食べます

1. 飲む　2. 書く　3. 行く
4. 歩く　5. 帰る　6. 来る

Drill 2: Formation

食べます ⟶ 食べるんです
食べません ⟶ 食べないんです

1. 飲みます　2. 飲みません　3. 行きます
4. 行きません　5. 帰りません　6. 帰ります

Drill 3: Formation

すし・て・食べます ⟶ すしはてで 食べます

1. さしみ・はし・食べます
2. ごはん・おちゃわん・食べます
3. ビール・グラス・飲みます
4. テスト・ペン・書きます
5. しゅくだい・えんぴつ・書きます

Task: Group Work

Work in a group of four or five. One of you acts as the waiter / waitress and others act as the customers who are about to order. (Use Dialog as a model.)

メニュー

お食事 (entree)		お飲みもの (drinks)	
さしみ定食	1,800 円	アサヒビール	400 円
すし	1,800 円	キリンビール	400 円
テリヤキ・チキン定食	1,200 円	さけ	700 円
てんぷら定食	1,800 円	コーラ	300 円
すきやき	1,800 円	スプライト	300 円
うなぎ	2,000 円	オレンジ・ジュース	400 円
* 定食 はごはんと、みそしると、サラダ付き			

(～付き *includes~*)

Vocabulary Collection (~pieces)	
1. 一つ (ひとつ)	2. 二つ (ふたつ)
3. 三つ (みっつ)	4. 四つ (よっつ)
5. 五つ (いつつ)	

Short Reading

父の湯飲みと、母の湯飲みはペアーです。父のは少し大きいです。母のは少し小さいです。父の箸と、母の箸もペアーです。父のは少し長いです。母のは少し短いです。

(湯飲み *tea cup exclusively for Japanese green tea,* 少し *a little bit,* 大きい *big,* 小さい *small,* 長い *long,* 短い *short*)

Writing 1

Write about an interesting aspect of eating customs in your country in English or Japanese.

Writing 2

Write all the katakana words that appear in this lesson several times each.

どこで朝ごはんを食べましたか　Breakfast

Notes Relating to This Lesson

Grammar and Usage	
5 ～で 98	10 ～ました, ～ませんでした 100
7 Daily time frame 99	**Culture**
8 ～する 99	Ⓒ ファーストフード・レストラン 102
9 ～を 100	

朝	昼
晩	昨

Basic Vocabulary and Kanji

アパ˥ート		*n. apartment*
プ˥ール		*n. swimming pool*
あ˥さ	朝	*n. morning* 7
ひる˥	昼	*n. noon, daytime* 7
ばん	晩	*n. evening, night* 7
あさご˥はん	朝御飯	*n. breakfast*
ひるご˥はん	昼御飯	*n. lunch*
ばんご˥はん	晩御飯	*n. supper, dinner*
きのう	昨日	*n. yesterday*
け˥さ	今朝	*n. this morning*
べんきょう(を)する	*irr.* 勉強(を)する	*vt. / vi. to study* 8
ねる	*e-ru* 寝る・寝ない・寝・寝て	*vi. to go to bed, to sleep*
およ˥ぐ	*g-u* 泳ぐ・泳がない・泳ぎ・泳いで	*vi. to swim*
～を		*prt. direct object marker* 9
～ました		*polite past affirmative suffix for verbs* 10
～ませんでした		*polite past negative suffix for verbs* 10

Newly introduced kanji:

朝(あさ)・昼(ひる)・晩(ばん)・昨日(きのう)・今朝(けさ)・今晩(こんばん)

Dialog

John Smith and Yoko Yamada talk about breakfast.

スミス：山田(やまだ)さん、今朝、朝ごはんを食(た)べましたか。

山田：いいえ、食べませんでした。

スミス：ああ、そうですか。

山田：スミスさんは。

スミス：私は食べました。

山田：どこで食べましたか。

スミス：ファースト・バーガーで食べました。

山田：何(なに)を食べましたか。

スミス：トーストを食べました。それから、コーヒーを飲みました。

Guess and Try 1

Do you know any fast food restaurants in Japan? Ⓒ

Guess and Try 2

Choose the appropriate options in the parentheses. 5 9

1. レストラン(で・に)行(い)きます。
2. レストラン(で・に)食(た)べます。
3. すし(を・で)食べます。
4. はし(を・で)食べます。

Guess and Try 3

Choose the appropriate options in the parentheses. 10

1. 昨日大学(だいがく)に行き(ます・ました)。
2. 明日(あした)大学に行き(ます・ました)。
3. 昨日大学に行き(ません・ませんでした)。

Drill 1: Mini-Conversation

食(た)べます ⟶ **S1:** 食べましたか
S2: いいえ、食べませんでした

1. 行きます
2. およぎます
3. ねます
4. 帰(かえ)ります
5. べんきょうします

Drill 2: Formation

りょう・べんきょうしました ⟶ りょうでべんきょうしました
りょう・行きました ⟶ りょうに行きました
朝ごはん・食べました ⟶ 朝ごはんを食べました

1. としょかん・べんきょうしました
2. としょかん・行きました
3. 日本ご・べんきょうしました
4. としょかん・日本ご・べんきょうしました
5. レストラン・食べました
6. 昼ごはん・食べました
7. うち・ねました
8. アパート・帰りました
9. プール・およぎました

Task 1: Survey

Ask four of your classmates whether they ate breakfast this morning, and if they did, ask them what they ate and where they ate it.

私(わたし)	
さん	
さん	
さん	
さん	

Task 2: Pair Work

Write down everything that you ate yesterday on a sheet of paper. Exclude beverages. Find out the food that both you and your partner had yesterday. (You can ask only yes / no questions.) Then find out which pair had the most items in common.

A：Bさんは昨日ピザを食(た)べましたか。

B：いいえ、食べませんでした。

A：ああ、そうですか。じゃあ、アイスクリームを食べましたか。

B：ええ、食べました。

A：ああ、そうですか。私も食べました。

Short Reading

朝ごはんはたいていりょうで食(た)べます。昼ごはんはたいてい食べません。ときどき、大学(だいがく)の食堂(しょくどう)で食べます。晩ごはんはたいていレストランで食べます。昨日の晩はうちですきやきを食べました。

(食堂(しょくどう) *dining hall, dining room, restaurant*)

Writing 1

Write where you usually eat and then write where you ate what last night.

Writing 2

Write the katakana words that appear in this lesson several times each.

ひまなときは何をしますか Pastime Activity

Notes Relating to This Lesson	
Grammar and Usage	14 The verbs that mean "to play" 101
2 それから 98	**Writing**
11 〜が 100	△C にんべん 102
12 〜つもりです 100	
13 〜んですか 100	

Basic Vocabulary and Kanji

えいが	映画	*n. movie, film*
てがみ	手紙	*n. letter*
しんぶん	新聞	*n. newspaper*
ざっし	雑誌	*n. magazine*
ようふく	洋服	*n. clothes*
する	*irr.* する・しない・し・して	*vt. to do* 14
よ˥む	***m*-u** 読む・読まない・読み・読んで	*vt. to read* (本を読む *to read a book*)
つく˥る	***r*-u** 作る・作らない・作り・作って	*vt. to make* (すしを作る *to make sushi*)
かう	***w*-u** 買う・買わない・買い・買って	*vt. to buy* (くつを買う *to buy shoes*)
つかう	***w*-u** 使う・使わない・使い・使って	*vt. to use* (ペンを使う *to use a pen*)
み˥る	***i*-ru** 見る・見ない・見・見て	*vt. to watch, to look* (テレビを見る *to watch TV*)
ひく	***k*-u** 弾く・弾かない・弾き・弾いて	*vt. to play string instruments and keyboards* (ピアノをひく *to play the piano*) 14
ふく	***k*-u** 吹く・吹かない・吹き・吹いて	*vt. to blow, to play (wind instruments)* (トランペットを吹く *to play the trumpet*) 14
〜が		*prt. subject marker* 11
〜つもりです		*I plan to do~* 12

Newly introduced kanji:

作(つく)る △C・使(つか)う △C・買(か)う・見(み)る

作	ノ イ 亻 仁 作 作 作	使	ノ イ 亻 仁 何 佢 使 使
買	' 冖 罒 罒 罒 罒 胃 胃 胃 冒 買 買	見	I 冂 冃 月 目 貝 見

Dialog

Ken Tanaka asks Mary Carter what she does when she is free.

田中(たなか)　：マリーさん。ひまなときは何(なに)をしますか。
(ひまな時(とき) *leisure time*)

カーター：しんぶんをよみます。それから、コンピューターゲームをします。それから、からてをします。

田中　：えっ、マリーさんがからてをするんですか。

カーター：はい。じゅうどうもします。けんどうもいつかするつもりです。
(いつか *someday*)

Guess and Try 1

What does それから in the above dialog mean? 2

Guess and Try 2

Fill in the blanks with appropriate Japanese verbs. 14

1. クラリネット *clarinet* を ____________
2. ギター *guitar* を ____________
3. ピアノ *piano* を ____________
4. テニス *tennis* を ____________
5. ゴルフ *golf* を ____________
6. チェス *chess* を ____________
7. トランプ *card* を ____________
8. かいもの *shopping* を ____________

Guess and Try 3

Choose the appropriate options in the parentheses: 11

1. 今日は父 (を・が) すし (を・が) 作ります。
2. 明日のクラスはこの本 (を・が) スミスさん (を・が) よみます。
3. 日本ごのクラスはしゅくだい (を・が) むずかしいです。

Guess and Try 4

Choose the appropriate options in the parentheses: 12

1. さしみを (食べる・食べます) つもりです。
2. さしみを (食べない・食べません) つもりです。

Guess and Try 5 (optional)

Why did Mr. Tanaka ask the underlined question in the dialog? 13

Drill 1: Conjugation

食べる ⟶ 食べる・食べない・食べます

1. 見る	2. 作る
3. 帰る	4. 買う
5. 使う	6. 書く
7. 行く	8. 歩く
9. する	10. 来る

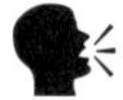

Drill 2: Formation

すし・食べます ⟶ すしを食べます
父・食べます ⟶ 父が食べます

1. ようふく・買います	2. コーヒー・飲みます
3. 母・飲みます	4. 父・えいが・見ます
5. あね・すし・作ります	6. 兄・てがみ・書きます
7. 兄・ざっし・よみます	8. 母・車・使います

Task: Classroom Activity

Each of you writes two pastime activities that you do on weekends on a piece of paper. Do not show them to others. Check with your classmates on their pastime activities and find out who has exactly the same pastime activities as yours. (See Dialog.)

ギャンブル
コンピューターゲーム, ブラブラ

Vocabulary Collection (Pastime Activities)

映画を見る *to watch a movie*	泳ぐ *to swim*
手紙を書く *to write a letter*	釣をする *to fish*
雑誌を読む *to read a magazine*	料理をする *to cook*
音楽を聞く *to listen to music*	掃除をする *to clean*
カラオケをする *to do karaoke*	絵を描く *to draw*
買物をする *to go shopping*	空手をする *to do karate*
ゴルフをする *to play golf*	
ジョギングをする *to jog*	
ピアノを弾く *to play the piano*	
ギャンブルをする *to gamble*	
コンピューターゲームをする *to play computer games*	
庭仕事をする *to do gardening*	
街をブラブラする *to walk around the town*	
写真を撮る *to take pictures*	
友達に電話をする *to phone one's friend*	
生け花をする *to do flower arranging*	

Short Reading

僕の趣味は料理です。暇な時はいつも料理をします。日本料理と、中華料理が好きです。特に、てんぷらが好きです。よく友達を招待します。みんな喜びます。先週は日本語の先生を招待しました。

(僕 *the first person singular pronoun for male (I),* 趣味 *hobby,* 料理 *cooking,* 中華料理 *Chinese cuisine,* ～が好きです *to like~,* 特に *especially,* 招待する *to invite,* みんな *everyone,* 喜ぶ *to be pleased*)

Writing 1

えいが, えいが, てがみ

Write about what you do in your free time. てがみ, しんぶん
しんぶん, ざっし, ざっし, ようふく, ようふく, する

Writing 2

する, よむ, よむ, 作る, 作る, 買う

Write the katakana words that appear in this lesson several times each. 買う, 使う, 使う, 見る, 見る, ようふく, カラオケ, ゴルフ, ジョギング, ピアノ

– Grammar and Usage –

1 Proportional frequency (たいてい, いつも, etc)

Adverbs such as たいてい *usually* and いつも *always* express proportional frequency of events. For example, たいてい in the following sentence means *most of the eating occasions* rather than *most of the time*:

私はたいていレストランで食べます。
I usually eat at a restaurant.

2 それから: And then / in addition [Multiple events]

The sentence connective word それから connects sentences that express temporarily ordered events (a) or randomly listed events (b):

(a) 今日は、まずテニスをします。それから、ともだちにてがみを書きます。
Today, I will play tennis, first. And then, I will write a letter to my friends.

(b) しゅうまつは、よくテニスをします。それから、ともだちにてがみを書きます。
On weekends, (I) often play tennis. In addition, I write letters to my friends.

3 ～かん [The duration of time]

The "absolute time" such as "2:15 pm" is expressed by a counter like ～時 and ～分, as in ごご 2 時 15 分. On the other hand, the "duration of time" is expressed by a counter like ～時間 and ～分(間). The following are some examples.

(a) 2 分(間) *two minutes*, 2 分 *two minutes*
(b) 2 時間 *two hours*, 2 時 *two o'clock*
(c) 2 日(間) *two days*, 2 日 *the second day*
(d) 2 ヶ月(間) *two months*, 2 月 *February*
(e) 2 年(間) *two years*, 2 年 *the second year*

4 ～ぐらい: Approximately～

The particle ～ぐらい means *approximately* or *about*, and follows a number phrase such as 2 時間 *two hours* and 2 時 *two o'clock*, as in 2 時間ぐらい *approximately two hours* and 2 時ぐらい *approximately two o'clock*.

5 ～で: By, with, in, at [How the action takes place]

The noun marked by the particle ～で shows "how" the action takes place. For example, it shows the form of transportation, instrument, mean, location and method that are used for the action denoted by the verb.

In the following sentence, the particle で specifies "how" one goes to New York:

(a) 私は車でニューヨークに行きます。
I will go to New York by car.

In sentence (b), はしで *by chopsticks* shows "how" one eats and in sentence (c), 日本語で *in Japanese* shows "how" one speaks.

(b) 私ははしで食べます。
I will eat with chopsticks.

(c) 母は日本語で話します。
My mother speaks in Japanese.

The location of activity is also marked by the particle ～で, as in the following sentence.

(d) 朝ごはんはどこで食べますか。
Where do you eat breakfast?
— カフェテリアで食べます。
— *I eat at the cafeteria.*

Here are some additional examples of で:

(e) 私は一人で食べます。
I will eat by myself.

(f) 私は裸足で歩きます。
I will walk barefoot.

(g) ぜんぶで 500 円です。
It is 500 yen in total.

In sentence (e), 一人で *by oneself* shows "how" one eats. In sentence (f), 裸足で *barefoot* shows "how" one walks. And in sentence (g), ぜんぶで *in total* shows "how" one came up with 500 yen.

6 ～んです: It is the case that～

The phrase ～んです, which is the contracted form of ～のです, is often added at a end of a sentence in conversation. ～んです directly follows the "plain" form of a verb or an adjective, as in 食べるんです and 高いんです. Note that だ in the plain form of the copula verb as well as na-type adjectives becomes な before ～んです, as in 日本人なんです *to be Japanese* and ハンサムなんです *to be handsome*. (As for the na-type adjectives, see Chapter Nine. As for the plain negative forms of copula verbs and adjectives, see Volume 2, Chapter Fifteen.)

(a) 私はよくテニスをするんです。
I often play tennis.

(b) 弟はあまり勉強しないんです。
My younger brother doesn't study very much.

(c) このカメラは高いんです。
This camera is expensive.

(d) あのカメラは高くないんです。
That camera is not expensive.

(e) この人は日本人なんです。
This person is a Japanese.

(f) 私は学生じゃないんです。
I am not a student.

～んです shows the speaker's willingness and openness for hearing the listener's comments on his / her statement. For this reason, ～んです is vital for conversational contexts where information is exchanged verbally between the speaker and listener, but not appropriate for written forms or presentations, where the information is one-directionally given from the author or speaker to the readers or audience. For example, for providing a new piece of information in a conversational context, (g) is more appropriate than (h), although (h) can be appropriate if it's an answer to the question like "What do you do on weekends?", or if the speaker is just making a statement in front of the audience.

(g) 私はよくテニスをするんです。

(h) 私はよくテニスをします。

7 Daily time frame (あさ, ばん, etc)

There are three ways of dividing a day. Firstly, based on the absolute time, a day can be divided into 午前 (a.m.: from 12 o'clock midnight to 12 o'clock noon) and 午後 (p.m.: from 12 o'clock noon to 12 o'clock midnight). Secondly, based on the "position of the sun", a day can be divided into 昼間 (daytime: from sunrise to sunset) and 夜 or 夜間 (night time: from sunset to sunrise). Thirdly, based on the combination of the absolute time and the position of the sun, a day can be divided into at least eight time frames as shown in the following table and diagram. 午後 is ambiguous between "p.m." and "afternoon".

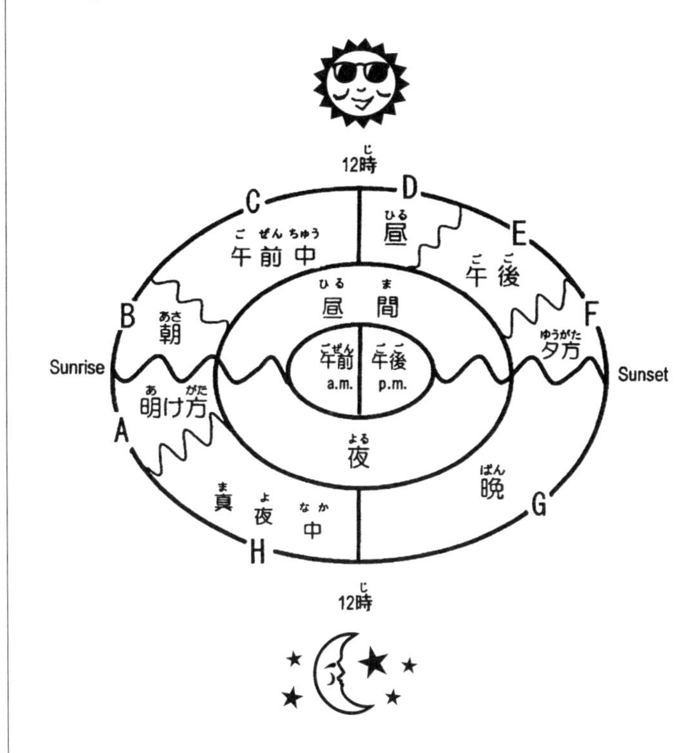

Daily Time Frame		
A	明け方	A few hours before sunrise
B	朝	A few hours after sunrise
C	午前中	After 朝, before noon
D	昼	From noon to 1 p.m.
E	午後	After 1 p.m., until 夕方
F	夕方	A few hours before sunset
G	晩	After sunset and before midnight
H	真夜中	After midnight and before sunrise

8 ～する [Verb formative]

Verbs from other languages such as Chinese and English can be adapted into Japanese by adding ～(を) する (for example, スケートをする *to skate*, 勉強 (を) する *to study*, コピー (を) する *to make a copy*, マリネードする *to marinade*).

The intervening を is optional in some cases, but must be dropped if the direct object is overtly stated along with を. So, sentence (a) to (c) are grammatical, but (d) is not.

(a) よく勉強します。
(b) よく勉強をします。
(c) よく日本語を勉強します。
(d) よく日本語を勉強をします。 (✕)
(Ungrammatical)

9 〜を [Direct object marker]

The direct object of a transitive verb is marked by the particle を in Japanese.

(a) 今日は本を読みます。
Today, (I) will read a book.
(b) 兄が弟をたたきました。
My older brother hit my younger brother.
(c) 今日は父がすしを作ります。
Today, my father will make sushi.

A noun can be the direct object of a sentence and it can be the topic of the sentence at the same time. In such a case, を must be absent and only the topic marker は occurs. Similarly, を must be deleted when followed by other pragmatic particles such as も.

(d) 今日は本を読みます。
As for today, I will read books.
(e) 本は今日読みます。
As for books, I will read (them) today.
(f) 今日は本も読みます。
As for today, I will read books, too.

10 〜ました, 〜ませんでした [Polite suffixes in the past tense]

The past tense of the polite suffixes are ました *affirmative* and ませんでした *negative*. They express habits and events in the past.

(a) よく東京に行きました。
I used to go to Tokyo often.
(b) あまり東京に行きませんでした。
I did not go to Tokyo very often.
(c) 昨日東京に行きました。
I went to Tokyo yesterday.
(d) 昨日東京に行きませんでした。
I did not go to Tokyo yesterday.

11 〜が [Subject marker]

The subject of a sentence is marked by the particle が in Japanese. The subject is スミスさん in (a), and it is これ in (b).

(a) スミスさんが来ます。
Mr. Smith will come (here).
(b) これがしゅくだいです。
This is the homework.

Unlike English sentences, Japanese sentences can be headed by a topic phrase, which is marked by the particle は (wa). In the following sentences, 今日 *today* is the topic:

(c) 今日はスミスさんが来ます。
As for today, Mr. Smith will come (here).
(d) 今日はこれがしゅくだいです。
As for today, this is the homework.

If the subject nouns スミスさん and これ are the topics as well, they are marked just by は.

(e) スミスさんは来ます。
As for Mr. Smith, (he) will come (here).
(f) これはしゅくだいです。
As for this, it is homework.

12 〜つもりです: It is planned that 〜[Plan]

つもり literally means *intention*. When つもりです is added at the end of a sentence, following a verb in the plain form, it shows that what is said is one's plan, schedule or intention and is subject to change.

(a) 明日ぎんこうに行くつもりです。
I plan to go to the bank tomorrow.
(b) 明日は大学に行かないつもりです。
I plan not to go to the university tomorrow.
(c) 父はアメリカに行かないつもりです。
My father intends not to go to the United States.
(d) 日本語を勉強するつもりですか。
Are you planning to study Japanese?

13 〜んですか: Is it the case that〜 ? [Confirming]

For confirming the statement you have just heard and inviting further information, use a question ending in 〜んですか. Suppose you have just heard that your partner is taking karate lessons, which happened to be a surprise to you, you can ask からてをするんですか *Is it true that you do karate?*. In this particular context, からてをしますか *Do you do karate?* is inappropriate as you already know it. If you ask からてをしますか in this context, your partner will get the impression that you did not hear what he / she said or you were not listening.

14 The verbs that mean "to play"

The English verb "to play" is a transitive verb and can be used along with things such as musical instruments, sports and games (for example, to play the piano, to play tennis, to play cards, to play a game). In Japanese, these activities are expressed by several different verbs. Playing games or sports is expressed by the verb する *to do* (for example, テニスをする、トランプをする and ゲームをする). Playing musical instruments requires a specific verb depending on the manner involved (for example, ピアノをひく *to play the piano* and フルートをふく *to play the flute*).

In many English or Japanese dictionaries, "to play" is translated as あそぶ, but the latter is mainly an intransitive verb that means *to play, to frolic, to enjoy oneself* or *to have fun* (for example, こうえんであそぶ *to play in the park*) and is rarely used as a transitive verb.

– Culture –

A Table manners

A typical Japanese dinner includes rice (ごはん) and "miso" soup (みそしる). Rice is served in a ceramic rice bowl, called ちゃわん. When the Japanese eat rice, they must lift the rice bowl with one hand and pick up a small amount of rice with chopsticks and bring it to the mouth. It is not as difficult as you may think because Japanese cooked rice (ごはん) is very sticky. Japanese chopsticks are pointy and are convenient for removing tiny bones in fish. Miso soup is served in a lacquered bowl called おわん. When the Japanese have miso soup, they also lift the bowl with one hand and sip the soup directly from the bowl, using chopsticks. Only young children have miso soup with a spoon.

The Japanese use many serving plates and dishes with different shapes, sizes, thickness, colors, materials and patterns. If you go to a Japanese-style inn (旅館（りょかん）), a meal for one person will be served using ten or twenty plates and dishes, as in the following photograph.

Table manners differ depending on the country and some manners that are very rude in some countries may be totally appropriate and permitted in other countries. It is not rude to sip miso soup directly from the bowl in Japan although soup bowls are usually not supposed to be lifted in Western countries. Noodles in soup (for example, ramen, udon and soba noodles) are served in a big bowl called どんぶり, and it is permitted to slurp up noodles in Japan, although it is extremely rude in Western countries. It is also acceptable and, in fact, preferred to eat sushi (with a rice ball) with your fingers in Japan.

B Rice

Rice is very essential for Japanese meals and culture. Many words describe the types of rice in Japanese. Cooked rice is ご飯（はん） and uncooked rice is お米（こめ）. Steamed rice is おこわ and porridge is お粥（かゆ）. For cerebrations, the Japanese eat 赤飯（せきはん） *steamed rice with red beans* and drink お酒（さけ） *rice wine*.

Ⓒ ファーストフード・レストラン

You see many American franchised fast food restaurants in Japan. The staff in these restaurants are trained to use a very polite speech style when talking with their customers, as in most Japanese restaurants. Some items are called differently in Japan. For example, French fries are called フライド・ポテト *fried potatoes* in Japan. And there are some items that you can find only in Japan (for example, テリヤキ・バーガー *teriyaki-burger*).

– Writing –

ⓐ もんがまえ

門	もんがまえ *door, gate, building*
	Example: 間(あいだ) *between,* 聞(き)く *to listen,* 問(と)う *to ask,* 開(ひら)く *to open,* 閉(し)まる *to close*

ⓑ しょくへん

飠	しょくへん *eating, food*
	Example: 飲(の)む *to drink,* ご飯(はん) *meal; rice,* 図書館(としょかん) *library*

ⓒ にんべん

亻	にんべん *people, people's activities and states*
	Example: 作(つく)る *to make,* 使(つか)う *to use,* 休(やす)む *to rest,* 働(はたら)く *to work*

– Kanji List –

でん車・じてん車・歩いて・〜時間・〜分(間)・食べる・飲む・書く・朝・昼・晩・昨日・今朝・今晩・作る・使う・買う・見る

Kanji	Readings / Meaning	Strokes	Examples
車	くるま・シャ *car*	[7]	電車(でんしゃ) *a train*; 自転車(じてんしゃ) *a bicycle*; 車(くるま) *a car*
歩	ある-く・ホ・ポ *walk*	[8]	歩(ある)く *to walk*; 歩(ある)いて *on foot*
時	とき・ジ *time, hour*	[10]	時(とき) *time*; 四時(よじ) *four o'clock*; 四時間(よじかん) *four hours*
間	あいだ・ま・カン *between, interval*	[12]	四時間(よじかん) *four hours*; 時間(じかん) *time*
分	わ-かれる・わ-かる・わ-ける・フン・ブン・プン *division, part, minute*	[4]	五分(ごふん) (間(かん)) *five minutes*; 分(わ)かる *to know, to understand*
食	た-べる・ショク *eat*	[9]	食(た)べる *to eat*
飲	の-む・イン *drink*	[12]	飲(の)む *to drink*
書	か-く・ショ *write, book, document*	[10]	書(か)く *to write*

朝 あさ・チョウ *morning*	一 十 𠀋 古 古 吉 直 卓 朝 朝 朝 朝 [12] Example: 朝(あさ) *morning* 今朝(けさ) *this morning*
昼 ひる・チュウ *noon, daytime*	一 コ 尸 尺 尽 昼 昼 昼 昼 [9] Example: 昼(ひる) *daytime, noon*
晩 バン *night*	丨 日 日 日 日' 日' 日' 晩 晩 晩 晩 晩 [12] Example: 晩(ばん) *evening, night* 今晩(こんばん) *tonight*
昨 サク *previous*	丨 日 日 日 日' 日' 昨 昨 昨 [9] Example: 昨日(きのう) or 昨日(さくじつ) *yesterday*
日 ひ・び・ニチ ・ニ・ジツ *sun, day*	丨 冂 日 日 [4] Example: 日曜日(にちようび) *Sunday* 昨日(きのう) *yesterday* 今日(きょう) *today,* 明日(あした) *tomorrow*
今 いま・コン *now, present*	ノ 人 亼 今 [4] Example: 今(いま) *now* 今日(きょう) *today* 今年(ことし) *this year*
作 つく-る・ サク・サ *make, produce*	ノ イ 亻 𠂉 竹 作 作 [7] Example: 作(つく)る *to make*
使 つか-う・シ *use*	ノ イ 仁 仁 佢 佢 使 使 [8] Example: 使(つか)う *to use*
買 か-う・バイ *buy*	丶 冖 罒 罒 罒 罒 胃 胃 冒 冒 買 買 [12] Example: 買(か)う *to buy*
見 み-る・ケン *see, look, view*	丨 冂 月 月 目 貝 見 [7] Example: 見(み)る *to look at*

– Review –

Q1. Write the pronounciation of the underlined kanji characters in hiragana.

1. すしを<u>食</u>べます。それから、コーヒーを<u>飲</u>みます。
2. 母はピザを<u>作</u>ります。オーブンを<u>使</u>います。
3. 今日はじしょを<u>買</u>います。それから、てがみを<u>書</u>きます。
4. <u>車</u>で行きます。<u>5 分</u>ぐらいです。
5. でん<u>車</u>を<u>使</u>います。

Q2. Fill in the blanks with either で or に.

1. 山田さんはとうきょう _に_ 来ます。
2. 山田さんはとうきょう _で_ べんきょうします。
3. スミスさんはりょう _で_ ねます。
4. スミスさんはりょう _に_ 帰ります。
5. 私はレストラン _に_ 行きます。
6. 私はレストラン _で_ 食べます。
7. えんぴつ _で_ てがみを書きます。
8. はし _で_ ごはんを食べます。

Q3. Fill in the blanks with either を or が.

1. 山田さん _が_ 食べます。
2. レストランですし _を_ 食べます。

3. レストランですし ____ 作ります。

4. 大学に兄 ____ 来ました。

5. 大学で日本ご ____ べんきょうします。

Q4. Fill in the blanks with を, が, に or で.

1. 明日、車 ____ 買います。

2. 明日、車 ____ 大学 ____ 行きます。

3. スプーン ____ ヨーグルト ____ 食べます。

4. とうきょう ____ 日本ご ____ べんきょうします。

5. 兄 ____ ここ ____ 来ます。

Q5. Rephrase the following sentences using ～んです, then rephrase them using ～つもりです.

1. 明日は日本に行きます。

2. 明日は大学に行きません。

Tips and Additional Knowledge: Wax Food Models at a Restaurant

Most restaurants in Japan have a display window full of wax food models at the entrance area. They are well made and look like real foods. Even if you don't speak Japanese well, you can place an order at a restaurant, just by pointing at the models.

CHAPTER SEVEN

Location of People and Things

Lesson 29
山田さんはどこにいますか **Campus** **106**

Lesson 30
本やは近くにありますか **Neighborhood** **108**

Lesson 31
ヒーターはどこにありますか **Things in Your Room** **110**

Lesson 32
ていきゅうびは金曜日です **Days of the Week** **112**

Grammar and Usage **114**

1 Verbs of existence (ある, いる and いらっしゃる) 114
2 ～は… にある: ~is at / in ... [The location of things and people] 114
3 Relative location 114
4 ～から: From～ [Starting point] 115
5 ～まで: Up to～, until～ [Ending point] 115
6 ～ようび [The days of the week] 115
7 ございます: To have, to be 115

Culture **115**

A Polite high pitch 115

Writing **116**

a しんにょう 116
b おのづくり 116

Kanji List **116**

Review **117**

Tips and Additional Knowledge: Japanese Address System **118**

山田さんはどこにいますか Campus

Notes Relating to This Lesson

Grammar and Usage

1 Verbs of existence 114
2 ～は…にある 114

Basic Vocabulary and Kanji

ちゅうしゃじょう	駐車場	*n. parking lot, parking garage*
き⌉	木	*n. tree*
さくら	桜	*n. cherry tree, cherry blossom*
ち⌉か	地下	*n. basement*
いる	***i*-ru** いる・いない・い・いて	*vi. to exist* 1
あ⌉る	***r*-u** ある・ない・あり・あって	*vi. to exist* 1
いらっしゃ⌉る	***r*-u** いらっしゃる・いらっしゃらない・いらっしゃい・いらっしゃって	*vi. to exist (honorific)* 1
～かい	～階	*c. ~th floor*

Newly introduced kanji:

木(き)

木	一 十 オ 木

Dialog

Ben Lee asks Yoko Yamada where John Smith is.

リー　：スミスさんはどこにいますか。

山田　：スミスさんはカフェテリアにいます。

リー　：ああ、そうですか。カフェテリアはどこにありますか。

山田　：カフェテリアはとしょかんの5かいにあります。

リー　：ああ、そうですか。

Guess and Try 1

Fill in the blanks. 1 2

1. 山田さんはあそこ ____ います。
2. 山田さんはあそこ ____ 行(い)きます。
3. 山田さんはあそこ ____ 食(た)べます。

Guess and Try 2

Choose the appropriate options in the parentheses. 1 2

1. 私の本(ほん)はあそこに(あります・います)。
2. 私の兄(あに)はあそこに(あります・います)。
3. 私の犬(いぬ)はあそこに(あります・います)。
4. さくらの木はあそこに(あります・います)。
5. 私の車(くるま)はあそこに(あります・います)。
6. バスはあそこに(あります・います)。

Guess and Try 3

Choose the appropriate options in the parentheses. 1 2

For example:

先生はあそこに(あります(✕)・います(✕)・いらっしゃいます(✓))。

1. スミスさんはあそこに(あります・います・いらっしゃいます)。
2. 私の母(はは)はあそこに(あります・います・いらっしゃいます)。
3. スミスさんのお母(かあ)さんはあそこに(あります・います・いらっしゃいます)。

Guess and Try 4

Circle the phrases that are not read as you would predict.

いっかい　：1 階
にかい　：2 階
さんかい　：3 階
よんかい　：4 階
ごかい　：5 階
ろっかい　：6 階
ななかい　：7 階
はっかい・はちかい　：8 階
きゅうかい　：9 階
じゅっかい　：10 階
なんかい　：何階

Drill 1: Substitution

山田（やまだ）さんはうちにいます

1. 本（ほん）や
2. ちゅうしゃじょう
3. としょかんのちか

Drill 2: Formation

山田さん・うち ──▶ 山田さんはうちにいます

1. 父（ちち）・フランス
2. 私の犬（いぬ）・うち
3. 山田さんのお父（とう）さん・とうきょう
4. カフェテリア・としょかんのちか
5. 私のうち・とうきょう

Task 1: Classroom Activity

Your teacher asks you where a particular student is in the room. Answer him / her and repeat several times.

For example:

Teacher　：パークさんはどこにいますか。

Students　：パークさんはあそこにいます。
(Pointing at Mr. Park.)

Task 2: Classroom Activity

Ask your classmates the location of the following on campus. Do not ask a classmate more than one question.

1. 自動販売機（じどうはんばいき） *vending machine*
2. カフェテリア
3. トイレ *toilet*
4. 公衆電話（こうしゅうでんわ） *public phone*
5. ATM

For example:

A　：すみません。スナックの自動販売機（じどうはんばいき）はどこにありますか。

B　：としょかんの1階（いっかい）にあります。

A　：ああ、そうですか。どうも。

B　：いいえ。

Vocabulary Collection (Campus)	
学生会館（がくせいかいかん） *student union*	カフェテリア *cafeteria*
図書館（としょかん） *library*	体育館（たいいくかん） *gym*
食堂（しょくどう） *dining hall / dining room*	

Short Reading

私の大学（だいがく）はニューヨークにあります。キャンパスは大（おお）きいです。カフェテリアは学生会館（がくせいかいかん）の1階（かい）にあります。L・L（エル・エル）教室（きょうしつ）は図書館（としょかん）の5階にあります。留学生課（りゅうがくせいか）も図書館の5階にあります。日本語（にほんご）の先生（せんせい）の研究室（けんきゅうしつ）は文学部（ぶんがくぶ）の建物（たてもの）の3階にあります。

(大（おお）きい *big; large,* 学生会館（がくせいかいかん） *student union building,*
L・L 教室（エルエルきょうしつ） *language lab,*
留学生課（りゅうがくせいか） *division for foreign students,*
研究室（けんきゅうしつ） *office; lab,* 文学部（ぶんがくぶ） *literature department*)

Writing

Write about your campus.

ちゅうしゃじょう, ちゅうしゃじょう
木, 木, さくら, さくら, ちか, ちか,
いま, あま, いらっしゃいませ

本やは近くにありますか Neighborhood

Notes Relating to This Lesson

Grammar and Usage	Writing
3 Relative location 114	Ⓐ しんにょう 116
4 〜から 115	Ⓑ おのづくり 116
5 〜まで 115	

Basic Vocabulary and Kanji

こうさてん	交差点	*n. intersection*
え˥き	駅	*n. railway station*
とおり˥	通り	*n. street*
きた	北	*n. north* 3
みなみ	南	*n. south* 3
ひがし	東	*n. east* 3
にし	西	*n. west* 3
ちか˥く	近く	*n. vicinity* 3
となり	隣	*n. next door, next position* 3
ま˥え	前	*n. front, front position* 3
あいだ	間	*n. the position between (two items)* 3
〜どおり	〜通り	*~street (三番通り 3rd street) (さんばんどおり)*
〜まで		*prt. up to, until* 5

Newly introduced kanji:

間(あいだ)・近(ちか)く Ⓐ Ⓑ

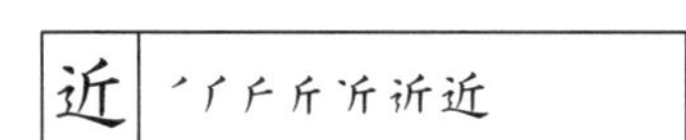

Dialog

Ben Lee wants to find out whether there is a bookstore in the neighborhood.

リー　：あのう、本(ほん)やは近くにありますか。

山田(やまだ)　：ええ。三番通(さんばんどお)りにあります。ここから車(くるま)で5分(ふん)ぐらいです。

リー　：三番通(さんばんどお)りのきたですか。みなみですか。

山田　：きたです。

リー　：ああ、そうですか。

山田　：ええ、レストランのとなりです。

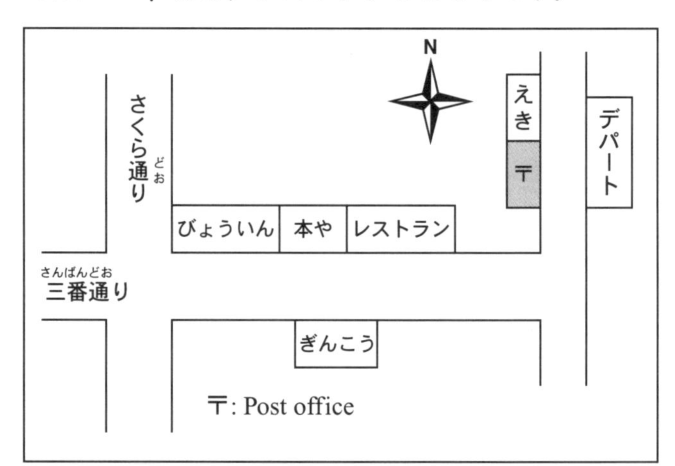

Guess and Try 1

Fill in the blanks. 4 5

1. 大学(だいがく) ________ えき ________ 歩(ある)きます。
   I will walk from the university to the railway station.

2. 2時(じ) ________ 3時 ________ 歩きます。
   I will walk from 2 o'clock to 3 o'clock.

3. 38ページ ________ 53ページ ________ 読(よ)みます。
   I will read from page 38 to page 53.

Guess and Try 2

Look at the above map and complete the following sentences. 3

1. デパートは ________________ にあります。
   in front of the railway station

2. えきは ______________________ にあります。
   next to the post office

3. 本やは ______________________ にあります。
   between the hospital and the restaurant

Drill 1: Substitution

ゆうびんきょくの近くにあります

1. まえ
2. となり
3. みなみ
4. ひがし

Drill 2: Formation

大学・近く ⟶ 大学の近くにあります

1. こうさてん・近く
2. 大学・まえ
3. デパート・となり
4. えき・きた
5. さくらどおり・ひがし
6. 本やと大学・間

Task: Classroom Activity

Pick one location (box) in the map as the location of your bank, then, ask other students where their banks are. Find out how many people go to the same bank as yours.

For example:

A ：B さんのぎんこうはどこにありますか。

B ：私のぎんこうは三番通り(さんばんどお)と、さくら通りのこうさてんにあります。

A ：三番通りのきたですか。みなみですか。

B ：きたです。…

A ：じゃあ、私のと同(おな)じです!
It's the same as mine!
(じゃあ、私のと違(ちが)います。)
(It's different from mine.)

こうさてん, こうさてん, えき, えき, みなみ, みなみ, ひがし, ひがし, にし, にし, きた, きた, とおり, とおり, 近く, 近く, 近く, となり, となり, まえ, まえ, あいだ, あいだ, 間, 間

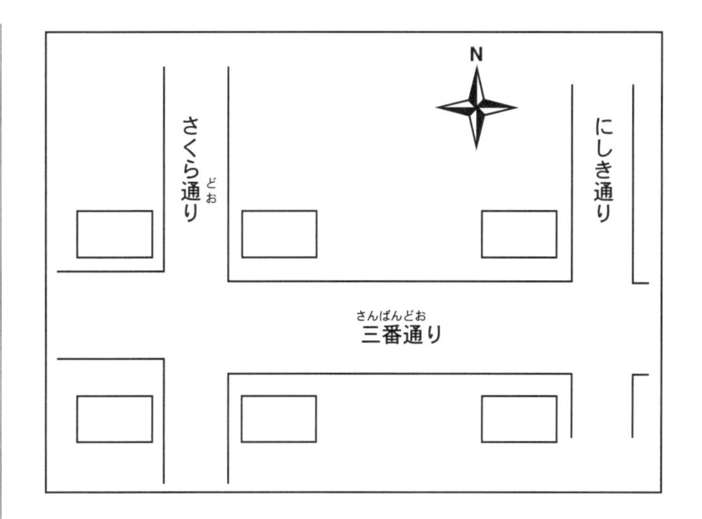

Short Reading

私の町(まち)は小(ち)さいです。小学校(しょうがっこう)は町の中心(ちゅうしん)にあります。郵便局(ゆうびんきょく)は小学校の北(きた)にあります。病院(びょういん)は三番通(さんばんどお)りにあります。図書館(としょかん)も三番通りにあります。大(おお)きいです。銀行(ぎんこう)は桜(さくら)通りにあります。スーパーマーケットは病院の隣(となり)にあります。私の家(いえ)からスーパーマーケットまで自転車(じてんしゃ)で5分(ふん)です。電車(でんしゃ)の駅(えき)はありません。

(町(まち) *town,* 小(ち)さい *small,* 小学校(しょうがっこう) *elementary school,* 中心(ちゅうしん) *center; middle part,* 大(おお)きい *big,* 家(いえ) *house*)

Writing

Write about your town, describing where the major buildings are located.

ヒーターはどこにありますか Things in Your Room

Notes Relating to This Lesson	
Grammar and Usage 3 Relative location 114	

Basic Vocabulary and Kanji

へや˥	部屋	*n. room*
で˥んき	電気	*n. electric light, electricity*
たんす	箪笥	*n. clothes chest*
ひきだし	引き出し	*n. drawer*
ほ˥んばこ	本箱	*n. bookcase*
しゃしん	写真	*n. photograph*
じ˥しょ	辞書	*n. dictionary*
うえ	上	*n. top part, above* 3
した	下	*n. bottom part, below, under* 3
な˥か	中	*n. inside, middle* 3
みぎ	右	*n. right* 3
ひだり	左	*n. left* 3
そ˥ば		*n. vicinity (cf. ちかく)* 3
よこ	横	*n. side* 3
うしろ	後	*n. behind* 3

Newly introduced kanji:

上(うえ)・下(した)・中(なか)・右(みぎ)・左(ひだり)

上	｜ ト 上	下	一 丅 下
右	ノ ナ 𠂇 右 右	左	一 ナ 𠂇 左 左

へや, へや, でんき, でんき, たんす, たんす, ひきだし, ひきだし, 本ばこ, 本んばこ しゃしん, しゃしん, じしょ, じしょ, 上, 上, 下 下, 下, 中, 中, 右, 右, 左, 左 右 右, 右, そば, よこ, よこ, うしろ, うしろ

Dialog

Mary Carter asked Yoko Yamada to wait for her for one hour in her apartment. Yoko asks Mary about the things in her room.

山田　　：ヒーターはどこにありますか。

カーター：ヒーターはつくえの左にあります。

山田　　：あ、これですね。

カーター：はい。

山田　　：それから、ざっしはありますか。

カーター：はい。ざっしはつくえのひきだしの中にあります。

山田　　：テレビは。

カーター：テレビはありません。

Guess and Try

Look at the above picture and answer the following questions. 3

1. たんすはどこにありますか。

____

2. しゃしんはどこにありますか。

____

3. ねこはどこにいますか。

____

4. シャツはどこにありますか。

____

(シャツ *shirt*)

Drill: Formation

テーブル・ベッド・よこ ⟶ テーブルはベッドのよこにあります

1. でんわ・たんす・上
2. 本(ほん)・じしょ・上
3. とけい・ほんばこ・中
4. カメラ・とけい・そば
5. しゃしん・つくえ・上
6. ねこ・つくえ・下

Task 1: Classroom Activity

Messages from thieves: Make five-member groups and line up in order (1st, 2nd, 3rd, 4th and 5th). Your teacher tells the 1st member in each group the location of something (for example, パスポート *passport*, おかね *money* and とけい *watch*) in the room illustrated below. Then, all the 1st members quietly pass the message to the 2nd members, pretending to be thieves. The 2nd members then pass the message to the 3rd members, the 3rd to 4th, and finally the 4th to 5th members. During the activity, participants are not allowed to point at the illustration or to take a note. The group that passes the message most accurately and quickly wins. Try a few times with different items in different locations.

For example:

Teacher : パスポートはベッドの下のかばんの中にあります。

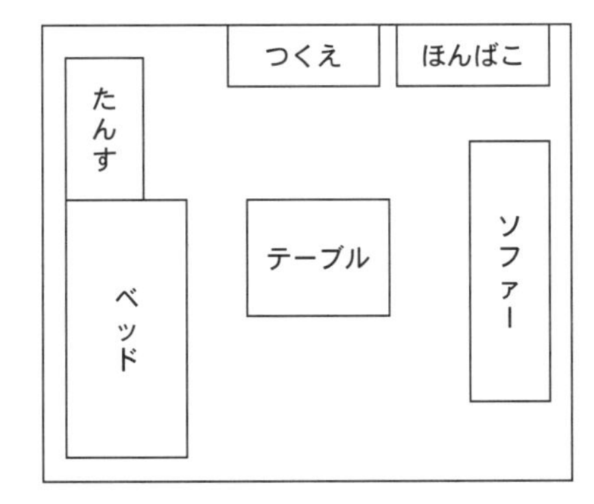

Task 2: Pair Work

Your partner draws the floor plan of his / her room which includes the location of furniture (for example, bed, desk, bookcase, chair and table) on a sheet of paper and gives it to you. Then, you ask him / her where the following things are: でんわ *telephone*, ようふく *clothes*, とけい *clock*, しゃしん *picture*, 本(ほん) *book* and じしょ *dictionary*.

For example:

A : でんわはどこにありますか。

B : でんわは ありません。

A : ああ、そうですか。じゃあ、じしょはどこにありますか。

B : じしょはつくえの上にあります。

A : ああ、ここですね。
(Pointing at the location of the dictionary in the picture.)

Vocabulary Collection (Things in Your Room)	
窓(まど) *window*	ドア *door*
壁(かべ) *wall*	天井(てんじょう) *ceiling*
床(ゆか) *floor*	机(つくえ) *desk*
棚(たな) *shelf*	本棚(ほんだな) *bookshelf*
本箱(ほんばこ) *bookcase*	箪笥(たんす) *clothes chest*
鏡台(きょうだい) *vanity*	椅子(いす) *chair*
冷蔵庫(れいぞうこ) *refrigerator*	ベッド *bed*
ソファー *sofa*	ヒーター/ストーブ *heater*
電気(でんき) *electric light*	電話(でんわ) *telephone*
人形(にんぎょう) *doll*	花瓶(かびん) *vase*
カレンダー *calendar*	ポスター *poster*
ナイトテーブル *night table*	
コーヒーテーブル *coffee table*	

Short Reading

机(つくえ)は窓(まど)の前(まえ)にあります。ベッドは壁(かべ)のそばにあります。本箱(ほんばこ)は机(つくえ)のよこにあります。たんすはありません。コンピューターは机の上にあります。

(壁(かべ) *wall*)

Writing

Write a short passage describing where the things are in your room.

ていきゅうびは金曜日です Days of the Week

Notes Relating to This Lesson	
Grammar and Usage	**Culture**
6 〜ようび 115	Ⓐ Polite high pitch 115
7 ございます 115	

Basic Vocabulary and Kanji

げつよ˥うび	月曜日	*n. Monday* 6
かよ˥うび	火曜日	*n. Tuesday* 6
すいよ˥うび	水曜日	*n. Wednesday* 6
もくよ˥うび	木曜日	*n. Thursday* 6
きんよ˥うび	金曜日	*n. Friday* 6
どよ˥うび	土曜日	*n. Saturday* 6
にちよ˥うび	日曜日	*n. Sunday* 6
も˥しもし		*Hello! (on the phone)*

Newly introduced kanji:

月曜日(げつようび)・火曜日(かようび)・水曜日(すいようび)・
木曜日(もくようび)・金曜日(きんようび)・土曜日(どようび)・日曜日(にちようび)

曜	丨 ⺆ 日 日 日⁷ 日⁷⁷ 旷 昕 昕 昕 昕 晍 曜 曜 曜 曜 曜		
火	丶 丷 火 火	水	亅 才 水 水
金	ノ 入 𠆢 今 今 仐 余 金	土	一 十 土

Vocabulary Collection		
月(つき) *the moon*	火(ひ) *fire*	水(みず) *water*
木(き) *tree*	金(きん) *gold*	土(つち) *soil*
日(ひ) *the sun*		

Dialog

Asking business hours at Tokyo Shoten (Tokyo Bookstore) over the phone.

てんいん：とうきょうしょてんでございます。
(東京書店(とうきょうしょてん) *Tokyo bookstore*)

きゃく　：あのう、ていきゅう日(び)は何曜日(なんようび)ですか。
(定休日(ていきゅうび) *closed days for business*)

てんいん：水曜日でございます。

きゃく　：ああ、水曜日ですね。

てんいん：はい。

きゃく　：えいぎょう時間(じかん)は?
(営業時間(えいぎょうじかん) *business hours*)

てんいん：ごぜん10時(じ)からごご9時まででございます。日曜日は6時まででございます。

きゃく　：ああ、そうですか。じゃあ、どうも。

てんいん：はい。よろしくおねがいいたします。
(おねがいいたします: The polite form of おねがいします)

Guess and Try 1

Is there any difference in the overall pitch between the customer and clerk? Ⓐ

Guess and Try 2

What is the difference between 水曜日です and 水曜日でございます? 7

Drill 1: Reading

1. 月火水

2. 月火水木

3. 金土日

4. 月火水木金土日

5. 月曜日-火曜日-水曜日-木曜日-金曜日-土曜日-日曜日

Repeat several times.

Drill 2: Formation

月曜日-火曜日 ⟶ 月曜日から火曜日まででございます

1. 月曜日-水曜日

2. 水曜日-金曜日

3. 金曜日-日曜日

4. 9 時-5 時

5. 7 時-4 時

6. 9 時はん-5 時はん

Task: Classroom Activity

Your teacher assigns each of you to be a worker at one of the places in the following table and informs you its business hours and its closed days. Find out the business hours and the closed days of other places by asking other students. You can pretend to be on the phone.

A：もしもし。山田スーパーさんですか。

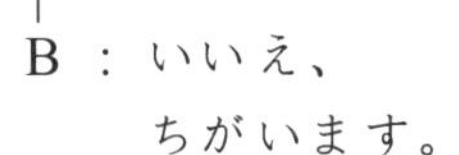

B：いいえ、ちがいます。　　B：はい。山田スーパーでございます。

A：あっ、すみません。　　A：…

B：いいえ。

	えいぎょう時間 *business hours*	ていきゅう日 *closed days*
山田スーパー *Yamada Supermarket*		
高橋びようしつ *Takahashi Beauty Parlor*		
旭しょくどう *Asahi Restaurant*		
高木しょてん *Takagi bookstore*		

Short Reading

月曜日と水曜日と金曜日は大学に行きます。火曜日は午前 11 時から午後 4 時まで本屋の中のコーヒーショップでアルバイトをします。木曜日はうちで勉強します。土曜日の午前中はうちの仕事をします。午後と晩はレストランでアルバイトをします。日曜日はゆっくりします。

(アルバイト *part-time job,* 仕事 *job; work,*
午前中 *in the morning (before noon),*
午後 *p.m.; in the afternoon (before dusk),*
ゆっくりする *vi. to relax*)

Writing

Write about your weekly schedule.

月	火	水	木	金	土	日
	1	2	3	4	5	6
7	8	9	10	11	12	13
14	15	16	17	18	19	20
21	22	23	24	25	26	27
28	29	30	31			

月曜日, 月曜日, 火曜日, 火曜日
水曜日, 水曜日, 木曜日, 木曜日
金曜日, 金曜日, 土曜日, 土曜日
日曜日, 日曜日

– Grammar and Usage –

1 Verbs of existence (ある, いる and いらっしゃる)

The verbs ある, いる and いらっしゃる mean *to exist*, and they are used along with two nouns: a noun that denotes the item that exists (X), and a noun that denotes the location (Y) where X exists. The former (X) is marked by the particle ～が and the latter is marked by the particle ～に, as in Y に X があります *X exists in Y*. The choice among ある, いる and いらっしゃる depends on the type of the item that exists: ある is for objects that do not move by themselves (for example, books, plants and chairs); いる is for items that can move by themselves (for example, people and animals); いらっしゃる is for one's superiors.

(a) あそこに本があります。
There is a book over there.

(b) ここに犬がいます。
Here is a dog.

(c) この大学に有名な先生がいらっしゃいます。
In this college, there is a famous professor.

Occasionally, いる is used for a non-human and non-animal item if it is moving (for example, a robot and a moving car).

Note that the verb いらっしゃる and ある are slightly irregular verbs. The polite form of いらっしゃる is "いらっしゃいます" and not いらっしゃります, and the plain negative form of ある is "ない" and not あない.

2 ～は… にある: ～is at / in ... [The location of things and people]

If you want to express the location (Y) of some item (X), make the item (X) the topic of the sentence, as in X は Y にあります or X は Y にいます. This will ensure that the item (X) is an old piece of information that both the speaker and listener know of its existence while highlighting the location (Y) as a new piece of information.

(a) あの本は私のうちにあります。
That book is at my house.

(b) 山田さんはとしょかんにいます。
Mr. Yamada is at the library.

(c) パンダはちゅうごくにいます。
Pandas are in China.

If you want to express what you have or what exists, make the location (Y) the topic of the sentence. (See Chapter Eight).

3 Relative location

The relative location is expressed by a relative location term such as 上 *top area* along with a reference item marked by the particle の. For example, つくえの上 means *the top of the desk*. Importantly, the reference item precedes the relative location term. Other relative location terms include 下 *lower area*, 中 *inside*, 右 *right*, 左 *left*, 前 *front*, 後 *rear; back*, 間 *between*, そば *vicinity*, 近く *vicinity*, 横 *side*, and 隣 *next-door; next to~*. Relative geographic location terms include 東 *east*, 西 *west*, 南 *south* and 北 *north*. 間 needs two reference items, as in A と B の間 *between A and B*.

(a) ボールはつくえの上にあります。
The ball is on the desk.

(b) ボールはつくえといすの間にあります。
The ball is between the desk and the chair.

(c) ぎんこうは大学の南にあります。
The bank is on the south of the university.

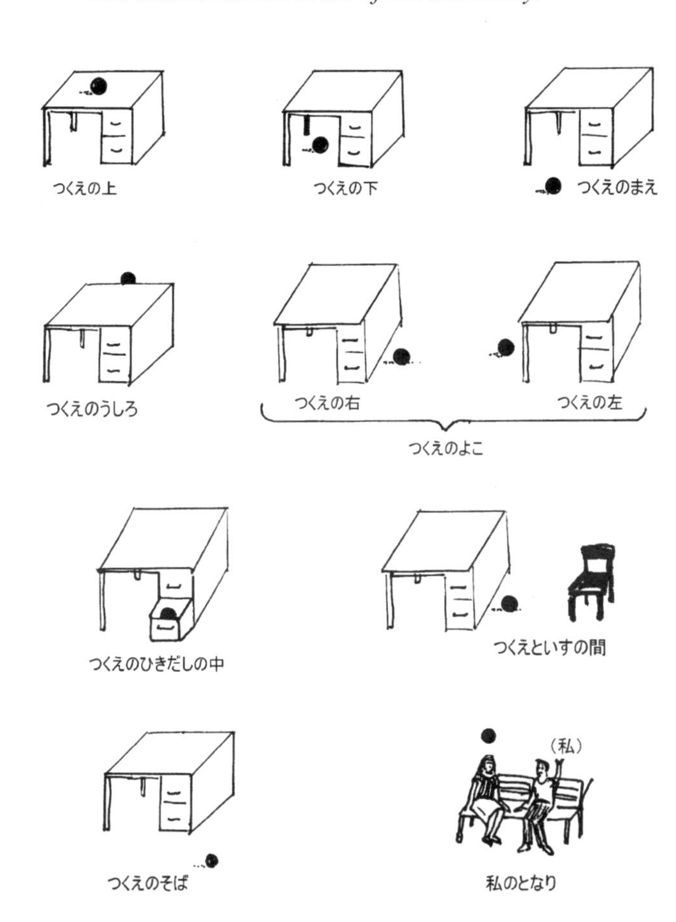

4 ～から: From～ [Starting point]

The particle ～から expresses the starting point.

(a) 3時からべんきょうします。
I will study from 3 o'clock.

(b) 大学からあるきます。
I will walk from the university.

(c) 大学から5分です。
It takes 5 minutes from the university.

(d) 38ページから読みます。
I will read from page 38.

5 ～まで: Up to～, until～ [Ending point]

The particle まで expresses the ending point.

(a) えきまであるきます。
I will walk to the station.

(b) 大学からえきまで5分です。
It takes 5 minutes from the university to the station.

(c) 3時から5時までべんきょうします。
I will study from 3 o'clock until 5 o'clock.

(d) 3ページから5ページまで読みます。
I will read from page 3 to page 5.

6 ～ようび [The days of the week]

In Japanese, a week starts from Monday and ends on Sunday. The following are the days of a week:

げつようび	月曜日	*Monday*
かようび	火曜日	*Tuesday*
すいようび	水曜日	*Wednesday*
もくようび	木曜日	*Thursday*
きんようび	金曜日	*Friday*
どようび	土曜日	*Saturday*
にちようび	日曜日	*Sunday*

7 ございます: To have, to be

In a commercial context such as at a store and a restaurant, clerks use super polite business-like expressions and sentence endings. The most obvious examples are ございます and ～でございます, which are the super-polite versions of あります and ～です, respectively.

(a) 本は5階にあります。
Books are on the fifth floor. (polite / neutral)

(b) 本は5階にございます。
Books are on the fifth floor.
(super polite / business-like)

(c) ぜんぶで500円です。
All together, it is 500 yen. (polite / neutral)

(d) ぜんぶで500円でございます。
All together, it is 500 yen.
(super polite / business-like)

– Culture –

Ⓐ Polite high pitch

In general, high pitch is perceived as a sign of politeness in Japan. The Japanese raise their overall pitch range when they talk to their superiors such as their bosses, teachers, customers and clients. Office workers and saleclerks in Japan are trained to speak in a higher pitch than their usual pitch range when they deal with customers and clients. You will be amazed at female clerks' overall high pitch when they make an announcement on floors and in elevators in a department store, and when they talk on the telephone. Japanese women's high pitch is also recognizable when they talk to young children.

– Writing –

Ⓐ しんにょう

辶	しんにょう *walk, way*
	Example: 近(ちか)い *near,* 遠(とお)い *far,* 週(しゅう) *week,* 道(みち) *street,* 返(かえ)す *to return,* 通(かよ)う *to commute,* 速(はや)い *fast,* 遅(おそ)い *slow,* 過(す)ぎる *to pass,* 遊(あそ)ぶ *to play,* 送(おく)る *to send*

Ⓑ おのづくり

斤	おのづくり *ax*
	Example: 近(ちか)い *near,* 新(あたら)しい *new,* 所(ところ) *place*

– Kanji List –

木・間・近く・上・下・中・右・左・月曜日・火曜日・水曜日・木曜日・金曜日・土曜日・日曜日

木	き・モク・ボク *tree*	一 十 才 木 [4]	Example: 木(き) *a tree*; 木曜日(もくようび) *Thursday*
間	あいだ・ま・カン *between, interval*	[12]	Example: 間(あいだ) *between*; 時間(じかん) *time*
近	ちか-い・キン *near, recent*	[7]	Example: 近(ちか)く *vicinity, near*
上	うえ・あ-がる・のぼ-る・ジョウ *above, up*	丨 ト 上 [3]	Example: 上(うえ) *above, top*
下	した・さ-がる・くだ-る・カ・ゲ *under, down*	一 丅 下 [3]	Example: 下(した) *under*
中	なか・チュウ・ジュウ *middle, inside*	中 [4]	Example: 中(なか) *inside*
右	みぎ・ウ・ユウ *right*	ノ ナ 右 [5]	Example: 右(みぎ) *the right*
左	ひだり・サ *left*	一 ナ 左 [5]	Example: 左(ひだり) *the left*
月	つき・ゲツ・ガツ *moon, month*	丿 月 [4]	Example: 月曜日(げつようび) *Monday*
曜	ヨウ *luminary day of the week*	曜 [18]	Example: 月曜日(げつようび) *Monday*
日	ひ・び・にち・に・ジツ *sun, day*	丨 日 [4]	Example: 日曜日(にちようび) *Sunday*; 日本(にほん) *Japan*; 明日(あした) *tomorrow*
火	ひ・カ *fire*	火 [4]	Example: 火曜日(かようび) *Tuesday*
水	みず・スイ *water*	亅 水 [4]	Example: 水曜日(すいようび) *Wednesday*

金 かね・キン *gold, metal, money*	ノ 𠆢 𠆢 今 全 全 金 金 [8] Example: 金曜日(きんようび) *Friday*
土 つち・ド *ground, earth, soil*	一 十 土 [3] Example: 土曜日(どようび) *Saturday*

– Review –

Q1. Choose the appropriate options in the parentheses.

1. (犬(いぬ)・じしょ)はつくえの下にいます。
2. ぎんこうは大学(だいがく)の(そば・間)にあります。
3. 今日(きょう)は(火曜日・9時)です。

Q2. Write the pronounciation of the kanji characters in hiragana.

1. うちの近く
2. 上と下
3. 右と左
4. 月曜日・火曜日・木曜日・日曜日・金曜日・土曜日・水曜日

Q3. Arrange the items in each set and create a grammatical sentence.

1. (います・山田(やまだ)さん・としょかん・に・は)
2. (あります・車(くるま)・ちゅうしゃじょう・は・に)
3. (あります・つくえ・本は・上・の・に)
4. (あります・レストランは・大学・みなみ・に・の)

Q4. Fill in the blanks with あります, います or いらっしゃいます.

1. 私の犬はあそこに ______________ 。
2. 母(はは)はうちに ______________ 。
3. 山田さんのお母(かあ)さんはあそこに ______________ 。
4. としょかんはあそこに ______________ 。
5. じしょはここに ______________ 。

Q5. Fill in the blanks with に or で.

1. 山田さんはとしょかん ____ 行(い)きます。
2. 山田さんはとしょかん ____ べんきょうします。
3. 山田さんはとしょかん ____ います。
4. ねこはたいていテーブルの下 ____ 食(た)べます。
5. ねこはたいていテーブルの下 ____ います。
6. しんぶんはソファーの上 ____ あります。

Q6. Read the following passage and figure out the seating position of each person.

田中(たなか)さんは私のまえにいます。田中さんのガールフレンドは田中さんのよこにいます。私のボーイフレンドは私の右にいます。私の兄(あに)は私の左にいます。父(ちち)は兄のまえにいます。

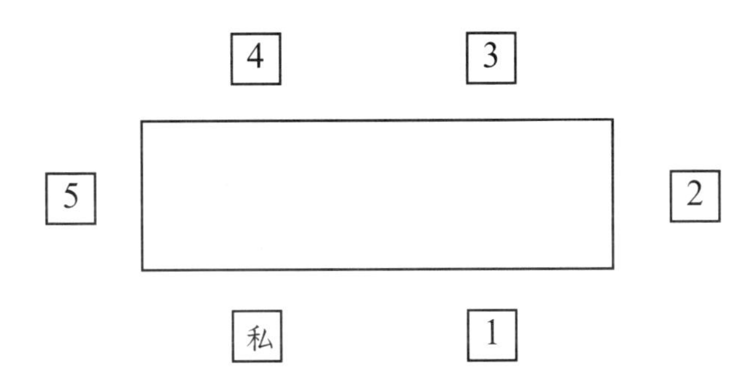

Tips and Additional Knowledge: Japanese Address System

Most Japanese streets don't have a name and street names are usually irrelevant for addresses. So, finding someone's house is more difficult in Japan than in countries where a house address includes the street name and house number on the given street.

An address in Japan is defined in terms of geographic / administrative area units. The largest area unit is 県 *prefecture*, as in 千葉県 *Chiba Prefecture*. The exceptions are 東京都, 大阪府, 京都府 and 北海道. Then, you have smaller area units such as 市 *city*, 区 *ward*, 郡 *county / township*, 村 *village*, 町 *town / city* and 丁目 *chome*. 丁目 is the smallest area unit and consists of only a few blocks and each 丁目 is numbered. In Japanese addresses, the zip code comes at the beginning, the larger area units precede smaller area units, and the number of the house or building is followed by the counter 番地 *number* and placed at the very end.

Someone's address will look like:

〒465-0123 愛知県名古屋市瑞穂区石山町三丁目16番地

〒465-0123 愛知県名古屋市瑞穂区石山町3の6

〒019-0555 秋田県平鹿郡西川村15番地

〒178-0078 東京都練馬区山川町2-12

The address is written on an envelop as below:

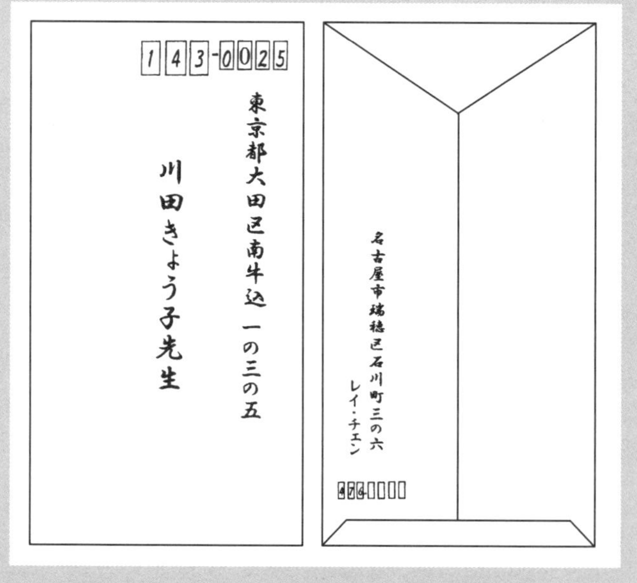

Front (receiver) Back (sender)

Note that the receiver's name must be followed by the respectful title 様. When 先生 is appropriate for him / her, 先生 is used instead of 様.

The logo 〒 is for zip code numbers. Red street mailboxes as in the photo below and post office buildings can be identified by 〒.

CHAPTER EIGHT

Expressing What You Have

Lesson 33
ノートが 3 冊あります **Things in Your Bag or Colors** 120

Lesson 34
へやにはつくえと本ばこがあります **Things in Your Room** 122

Lesson 35
私は兄が 2 人います **Family** 124

Lesson 36
明日はしけんがあります **Daily Schedule** 126

Grammar and Usage 128

1 Colors 128
2 ～には… がある: There is an... in～, I have an... in～ [Existence] 128
3 Number phrases [Numeral + counter] 129
4 ですから: Therefore [Consequence] 129
5 すこし: A few / a little / slightly [Quantity / amount / degree] 129
6 Imitating words (ワンワン, ネバネバ, etc) 129
7 ～と: With～ [Accompaniment] 130

Culture 130

A ふとん: Futon mattress 130

Writing 130

a きへん 130
b ぼくづくり 130
c おんなへん 130
d ゆみへん 130

Kanji List 131

Review 131

Tips and Additional Knowledge: Animal Sounds 132

ノートが3冊あります Things in Your Bag or Colors

Notes Relating to This Lesson	
Grammar and Usage	**Writing**
1 Colors 128	ⓐ きへん 130
2 ～には… がある 128	ⓑ ぼくづくり 130
3 Number phrases 129	

Basic Vocabulary and Kanji

きって⌉	切手	*n. stamp*
けしゴム	消しゴム	*n. eraser*
ノ⌉ート		*n. notebook*
いろ⌉	色	*n. color*
あ⌉か	赤	*n. red color* 1
あ⌉お	青	*n. blue color* 1
く⌉ろ	黒	*n. black color* 1
～つ		*c. a native counter for a variety of objects*
～ほん / ぼん / ぽん	～本	*c. a counter for cylindrical objects*
～まい	～枚	*c. a counter for flat objects*
～さつ	～冊	*c. a counter for bound objects such as books and magazines*

Newly introduced kanji:

～本・～枚 ⓐ ⓑ・～冊

枚	一 十 才 木 木' 木' 朩 枚	冊	丨 冂 冂 冊 冊

Vocabulary Collection (Colors) 1		
赤 *red*	青 *blue*	白 *white*
黒 *black*	黄色 *yellow*	緑 *green*
紫 *purple*	ピンク *pink*	灰色 *gray*
ベージュ *beige*	オレンジ色 *orange*	茶色 *brown*

Dialog

A woman has claimed that the bag the police officer is holding is hers, and the police officer starts asking her questions.

Police officer ： かばんの中には何がありますか。

女の人 ： そのかばんの中にはノートが3冊あります。

Police officer ： 何色ですか。

女の人 ： 赤と青と黒です。

Police officer ： それから。

女の人 ： それから、ボールペンが2本あります。

Police officer ： はい。じゃあ、どうぞ。

Guess and Try 1

What is the difference between the following two sentences. 2

1. 日本ごの本はかばんの中にあります。
2. かばんの中には日本ごの本があります。

Guess and Try 2

Underline the phrases that are not read as you would predict.

1. ボールペン *ballpoint pen*・えんぴつ *pencil*・バナナ *banana*・かさ *umbrella*

いっぽん (1 本)	にほん (2 本)
さんぼん (3 本)	よんほん (4 本)
ごほん (5 本)	ろくほん / ろっぽん (6 本)
ななほん (7 本)	はちほん / はっぽん (8 本)
きゅうほん (9 本)	じゅっぽん (10 本)
なんぼん (何本)	

2. かみ *paper*・きって *stamp*・ポスター *poster*・チケット *ticket*・のり *seaweed*

いちまい (1 枚)	にまい (2 枚)
さんまい (3 枚)	よんまい (4 枚)
ごまい (5 枚)	ろくまい (6 枚)
ななまい (7 枚)	はちまい (8 枚)

きゅうまい(9 枚)　　じゅうまい(10 枚)
なんまい(何枚)

3. けしゴム *eraser*・ホッチキス *stapler*・ふでいれ *pencil case*・はさみ *scissors*・りんご *apple*・つくえ *desk*

ひとつ(1 つ)　　ふたつ(2 つ)
みっつ(3 つ)　　よっつ(4 つ)
いつつ(5 つ)　　むっつ(6 つ)
ななつ(7 つ)　　やっつ(8 つ)
ここのつ(9 つ)　　とお(10 つ)
いくつ(幾つ)

4. 本 *book*・ざっし *magazine*・ノート *notebook*・テキスト *textbook*

いっさつ(1 冊)　　にさつ(2 冊)
さんさつ(3 冊)　　よんさつ(4 冊)
ごさつ(5 冊)　　ろくさつ(6 冊)
ななさつ(7 冊)　　はっさつ(8 冊)
きゅうさつ(9 冊)　　じゅっさつ(10 冊)
なんさつ(何冊)

Guess and Try 3

State where you place a quantity phrase like 2 冊 and 2 本 in a sentence. 3

Drill 1: Reading

1.	1 枚	2 枚	3 枚
2.	1 本	2 本	3 本
3.	1 冊	2 冊	3 冊
4.	1 つ	2 つ	3 つ

Repeat several times.

Drill 2: Formation

ボールペン ⟶ ボールペンを一本ください

1. えんぴつ
2. けしゴム
3. ノート
4. 30 円(えん)のきって
5. 50 円(えん)のきって

Task: Classroom Activity

Your teacher shows the class six small items (for example, a notebook, pencil or wallet). He / she then secretly selects only three items and puts them in a bag. Pretend that your teacher is the police officer, claim the bag to be yours by stating the content of the bag. The student who can state the content of the bag correctly wins.

Police officer ： かばんの中には何がありますか。

Person A ： ノートが 1 冊あります。

Police officer ： 何色(なにいろ)ですか。

Person A ： くろです

Police officer ： はい。それから。

Person A ： けしゴムが 1 つあります。

Police officer ： ちがいますね。つぎの人(ひと)、どうぞ。 (Next person, please.)

Person B ： はい。

Police officer ： かばんの中には何がありますか。

Vocabulary Collection (Inside the Bag)	
財布(さいふ) *wallet*	携帯電話(けいたいでんわ) *cellular phone*
眼鏡(めがね) *eyeglasses*	化粧品(けしょうひん) *cosmetics*
薬(くすり) *medication*	ちり紙(がみ) *tissue paper*
ハンカチ *handkerchief*	アドレス帳(ちょう) *address book*
傘(かさ) *umbrella*	サングラス *sunglasses*
ボールペン *ball-point pen*	筆入れ(ふでいれ) *pen case*
シャーペン(シャープペンシル) *mechanical pencil*	
フロッピーディスク *floppy disc*	

Short Reading

私のかばんの中(なか)にはノートが 2 冊と、財布(さいふ)が 1 つと、傘(かさ)が 1 本と、筆入れ(ふでいれ)が 1 つあります。筆入れの中には青(あお)の万年筆(まんねんひつ)が 1 本と、シャーペンが 3 本あります。

(筆入れ(ふでいれ) *pen case*, 万年筆(まんねんひつ) *fountain pen*,
シャーペン(シャープ・ペンシル) *mechanical pencil*)

Writing

List what you have in your backpack.

ざっし, ざっし, けしゴム, けしゴム
ノート, ノート, いち, いち, 一本, 一本
一枚, 一枚, 一冊, 一冊, 二枚

へやにはつくえと本ばこがあります Things in Your Room

Notes Relating to This Lesson

Grammar and Usage	
2 ～には… がある 128	5 すこし 129
3 Number phrases 129	**Culture**
4 ですから 129	A ふとん 130

Basic Vocabulary and Kanji

れいぞ˥うこ	冷蔵庫	*n. refrigerator*
ふとん	布団	*n. futon mattress* A
ベ˥ッド		*n. bed*
で˥すから		*con. therefore, so* 4
たくさん	沢山	*adv. a lot*
すこ˥し	少し	*adv. a little, a few, slightly* 5
ぼく	僕	*pron. I, me (the first person pronoun for male)*
～だい	～台	*c. a counter for mechanical objects*

Newly introduced kanji:

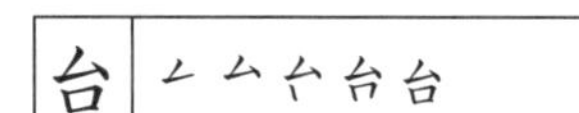

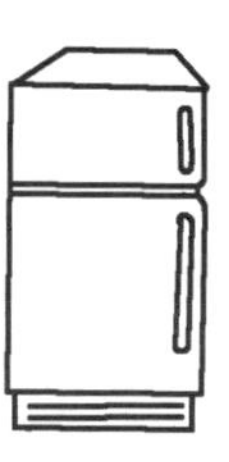

Dialog

Yoko Yamada and John Smith talk about their rooms.

スミス　：山田さんのへやには何(なに)がありますか。

山田　　：私のへやにはつくえと、本(ほん)ばこがあります。

スミス　：ベッドは。

山田　　：ベッドはありません。ですから、ふとんでねます。スミスさんのへやは。

スミス　：ぼくのへやにはベッドが1つと、つくえが1つと、コンピューターが2台あります。それから、CDがたくさんあります。コンピューターゲームもすこしあります。

Guess and Try 1

Choose the appropriate options in the parentheses. 4

1. 私は日本人です。(ですから・でも)、はしを使います。

2. 私は日本人です。(ですから・でも)、はしを使いません。

Guess and Try 2

Underline the phrases that are not read as you would predict.

テレビ *TV*・コンピューター *computer*・車 *car*・タイプライター *typewriter*・れいぞうこ *refrigerator*

いちだい(1台)	にだい(2台)
さんだい(3台)	よんだい(4台)
ごだい(5台)	ろくだい(6台)
ななだい(7台)	はちだい(8台)
きゅうだい(9台)	じゅうだい(10台)
なんだい(何台)	

Guess and Try 3

Fill in the blanks with an appropriate particle **if necessary**. 2 3

1. 私のへやにはいす____ あります。
   I have a chair in my room.

2. 私のへやにはいす____ 2つ____ あります。
   I have two chairs.

3. 私のへやにはいす____ 2つ____、テレビ____ 2台____ あります。
   There are two chairs and two TVs in my room.

Drill 1: Reading

1. 1 台　　2 台　　3 台
   4 台　　5 台

2. 1 つ　　2 つ　　3 つ
   4 つ　　5 つ

Repeat several times.

Drill 2: Formation

テレビ ⟶ テレビが 1 台あります

1. 車(くるま)
2. ステレオ
3. ベッド
4. れいぞうこ
5. いす

Drill 3: Formation

テレビ (1)・ソファー (2) ⟶ テレビが 1 台と、ソファーが 2 つあります

1. ステレオ (1)・テレビ (2)
2. テレビ (2)・コンピューター (3)
3. ソファー (1)・いす (2)
4. ベッド (1)・テーブル (2)
5. ソファー (1)・いす (1)・テレビ (1)

Task 1: Pair Work

Find out what your partner has in his / her room. Use the dialog as a model.

Vocabulary Collection (Inside Your Room)	
机(つくえ) *desk*	本箱(ほんばこ) *bookcase*
椅子(いす) *chair*	洋服(ようふく) *clothes*
箪笥(たんす) *clothes chest*	鏡台(きょうだい) *dresser*
ステレオ *stereo*	テレビ *TV*
ベッド *bed*	テーブル *table*
ソファー *sofa*	コンピューター *computer*

Task 2: Survey

Ask two of your classmates how many of the following items they have at home.

	私	さん	さん
車(くるま) *car*			
冷蔵庫(れいぞうこ) *refrigerator*			
テレビ *televison*			
コンピューター *computer*			

For example:

A ：B さんのうちには車が何台(なんだい)ありますか。

B ：3 台あります。(うちには車はありません。)

A ：ああ、そうですか。じゃあ、テレビは何台ありますか。

B ：テレビは…

Short Reading

私のうちにはテレビが 3 台あります。台所(だいどころ)に 1 台と、居間(いま)に 1 台と、弟(おとうと)の部屋(へや)に 1 台あります。私はあまりテレビを見(み)ません。弟はよく見ます。

(台所(だいどころ) *kitchen,* 居間(いま) *living room,* 借(か)りる *to borrow,* 新(あたら)しい *new,* 小(ちい)さい *small*)

Writing

Write a short passage describing how many computers (コンピューター) there are in your house and who uses them.

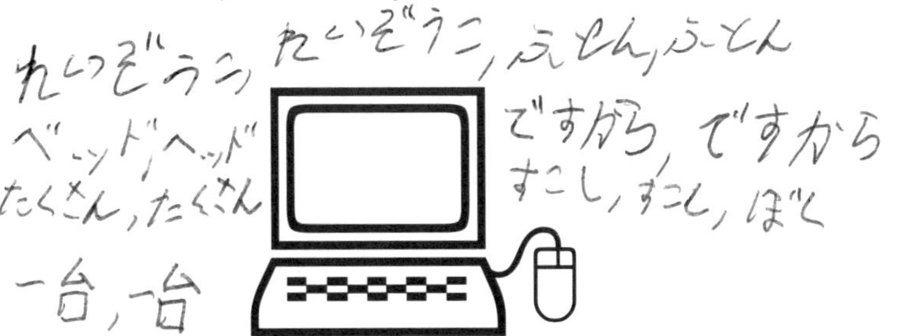

私は兄が２人います Family

Notes Relating to This Lesson	
Grammar and Usage	**Writing**
2 〜には…がある 128	ⓒ おんなへん 130
3 Number phrases 129	
6 Imitating words 129	

Basic Vocabulary and Kanji

きょ˥うだい・ごきょ˥うだい	兄弟・御兄弟	*n. siblings*
りょ˥うしん・ごりょ˥うしん	両親・御両親	*n. parents*
そ˥ふ・おじ˥いさん	祖父・おじいさん	*n. grandfather*
そ˥ぼ・おば˥あさん	祖母・おばあさん	*n. grandmother*
い˥とこ	従兄弟	*n. cousin*
ひとり˥っこ	一人っ子	*n. only one child*
さびし˥い	寂しい・寂しくない	*adj. lonely*
うるさ˥い	うるさい・うるさくない	*adj. noisy*
〜にん／り	〜人	*c. a counter for people*
〜ひき／びき／ぴき	〜匹	*c. a counter for animals*

Newly introduced kanji:

姉(あね)・お姉(ねえ)さん・妹(いもうと) ⓒ・
兄弟(きょうだい)・弟(おとうと)・〜匹(ひき・びき・ぴき)・〜人(にん・り)

姉	ㄑ女女'女'女'女'妒姉	妹	ㄑ女女女'女'妹妹妹
弟	丶丷丷当当弟弟	匹	一丆兀匹

Vocabulary Collection (Non-blood-related Family)	
義理(ぎり)の母(はは)(継母(ままはは)) *stepmother*	義理(ぎり)の父(ちち) *stepfather*
義理(ぎり)の弟(おとうと) *stepbrother*	義理(ぎり)の兄弟(きょうだい) *stepsibling*
養母(ようぼ) *foster / adoptive mother*	
養父(ようふ) *foster / adoptive father*	

Dialog

Mary Carter asks her professor about her family.

カーター：先生にはご兄弟がいらっしゃいますか。

先生　　：ええ、２人(ふたり)います。姉が１人(ひとり)と兄(あに)が１人です。

カーター：ああ、そうですか。

先生　　：マリーさんは。

カーター：私は兄弟がいません。一人っ子(ひとりっこ)です。

先生　　：じゃあ、ちょっとさびしいですね。

カーター：ええ。でも、うちには犬(いぬ)が３匹(さんびき)います。<u>ワンワン</u>うるさいです。

Guess and Try 1

Interpret the underlined part in above dialog. 6

Guess and Try 2

Underline the phrases that are not read as you would predict.

1. ひとり (1 人)　ふたり (2 人)
   さんにん (3 人)　よにん (4 人)
   ごにん (5 人)　ろくにん (6 人)
   ななにん／しちにん (7 人)
   はちにん (8 人)　きゅうにん (9 人)
   じゅうにん (10 人)　なんにん (何人)

2. いっぴき (1 匹)　にひき (2 匹)
   さんびき (3 匹)　よんひき (4 匹)
   ごひき (5 匹)　ろくひき／ろっぴき (6 匹)
   ななひき (7 匹)　はちひき／はっぴき (8 匹)
   きゅうひき (9 匹)　じゅっぴき (10 匹)
   なんびき (何匹)

Guess and Try 3

Fill in the blanks with appropriate particles **if necessary**. 2 3

1. 私は兄弟 ____ います。

2. 私は姉 ____ 兄がいます。

3. 私は姉＿＿兄＿＿弟がいます。

4. 私は姉＿＿2人＿＿います。

5. 私は姉＿＿2人＿＿兄＿＿3人＿＿います。

Drill 1: Reading

1. 1人　2人　3人
   4人　5人　6人
   7人　8人　9人
   10人

2. 1匹　2匹　3匹
   4匹　5匹　6匹
   7匹　8匹　9匹
   10匹

Repeat several times.

Drill 2: Formation

姉が2人 ⟶ 姉が2人います
姉が2人・弟が1人 ⟶ 姉が2人と、弟が1人います

1. 兄が2人
2. 弟が1人
3. 兄が2人・弟が1人
4. 姉が3人・妹が3人
5. 兄弟が4人
6. いとこが5人
7. 日本人のともだちが6人

Task 1: Survey

Ask some of your classmates how many siblings they have, and where they are now.

For example:

A：Bさんはご兄弟がいらっしゃいますか。

B：はい、4人います。姉が1人と兄が3人です。

A：お姉さんは今(いま)どこにいらっしゃいますか。

B：今ホンコンにいます。

A：ああ、そうですか。じゃあ、一番目(いちばんめ)のお兄さんは今どこにいらっしゃいますか。

B：今ボストンにいます。

(一番目(いちばんめ)の〜 *the first~*, 二番目(にばんめ)の〜 *the second~*)

Task 2: Classroom Activity

Find out who has the greatest number of cousins in the class.

For example:

先生：Aさんはいとこがいますか。

A：はい。15人います。

B：ああ、多(おお)いですね。

(多(おお)いですね *That is a lot!*, 少(すく)ないですね *That is so few!*)

Task 3: Classroom Activity

Find out who has the greatest number of Japanese friends in the class.

For example:

先生：Aさんは日本人(にほんじん)のともだちがいますか。

A：はい。3人います。よう子(こ)さんと、ゆき子(こ)さんと、さと子(こ)さんです。

B：ああ、ぜんぶ女(おんな)の人(ひと)ですね。
Oh, they are all women!

Short Reading

僕(ぼく)は兄弟がいません。一人(ひとり)っ子(こ)です。でも、従兄弟(いとこ)が13人います。僕の父(ちち)は兄弟が3人います。母(はは)は兄弟が5人います。父の方(ほう)の従兄弟は4人います。母の方の従兄弟は9人います。

(〜の方(ほう) *~'s side*)

Writing

Write about your family and relatives.

明日はしけんがあります Daily Schedule

Notes Relating to This Lesson	
Grammar and Usage	**Writing**
2 〜には…がある 128	d ゆみへん 130
7 〜と 130	

Basic Vocabulary and Kanji

しゃか˥いがく	社会学	*n. sociology*
けいざ˥いがく	経済学	*n. economics*
し˥けん	試験	*n. exam, test* (試験をうける *to take an exam*)
しごと	仕事	*n. job* (仕事をする *to work*)
めんせつ	面接	*n. interview*
デ˥ート		*n. date*
アルバ˥イト		*n. part-time job (the German word, Arbeit)*
ごぜんちゅう	午前中	*n. after dawn before noon (morning)* (*c.f.* ごぜん *a.m.*)
あさ˥って	明後日	*n. the day after tomorrow*
おもしろ˥い	面白い・面白くない	*adj. funny, interesting, amusing*

Newly introduced kanji:

勉強(べんきょう)する *to study* d

勉	ノ ク ク 各 缶 缶 争 免 勉 勉	強	⁷ ⁷ 弓 弘 弘 弘 弘 弘 弾 強 強

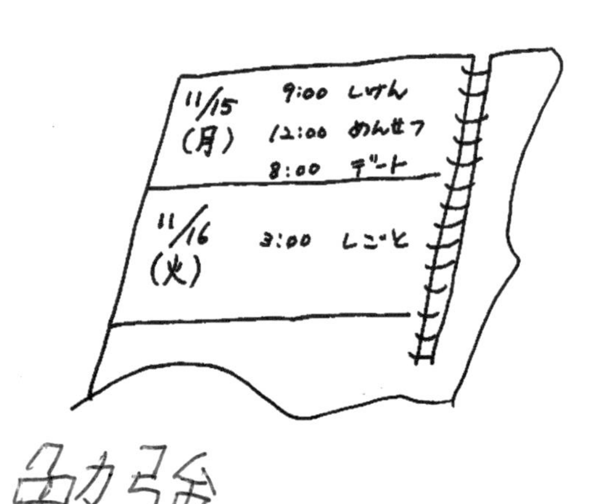

Dialog

Ben Lee feels lonesome. He tries to find someone who can do something with him.

リー　：川口さん、ジムに行(い)きませんか。

川口　：すみません。今(いま)から、田中(たなか)さんと、勉強するんです。

リー　：ああ、そうですか。じゃあ、ごごは。

川口　：すみません。ごごは、アルバイトがあります。

リー　：ああ、そうですか。じゃあ、今晩(こんばん)、いざかやに行きませんか。

川口　：すみません。今晩はデートがあるんです。

リー　：ああ、そうですか。

Guess and Try 1

What does the underlined part in the above dialog mean? 7

Guess and Try 2

What do the following sentences mean? 2

1. 兄(あに)は明日(あした)しけんがあります。
2. 私は今日(きょう)クラスがありません。

Drill: Formation

明日(あした)・しけん ⟶ 明日はしけんがあります

1. あさって・めんせつ
2. 今日(きょう)・しごと
3. 明日の晩(ばん)・デート
4. 今晩(こんばん)・アルバイト
5. 明日のごぜんちゅう・けいざい学(がく)のクラス
6. 明日のごご・しゃかい学のしけん

Task 1: Classroom Activity

Insert the following four events in your schedule as you like, then, look for those who can spend time with you studying Japanese in your free time during the following three days. Find as many people as possible.

1. コンパ (informal party among college students)
2. デート
3. しごと
4. Your choice?

	今日 *today*	明日 *tomorrow*	あさって *the day after tomorrow*
ごぜんちゅう *morning*	しけん		
ごご *afternoon*	めんせつ		
晩 *evening / night*			

For example:

A ： 明日のごごはひまですか。

B ： ええ、ひまですよ。

A ： 私と日本ごを勉強しませんか。

B ： いいですよ。

Task 2: Group Work

Pick one fun activity that you often do (for example, fishing, playing tennis, cooking and shopping) and find at least three people with whom you can do it together. With each person, arrange the time and the place for it.

For example:

A ： こんど私とバスケットボールをしませんか。
(こんど *sometime soon*)

B ： ええ、いいですよ。(あのう、ちょっと。)

A ： 月曜日のごごはひまですか。

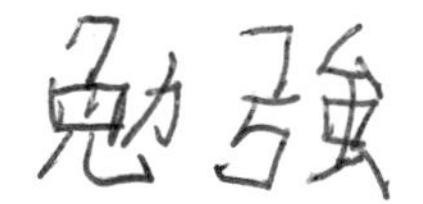

B ： 月曜日のごごは しごとがあります。

A ： じゃあ、…

Short Reading

明日の晩は魚一屋でテニス部のコンパがあります。魚一屋は安いすし屋です。大学の近くにあります。大学から、歩いて 5 分です。座敷があります。とても安いです。1 人 1,500 円ぐらいです。いつも学生がたくさんいます。明日のコンパは 30 人ぐらい来ます。とても楽しみです。

(テニス部 *tennis club,*
コンパ *an informal party for college students,*
すし屋 *sushi restaurant,* 座敷 *Japanese-style room,*
楽しみです *to be looking forward to~*)

Writing

Write about your weekly schedule.

しゃかい学，しゃかい学，しけん
けいざい学，けいざい学，しけん
しごと，しごと，めんせつ，めんせつ
デート，デート，アルバイト，アルバイト
午前中，午前中，あさって，あさって
おもしろい，おもしろい，
勉強，勉強

– Grammar and Usage –

1 Colors

The following table lists the basic color terms in Japanese. One interesting aspect of Japanese people's perception on colors is that 青(あお) *blue* and 緑(みどり) *green* are occasionally merged to 青(あお). The colors of traffic lights are actually *red*, *yellow* and *green* in Japan, but the Japanese call it 赤(あか) *red*, 黄色(きいろ) *yellow* and 青(あお) *blue*. And the Japanese call green leafy vegetables in general 青(あお)いもの *blue things*.

Nouns	Adjectives
緑(みどり) *green*	緑の *green~*
紺(こん) *navy*	紺の *navy~*
橙(だいだい) *orange*	橙の *orange~*
紫(むらさき) *purple*	紫の *purple~*
赤(あか) *red*	赤い・赤の *red~*
白(しろ) *white*	白い・白の *white~*
灰色(はいいろ) *gray*	灰色の *gray~*
黄色(きいろ) *yellow*	黄色い・黄色の *yellow~*
黒(くろ) *black*	黒い・黒の *black~*
青(あお) *blue*	青い・青の *blue~*
茶色(ちゃいろ) *brown*	茶色い・茶色の *brown~*

2 ～には… がある: There is an ... in～, I have an ... in～ [Existence]

The existential verbs ある, いる and いらっしゃる express not only the location of things, but also what exists or what one has. For example, in (a), the fact that the speaker has a dog is already known and the location of the dog is highlighted as a new piece of information, whereas in (b), the fact that the speaker has a dog is highlighted as a new piece of information.

(a) 犬(いぬ)はうちにいます。
The dog is at home. (location)

(b) うちに(は) 犬(いぬ)がいます。
There is a dog at home. / We have a dog at home. (existence)

The difference between these sentences is the choice of the topic. To express what one has and what exists, the item (X) should not be the topic marked by は, but the subject marked by the particle が, as in (b). The following are other examples that express what one has (had) or what exists (existed):

(c) 私の車(くるま)にはテレビがあります。
In my car, there is a TV.

(d) 図書館(としょかん)にはコンピューターがあります。
In the library, there is a computer.

(e) 空港(くうこう)には警察官(けいさつかん)がいました。
In the airport, there was a police officer.

(f) 中国(ちゅうごく)にはパンダがいます。
In China, there are pandas.

(g) 私(に)は車(くるま)があります。
I have a car.

(h) 父(ちち)(に)はお金(かね)があります。
My father has money.

(i) 私(に)は兄(あに)がいます。
I have a brother.

(j) 私(に)はガールフレンドがいます。
I have a girl friend.

(k) 私(に)はともだちがいません。
I do not have a friend.

(l) スミスさん(に)はピアノの才能(さいのう)があります。
Mr. Smith has a talent for the piano.

(m) 私(に)は勇気(ゆうき)がありません。
I do not have courage.

Note that the particle に tends to be deleted when it occurs before the particle は. When X is an event, に is almost always absent before the particle は.

(n) 私は明日(あした)パーティーがあります。
I have a party tomorrow.

(o) 私は明日しけんがあります。
I have an exam tomorrow.

(p) 私は明日デートがあります。
I have a date tomorrow.

3 Number phrases [Numeral + counter]

The quantity or the amount of things and people must be expressed by a numeral and a counter. The counter to be used depends on the type, shape, function and size of the item you are counting or measuring.

Counters and Number Phrases	Type of the Items	Examples
〜本(ほん) (1本(いっぽん)・2本(にほん)・3本(さんぼん))	*cylindrical shaped objects*	*banana, pencil, pen, cigarette, pillar*
〜枚(まい) (1枚(いちまい)・2枚(にまい)・3枚(さんまい))	*flat shaped objects*	*paper, sheet, ticket, stamp*
〜台(だい) (1台(いちだい)・2台(にだい)・3台(さんだい))	*mechanical objects*	*TV, radio, computer, refrigerator*
〜匹(ひき) (1匹(いっぴき)・2匹(にひき)・3匹(さんびき))	*small or medium sized animals*	*fish, dog, cat*
〜冊(さつ) (1冊(いっさつ)・2冊(にさつ)・3冊(さんさつ))	*books and magazines*	*book, dictionary, notebook*
〜人(にん) (1人(ひとり)・2人(ふたり)・3人(さんにん))	*people*	*students, children*
〜つ* (1つ(ひとつ)・2つ(ふたつ)・3つ(みっつ))	*a variety of non-animate items*	*chair, bed, apple, candy*

* つ is a native Japanese counter and the numerals that precede it are also native Japanese numerals. Native Japanese numerals are available only under ten and most of them are not used independently in modern Japanese. They are used only with native counters such as つ. Accordingly, the counter つ may not be used for numbers over ten. For counting ten or more items, use 個(こ) instead of 〜つ.

A number phrase most commonly occurs right after the associated item and its particle:

(a) 私はペンを2本買(か)いました。
I bought two pens.

(b) ここにペンが2本あります。
Here are two pens.

(c) 学生(がくせい)が3人先生(せんせい)のオフィスに来(き)ました。
Three students came to the teacher's office.

When two or more nouns with their respective number phrases are listed, the relevant grammatical particle must appear repeatedly, as follows:

(d) 私はペンを2本と、鉛筆(えんぴつ)を3本買(か)いました。
I bought two pens and three pencils.

(e) ここにペンが2本と、鉛筆が3本あります。
Here are two pens and three pencils.

4 ですから: Therefore [Consequence]

The connective word ですから shows that the following sentence is the conclusion or the consequence with respect to the preceding sentence:

(a) 私は日本人(にほんじん)です。ですから、日本語(にほんご)を話(はな)します。
I am a Japanese. Therefore, I speak Japanese.

(b) 私のうちにはねこが2匹(ひき)います。ですから、ねずみがいません。
I have two cats at home. Consequently, I do not have any mice at home.

(c) 私のうちにはテレビがありません。ですから、ともだちのうちでテレビを見ます。
There is no TV in my house. So, I watch TV in my friend's house.

5 すこし: A few / a little / slightly [Quantity / amount / degree]

少(すこ)し means *a few* or *a little* and it occurs where a number phrase usually occurs.

(a) うちにはCDが少(すこ)しあります。
I have a few CDs at home.

(b) コーヒーに砂糖(さとう)を少し入(い)れます。
I put a little sugar in my coffee.

少(すこ)し also means *slightly*, just like ちょっと, being used with a predicate that expresses an unfavorable situation or state:

(c) 日本語(にほんご)は少(すこ)し難(むずか)しいです。

(d) 日本語(にほんご)はちょっと難(むずか)しいです。

Unlike ちょっと, 少(すこ)し cannot be used for indicating hesitation, nor for attracting attention.

6 Imitating words (ワンワン, ネバネバ, etc)

Japanese has a huge inventory of imitating words called 擬声語(ぎせいご) and 擬態語(ぎたいご). 擬声語(ぎせいご) (phonomimes, onomatopoeia) are words that describe the sounds associated with the actions and movements of people, animals, and things, and they are formed by actually imitating those sounds. On the other hand, 擬態語 (phenomimes, psychomimes) describe the states, manner, and feelings associated with items and their actions and movements, and they are created by imitating them impressionistically. 擬声語 and 擬態語 consist of the repetition of one (or two) syllable(s), and they are conventionally written in katakana. The following are some examples:

(a) 犬がワンワンほえます。
The dog barks "wan-wan".

(b) ネバネバのごはん
sticky rice

(c) パサパサのごはん
non-sticky rice / fluffy rice

(d) 雨がザーザーふります。
It rains very heavily.

(e) 風がビュービューふきます。
The wind blows very heavily.

(f) うなぎがニョロニョロうごきます。
The eel moves in a smooth manner.

(g) この板はツルツルです。
This board has a smooth and polished surface.

(h) この板はザラザラです。
This board has a rough surface.

(i) 母がプンプンしています。
My mother is in a bad mood.

7 〜と: With〜 [Accompaniment]

Besides listing nouns, the particle と specifies the person (or animal) who accompanies the performer (agent) of the event. For example, in the following sentence, Mr. Tanaka will study, and he will do it with Mary.

(a) 田中さんはマリーさんと勉強します。
Mr. Tanaka will study with Mary.

Sentence (b) also means that both Mr. Tanaka and Mary will study, but they do not necessarily study together.

(b) 田中さんとマリーさんは勉強します。
Mr. Tanaka and Mary will study.

– Culture –

A ふとん: Futon mattress

Futon is a Japanese mattress and bedding. At night, you can take the 敷布団 (futon mattress) out of the closet, spread it out on the floor and sleep on it. You can use 掛け布団 (futon comforter) for covering your body. In the morning, you can fold them up and put them right back into the closet. This way, a room can function as a bedroom at night and a living room during the day time.

– Writing –

a きへん

木	きへん *tree*
	Example: 村 *village,* 林 *woods,* 学校 *school,* 〜枚 *counter for flat items*

b ぼくづくり

攵	ぼくづくり *strike, attack*
	Example: 〜枚 *counter for flat items,* 教える *to teach,* 数学 *mathematics*

c おんなへん

女	おんなへん *woman*
	Example: 姉 *older sister,* 妹 *younger sister,* 嫁 *bride,* 結婚 *marriage*

d ゆみへん

弓	ゆみへん *bow*
	Example: 強い *strong,* 引く *to pull,* 弱い *weak*

– Kanji List –

〜本・〜枚・〜冊・〜台・姉・お姉さん・妹・兄弟・弟・〜匹・〜人・勉強する

本	もと・ホン *root, origin, true, main*	一 十 才 木 本 [5]	Example: 本(ほん)や *a bookstore* 日本(にほん) *Japan* 2本(ほん) *two (for cylindrical items)*
枚	マイ *a counter for flat items*	一 十 オ 木 木' 朴 枚 枚 [8]	Example: 1枚(いちまい) *one (for flat items)*
冊	サツ *a counter for books*	丨 冂 冂 冊 冊 [5]	Example: 1冊(いっさつ) *one (book)*
台	ダイ・タイ *board, table, base, a counter for machines*	㇜ ム 厶 台 台 [5]	Example: 1台(いちだい) *one (for machines)*
姉	あね・シ *elder sister*	く 女 女 女' 女' 女' 姉 姉 [8]	Example: 姉(あね) *one's elder sister* お姉(ねえ)さん *someone else's elder sister*
妹	いもうと・マイ *younger sister*	く 女 女 女' 女' 妹 妹 妹 [8]	Example: 妹(いもうと) *one's younger sister*
兄	あに・ケイ・キョウ *elder brother*	丨 口 口 尸 兄 [5]	Example: 兄(あに) *one's elder sister* 兄弟(きょうだい) *siblings* お兄(にい)さん *someone else's elder brother*
弟	おとうと・テイ・ダイ *younger brother*	ヽ ソ 㔾 当 当 弟 弟 [7]	Example: 兄弟(きょうだい) *siblings* 弟(おとうと) *one's younger brother*
匹	ヒキ・ビキ *a counter for animals*	一 ア 兀 匹 [4]	Example: 1匹(いっぴき) *one (for animals)*
人	ひと・ジン・ニン *person*	ノ 人 [2]	Example: 3人(さんにん) *three (people)* あの人(ひと) *that person* 日本人(にほんじん) *Japanese people*
勉	ベン *endeavor*	ノ ク 各 各 各 争 免 免 勉 勉 [10]	Example: 勉強(べんきょう)する *to study*
強	つよ-い・キョウ *force, strong*	7 コ 弓 弘 弘 弘 弹 弹 強 強 強 [11]	Example: 勉強(べんきょう)する *to study*

– Review –

Q1. Read the following phrases.

1.	1 台	2 台	3 台
2.	1 匹	2 匹	3 匹
3.	1 つ	2 つ	3 つ
4.	1 本	2 本	3 本
5.	1 人	2 人	3 人
6.	1 冊	2 冊	3 冊

Q2. Fill in the blanks with one of the following number phrases:

2枚・2台・2本・2人・2匹・2冊・2つ

1. 私は妹が ________ います。
2. えんぴつを ________ 買います。それから、けしゴムを ________ 買います。
3. うちには犬が ________ います。それから、ねこも ________ います。
4. 私のへやにはいすが ________ あります。それから、テレビが ________ あります。

5. 本を ________ よみます。それから、ざっしを ________ よみます。

Q3. Insert the given number phrase into the sentence appropriately. Make any necessary changes.

1. ここにいすがあります。(3 つ)
2. 私は姉と兄がいます。(2 人・2 人)
3. 私は明日ゆうびんきょくできってを買います。(3 枚)
4. 私は明日ゆうびんきょくできってを買います。(たくさん)

Q4. Fill in the blanks with an appropriate particle if necessary.

1. 私のへやにはテレビ ____ あります。
2. 兄のへやにはテレビ ____ ラジオ ____ コンピューター ____ あります。
3. 姉のへやにはテレビ ____ 1 台 ____ ラジオ ____ 2 台 ____ あります。

Q5. Fill in the blanks with one of the following words:

ですから・でも・それから

1. 私のへやにはコンピューターがあります。____________、いつもへやで勉強します。
2. 私のへやにはコンピューターがあります。____________、ステレオもあります。
3. この本は私のです。____________、あの本は私のじゃありません。
4. マリーさんはフランス人です。____________、よくワインを飲みます。

Q6. What would you say in Japanese in the following situations?

1. You want to say that you have a TV at home.
2. You want to say that the TV is at home.
3. You want to say that you have two older sisters.
4. You want to say that you have a class tomorrow.

Tips and Additional Knowledge: Animal Sounds

Dogs bark with a "wan-wan", not a "bow-wow", in Japan.

No.	Animal	Language	Sound
1.	dog	English	: Bow-wow
		Japanese	: ワンワン
		Chinese*	: Wang-wang
		Korean	: Mong-mong
2.	mouse	English	: Squeak-squeak
		Japanese	: チューチュー
		Chinese*	: Chee-chee or Zi-zi
		Korean	: Chit-chit
3.	pig	English	: Oink-oink
		Japanese	: ブーブー
		Chinese*	: Hu-lu
		Korean	: Ggooll-ggooll
4.	rooster	English	: Cock-a-doodle-doo
		Japanese	: コケコッコー
		Chinese*	: Wo-wo-wo
		Korean	: Ko-kee-o
5.	sheep	English	: B-a-a-a-a
		Japanese	: メーメー
		Chinese*	: M-i-e-h
		Korean	: Mieh-mieh
6.	bee	English	: Bzzz
		Japanese	: ブンブン
		Chinese*	: Weng-weng
		Korean	: Weng-weng
7.	bird	English	: Tweet-tweet
		Japanese	: ピーピー
		Chinese*	: Ji-ji
		Korean	: Jjakk-jjakk
8.	crow	English	: Caw-caw
		Japanese	: カーカー
		Chinese*	: Gua-gua
		Korean	: Ggakk-ggakk
9.	cat	English	: Meow
		Japanese	: ニャンニャン
		Chinese*	: Mi-mi or Myao-myao
		Korean	: Yaong-yaong
10.	cow	English	: Moo
		Japanese	: モーモー
		Chinese*	: Moo-moo
		Korean	: Um-moo

* Varies depending on the dialect.

CHAPTER NINE

Describing the Property of Things and People

Lesson 37
どんなたてものですか **Describing Buildings** **134**

Lesson 38
リーさんのへやはどうですか **Describing Rooms** **136**

Lesson 39
日本語はむずかしくありません **Foreign Languages** **138**

Grammar and Usage **140**

1 ふるい: Old 140
2 どんな: What kind of ~ [Question word for a property (prenominal)] 140
3 Adjectives (高い, 高価な, etc) 140
4 ~の: One [Pronominal element] 140
5 どう: How [Question word for a property (predicate)] 141
6 それに: Furthermore [Additional fact] 141
7 おじゃまします [When entering someone else's residence] 141
8 Degree adverbs (とても, ぜんぜん, まあまあ, etc) 141

Writing **142**

a まだれ 142
b ごんべん 142

Kanji List **142**

Review **143**

Tips and Additional Knowledge 1: Gender / Age Sensitive Friendly Addressing Terms for Strangers **144**

Tips and Additional Knowledge 2: Blowfish **144**

CHAPTER NINE | Lesson 37

どんなたてものですか Describing Buildings

Notes Relating to This Lesson	
Grammar and Usage	
1 ふるい 140	3 Adjectives 140
2 どんな 140	4 ～の 140

Basic Vocabulary and Kanji

おおき˥い	*irr.* 大きい・大きくない	*adj. big (variation:* 大きな*)*
ちいさ˥い	*irr.* 小さい・小さくない	*adj. small (variation:* 小さな*)*
あたらし˥い	新しい・新しくない	*adj. new*
ふる˥い	古い・古くない	*adj. old (for non-animate items)* 1
ひく˥い	低い・低くない	*adj. low, not tall*
きたな˥い	汚い・汚くない	*adj. dirty*
りっぱ(な)	立派だ・立派じゃない	*adj. splendid, great, gorgeous, elegant*
ど˥んな		*q. what kind of~* 2

Newly introduced kanji:

大(おお)きい・小(ちい)さい・新(あたら)しい・古(ふる)い

小	亅 小 小	新	丶 亠 亣 立 立 辛 辛 亲 亲 新 新 新 新
古	一 十 廾 古 古		

Dialog

Ben Lee asks a stranger whether there is a post office nearby.

リー　：ちょっと、すみません。ゆうびんきょくは近(ちか)くにありますか。

女(おんな)の人　：ええ。あそこに高(たか)いたてものがありますね。

リー　：ああ、あのりっぱなたてものですね。

女の人　：はい。あれはぎんこうです。あのぎんこうのうしろにあります。

リー　：どんなたてものですか。

女の人　：きれいなたてものです。でも、小さいです。

リー　：ああ、そうですか。どうも。

女の人　：いいえ。

Guess and Try 1

There are two types of adjectives: those that end in な (な-type) and those that end in い (い-type) when they occur right before a noun. Fill in the blanks appropriately and state the generalization on how these two types of adjectives pattern. 3

1. A. あれは ________ たてものです。
   That is a tall building.

   B. あのたてものは高いです。
   That building is tall.

2. A. あれは ________ たてものです。
   That is a splendid building.

   B. あのたてものはりっぱです。
   That building is splendid.

3. A. あれはきれいなたてものです。
   That is a beautiful building.

   B. あのたてものは ________ です。
   That building is beautiful.

Guess and Try 2

Make a sentence using the word どんな. 2

Guess and Try 3

The noun right after an adjective can be replaced by の if contextually understood. What do you think each occurrence of の in the following passage stands for? 4

あの高いたてものはびょういんです。あの小さい<u>の</u>は本やです。あのりっぱな<u>の</u>はホテルです。

Drill 1: Formation

きれいなたてものです ⟶ きれいです

1. 古いたてものです
2. 新しい本です
3. りっぱな車(くるま)です
4. 小さい犬(いぬ)です
5. きれいなレストランです
6. 高(たか)いとけいです

Drill 2: Formation

小さいです・ゆうびんきょくです ⟶ 小さいゆうびんきょくです

りっぱです・ゆうびんきょくです ⟶ りっぱなゆうびんきょくです

1. 大きいです・大学です
2. 古いです・こうこうです
3. りっぱです・ぎんこうです
4. きれいです・レストランです
5. 新しいです・びょういんです
6. きたないです・えきです

Task: Group Work

Each of you secretly picks a building on campus. Let other students guess which building it is by asking you questions. The student who could guess correctly wins. Take turns.

For example:

A：小さいですか。

B：いいえ、まあまあ大きいです。

C：古いですか。

B：はい、とても古いです。

D：ああ、けいざい学部(がくぶ)のたてものですね。

B：はい、そうです。

(～学部(がくぶ) *(academic) department of~*)

Short Reading

私の大学(だいがく)の図書館(としょかん)は五階建(ごかいだ)てです。まあまあ新しいです。とてもきれいです。エレベーターは三(みっ)つあります。地下(ちか)には本屋(ほんや)があります。一階(いっかい)には小さいカフェテリアがあります。

(五階建(ごかいだ)て *five-story building,* エレベーター *elevator*)

Writing

Write about the nicest building on your campus.

りっぱな どんな どんな
大きい, 大きい, 小さい, 小さい,
新し, 新しい, 新しい, 新しい
古い, 古い, ひくい, ひくい,
きたない, きたない, りっぱな

リーさんのへやはどうですか Describing Rooms

Notes Relating to This Lesson	
Grammar and Usage	**Writing**
5 どう 141	ⓐ まだれ 142
6 それに 141	
7 おじゃまします 141	

Basic Vocabulary and Kanji

いえ	家	*n. house*
やちん	家賃	*n. rent for houses and apartments*
あかるい	明るい・明るくない	*adj. bright, cheerful*
くらい	暗い・暗くない	*adj. dark, gloomy*
ひろい	広い・広くない	*adj. spacious, wide*
せまい	狭い・狭くない	*adj. non-spacious, narrow (狭いへや a small room)*
しずか(な)	静かだ・静かじゃない	*adj. quiet*
べんり(な)	便利だ・便利じゃない	*adj. convenient (便利なじしょ a convenient dictionary)*
ふべん(な)	不便だ・不便じゃない	*adj. inconvenient*
ちかい	近い・近くない	*adj. near (c.f. 近く vicinity)*
とおい	遠い・遠くない	*adj. far*
どう		*q. how* 5
それに		*con. furthermore, moreover* 6
おじゃまします	お邪魔します	*I'll come in (lit. I am going to disturb you.)* 7

Newly introduced kanji:

明(あか)るい・暗(くら)い・広(ひろ)い ⓐ・近(ちか)い

暗	丨 冂 日 日 日' 日ˆ 日ᅮ 日ᅲ 暗 暗 暗 暗 暗	広	' 亠 广 広 広

Dialog

Ben Lee enters Ken Kawaguchi's room.

川口　：どうぞ。

リー　：おじゃまします。きれいなへやですね。

川口　：そうですか。

リー　：ええ、きれいですよ。それに、とても広いですね。

川口　：ああ、どうも。リーさんのアパートはどうですか。

リー　：ちょっとせまいです。

川口　：やちんはいくらですか。

リー　：3万円です。

川口　：安いですね。

Guess and Try 1

What should you say when you are entering your friend's house, teacher's office and teacher's house? 7

Guess and Try 2

Choose the appropriate option(s). 6

兄のアパートは新しいです。(それに・それから・ですから・でも)、きれいです。

Guess and Try 3

Choose the appropriate options in the parentheses. 5

1. 新しいルームメートは(どう・どんな)ですか。
2. 新しいルームメートは(どう・どんな)人ですか。

Drill 1: Formation

しずかなへやです ⟶ しずかです

1. 暗いへやです
2. 大きい大学です
3. りっぱなたてものです
4. きれいな大学です
5. 新しいアパートです
6. 明るいアパートです
7. べんりなりょうです
8. 広いキャンパスです

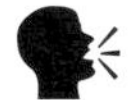

Drill 2: Formation

しずかです ⟶ しずかなへやです

1. 広いです
2. 明るいです
3. りっぱです
4. きたないです
5. べんりです
6. きれいです

Task 1: Pair Work

Ask your partner about his / her apartment (for example, new?, clean?, bright?, quiet?, spacious?, convenient?, expensive?, any roommates?).

For example:

A：Bさんはりょうですか。

B：いいえ。アパートです。

A：ああ、そうですか。Bさんのアパートは新しいですか。

B：いいえ。ちょっと古いです。

A：大学(だいがく)から近(ちか)いですか。

B：はい、車(くるま)で5分(ふん)です。

A：ルームメートはいますか。

B：はい。一人(ひとり)います。

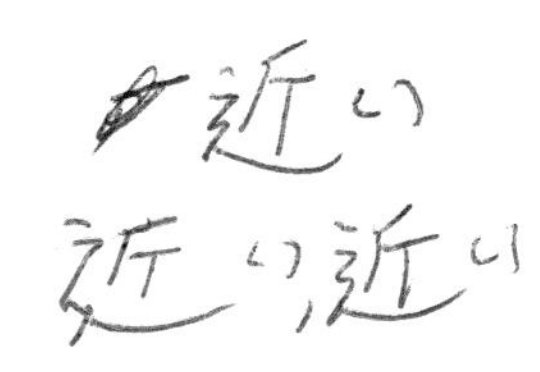

Vocabulary Collection (Residence)

アパート *apartment*
両親(りょうしん)の家(いえ) *parents' house*
自宅(じたく) *one's own house*
一軒家(いっけんや) *solitary house*
寮(りょう) *dormitory*
家賃(やちん) *rent*
下宿(げしゅく) *lodging house, boarding house*
マンション *apartment or condominium in a neat-looking multistory building*
ルームメート *roommate*
寮費(りょうひ) *dormitory fee*

Task 2: Skit

Act out the scene where two of your classmates visit your place for the very first time. Start from opening the door and let them enter (see Dialog).

Short Reading

私の寮(りょう)の部屋は明るいです。窓(まど)は南向きです。日がよく入ります。ですから、冬はとても暖(あたた)かいです。でも、少しせまいです。それに、少しうるさいです。となりの部屋の学生はよくロック・ミュージックを聞きます。ルームメートはいい人です。寮費(りょうひ)は一ヶ月に一万円です。大学まで歩いて一分です。

(南向き(みなみむき) *facing south,* 日(ひ) *sun; sunlight,* 入る(はいる) *enter,* 冬(ふゆ) *winter,* 暖かい(あたたかい) *warm,* 聞く(きく) *to listen to,* 寮費(りょうひ) *dormitory fee,* 一ヶ月(いっかげつ) *one month*)

Writing

Write about your room.

日本語はむずかしくありません Foreign Languages

Notes Relating to This Lesson	
Grammar and Usage	**Writing**
3 Adjectives 140	Ⓑ ごんべん 142
8 Degree adverbs 141	

Basic Vocabulary and Kanji

がいこくご	外国語	*n. foreign language*
かいわ	会話	*n. conversation*
ききとり	聞き取り	*n. listening comprehension*
さくぶん	作文	*n. composition*
たんご	単語	*n. word, vocabulary*
はつおん	発音	*n. pronunciation*
ぶんぽう	文法	*n. grammar*
ぶ˥ん	文	*n. sentence*
たのし˥い	楽しい・楽しくない	*adj. fun, entertaining, amusing*

Newly introduced kanji:

日本語(にほんご) Ⓑ・文(ぶん)・作文(さくぶん)・文(ぶん)ぽう (文法(ぶんぽう))・文学(ぶんがく)

語	丶 亠 亖 言 言 言 言 訂 訐 語 語 語 語 語	文	丶 亠 ナ 文

ぶんぽう
Verb?
adjective?
-は?
-が?

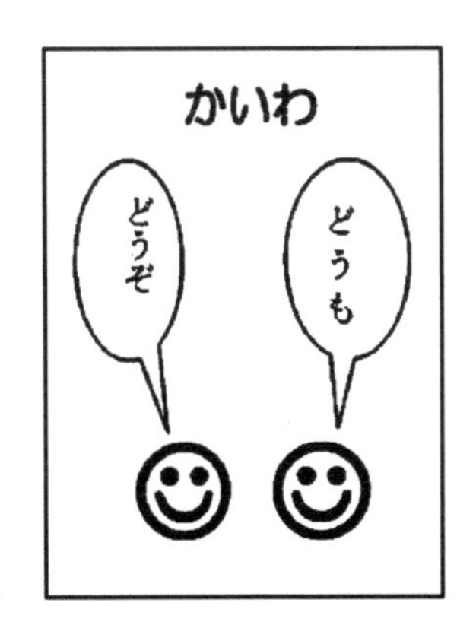

Dialog

Yoko Yamada asks John Smith how he finds the Japanese language.

山田　：日本語のはつおんはむずかしいですか。

スミス　：いいえ、あまりむずかしくありません。まあまあかんたんです。

山田　：文ぽうはかんたんですか。

スミス　：いいえ、文ぽうはあまりかんたんじゃありません。ちょっと、むずかしいです。

山田　：かいわは。

スミス　：かいわはたのしいです。

Guess and Try 1

Fill in the blanks. 3

1. むずかしいですか。
—いいえ、＿＿＿＿＿＿＿＿＿＿ません。

2. かんたんですか。
—いいえ、＿＿＿＿＿＿＿＿＿＿ません。

3. いいですか。
—いいえ、＿＿＿＿＿＿＿＿＿＿ません。

Guess and Try 2

Choose the appropriate options in the parentheses. 8

1. ちゅうごく語はぜんぜん(むずかしいです・むずかしくありません)。

2. えい語はとても(むずかしいです・むずかしくありません)。

3. フランス語はちょっと(むずかしいです・むずかしくありません)。

Drill 1: Mini-Conversation

たのしいですか ⟶ あまりたのしくありません

1. むずかしいですか
2. かんたんですか
3. おもしろいですか
4. きれいですか
5. しずかですか
6. 新(あたら)しいですか
7. いいですか

Drill 2: Formation

あまり・たのしいです ⟶ あまりたのしくありません

とても・たのしいです ⟶ とてもたのしいです

1. ぜんぜん・かんたんです
2. ちょっと・むずかしいです
3. まあまあ・おもしろいです
4. あまり・きれいです
5. ぜんぜん・べんりです

Task 1: Survey

Ask two of your classmates how they like Japanese.

Task 2: Survey

Find the students who know foreign languages besides Japanese and ask them about the following: はつおん・ぶんぽう・アクセント・たんご

안녕하세요?

Bonjour!

こんにちは！

你　好！

For example:

A：どの外国語(がいこくご)をしっていますか。
(Which foreign language(s) do you know?)

B：スペイン語(ご)をしっています。

A：スペイン語のはつおんはどうですか。

B：まあまあかんたんです。

Vocabulary Collection (Languages)

中国語(ちゅうごくご) *Chinese*	韓国語(かんこくご) *Korean*
英語(えいご) *English*	フランス語(ご) *French*
スペイン語(ご) *Spanish*	ラテン語(ご) *Latin*
イタリア語(ご) *Italian*	ロシア語(ご) *Russian*

Short Reading

私は今、日本語をとっています。日本語の会話はあまり難(むずか)しくありません。日本語の発音はとても簡単(かんたん)です。日本語のアクセントは英語のアクセントとちょっと違(ちが)います。でも、ぜんぜん難しくありません。漢字は少し難しいです。でも、面白いです。先生はとてもやさしいです。

(〜をとっています *to be taking〜,* アクセント *accent,* 〜と違(ちが)う *to be different from〜,* やさしい *kind*)

Writing

Write what you think about the Japanese language.

– Grammar and Usage –

1 ふるい: Old

ふるい means *old* but it applies only to inanimate objects and may not apply to people and animals.

(a) この車は古いです。
This car is old.

(b) イギリスには古いたてものがたくさんあります。
There are many old buildings in England.

When a person is old, you can say 年がいっています, 高齢です or 年です.

2 どんな: What kind of～ [Question word for a property (prenominal)]

どんな is a question word used for asking the property or the state of things and people. どんな must be used before a noun:

(a) ルームメートはどんな人ですか。
What kind of person is your roommate?

(b) 図書館はどんな建物ですか。
What kind of building is the library?

3 Adjectives (高い, 高価な, etc)

Japanese adjectives are classified into i-type adjectives and na-type adjectives based on their conjugation patterns. When followed by a noun (at a pre-nominal position), i-type adjectives end with い and na-type adjectives end with な. For example, 高い and 高価な both mean *expensive*, but the former is an i-type adjective and the latter is a na-type adjective.

(a) これは高い本です。
This is an expensive book.

(b) これは高価な本です。
This is an expensive book.

The part of the adjective without the inflectional part い and な (for example, 高 and 高価) are called "stems". How adjectives conjugate is summarized in the following table.

		Adjectives in Japanese	
		I-type Adjectives	**Na-type Adjectives**
Pre-nominal Modifier (Before a noun)		Stem + い For example: これは高い本です。	Stem + な For example: これは高価な本です。
Sentence Predicate (At the end of a sentence)	**Affirmative**	Stem + いです For example: これは高いです。	Stem + です For example: これは高価です。
	Negative	Stem + くありません For example: これは高くありません。	Stem + じゃありません* For example: これは高価じゃありません。
	Negative	Stem + くないです For example: これは高くないです。	Stem + じゃないです* For example: これは高価じゃないです。

* じゃ in the negative form can be では (dewa).

Irregular adjectives include 大きい *big*, 小さい *small* and いい *good*. 大きい and 小さい are i-type adjectives, but when used as pre-nominal modifiers, they have additional forms, which are 大きな and 小さな. The negative form of いい is よくありません or よくないです.

4 ～の: One [Pronominal element]

The noun that occurs after an adjective may be replaced by ～の if contextually understood.

(a) 山田さんの本は高い本です。
Mr. Yamada's book is an expensive book.

(b) 山田さんの本は高いのです。
Mr. Yamada's book is an expensive one.

(c) 山田さんの本は高価な本です。
Mr. Yamada's book is an expensive book.

(d) 山田さんの本は高価なのです。
Mr. Yamada's book is an expensive one.

5 どう: How [Question word for a property (predicate)]

どう is a question word used for asking the property or the state of things and people. Unlike どんな, which must occur before a noun, どう must occur as a part of a sentence predicate.

(a) 日本語のクラスはどうですか。
How is the Japanese class?

(b) 仕事はどうですか。
How is the job?

6 それに: Furthermore [Additional fact]

The sentence connective word それに shows that each of the following sentences expresses information additional to the fact expressed by the previous sentence.

(a) この部屋は明るいです。それに、きれいです。
This room is bright. And it is clean.

(b) この部屋は暗いです。それに、きたないです。
This room is dark. And it is dirty.

The two sentences connected by それに must be making the same point in the context. For example, both sentences in (a) state positive characteristics of the room. Similarly, both sentences in (b) state negative characteristics of the room. Accordingly, (c) is inappropriate since the first sentence states a negative characteristic but the second sentence states a positive characteristic:

(c) この部屋は暗いです。それに、きれいです。(✕)
(Inappropriate)

If それに is replaced by でも, (c) becomes appropriate. The same condition applies to the sentence connective word それから, but its effect is observed more strongly with それに than with それから.

7 おじゃまします [When entering someone else's residence]

When entering someone else's house or apartment, say おじゃまします, which literally means *I will disturb you*. When entering someone else's business offices, say しつれいします, which literally means *I will be rude*. These are some of the essential Japanese set phrases for showing respect to others.

8 Degree adverbs (とても, ぜんぜん, まあまあ, etc)

Adverbs such as とても *very much*, まあまあ *more or less*, 少し *slightly*, ちょっと *a little*, あまり *(not) very much* and ぜんぜん *(not) at all* specify the degree of the property expressed by adjectives.

あまり and ぜんぜん must be used with a negative verb (for example, きれいじゃありません).

(a) あまりきれいじゃありません。
It is not very pretty.

(b) ぜんぜんきれいじゃありません。
It is not pretty at all.

(c) あまりきれいです。 (✕)
(Ungrammatical)

+10	とても *very much*
+5	まあまあ *more or less* (少し *slightly,* ちょっと *a little,* あまり *(not) very much)*
0	ぜんぜん *(not) at all*

On the other hand, other adverbs (for example, とても・まあまあ・ちょっと・すこし) are usually used with a verb in the affirmative form. But among them, まあまあ, ちょっと and すこし are further restricted: まあまあ is used only when the speaker's feeling toward the state is favorable, whereas ちょっと and すこし are used when it is unfavorable.

(d) まあまあきれいです。
It is more or less pretty, (and I am happy with it).

(e) ちょっときたないです。
It is slightly dirty, (and I am unhappy with it.)

– Writing –

ⓐ まだれ

广	まだれ *linen, flax*
	Example: 広(ひろ)い *spacious; wide,* 店(みせ) *store,* ～度(ど) *counter for occasions, degree*

ⓑ ごんべん

言	ごんべん *word, speech, expression*
	Example: 話(はな)す *to speak,* 読(よ)む *to read,* ～語(ご) *language,* 説(と)く *to explain*

– Kanji List –

大きい・小さい・新しい・古い・明るい・暗い・広い・近い・日本語・文・作文・文ぽう・文学

Kanji	Readings / Meaning	Stroke order	Strokes	Example
大	おお-きい・ダイ・タイ *big, great*	一 ナ 大	[3]	大(おお)きい *big*; 大学(だいがく) *a university*
小	ちい-さい・こ・お・ショウ *small, little*	亅 小 小	[3]	小(ちい)さい *small*
新	あたら-しい・シン *new*	丶 亠 亠 立 立 辛 辛 亲 亲 新 新 新 新	[13]	新(あたら)しい *new*
古	ふる-い・コ *old*	一 十 十 古 古	[5]	古(ふる)い *old*
明	あか-るい・あ-ける・メイ *bright, light*	丨 冂 日 日 日) 明 明 明	[8]	明(あか)るい *bright*; 明日(あした) *tomorrow*
暗	くら-い・アン *dark*	丨 冂 日 日 日' 日亠 日立 日立 暗 暗 暗 暗 暗	[13]	暗(くら)い *dark*
広	ひろ-い・コウ *wide, spacious*	丶 亠 广 広 広	[5]	広(ひろ)い *spacious*
近	ちか-い・キン *near, recent*	ノ 厂 斤 斤 斤 近 近	[7]	近(ちか)い *close, near*; 近(ちか)く *vicinity*
日	ひ・び・ニチ・ニ・ジツ *sun, day*	丨 冂 日 日	[4]	日本(にほん) *Japan*; 月曜日(げつようび) *Monday*
本	もと・ホン *root, origin, true, main*	一 十 才 木 本	[5]	本(ほん) *book*; 日本(にほん) *Japan*
語	かた-る・ゴ *word, language*	丶 亠 亠 亠 言 言 言 訂 訂 語 語 語 語 語	[14]	日本語(にほんご) *Japanese language*

	゛ 亠 ナ 文 [4]
ブン・モン・(ふみ) *pattern, letter, sentence*	Example: 文(ぶん) *a sentence,* 文法(ぶんぽう) *grammar,* 作文(さくぶん) *composition,* 文学(ぶんがく) *literature*

– Review –

Q1. Fill in the blanks.

1.

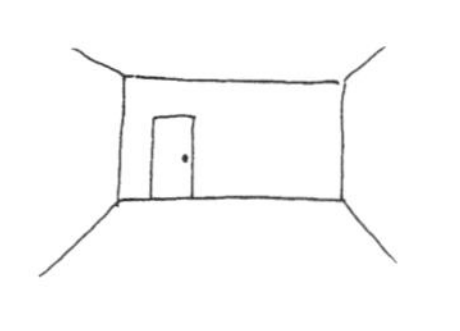

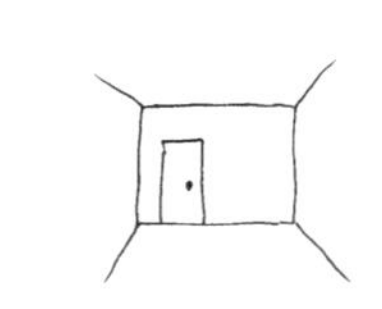

__________ へや　__________ へや

2.

__________ たてもの　__________ たてもの

3.

__________ ぼうし　__________ ぼうし

4.

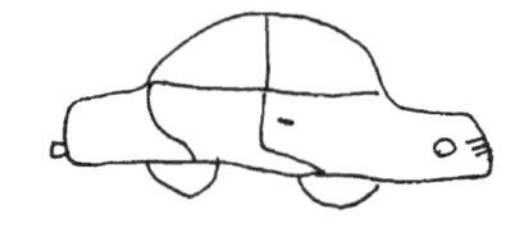

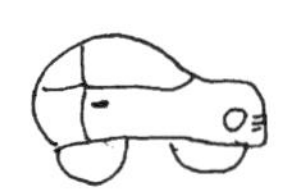

__________ 車　__________ 車

Q2. Write the pronounciation of the underlined kanji in hiragana.

1. たいいくかんは広いです。それに、新しいです。でも、としょかんは古いです。

2. 大きいじしょは高いです。でも、小さいじしょは安いです。

3. 私のへやは明るいです。でも、兄のへやはちょっと暗いです。

Q3. Match the words that have the opposite meaning.

1. きれいです	a. せまいです
2. 新しいです	b. ひくいです
3. べんりです	c. きたないです
4. 明るいです	d. 暗いです
5. しずかです	e. 古いです
6. 広いです	f. ふべんです
7. 高いです	g. うるさいです

Q4. Fill in the blanks appropriately.

1. このへやは広いです。でも、ちょっと __________ です。

2. 私の車は大きいです。それに、とても __________ 。

3. 日本ごはちょっとむずかしいです。でも、とても __________ 。

4. 日本ごのしけんはぜんぜん __________ 。

5. 私のへやはとても明るいです。でも、弟のへやはあまり __________ 。

6. 私のアパートは大学から近いです。ですから、とても __________ 。

Tips and Additional Knowledge 1: Gender / Age Sensitive Friendly Addressing Terms for Strangers

In a relatively friendly context, the Japanese address strangers by the age or gender sensitive address terms such as おじいさん *elderly gentlemen* and おばさん *middle-aged woman*. Since these terms reflect how people appear in terms of their age, they must be used very carefully.

Friendly Addressing Terms for Strangers

ぼうや *young boys*	おにいさん *young men*
おじさん *middle-aged men*	おじいさん *elderly men*
おじょうさん *young girls*	おねえさん *young women*
おばさん *middle-aged women*	おばあさん *elderly women*

Tips and Additional Knowledge 2: Blowfish

Blowfish (河豚 (ふぐ)) has been one of the most expensive delicatessens in Japan for a long time. But there is one problem. Its ovary and liver are extremely poisonous, and people could die from eating it. For this reason, only a trained and licensed chef is allowed to prepare and serve blowfish. Blowfish is most commonly served as sashimi (sliced raw fish) or as "nabe" (casserole). Hot sake with roasted blowfish fin in it is delicious. The next time when you go to Japan, try this exquisite cuisine if you can afford it. Don't ever try to save money by cooking it yourself!

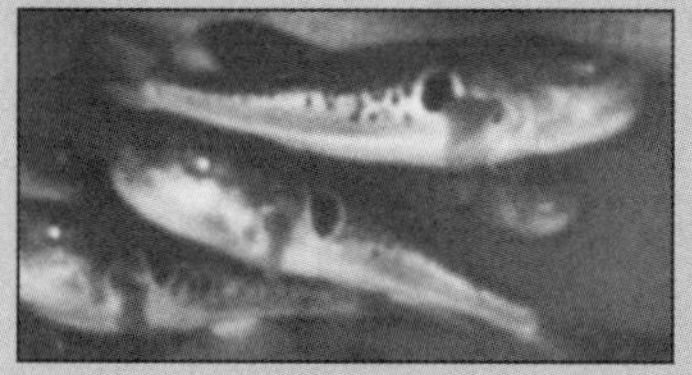

CHAPTER TEN

Requesting

Lesson 40
Te-forms 146

Lesson 41
テープをかして下さい **Request** 148

Lesson 42
もう少しきれいに書いて下さい **Manners** 150

Lesson 43
この道をまっすぐ行って下さい **Giving Directions** 152

Grammar and Usage 154

1 The te-form of verbs (〜て / で) 154
2 もっていく, もってくる: To take / to bring 154
3 しつれいします [Entering and leaving someone else's office] 154
4 〜てください (ませんか): Please do〜, could you do〜 [Requesting] 155
5 〜ましょうか: Shall we〜 ?, shall I〜 ? [Making a suggestion / offering help] 155
6 はやい: Early / fast 155
7 Verbs for learning (ならう, まなぶ, べんきょうする, etc) 155
8 Adverbs derived from adjectives (〜く and 〜に) 155
9 〜くする, 〜にする: To make something〜 / to make oneself〜 [Change] 156
10 いいです: Good / no, thank you 156
11 そうすると: Then [Subsequent fact] 156
12 X という Y: Y called X [Introducing a new item with its proper name] 156
13 〜め: 〜th [Creating ordinal numbers] 157
14 〜を [Direct object marker: the domain of movement] 157

Culture 157

A こうばん: Police boxes 157

Kanji List 157

Review 158

Tips and Additional Knowledge: Handling Money 160

Te-forms

Notes Relating to This Lesson	
Grammar and Usage 1 The te-form of verbs 154	

Basic Vocabulary and Kanji

いう	*w*-**u** 言う・言わない・言い・言って	*vt. to say* (こたえを言う *to say the answer)*
はな˥す	*s*-**u** 話す・話さない・話し・話して	*vt. to tell, to talk* (ともだちと話す *to talk with one's friend)*
きく	*k*-**u** 聞く・聞かない・聞き・聞いて	*vt. to listen, to inquire, to ask* (おんがくをきく *to listen to the music)* (先生にきく *to ask the teacher)*

Newly introduced kanji:

言う・話す・読む・聞く

言	' 亠 亠 亖 言 言 言	話	' 亠 亠 亖 言 言 言 言' 言' 許 許 話 話
読	' 亠 亠 亖 言 言 言 言 訁 訁 訁 読 読 読		
聞	丨 ㄗ ㄗ ㄗ ㄗ 門 門 門 門 門 門 門 門 聞		

Verbs must be in the te-form when followed by another verb or by a certain suffix. Te-forms all end in て or で, as shown in the following tables.

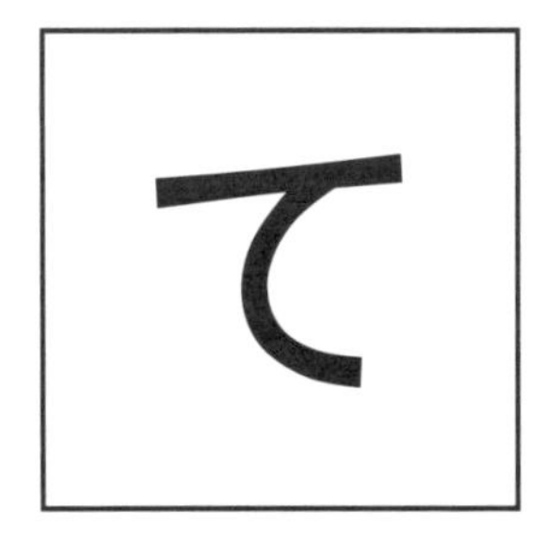

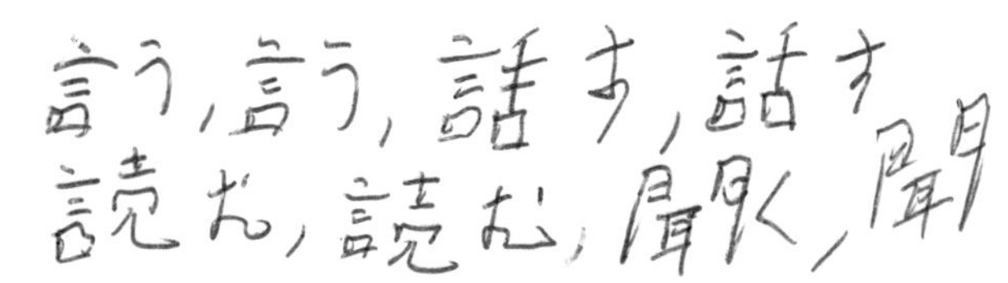

Verb Classes	Patterns	Examples
Irregular verbs	Stem + て	来る → 来て する → して
Ru-verbs	～る → ～て (or Stem + て)	食べる → 食べて 見る → ①________
U-verbs	～す → ～して (or Stem + て)	話す → 話して だす → だして かす → ②________
	～く → ～いて ～ぐ → ～いで	書く → 書いて 歩く → 歩いて およぐ → およいで 聞く → ③________ とぐ → ④________ *行く → 行って (Irregular)
	～む ～ぬ → ～んで ～ぶ	読む → 読んで しぬ → しんで あそぶ → あそんで はこぶ → ⑤________ 飲む → ⑥________
	～う ～る → ～って ～つ	買う → 買って とる → とって 帰る → 帰って かつ → かって 使う → ⑦________ 作る → ⑧________ たつ → ⑨________

Guess and Try

Fill in the blanks in the above table. Do not worry about the meaning of the verbs. 1

Drill 1: Conjugation

食べる → 食べて

Repeat each of the following several times.

～る・～す → stem + て

1. 見る
2. 食べる
3. 来る
4. ねる
5. する
6. 話す

～く・～ぐ → ～いて・～いで

1. 書く
2. およぐ
3. 歩く
4. 聞く
5. 行く*

～む・～ぬ・～ぶ → ～んで

1. 読む
2. 飲む
3. しぬ *to die*
4. あそぶ *to play*
5. やすむ *to rest*

～う・～る・～つ → ～って

1. 買う
2. 使う
3. 作る
4. 帰る
5. たつ *to stand up*

Drill 2: Conjugation

食べる → 食べて

1. ねる
2. 書く
3. 読む
4. およぐ
5. 行く
6. 帰る
7. 買う
8. 作る
9. 使う
10. 来る
11. する
12. 飲む

Writing

Write the te-forms of the following verbs several times each.

食(た)べる	食べて	食べて	食べて
飲(の)む	飲んで	飲んで	飲んで
書(か)く	書いて	書いて	書いて
聞(き)く	聞いて	聞いて	聞いて
読(よ)む	読んで	読んで	読んで
見(み)る	見て	見て	見て
作(つく)る	作って	作って	作って
使(つか)う	使って	使って	使って
買(か)う	買って	買って	買って
言(い)う	言って	言って	言って
する	して	して	して
勉強(べんきょう)する	勉強して	勉強して	勉強して
帰(かえ)る	帰って	帰って	帰って
行(い)く	行って	行って	行って
来(く)る	来て	来て	来て

テープをかして下さい Request

Notes Relating to This Lesson	
Grammar and Usage	
2 もっていく, もってくる 154	4 ～てください (ませんか) 155
3 しつれいします 154	5 ～ましょうか 155

Basic Vocabulary and Kanji

あつめ˥る	*e*-**ru** 集める・集めない・集め・集めて	*vt. to collect*
かす	*s*-**u** 貸す・貸さない・貸し・貸して	*vt. to loan, to lend*
すわる	*r*-**u** 座る・座らない・座り・座って	*vi. to sit (いすにすわる sit on the chair)*
た˥つ	*t*-**u** 立つ・立たない・立ち・立って	*vi. to stand up*
だ˥す	*s*-**u** 出す・出さない・出し・出して	*vt. to hand in, to take out (しゅくだいを出す to hand in one's homework)*
なくす	*s*-**u** なくす・なくさない・なくし・なくして	*vt. to lose (さいふをなくす to lose one's purse)*
は˥いる	*r*-**u** 入る・入らない・入り・入って	*vi. to enter (へやに入る to enter the room)*
みせ˥る	*e*-**ru** 見せる・見せない・見せ・見せて	*vt. to show*
おねがいする	*irr.* お願いする	*vt. to ask a favor of someone*
もってく˥る	持って来る	*to bring (something) (here)* 2
もっていく	持って行く	*to take (something) (there)* 2
しつれいします	失礼します	*I'll come in / I'll leave* 3 *(lit. I will be rude)*
(～て)ください	(～て) 下さい	*please do~* 4

Newly introduced kanji:

下(くだ)さい・立(た)つ・出(だ)す・入(はい)る・見(み)せる

立	丶 亠 亣 立 立	出	丨 屮 屮 出 出
入	ノ 入		

Dialog 1

A student, Emily Wong, comes to her teacher's office to borrow the audio tape for the textbook.

先生　：ああ、ワンさん、入って下さい。

学生　：はい。しつれいします
(Ms. Wong enters the room.)
先生(せんせい)、テープをかして下さいませんか。

先生　：はい。どうぞ。

学生　：どうもありがとうございます。

先生　：なくさないで下さいね。

学生　：はい。じゃあ、しつれいします。また、クラスで。
(Ms. Wong closes the door.)

Guess and Try 1

How do you ask someone to eat? How do you ask someone not to eat? 4

to eat　: ______________________

not to eat　: ______________________

Guess and Try 2

What is the difference between かして下さいませんか and かして下さい. 4

Guess and Try 3

When do they say しつれいします? 3

Dialog 2

Your teacher is about to collect homework in the classroom.

先生　：じゃあ、しゅくだいを出して下さい。

学生　：先生、私があつめましょうか。

先生　：じゃあ、おねがいします。

学生　：はい。

Guess and Try 4

What would you say when you want to clean (そうじする) a room for someone? 5

Drill 1: Conjugation

食べる ⟶ 食べて

1. 見る
2. 見せる
3. 勉強(べんきょう)する
4. かす
5. あつめる
6. 出す
7. もって行く
8. もって来る
9. 書く
10. およぐ
11. 読(よ)む
12. 入る
13. すわる
14. 立つ

Drill 2: Formation

Variation 1:

ここでねる ⟶ ここでねて下さい

Variation 2:

ここでねる ⟶ ここでねないで下さい

1. てがみを見せる
2. へやに入る
3. いすにすわる
4. ここに立つ
5. じしょをもって来る

Task 1: Pair Work

Ask your partner to perform the following. Take turns.

1. 左を見る
2. うしろを見る
3. こくばん *(chalkboard)* を見る
4. ノートを見せる
5. 立つ
6. すわる

Task 2: Roll Play / Skit

S1:

You are about to enter the Japanese teacher's office to ask him / her something.

S2:

You are a Japanese language teacher, and one of your students is about to visit you at your office.

Writing

Write the te-forms of the verbs listed in Drill 1.

あつめて, あつめて, かして, かして
すわって, すわって, 立って, 立って
出して, 出して, なくてて, なくして
入って, 入って, 見せて, 見せて
おねがいして, おねがいして
もって来て, もって来て, もって行って
もって行って, しつれいします,
しつれいします

もう少しきれいに書いて下さい Manners

Notes Relating to This Lesson

Grammar and Usage	
6 はやい 155	8 Adverbs derived from adjectives 155
7 Verbs for learning 155	9 〜くする, 〜にする ..156
	10 いいです 156

Basic Vocabulary and Kanji

おと˥	音	*n. sound, volume*
ねだん	値段	*n. price*
きびし˥い	厳しい・厳しくない	*adj. strict*
はや˥い	早い・早くない	*adj. early* 6
はや˥い	速い・速くない	*adj. fast, speedy* 6
やさしい	優しい・優しくない	*adj. kind, nice*
まじめ(な)	真面目だ・真面目じゃない	*adj. studious, serious, honest*
れんしゅう(を)する	*irr.* 練習(を)する	*vt. / vi. to practice*
ふくしゅう(を)する	*irr.* 復習(を)する	*vt. / vi. to review*
なら˥う	*w-u* 習う・習わない・習い・習って	*vt. to learn* 7
もうすこ˥し	もう少し	*adv. a little more*

Newly introduced kanji:

早(はや)い・速(はや)い・習(なら)う・れん習(しゅう)・ふく習(しゅう)

早	㇑ 冂 日 日 旦 早	速	一 ㇐ ㇐ ㇐ 申 束 束 㔾束 涑 速
習	㇕ ㇕ ㇕ 羽 羽 羽 羽 翌 習 習 習		

Dialog 1

In the Japanese classroom.

先生　：ジョンさん、カタカナで名前(なまえ)を書(か)いて下(くだ)さい。

ジョン：はい。
(John writes his name on the whiteboard.)

先生　：もう少(すこ)し大(おお)きく書いて下さい。

ジョン：はい。
(John writes it bigger.)

先生　：あのう、もう少しきれいに書いて下さい。

ジョン：ああ、すみません。

Guess and Try 1

Using the given words, complete the sentences and interpret them. 8

1. 速い: すみません。もう少し ＿＿＿＿＿＿ 歩(ある)いて下さい。
2. しずか(な): すみません。もう少し ＿＿＿＿＿＿ 食(た)べて下さい。
3. いい: もう少し ＿＿＿＿＿＿ ふく習して下さい。

Dialog 2

At the store.

きゃく　：ちょっと高(たか)いですね。①もう少(すこ)しねだんを安(やす)くして下(くだ)さい。

てんいん：ちょっと… それは…

きゃく　：②じゃあ、いいです。

Guess and Try 2

Guess what the underlined part ① in the above dialog means, and interpret the following sentences. 9

1. ラジオのおとをもう少し小(ちい)さくして下さい。
2. もう少しへやをきれいにして下さい。
3. もう少しやさしくして下さい。
4. もう少しまじめにして下さい。

Guess and Try 3

What does the underlined part ② in the dialog mean? 10

Drill 1: Formation

大きいです ⟶ 大きく(します)
しずかです ⟶ しずかに(します)

1. やさしいです
2. きびしいです
3. きれいです
4. いいです
5. 速いです
6. 早いです
7. 安いです
8. 高いです
9. まじめです

Drill 2: Formation

大きいです・書いて下さい ⟶ 大きく書いて下さい

1. きれいです・書いて下さい
2. きれいです・して下さい
3. 速いです・歩(ある)いて下さい
4. 早いです・来て下さい
5. いいです・れん習して下さい
6. やさしいです・話(はな)して下さい
7. やさしいです・して下さい
8. まじめです・して下さい

Task 1: Classroom Activity

Your teacher draws someone's face on a big sheet of paper and shows it to all of you except one. The student who does not see it draws the face on the board, just by guessing. Then other students give suggestions like, もう少(すこ)し目(め)を大(おお)きくして下(くだ)さい, so that he / she can make his / her drawing closer to the teacher's drawing. Give at most five suggestions.

Vocabulary Collection	
長(なが)い *long*	短(みじか)い *short*
大(おお)きい *big*	小(ちい)さい *small*
広(ひろ)い *wide*	狭(せま)い *narrow, small*
細(ほそ)い *skinny, thin*	太(ふと)い *thick*
丸(まる)い *round*	

Task 2: Roll Play / Skit

S1:
You have many complaints with your roommate, and you have decided to discuss the problems with him / her. You want to make specific requests politely, but firmly.

S2:
Your roommate complains about how you use the room, but you do not completely agree with him / her.

For example:

S1: もう少(すこ)しキッチンをきれいに使(つか)って下(くだ)さいませんか。

S2: はい、わかりました。/いいえ、それはちょっと。

Short Reading

<先生(せんせい)へのお願(ねが)い>

もう少(すこ)しゆっくり話(はな)して下(くだ)さい。それから、試験(しけん)の問題(もんだい)を少(すく)なくして下さい。それから、黒板(こくばん)の字(じ)をきれいにして下さい。

(お願(ねが)い *request,* 試験(しけん) *test,* 少(すく)ない *few,* 問題(もんだい) *question; problem,* 黒板(こくばん) *blackboard,* 字(じ) *characters*)

Writing

Write your requests to your teacher.

おも, よそ, ねだん, ねだん, きびしい, きびしい, 早い, 早い, 速い, 速い, やさしい, やさしい, まじめな, まじめな, れん習, れん習, ふく習, ふく習, 習う, 習う, 習う, も少し, もう少し

この道をまっすぐ行って下さい Giving Directions

Notes Relating to This Lesson	
Grammar and Usage	
11 そうすると 156	14 〜を 157
12 X という Y 156	**Culture**
13 〜め 157	A こうばん 157

Basic Vocabulary and Kanji

か⌉ど	角	*n. corner*
はし⌉	橋	*n. bridge*
みち	道	*n. street, road*
つきあたり	突き当たり	*n. dead-end*
まがる	***r*-u** 曲がる・曲がらない・曲がり・曲がって	*vt. to make a turn*
わたる	***r*-u** 渡る・渡らない・渡り・渡って	*vt. to cross, to cross over*
すぎ⌉る	***i*-ru** 過ぎる・過ぎない・過ぎ・過ぎて	*vt. to pass*
まっす⌉ぐ		*adv. straight*
そうすると		*if (you do) so, in that case* 11
〜という		*called~* 12
〜め	〜目	*c. a counter for ordinal numbers (一つ目 the first)* 13

Newly introduced kanji:

道・曲がる・東 (east)・西 (west)・南 (south)・北 (north)

道	丶丷䒑丷产䒑首首首首道道	曲	丨冂巾巾曲曲
東	一丆戸戸百申東東	西	一丆丙丙两西
南	一十冂冂冂冂両南南	北	丨丬丬北北

Dialog

Ben Lee is looking for a restaurant called "Bluebird". He asks a woman where it is on the street.

リー　：すみません。<u>ブルーバードというレストラン</u>をしっていますか。
(〜を知っていますか *Do you know~?*)

女の人：はい。

リー　：どこにありますか。

女の人：この道をまっすぐ行って下さい。それから、三つ目のかどを右に曲がって下さい。そうすると、つきあたりにあります。

リー　：ああ、そうですか。どうも。

女の人：いいえ。

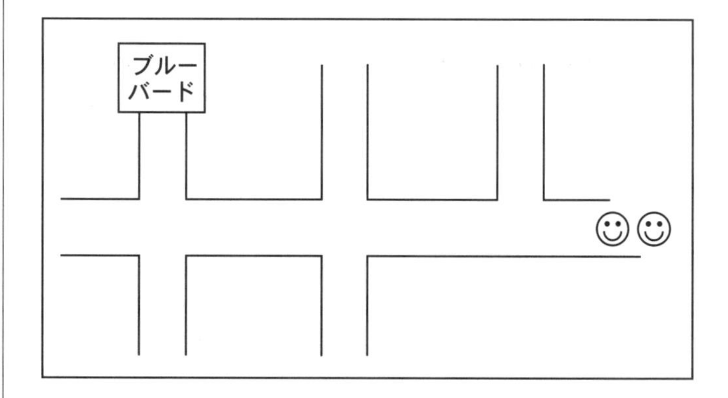

Guess and Try 1

What does the underlined part mean? 12

Guess and Try 2

Fill in the blanks with appropriate particles and interpret the sentences. 14

1. あのこうさてん＿＿右＿＿曲がって下さい。
2. この道＿＿北＿＿行って下さい。
3. あのこうさてん＿＿わたって下さい。
4. このはし＿＿わたって下さい。
5. ゆうびんきょく＿＿すぎて下さい。

Guess and Try 3

Choose the appropriate options in the parentheses. 11

1. あのこうさてんを右に曲がってください。(そうすると・それから)、左にぎんこうがあります。
2. あのこうさてんを右に曲がってください。(そうすると・それから)、まっすぐ行って下さい。

Drill: Formation

三番通り・東・行く ⟶ 三番通りを東に行って下さい

1. この道・南・行く
2. あのこうさてん・左・曲がる
3. あのこうさてん・わたる
4. このはし・わたる
5. ぎんこう・すぎる

Task 1: Classroom Activity

Pretend that there are streets and intersections in the classroom. One student gives the directions to another student's seat in the class (for example, まっすぐ行って下さい, かどを曲がって下さい, はしをわたって下さい and ぎんこうをすぎて下さい) without telling whose seat it is. The rest of the students guess whose seat the destination is. Take turns.

Task 2: Classroom Activity

Imagine that you are at ☺ in the following map. Complete the directions that follow.

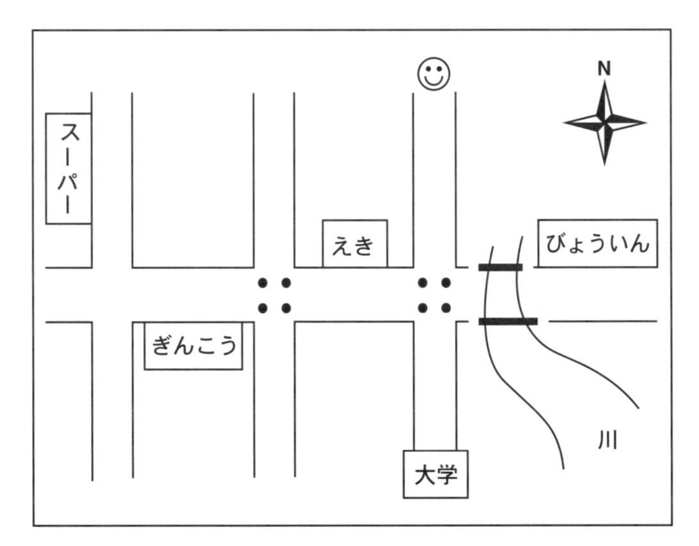

1. この道をまっすぐ行って下さい。そうすると、つきあたりに ________ があります。
2. この道をまっすぐ行って下さい。それから、一つ目のこうさてんを右に曲がって下さい。そうすると、右に ________ があります。
3. この道をまっすぐ行って下さい。それから、一つ目のこうさてんを左に曲がって下さい。そうすると、はしがあります。そのはしをわたって下さい。びょういんは ________ にあります。

Task 3: Pair Work

Name the following places as you like and mark their locations randomly on the map in Task 2, then tell your partner where they are without showing your map.

1. Your favorite fast food restaurant.
2. Your favorite movie theater.
3. Your favorite bookstore.

Short Reading Ⓐ

日本は安全な国で有名です。日本には交番がたくさんあります。交番にはいつも警察官が一人か二人います。交番の警察官はよく自転車で町の中を見回ります。

(安全(な) *safe,* 〜で有名です *to be famous as / for〜,* 交番 *police box,* 警察官 *police officer,* A か B *A or B,* 町 *town,* 見回る *to patrol*)

Writing

Write the directions to your house from the school, or to your dorm from the class.

– Grammar and Usage –

1 The te-form of verbs (〜て / で)

Verbs must be in the te-form when followed by another verb or by an auxiliary verb in a sentence. All the te-forms end in either て or で, but depending on the type of verbs, how to form a te-form differs.

1. For the major irregular verbs, する and くる, all the **ru**-verbs and the **u**-verbs that end in す, just add て to their stem forms.

   For example: する → して, くる → きて,
   たべる → たべて, はなす → はなして

2. For **u**-verbs that end in く or ぐ, replace these endings with いて and いで, respectively.

   For example: かく → かいて, およぐ → およいで

3. For **u**-verbs that end in む, ぬ or ぶ, replace these endings with んで.

   For example: のむ → のんで, しぬ → しんで,
   あそぶ → あそんで

4. For **u**-verbs that end in う, る or つ, replace these endings with って.

   For example: かう → かって, とる → とって,
   かつ → かって

5. The only exception is the verb 行く, whose te-form is 行って, rather than 行いて.

Verb Class	Pattern	Examples
Irregular verbs	Stem + て	来る → 来て する → して
Ru-verbs	〜る → 〜て (or Stem + て)	食べる → 食べて 見る → 見て
U-verbs	〜す → 〜して (or Stem + て)	話す → 話して だす → だして かす → かして
U-verbs	〜く → いて 〜ぐ → いで	書く → 書いて 歩く → 歩いて およぐ → およいで 聞く → 聞いて とぐ → といで *行く → 行って (Irregular)
	〜む 〜ぬ → 〜んで 〜ぶ	読む → 読んで しぬ → しんで あそぶ → あそんで はこぶ → はこんで 飲む → 飲んで
	〜う 〜る → 〜って 〜つ	買う → 買って とる → とって 帰る → 帰って かつ → かって 使う → 使って 作る → 作って たつ → たって

2 もっていく, もってくる: To take / to bring

The action to bring something is expressed by a complex phrase composed of the verb もつ *to hold* in the te-form (もって) and a motion verb such as 行く *to go*, 来る *to come* and 帰る (to return).

(a) ジョンは本をもって行きました。
John took a book (there).

(b) ジョンは本をもって来ました。
John brought a book (here).

(c) ジョンは本をもって帰りました。
John took a book home.

3 しつれいします [Entering and leaving someone else's office]

しつれいします literally means *(I) will be rude*, but it is a formal expression used when one enters or leaves someone else's business offices and possibly houses and rooms. Slightly less formal expressions are おじゃまします *I will disturb you* and おじゃましました *I have disturbed you*; the former is used when one enters someone else's room or house, and the latter is used when one leaves it. When you use these expressions, do not forget to bow to the person.

4 〜てください(ませんか): Please do〜, could you do〜 [Requesting]

For requesting a service of other people, add 下さい at the end of the verb in the te-form. 下さい literally means *to give (it to me please)* and the combination of a verb in the te-form and 下さい means *Do~ and give me that (as a service)* or *(Please) do~*.

(a) これを食べて下さい。
Please eat this.

(b) ここに来て下さい。
Please come here.

(c) 静かにして下さい。
Please be quiet.

To ask someone not to do something, use the plain present negative form plus で and 下さい:

(d) これを食べないで下さい。
Please do not eat this.

(e) ここに来ないで下さい。
Please do not come here.

(f) うるさくしないで下さい。
Please don't make a noise.

For making your request very polite, add ませんか to this form and say it with a rising intonation.

(g) これを食べて下さいませんか。
Would you please eat this?

(h) これを食べないで下さいませんか。
Would you please not eat this?

(i) この手紙を読んで下さいませんか。
Would you please read this letter?

(j) この手紙を読まないで下さいませんか。
Would you please not read this letter?

5 〜ましょうか: Shall we〜?, shall I〜? [Making a suggestion / offering help]

〜ましょうか follows a verb in the stem form and is used either for making a suggestion or for offering help.

(a) このへやをそうじしましょうか。
Shall I (we) clean this room?

(b) コーヒーを飲みましょうか。
Shall we drink coffee?

(c) テレビを見ましょうか。
Shall we watch TV?

(d) これをコピーしましょうか。
Shall I (we) make a copy of this?

6 はやい: Early / fast

早い and 速い are homonyms, and their meanings are both related to time. But 早い is about the timing *early* and 速い is about the speed *fast*.

(a) 早く起きました。
I woke up early.

(b) 速く走ります。
I run fast.

7 Verbs for learning (ならう, まなぶ, べんきょうする, etc)

The verbs 習う, 勉強する and 学ぶ all mean *to study* or *to learn*, but they are used differently. 習う is used for non-academic skills such as karate, piano, swimming and flower arranging. 勉強する is used for academic subjects in science and humanities. Languages can be studied as academic subjects or can be learned as skills, and thus they can be used with either 習う or 勉強する. The verb 学ぶ is used not only for academic and non-academic matters, but also for philosophical, moral and religious matters. Unlike 習う and 勉強する, 学ぶ emphasizes the learner's modest attitude and deep respect toward the field in which he is learning.

8 Adverbs derived from adjectives (〜く and 〜に)

Adjectives describe the property and the state of things and people, whereas adverbs describe the manner of actions. We can create adverbs from adjectives by adding に and く to the stem of a na-type adjective and the stem of an i-type adjective, respectively.

(a) すみません。もう少ししずかに食べて下さい。
Excuse me, please eat a little more quietly.

(b) まじめに勉強して下さい。
Please study seriously.

(c) 早く帰って下さい。
Please come home early.

(d) 速く話せません。
I cannot speak fast.

(e) もう7時ですよ。早くおきて下さい。
It's already 7 o'clock. Wake up quickly.

(f) ちがいますよ。よく見(み)て下さい。
It is wrong. Look at it carefully.

	Prenominal Form	Adverbs
I-type adjective	うまい *skillful*	うまく *skillfully*
Na-type adjective	しずか(な) *quiet*	しずかに *quietly*
Irregular	いい *good*	よく *well*

9 〜くする, 〜にする: To make something〜 / to make oneself〜 [Change]

When the verb する is used with an adverb, it means *to change the state of something in a specified way*. For example, へやをきれいにする means *to make the room clean*.

(a) 私は髪(かみ)を短(みじか)くしました。
I made my hair short.

(b) 私は成績(せいせき)をよくします。
I will make my grades better.

(c) うるさいですよ。ラジオの音(おと)を小(ちい)さくして下(くだ)さい。
It is noisy. Turn down the volume of the radio.

The item that changes (the direct object) is often unspoken if understood in the context.

(d) 安(やす)くして下さい。
Make (the price) cheaper.

(e) やさしくします。
(I) will make (myself) kind / (I) will be kind.

(f) 学生(がくせい)にやさしくして下さい。
Please be kind to the students.

(g) まじめにします。
(I) will make myself serious / (I) will be serious.

(h) しずかにして下さい。
(Please) make (yourself) quiet / Please be quiet.

10 いいです: Good / no, thank you

いいです and 結構(けっこう)です literally mean *good*, but they may mean *no, thank you* in some contexts.

(a) ビールを飲(の)みませんか。
Would you like to drink beer?
— いいえ、いいです / いいえ、結構(けっこう)です。
— *No, thank you.*

(b) おつりはいいです / おつりは結構(けっこう)です。
(I) do not need the change. / Keep the change.

結構(けっこう)です is more formal than いいです. It is important to use these expressions with a hesitant intonation and facial expression if you mean *no, thank you*.

11 そうすると: Then [Subsequent fact]

The word そうすると connects two sentences that express the preceding and the following events or situations. When the sentence is in the present tense, そうすると introduces an automatic consequence of the event expressed by the previous sentence.

(a) あの交差点(こうさてん)を右(みぎ)に曲(ま)がって下さい。そうすると、銀行(ぎんこう)があります。
Please make a right turn at that intersection. Then, you will see a bank.

In this case, the sentence that follows そうすると should express what one finds or what happens and may not be a command, request or speculation. The following sentence is ungrammatical for this reason.

(b) あの交差点(こうさてん)を右(みぎ)に曲(ま)がって下さい。そうすると、まっすぐ行(い)って下さい。 (✕)
(Ungrammatical)

By contrast, (c) is grammatical:

(c) あの交差点(こうさてん)を右(みぎ)に曲(ま)がって下さい。それから、まっすぐ行(い)って下さい。

12 X という Y: Y called X [Introducing a new item with its proper name]

For introducing a specific item that the listener may have never heard of, make a noun phrase using 〜という. と is the particle that marks a quotation, and いう is the verb *to say*. Using という, combine its proper name and common name. For example, ブルーバードというレストラン means *a restaurant called Bluebird*.

(a) 山田(やまだ)さんという日本人(にほんじん)が来(き)ました。
A Japanese person called Mr. Yamada came.

(b) 北海道という所で勉強しました。
I studied in a place called Hokkaido.

(c) アキタという犬がいます。
There is a breed of dog called Akita.

13 ～め: ～th [Creating ordinal numbers]

You can create ordinal numbers such as *the first, the third and the fourth* just by adding 目 at the end of a quantity phrase such as 一つ, 二つ, 一本 and 三台. When you place an ordinal number before a noun, add the particle の after the ordinal number.

(a) 二つ目のこうさてんを右に曲がって下さい。
Turn right at the second intersection, please.

(b) この車は三台目です。
This car is the third one.

(c) 三本目の道をまっすぐ南に行って下さい。
Please go straight on the third street to the south.

14 ～を [Direct object marker: the domain of movement]

Motion verbs such as 曲がる *to turn* and 行く *to go* are used with a noun that expresses the area or location over which the movement takes place. Mark it with the particle を. For example, この道をまっすぐ行きます means *(I) will go straight on this street.*

(a) 交差点を渡りました。
I crossed the intersection.

(b) 橋を渡りました。
I crossed over the bridge.

(c) 銀行を過ぎました。
I passed the bank.

(d) 階段をのぼりました。
I went up the stairs.

(e) 山をのぼりました。
I climbed up the mountain

(f) 山をこえました。
I went over the mountain.

(g) 空を飛びました。
I flew through the sky.

(h) こうえんを歩きました。
I walked (all over) the park.

(i) 銀座を歩きました。
I walked around in Ginza.

(j) 川を泳ぎました。
I swam along the river.

For specifying the direction of movement such as east, west, right and left, use the particle に.

(k) この道を南にまっすぐ行きます。
I will go straight on this street to the south.

(l) 交差点を右に曲がります。
I will make a right turn at the intersection.

– Culture –

A こうばん: Police boxes

There are many small police buildings called 交番 in most cities and towns in Japan. There are one or two police officers in a 交番, and they patrol the neighborhood to prevent crimes. If you get lost, you can go to a 交番 and ask for help. They are usually open 24 hours a day and have detailed maps.

– Kanji List –

言う・話す・読む・聞く・下さい・立つ・出す・入る・見せる・早い・速い・習う・れん習・ふく習・道・曲がる・東・西・南・北

Kanji	Stroke order / Examples
言	[7]
い-う・ゲン・ゴン *say*	Example: 言う *to say* 言語学 *linguistics*
話	[13]
はな-す・はなし・ワ *talk*	Example: 話す *to speak* 話 *story, talk* 電話 *telephone*
読	[14]
よ-む・ドク *read*	Example: 読む *to read* 読書 *reading*

Kanji	Readings / Meaning	Strokes	Examples
聞	き-く・き-こえる・ブン *to hear, to listen*	[14]	Example: 聞(き)く *to listen* 新聞(しんぶん) *newspaper*
下	した・さ-がる・くだ-る・カ・ゲ *under, down, inferior*	[3]	Example: 下(した) *under* 下手(へた)な *unskillful* 下(くだ)さい *(please) give me*
立	た-つ・た-てる・たち-・リツ *stand, establish*	[5]	Example: 立(た)つ *to stand*
出	で-る・だ-す・シュツ・シュッ *come, go out*	[5]	Example: 出(で)る *to come out* 出(だ)す *to hand in, to take out*
入	はい-る・い-れる・ニュウ *enter, put in*	[2]	Example: 入(はい)る *to enter*
見	み-る・ケン *see, look, view*	[7]	Example: 見(み)る *to look at* 見(み)せる *to show*
早	はや-い・ソウ *early*	[6]	Example: 早(はや)い *early* 早(はや)く *early, soon*
速	はや-い・ソク *speedy*	[10]	Example: 速(はや)い *speedy* 速(はや)く *fast*
習	なら-う・シュウ *practice*	[11]	Example: 習(なら)う *to learn* 復習(ふくしゅう)する *to review*
道	みち・ドウ *street, way*	[12]	Example: 道(みち) *street* 北海道(ほっかいどう) *Hokkaido*
曲	ま-がる・ま-げる・キョク *bend, curve, melody*	[6]	Example: 曲(ま)がる *to make a turn*
東	ひがし・トウ *east*	[8]	Example: 東(ひがし) *east* 東京(とうきょう) *Tokyo*
西	にし・セイ・サイ *west*	[6]	Example: 西(にし) *west*
南	みなみ・ナン *south*	[9]	Example: 南(みなみ) *south*
北	きた・ホク・ホッ *north*	[5]	Example: 北(きた) *north* 北海道(ほっかいどう) *Hokkaido*

– Review –

Q1. Choose the appropriate options in the parentheses.

1. (早く・速く) 歩(ある)いて下さい。
2. どうぞ(入・人)って下さい。
3. あの(道・近)をまっすぐ行って下さい。

Q2. Fill in the blanks appropriately.

1. すみません。ラジオのおとを ＿＿＿＿＿ して下さい。

2. 高いですよ。もう少し ________ して下さい。

3. きたないですよ。もう少し ________ して下さい。

4. もう少し ________ 勉強して下さい。

Q3. Conjugate the following verbs into te-forms.

For example:

たべる ➝ たべて

1. よむ ➝ ________________
2. いう ➝ ________________
3. きく ➝ ________________
4. はなす ➝ ________________
5. みせる ➝ ________________
6. すわる ➝ ________________
7. はいる ➝ ________________
8. かえる *to return* ➝ ________________
9. つくる ➝ ________________
10. とる ➝ ________________
11. する ➝ ________________
12. くる ➝ ________________

Q4. What would you say in the following situations?

1. You want to ask your teacher to loan you his / her dictionary.

2. In the movie theater, a man behind you is making noise. You want to ask him to be quiet.
3. You have found a nice camera at a store, but it is too expensive. You want to ask the clerk to give you a discount.
4. Your teacher is about to collect homework, and you want to help her do it.
5. Your friend offered you a cup of coffee, but you don't feel like drinking it.
6. You are about to enter the teacher's office.
7. You are about to leave the teacher's office.

Tips and Additional Knowledge: Handling Money

In Japan, to open a bank account, one should know that a checking account is usually unavailable for individuals. One should also know that Japanese use a 印鑑(いんかん) (personal seal) for opening a bank account. 印鑑(いんかん), which is also known as a 判子(はんこ), is a horn, wood or stone seal imprinted with the bearer's name, and it's sort of like a signature for a Westerner. You can order a 印鑑(いんかん) at a special store. Each 印鑑(いんかん) is a one-of-a-kind item, and it must be registered at the local government office. You need a 印鑑(いんかん) to authorize all important transactions involving money and personal property, as well as all business contracts. For everyday use, such as for receiving delivered items and sending a business memo or letter, you can use an inexpensive ready-made seal sold at local stationary stores. The following terms are useful for handling your money.

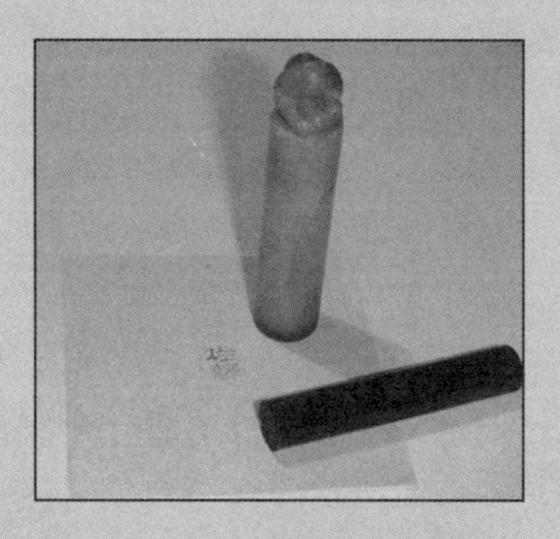

現金(げんきん)(キャッシュ) *cash*	キャッシュ・カード *ATM card*
エー・ティー・エム *ATM*	普通預金口座(ふつうよきんこうざ) *savings account*
トラベラーズ・チェック *travelers check*	両替(りょうがえ) *exchange*
クレジット・カード *credit card*	預金(よきん) *deposit*
引(ひ)き出(だ)し *withdrawal*	利息(りそく) *interest*
定期預金口座(ていきよきんこうざ) *fixed-deposit account / CD*	

CHAPTER ELEVEN

Expressing the Characteristics of People and Things

Lesson 44
かのじょは目がきれいです **Appearance of People** 162

Lesson 45
おみやげは何がいいですか **Souvenir** 164

Lesson 46
何がとくいですか **Skills and Preferences** 166

Lesson 47
カタカナで名前が書けますか **Abilities and Potentials** 168

Lesson 48
何が一ばんほしいですか **Desire** 170

Lesson 49
しょうらいは何をしたいですか **Your Future** 172

Grammar and Usage 174

1. おおい, すくない: Numerous, scarce 174
2. ～は～が～です: As for ～, ～ is ～ 174
3. ～や: And so on, etc [Example-listing] 175
4. ～か: Or [Disjunctive listing] 175
5. こんど: This time / next time 175
6. Skills (とくい (な), にがて (な), etc) 175
7. ～が: But [Conflict / contrast] 176
8. ～の [Noun-maker] 176
9. ～は [Contrast] 176
10. ～(ら) れ: Can do～ [Potential] 176
11. ～ことができる: Can do～ [Potential] 177
12. ほしい: To want something [Desire for items] . . . 177
13. ～たい: To want to do～ [Desire for action] 178
14. Working (はたらく and つとめる) 178
15. それか: Or [Alternative idea] 178

Writing 179

- a. くにがまえ 179
- b. しめすへん 179

Kanji List 179

Review 181

Tips and Additional Knowledge:
Tongue Twisters 182

かのじょは目がきれいです Appearance of People

Notes Relating to This Lesson	
Grammar and Usage 1 おおい, すくない.....174 2 ～は～が～です......174	

Basic Vocabulary and Kanji

か˥のじょ	彼女	*pron.* her, she
か˥れ	彼	*pron.* he, him
かみ˥	髪	*n.* hair of the head
あたま˥	頭	*n.* head
せ˥ / せ˥い	背	*n.* height of people and animals
なが˥い	長い・長くない	*adj.* long (length)
みじか˥い	短い・短くない	*adj.* short (length)
おお˥い	多い・多くない	*adj.* many, a lot 1
すくな˥い	少ない・少なくない	*adj.* scarce, little, few 1

Newly introduced kanji:

口(くち)・目(め)・耳(みみ)・足(あし)・手(て)・背(せ/せい)・長(なが)い・短(みじか)い・多(おお)い・少(すく)ない・少(すこ)し

目	丨 冂 冃 月 目	耳	一 丅 下 F 王 耳
足	' 口 口 早 早 尸 足	手	´ 二 三 手
背	' ｲ ﾇ ﾇ' 北 北 背 背 背	長	丨 「 F F 王 手 手 長
短	´ ㇒ 亠 チ 矢 矢 矢 矢 短 短 短 短	多	ノ ク タ タ 多 多
少	亅 小 小 少		

Dialog

スミス　：川口(かわぐち)さんのガールフレンドはどんな人ですか。

川口　　：やさしい人です。それに、まじめです。

スミス　：きれいですか。

川口　　：まあまあです。かのじょは目がきれいです。スミスさんのガールフレンドは。

スミス　：ぼくはガールフレンドはいませんよ。

Guess and Try 1

Interpret the following sentences. 2

1. 姉(あね)は背が高(たか)いです。
______
2. 妹(いもうと)は背がひくいです。
______
3. 姉はかみが長いです。
______
4. 父(ちち)はかみが少ないです。
______
5. 兄(あに)ははなが高いです。
______
6. 弟(おとうと)ははながひくいです。
______
7. 姉は目が大(おお)きいです。
______
8. 姉は目がきれいです。
______
9. 姉は目がいいです。
______
10. スミスさんはあたまがいいです。
______

Guess and Try 2

What is the difference between the following two sentences? 2

1. ようこさんは目がきれいです。
2. ようこさんの目はきれいです。

Drill: Formation

父・背・高いです ⟶ 父は背が高いです

1. 母・口・小さいです
2. 私・かみ・長いです
3. 兄・足・長いです
4. 妹・背・ひくいです
5. 姉・目・きれいです

Task 1: Classroom Activity

When your teacher reads out a body part, touch that part on yourself.

Task 2: Classroom Activity

Describe the appearance of the following people.

Vocabulary Collection (Body Parts)	
目(め) *eye*	口(くち) *mouth*
耳(みみ) *ears*	鼻(はな) *nose*
額(ひたい)・おでこ *forehead*	顎(あご) *jaw*
頬(ほお) *cheek*	顔(かお) *face*
頭(あたま) *head*	腕(うで) *arm*
手(て) *hand (and arm)*	ひじ *elbow*
足(あし) *foot (and leg)*	膝(ひざ) *knee*
胸(むね) *chest*	背中(せなか) *back*
お腹(なか) *belly, stomach*	腰(こし) *hip*

Task 3: Classroom Activity

Your teacher has a photograph of some people (for example, his / her family members, friends and celebrities). Without showing the photograph to you, he / she describes their faces (for example, 口が大きいです。それから、はながひくいです。それから、…). Listen to his / her description, draw the faces on your notebook, then, look at the photograph and compare it with everyone's drawing. Evaluate whose drawing looks most similar to the photograph.

Task 4: Pair Work

Compliment each other's appearances as much as possible.

For example:

A ：B さんはかみがきれいですね。

B ：いいえ、ぜんぜんきれいじゃありませんよ。
A さんこそかみがきれいですよ。

A ：そうですか。

(～こそ *a emphatic particle*. For example, ～こそ…です *It is~ that is...*)

Short Reading

私の兄は背が高いです。よくテニスをします。ですから、色が少し黒いです。髪は短いです。私の姉は背が低いです。髪が長いです。父はお腹が大きいです。白髪が少しあります。ガールフレンドは髪が長いです。それから、目がとてもきれいです。

(色(いろ) *color; skin complexion,* 黒(くろ)い *black; dark,* お腹(なか) *belly,* 白髪(しらが) *gray hair*)

Writing

Write about the appearance of your parents, siblings, or some of your friends.

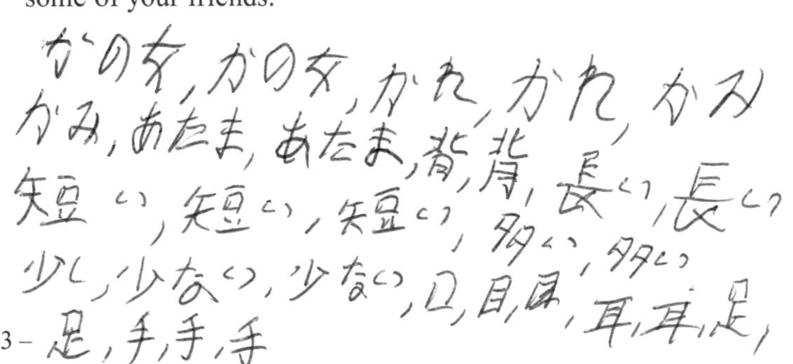

おみやげは何がいいですか Souvenir

Notes Relating to This Lesson	
Grammar and Usage	**Writing**
2 ～は～が～です 174	ⓐ くにがまえ 179
3 ～や 175	
4 ～か 175	

Basic Vocabulary and Kanji

りょこう	旅行	*n. traveling*
たべ˥もの	食べ物	*n. food*
ところ˥	所	*n. place*
もの˥	物	*n. thing, item, object*
おみやげ	お土産	*n. souvenir*
くに	国	*n. country, home country*
ら˥いげつ	来月	*n. next month*
おいし˥い	美味しい・美味しくない	*adj. delicious, tasty*
まず˥い	まずい・まずくない	*adj. not delicious*
にぎ˥やか (な)	にぎやかだ・にぎやかじゃない	*adj. bustling, cheerful, lively, crowded*
もち˥ろん	勿論	*adv. surely, certainly*
～や		*prt. and so on, etc.* 3
～か		*prt. or* (A か B *A or B*) 4

Newly introduced kanji:

国（くに）ⓐ・中国（ちゅうごく） (China)・かん国（こく） (韓国（かんこく） Korea)・来月（らいげつ）・食（た）べもの

国	丨冂冂冂用国国国

にぎやか
もちろん
もちろん
りょこう, りょこう, 食べもの, 食べもの
ところ, ところ, もの, もの, おみやげ, おみやげ
国, 国, 国, 中国, 中国, 来月, 来月
おいしい, おいしい, まずい, まずい, にぎやか

Dialog

Yoshio Tanaka talks with Ann Harvey about traveling.

田中　：アンさんはよくりょこうをしますか。

ハーヴィー：はい。よくオーストラリアやアメリカに行（い）きます。アフリカにも行きます。来月はフランスに行くんですよ。

田中　：ああ、そうですか。フランスは古いたてものがいいですよね。

ハーヴィー：ええ。田中さん、おみやげは何（なに）がいいですか。

田中　：いいんですか。

ハーヴィー：ええ、もちろん。

田中　：じゃあ、ワインかチーズをおねがいします。

Guess and Try 1

Fill in the blanks and interpret the sentences. 2

1. 日本（にほん）は山（やま）＿＿ きれいです。
2. 中国は食べもの＿＿ おいしいです。
3. アメリカはニューヨーク＿＿ にぎやかです。

Guess and Try 2

Interpret the following sentences. 3 4

1. ワインと ビールを飲（の）みます。
2. ワインや ビールを飲みます。
3. ワインか ビールを飲みます。

Drill: Formation

フランス・ちかてつ・べんりです ⟶ フランスはちかてつが べんりです

1. 日本・さかな *fish*・おいしいです
2. ドイツ・ビール・おいしいです
3. イギリス・たてもの・古いです
4. 日本・ホテル・高いです
5. かん国・ソウル・にぎやかです

Task: Classroom Activity

おみやげリスト: Your teacher assigns each student a (possibly different) country. Each student pretends that he / she is going there and starts preparing a list of souvenirs to obtain for his / her classmates. At the end of the activity, share the information in the class. Use the dialog in this lesson as the model.

Your destination: ( )	
1. ________	さん: ________
2. ________	さん: ________
3. ________	さん: ________
4. ________	さん: ________
5. ________	さん: ________
6. ________	さん: ________
7. ________	さん: ________
8. ________	さん: ________
9. ________	さん: ________
10. ________	さん: ________
11. ________	さん: ________
12. ________	さん: ________

Short Reading

香港(ほんこん)はにぎやかです。観光客(かんこうきゃく)がたくさん行きます。店(みせ)がたくさんあります。化粧品(けしょうひん)や、香水(こうすい)が安いです。レストランもたくさんあります。フランスは古い建物が多いです。カフェもたくさんあります。でも、ホテルはちょっと高いです。フランスには私の友達がいます。恵子(けいこ)さんです。恵子さんはパリ大学の学生です。

(観光客(かんこうきゃく) *tourist,* 化粧品(けしょうひん) *cosmetic,* 香水(こうすい) *perfume,* パリ大学(だいがく) *University of Paris*)

Writing

Write about some countries or cities you visited in the past.

何がとくいですか Skills and Preferences

Notes Relating to This Lesson	
Grammar and Usage	
2 ～は～が～です 174	7 ～が 176
5 こんど 175	8 ～の 176
6 Skills 175	9 ～は 176

Basic Vocabulary and Kanji

りょ˥うり	料理	*n. cooking*
ど˥くしょ	読書	*n. reading*
うた˥	歌	*n. song*
お˥んがく	音楽	*n. music*
こ˥んど	今度	*n. next time, this time* 5
すき˥(な)	好きだ・好きじゃない	*adj. to be fond of~, (to like~)*
だ˥いすき(な)	大好きだ・大好きじゃない	*adj. to be extremely fond of~*
きらい(な)	嫌いだ・嫌いじゃない	*adj. hating (to hate~)*
とく˥い(な)	得意だ・得意じゃない	*adj. skillful* 6
にがて(な)	苦手だ・苦手じゃない	*adj. unskillful* 6
じょうず˥(な)	上手だ・上手じゃない	*adj. skillful (to be good at~)* 6
へた˥(な)	下手だ・下手じゃない	*adj. unskillful (to be not good at~)* 6
～が		*con. but* 7

Newly introduced kanji:

読書(どくしょ)・好(す)き・大好(だいす)き・上手(じょうず)・下手(へた)

好	く 女 女 女' 好 好

Dialog

Yoko Yamada asks Kyungtaek Park what he is good at.

山田(やまだ)　：パクさんは何がとくいですか。

パク　：ぼくはうたをうたうのがとくいです。山田さんは。

山田　：私はりょうりがとくいです。

パク　：ああ、そうですか。

山田　：パクさんはりょうりが好きですか。

パク　：ぼくは食べるのは好きですが、りょうりをするのはにがてです。

山田　：そうですか。こんど、いっしょにりょうりをしませんか。

パク　：いいえ、いいです。

Guess and Try 1

Choose the appropriate options in the parentheses. 2

1. 私はりょうり（を・が）きらいです。
2. 兄(あに)はおんがく（を・が）大好きです。

Guess and Try 2

Fill in the blanks appropriately. 7

1. クッキーは好きです＿＿＿、あまり食(た)べません。
2. クッキーは好きです。＿＿＿＿＿、あまり食べません。

Guess and Try 3

Fill in the blanks. 8

1. 私は＿＿＿＿＿が好きです。
   I like reading newspapers.

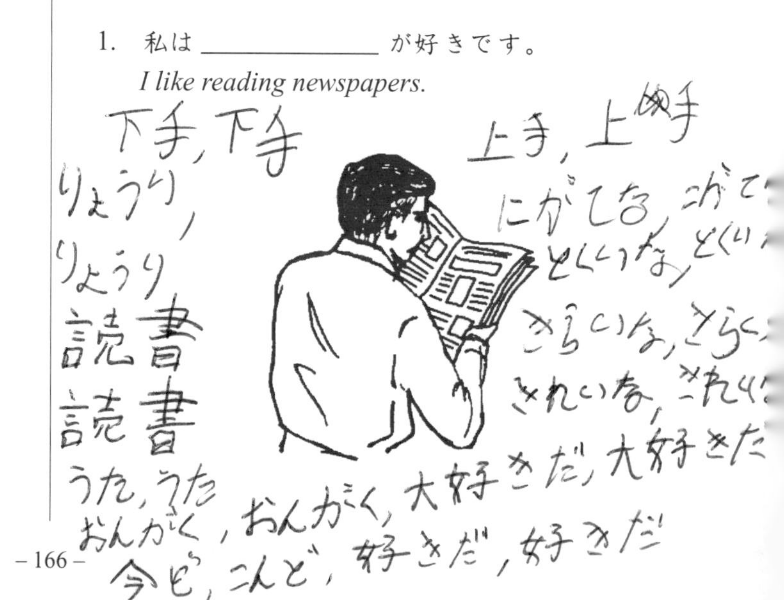

Guess and Try 4

Choose the appropriate options in the parentheses. 9

私は犬 (が・は) 好きですが、ねこ (が・は) 好きじゃありません。

Drill: Formation

テニス・好きです ⟶ テニスが好きです
食べる・好きです ⟶ 食べるのが好きです

1. 読書・好きです
2. じゅうどう・大好きです
3. りょうり・とくいです
4. 作文・にがてです
5. 話す・下手です
6. うたう・上手です

Task: Classroom Activity

Ask each of your classmate what he / she is good at. Use Dialog as the model.

Vocabulary Collection (Skills)	
車を修理する *to fix a car*	
ピアノをひく *to play the piano*	
おどる *to dance*	
コンピューターを使う *to use a computer*	
魚を料理する *to cook fish*	
絵を描く *to draw*	
写真を撮る *to take photographs*	
英語を教える *to teach English*	
書道 *calligraphy*	
そろばん *abacus*	生け花 *flower arranging*
計算 *calculation*	暗算 *mental calculation*
タイプ *typing*	デザイン *designing*

Short Reading

私はよく大学の友達とテニスをします。兄と弟は野球が好きです。私は野球はしませんが、テレビで野球の試合をよく見ます。父はゴルフと、釣りが好きです。毎週日曜日はゴルフか、釣りをします。母は運動は全然しません。

(野球 *baseball,* 試合 *game; match,* ゴルフ *golf,* 釣り *fishing,* 毎週日曜日 *every Sunday,* 運動 *exercise*)

Writing

Write about your favorite sport activities. You can also write about your family members' favorite sport activities

カタカナで名前が書けますか Abilities and Potentials

Notes Relating to This Lesson	
Grammar and Usage 10 〜(ら)れ . . . . .176 11 〜ことができる 177	

Basic Vocabulary and Kanji

さけ・おさけ	酒・お酒	*n. rice wine, alcoholic beverage in general*
おどる	*r*-**u** 踊る・踊らない・踊り・踊って	*vi. to dance*
うんてんする	*irr.* 運転する	*vt. to drive*
おしえる	*e*-**ru** 教える・教えない・教え・教えて	*vt. to teach*

Newly introduced kanji:

名前・運転・教える

名	ノクタタ名名	前	` ` 丷 䒑 产 前 前 前 前
運	' 冖 冖 冖 冐 冐 冒 軍 軍 渾 運	転	一 ｢ 百 百 百 亘 車 車 転 転 転
教	一 + 土 耂 耂 孝 孝 孝 孝 教 教		

  Dialog

Mike Falk asks Kyungtaek Park whether he can write his name in katakana.

フォーク：パクさんはカタカナで名前が書けますか。

パク　　：ええ、書けますよ。

フォーク：いいですね。

パク　　：マイクさんは。

フォーク：ぼくはまだ書けません。

Guess and Try 1

What is the difference between 書きます and 書けます? 10

Guess and Try 2

Fill in the blanks and state how the potential forms are created. 10

1. 書く → 書ける・書けます (potential)
2. 読む → 読める・読めます
3. 作る → ＿＿＿＿＿＿・＿＿＿＿＿＿
4. およぐ → ＿＿＿＿＿＿・＿＿＿＿＿＿
5. 買う → ＿＿＿＿＿＿・＿＿＿＿＿＿
6. 食べる → 食べられる・食べられます
7. 見る → ＿＿＿＿＿＿・＿＿＿＿＿＿
8. 来る → 来られる・＿＿＿＿＿＿
9. する → できる・＿＿＿＿＿＿

Guess and Try 3

Choose the appropriate particles in the parentheses. 10

1. 私は日本語(を・が)話します。
2. 私は日本語(を・が)話せます。
3. 私はからて(を・が)できます。

Guess and Try 4

Complete the following sentences. 10

1. 今、お金 *money* がありません。ですから、車が ＿＿＿＿＿＿＿＿＿＿。
2. このへやは暗いです。ですから、本が＿＿＿＿ ＿＿＿＿＿＿＿＿＿＿。

Guess and Try 5

What does the following sentence mean? 11

私は日本語を話すことができます。

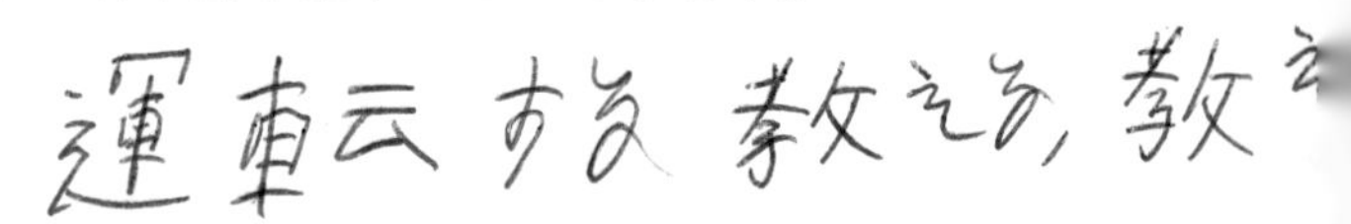

Drill 1: Conjugation

Variation 1:

話す ──► 話せる

Variation 2:

話す ──► 話せる・話せます

1. 書く
2. およぐ
3. 買う
4. 飲む
5. 作る
6. 帰る
7. おどる
8. 来る
9. 運転する
10. 食べる
11. 見る
12. 教える

Drill 2: Formation

日本語を話す ──► 日本語が話せます

1. すしを作る
2. おさけを飲む
3. はしで食べる
4. すう学を教える
5. 車を運転する

Task 1: Pair Work

Find out whether your partner can do the following.

1. カタカナで名前を書く
2. およぐ *to swim*
3. はしで食べる *to eat with chopsticks*
4. 耳をうごかす *to wiggle one's ears*

Task 2: Classroom Activity

Practice saying the following 早口言葉 *tongue twisters*, then each of you say it one by one. Find out who can say them the fastest (だれがはやく言えますか).

1. なまむぎ　なまごめ　なまたまご
   生麦　生米　生卵
2. すもももも　ももも　もものうち
   スモモも　桃も　桃のうち
3. あかぱじゃま　きぱじゃま　ちゃぱじゃま
   赤パジャマ　黄パジャマ　茶パジャマ

For more tongue twisters, see Tips and Additional Knowledge in this chapter.

Task 3: Classroom Activity

Find the person who can do something that you wish you could do (for example, 暗算 *arithmetic calculation* ができる, 逆立ち *handstand* ができる, フランス語が話せる, 車が運転できる, バイオリンがひける, およげる, and フラメンコがおどれる). Ask all of your classmates questions.

Short Reading

ゆみ子さんのお母さんは日本人ですが、お父さんはアメリカ人です。ゆみ子さんはアメリカで生まれました。ですから、日系アメリカ人です。ゆみ子さんのお父さんは日本語が少しできますが、うちではたいてい英語で話します。ゆみ子さんはお母さんの日本語がわかります。でも、日本語で話すことができません。ですから、ゆみ子さんのお母さんはゆみ子さんに日本語で話しますが、ゆみ子さんはお母さんに英語で話します。ゆみ子さんはひらがなとカタカナは書けます。でも、漢字はあまり書けません。ゆみ子さんは来年大学で日本語をとるつもりです。

(生まれる *to be born,* 日系アメリカ人 *Japanese American,* 来年 *next year,* とる *to take*)

Writing

Write about one of your friends who can speak more than one language.

何が一ばんほしいですか Desire

Notes Relating to This Lesson	
Grammar and Usage	**Writing**
12 ほしい 177	ⓑ しめすへん 179
13 〜たい 178	

Basic Vocabulary and Kanji

じかん	時間	*n. time*
おかね	お金	*n. money*
しゃちょう・しゃちょうさん	社長・社長さん	*n. company president*
かいしゃ	会社	*n. company*
ほし˥い	欲しい・欲しくない	*adj. to want (some items)* 12
やす˥む	**m-u** 休む・休まない・休み・休んで	*vi / vt. to rest, to take a day off, to be absent from~*
かりる	**i-ru** 借りる・借りない・借り・借りて	*vt. to borrow*
いちばん	一番	*adv. the most, the best*
べつに	別に	*adv. (not) particularly*
じつ˥は	実は	*adv. as a matter of fact*
あそびにいく	遊びに行く	*to visit somewhere or someone for fun*
あそびにく˥る	遊びに来る	*to be visited by someone*
〜たい	〜たい・〜たくない	*aux. to want to do something* (食べたい *to want to eat*) 13

Newly introduced kanji:

お金（かね）・休（やす）む・社長（しゃちょう）ⓑ・
会社（かいしゃ）・社会学（しゃかいがく）(sociology)

休	ノ イ 仁 什 付 休	社	` ラ ネ ネ ネ 社 社
会	ノ 人 へ 会 会 会		

Dialog 1

John Smith asks Yoko Yamada what she wants the most now.

スミス　：山田さんは今（いま）何（なに）が一（いち）ばんほしいですか。

山田　：そうですね。今はべつに…。スミスさんは。

スミス　：ぼくは新（あたら）しい車がほしいです。

山田　：ああ、そうですか。

Guess and Try 1

Choose the appropriate particle in the parentheses. 12

私はお金（が・を）ほしいです。
I want money.

Dialog 2

Mr. Tanaka talks to the president of the company where he works for.

田中　：あのう、社長。ちょっと明日（あした）休みたいんですが。

社長　：ああ、どうぞ。

田中　：それから、ちょっと会社の車（くるま）をかりたいんですが。

社長　：それは、ちょっと…

田中　：じつは、明日（あした）、父（ちち）と母（はは）がいなかからあそびに来（く）るんです。
（いなか *countryside, hometown*）

社長　：ああ、じゃあ、どうぞ。

Guess and Try 2

Tell your partner that you want to borrow his / her pen. 13

Drill 1: Substitution

(私は) 新しいじてん車がほしいです

1. プリンター
2. 広いへや
3. やきゅうのバット *baseball bat*
4. お金
5. ともだち

Drill 2: Formation

見る ⟶ 見たい

1. 書く	2. およぐ
3. 読む	4. 話す
5. 買う	6. 作る
7. かりる	8. する
9. 来る	

Drill 3: Formation

車をかります ⟶ 車をかりたいんですが

1. お金をかります
2. うちに帰ります
3. パーティーに行きます
4. クラスを休みます
5. へやで休みます

Task 1: Classroom Activity

Write down the item that you want to get the most now (other than money), on a sheet of paper, but do not show it to anyone. Then, look for the people who wrote exactly the same thing as you did, by asking questions in Japanese. (See Dialog 1.)

Task 2: Skit

Make up a skit where you try to borrow money from your partner. Make up a good reason for borrowing the money.

For example:

A : 少しお金をかりたいんですが。

B : ああ、いいですよ。/ すみませんが、ちょっと…。

A : じつは、コンピューターの会社をはじめたいんです。
(始める *to start*)

B : ああ、いいですね。/ ああ、そうですか。でも、…。

Short Reading

私は今運転免許が一番ほしいです。でも、30万円から40万円かかります。二番目には一人の部屋がほしいです。今は妹とアパートに住んでいます。よくけんかします。三番目には携帯電話がほしいです。これは来月買うつもりです。

(運転免許 *driver's license,* 30万円から40万円 *from ¥300,000 to ¥400,000,* かかる *to cost,* 二番目に *secondly,* ～に住んでいます *to live in~,* けんか(を)する *to fight,* 三番目に *thirdly,* 携帯電話 *cellular phone*)

Writing

Write three things that you want to get the most now.

しょうらいは何をしたいですか Your Future

Notes Relating to This Lesson	
Grammar and Usage	
14 Working 178	
15 それか 178	

Basic Vocabulary and Kanji

しょ˥うらい	将来	*n. future*
いしゃ・おいしゃさん	医者・お医者さん	*n. medical doctor*
かいしゃ˥いん・かいしゃ˥いんさん	会社員・会社員さん	*n. company employee*
きょ˥うし・せんせ˥い	教師・先生	*n. teacher*
べんご˥し・べんご˥しさん	弁護士・弁護士さん	*n. lawyer*
ぼうえき	貿易	*n. trading* (貿易会社(ぼうえきがいしゃ) *trading company*)
けいえいする	*irr.* 経営する	*vt. to run (a business)* (レストランを経営する *to run a restaurant*)
はたらく	***k*-u** 働く・働かない・働き・働いて	*vi. to work* (レストランで働く *to work at a restaurant*) 14
な˥る	***r*-u** なる・ならない・なり・なって	*vt. to become* (学生になる *to become a student*)
それか		*con. or* (*cf.* それとも) 15

Newly introduced kanji:

会社(かいしゃ)いん(会社員(かいしゃいん))・働(はたら)く

働	ノイイ'仁仁仁佰佰俥俥傅働働

Dialog

Jason Chen asks John Smith what he wants to do in the future.

チェン　：スミスさんはしょうらい何(なに)をしたいですか。

スミス　：ぼくは日本でえい語(ご)をおしえたいです。

チェン　：ああ、そうですか。日本が好きなんですね。

スミス　：ええ、大好きです。チェンさんは。

チェン　：ぼくはぼうえき会社で働きたいです。それか、ぎんこうで働きたいです。

スミス　：ああ、お金が好きなんですね。

チェン　：ええ、大好きです。

Vocabulary Collection (Occupation)

- 医者(いしゃ) *medical doctor*
- 学者(がくしゃ) *scholar*
- 弁護士(べんごし) *lawyer*
- 看護士(かんごし) *nurse*
- 教師(きょうし) *teacher*
- 社長(しゃちょう) *company president*
- 学長(がくちょう) *university president*
- 店長(てんちょう) *store manager*
- ～のオーナー *owner of~*
- アーティスト *artist*
- 映画監督(えいがかんとく) *movie director*
- 作家(さっか) *writer*
- イラストレーター *illustrator*
- デザイナー *designer*
- ファッションモデル *fashion model*
- 国家公務員(こっかこうむいん) *government employee*
- 歌手(かしゅ) *singer*
- 俳優(はいゆう) *actor*
- 女優(じょゆう) *actress*
- コメディアン *comedian*
- パイロット *pilot*

Vocabulary Collection (Institutions / Companies)

- 大学(だいがく) *college*
- 高校(こうこう) *high school*
- 中学校(ちゅうがっこう) *junior high school*
- 幼稚園(ようちえん) *kindergarten*
- 専門学校(せんもんがっこう) *vocational school*
- 小学校(しょうがっこう) *elementary school*
- 工場(こうじょう) *factory*
- 銀行(ぎんこう) *bank*
- 貿易会社(ぼうえきがいしゃ) *trading company*
- 旅行会社(りょこうがいしゃ) *travel agency*
- 病院(びょういん) *hospital*
- 郵便局(ゆうびんきょく) *post office*
- 店(みせ) *store*
- レストラン *restaurant*
- 農家(のうか) *farmhouse*

Guess and Try 1

Choose the appropriate particle in the parenthesis. 14

会社(で・に)働きます。

Guess and Try 2

Complete the sentence appropriately. 15

今日(きょう)は勉強(べんきょう)します。それから、__________。

Drill 1: Formation

食べる ⟶ 食べたいです

1. 飲む
2. 見る
3. 帰る
4. 買う
5. 教える
6. 働く

Drill 2: Formation

社長になる ⟶ 社長になりたいです

1. きょうしになる
2. 大学で教える
3. いしゃになる
4. びょういんで働く
5. ぎんこうで働く
6. ぼうえき会社(がいしゃ)をけいえいする
7. りょこう会社(がいしゃ)をけいえいする

Task: Survey

Ask four of your classmates what they want to do in the future. Also ask them what their major is.

	Future	Major
私		
さん		
さん		
さん		
さん		

Short Reading

私の父は貿易会社(ぼうえきがいしゃ)の社長です。父は英語と、中国語と、日本語を話します。韓国(かんこく)語も少し話します。父の会社はホンコンにあります。来年父は日本に行きます。東京に一年いる予定です。私も父と日本に行きます。日本の大学で一年間勉強するつもりです。日本では日本語を勉強します。日本人の友達をたくさん作りたいです。将来(しょうらい)は父の会社で働きたいです。

周肖鳴(しゅうしょうめい) 23歳(さい)

(来年(らいねん) *next year,* 予定(よてい) *plan*)

Writing

Write about your future plans.

– Grammar and Usage –

1 おおい, すくない: Numerous, scarce

多い *many* and 少ない *scarce* are placed at the end of a sentence, but may not be placed right before a noun.

(a) 日本人は多いです。
There are many Japanese (here.)

(b) 日本人は少ないです。
There are not so many Japanese (here).

(c) 多い人が来ました。 (✕)
(Ungrammatical) Intended meaning: *Many people came.*

(d) 少ない人が来ました。 (✕)
(Ungrammatical) Intended meaning: *Few people came.*

The intended readings of (c) and (d) can be (e) and (f), respectively.

(e) 人がたくさん来ました。
(f) 人はあまり来ませんでした。

2 ～は～が～です: As for ～, ～ is ～

Adjectives describe the property of things and people. For example, (a) means that Yoko is pretty in general:

(a) ようこさんはきれいです。
Yoko is pretty.

For saying that Yoko is pretty as far as her eyes are concerned, rather than she is pretty in general, (b) is more appropriate than (a):

(b) ようこさんは目がきれいです。
As for Yoko, her eyes are pretty.

Expectedly, (b) can be rephrased as (c):

(c) ようこさんの目はきれいです。
As for Yoko's eyes, they are pretty.

The difference between (b) and (c) is that (b) is a statement about the person Yoko, but (c) is a statement about Yoko's eyes. It is easy to see in (d) and (e):

(d) 山田さんは髪がきれいです。それに、山田さんは目がきれいです。
Ms. Yamada has beautiful hair. In addition, she has beautiful eyes.

(e) 山田さんの目は大きいです。それに、山田さんの目はきれいです。
Ms. Yamada's eyes are big. In addition, they are pretty.

～は～が～です construction can be used for various purposes. The following are some examples.

A. Describing People

(a) 姉は背が高いです。
My older sister is tall.

(b) 妹は背がひくいです。
My younger sister is short.

(c) 姉は目が大きいです。
As for my older sister, her eyes are big.

(d) 弟は鼻が高いです。
As for my younger brother, he has a long nose.

(e) 姉は髪がながいです。
My older sister has long hair.

(f) 母は髪が多いです。
My mother has thick hair.

(g) 姉は頭がいいです。
My sister is smart.

(h) 姉は目がいいです。
My sister has good eyesight.

(i) 姉はともだちが多いです。
My sister has many friends.

B. Describing Places

(a) 日本は山がきれいです。
As for Japan, the mountains are beautiful.

(b) 東京は地下鉄が便利です。
In Tokyo, subways are convenient.

(c) フロリダはオレンジがおいしいです。
As for Florida, the oranges are delicious.

(d) アメリカはニューヨークがおもしろいです。
As for the United States, New York is interesting.

(e) 中国は自転車が多いです。
As for China, there are a lot of bicycles there.

(f) 秋葉原はカメラやテレビが安いです。
As for Akihabara, items such as cameras and TVs are cheap there.

C. Describing Skills, Preferences and Desire

(a) 私はゴルフが好きです。
I like golf.

(b) 私はバスケットボールが嫌いです。
I hate basketball.

(c) 私はテニスが下手です。
I am not good at tennis.

(d) スミスさんは料理が上手です。
Mr. Smith is good at cooking.

(e) 私はラケットがほしいです。
I want a racket.

3 〜や: And so on, etc [Example-listing]

Use the particle 〜や for randomly listing two or more nouns as examples, as in "A, B, C and so on or "A, B, C, etc".

(a) 私はビールや、お酒を飲みました。
I drank beer, sake, etc.

(b) 中国や、韓国や、日本に行きました。
(I) went to China, Korea, Japan, etc.

Unlike the particle 〜と, 〜や strongly implies that there are other items besides the listed items. For example, (c) strongly implies that there are other items besides the desk and chair in the room, but (d) does not.

(c) 私の部屋には机や、椅子があります。
There are a desk, a chair (and other things) in my room.

(d) 私の部屋には机と、椅子があります。
There are a desk and a chair in my room.

4 〜か: Or [Disjunctive listing]

Use the particle 〜か for listing two or more nouns disjunctively, as in "A, B or C".

(a) 私は英語か、フランス語か、スペイン語を習うつもりです。
I am planning to learn English, French or Spanish.

(b) 図書館か、うちで勉強します。
I study at the library or at home.

(c) このネクタイは父か、兄にあげます。
As for this necktie, I will give it to my father or my brother.

(d) あの人は中国人か、日本人です。
That person is Chinese or Japanese.

The particle か can be used for verbs and adjectives. In this case, か also appears after the last item, as in the following examples:

(e) 私はテレビを見るか、ねるかします。
I will watch TV or sleep.

(f) まだあの車は売れていません。あの車は高いか、悪いかです。
That car has not been sold yet. That car is either expensive or bad.

For listing statement sentences, use それか and for listing question sentences, use それとも, as in the following examples.

(g) 英語を話します。それか、フランス語を話します。
I will speak English. Or, I will speak French.

(h) バスで行きます。それか、車で行きます。
I will go (there) by bus. Or, I will go (there) by car.

(i) 英語を話しますか。それとも、フランス語を話しますか。
Will you speak English? Or, will you speak French?

(j) バスで行きますか。それとも、車で行きますか。
Will you go there by bus? Or, will you go there by car?

5 こんど: This time / next time

The word 今度 has two different meanings. When it occurs with a past tense predicate, as in (a), it means *this time*, but when it occurs with a present tense predicate, as in (b), it means *next time*:

(a) 今度は私が書きました。
I wrote (it) this time.

(b) 今度は私が書きます。
I will write (it) next time.

6 Skills (とくい (な), にがて (な), etc)

The adjectives 上手(な), うまい and とくい(な) all mean *skillful*, but there are some differences between とくい(な) on one hand, and 上手 (な) and うまい, on the other. 上手 (な) and うまい express the absolute skill, but とくい(な) expresses the relative skill (one's strong point) and emphasizes that one likes the activity. For example, you can use とくい(な) when you think you are good at something and you like it, even if you are not very skilled at it compared with other people. When you want to express your own skill, とくい(な) is more appropriate than 上手 (な) and うまい because the former sounds more modest than the latter. On the other hand, when you want to compliment someone else's skill, 上手 (な) or うまい is more appropriate than とくい(な).

The parallel difference holds between 苦手(な) and 下手(な): 苦手(な) emphasizes the negative feelings toward the relevant activity, but 下手(な) merely refers to the absolute degree of one's skill.

7 〜が: But [Conflict / Contrast]

The particle 〜が connects two clauses that express conflicting or contrasting ideas.

(a) 日本語のクラスは難しいですが、楽しいです。
The Japanese class is difficult, but fun.

(b) 兄は 15 才ですが、おさけを飲みます。
My brother is 15 years old, but he drinks alcohol.

(c) 犬は好きですが、ねこは好きじゃありません。
I like dogs, but I do not like cats.

For connecting two separate sentences, use the connective word でも instead of the particle が, as in the following examples:

(d) 日本語のクラスは難しいです。でも、楽しいです。
(e) 兄は 15 才です。でも、おさけを飲みます。
(f) 犬は好きです。でも、ねこは好きじゃありません。

In some cases, が does not specify conflict nor contrast, but simply relates two clauses:

(g) もしもし、山田ですが、スミスさんをおねがいします。
Hello, I am Mr. Yamada. May I talk to Mr. Smith.

(h) 明日山田さんが来ますが、あなたも来ませんか。
Tomorrow, Mr. Yamada is coming, but would you like to come, too?

8 〜の [Noun-maker]

For having a verb at the places where nouns are usually placed, for example, before a particle like が and は, make the verb noun-like by adding a noun-maker の. The verb must be in the plain form in this case. For example, in the following sentence, the verb 食べる is followed by the noun-maker の and occurs before the particle が.

(a) 私は食べるのが好きです。
I like eating.

A verb must be in the plain form when followed by の and it can be preceded by other phrases related to the verb such as its direct object, as in the following sentences:

(b) ジョンさんはうたをうたうのがとくいです。
John is good at singing songs.

(c) かんじを書くのはむずかしいです。
Writing kanji is difficult.

Most of the time, the noun-maker の can be replaced by こと, but in the above examples, の is preferred to こと. For the use of こと, see Grammar and Usage Note 11 in this chapter.

9 〜は [Contrast]

The pragmatic particle は can function as a contrastive marker as well as a topic marker. When it functions as a contrastive marker, it shows that the status of the item marked by は contrasts sharply with the status of something else, understood in the context. For example, sentence (a) strongly implies the fact that the speaker likes 山田さん but does not like someone else understood in the context, say 田中さん, about whom they know they have been talking or thinking.

(a) 私は山田さんは好きです。
I like Ms. Yamada, (but I do not like Mr. Tanaka).

When the two items in contrast are pronounced, both of them are marked by the particle は.

(b) 私は山田さんは好きです。でも、田中さんは好きじゃありません。
I like Ms. Yamada. But I do not like Mr. Tanaka.

(c) 山田さんは来ました。でも、田中さんは来ませんでした。
Mr. Yamada came. But Mr. Tanaka did not.

10 〜(ら)れ: Can do〜 [Potential]

One's ability and potential can be expressed by adding the potential suffix **-e** or **-rare** to a verb root. The potential suffix is **-e** for an **u**-verb (for example, kak → kak-e) and it is **-rare** for a **ru**-verb (for example, tabe → tabe-rare). Younger people tend to use **re** rather than **rare** for **ru**-verb (for example, **tabe** → **tabe-re**). By adding the potential suffix to a verb root, you are creating a new **ru**-verb root that means "can do~", which can be followed by other inflectional suffixes such as **-ru** and **-masu** (for example, たべられる, たべられます). The verbs する and くる are exceptions as usual: their potential forms are できる and こられる, respectively. When the verbs are in their potential forms, the direct object is usually marked by the particle が, although を is also used in some cases. When the potential verb is できる, the direct object must be marked by the particle が.

(a) 私は日本語を話します。
I speak Japanese.

(b) 私は日本語が / を話せます。
I can speak Japanese.

(c) 私はからてをします。
I do karate.

(d) 私はからてができます。
I can do karate.

Some verbs such as 見える *to see*, 聞こえる *to hear* and わかる *to understand* include potential meaning to start with, and they are rarely used with a potential suffix because it would be redundant. These verbs also take the particle が for their direct object.

(e) 山が見えます。
I see a mountain.

(f) 音楽が聞こえます。
I hear music.

(g) 日本語が分かりますか。
Do you understand Japanese?

Dictionary Form	Potential Form
たべる *to eat*	tabe-rare-ru たべられる
みる *to watch*	mi-rare-ru みられる
かく *to write*	kak-e-ru かける
およぐ *to swim*	oyog-e-ru およげる
あそぶ *to play*	asob-e-ru あそべる
よむ *to read*	yom-e-ru よめる
しぬ *to die*	shin-e-ru しねる
まつ *to wait*	mat-e-ru まてる
はなす *to speak*	hanas-e-ru はなせる
つくる *to make*	tsukur-e-ru つくれる
かう *to buy*	kaw-e-ru かえる
する *to do*	dekiru できる
くる *to come*	korareru こられる

11 〜ことができる: Can do〜 [Potential]

One's potential or ability can be expressed by using the verb できる, as in (a), as well as by the potential form of a verb, as in (b):

(a) 日本語を話すことができます。
(I) can speak Japanese.

(b) 日本語が話せます。
(I) can speak Japanese.

こと in (a) is a noun-maker, but it cannot be replaced by the other noun-maker の in this context.

(c) 私は日本語を話すのができます。 (✕)
(Ungrammatical)

12 ほしい: To want something [Desire for items]

The desire for things is expressed by the adjective ほしい. The wanted item is marked by the particle が:

(a) 私はコンピューターがほしいです。
I want a computer.

(b) 今何が一番ほしいですか。
What do you want the most now?

And ほしい cannot be used to describe what is wanted by a third person. The latter is expressed by the complex phrase ほしがる (see Chapter Twenty-two).

Remember that the question ほしいですか *Do you want ...?* is not appropriate for offering food and beverages to your guests. For example, コーヒーがほしいですか sounds too direct and rude, so you should use one of the following for offering a cup of coffee to your guests.

(c) コーヒーはどうですか。
How about coffee?

(d) コーヒーはいかがですか。
How about coffee?

(e) コーヒーをのみませんか。
How about drinking coffee?

(f) コーヒーをのみましょうか。
Shall we drink coffee?

13 ～たい: To want to do～ [Desire for action]

The desire for things is expressed by the adjective ほしい (for example, 私は本がほしいです *I want a book*), but the desire for doing some actions must be expressed by the suffix ～たい, and not by ほしい. The suffix ～たい follows a verb in the stem form.

(a) 私はうちで寝(ね)たいです。
I want to sleep at home.

(b) 私は医者(いしゃ)になりたいです。
I want to become a doctor.

(c) 私はガールフレンドに会(あ)いたいです。
I want to see my girlfriend.

(d) 私はひとりで勉強(べんきょう)したいです。
I want to study by myself.

(e) どうしましたか。
What happened?
— すみません。電話(でんわ)をかりたいんですが。
— *Sorry, but I want to use your phone.*

(f) 昨日(きのう)はすきやきを食(た)べました。今日(きょう)はさしみが食べたいです。
Yesterday, I ate sukiyaki. Today, I want to eat sashimi.

The direct object of the verb may be marked by が or を, but the focus of the sentence changes depending on the choice between the two. The following two sentences are almost synonymous, but (g) focuses on what one wants to do and (h) focuses on what one wants to eat.

(g) 私はてんぷらを食べたいです。
I want to eat tempura.

(h) 私はてんぷらが食べたいです。
I want to eat tempura.

You can seek permission by using たい. In this case, it is often followed by ～んです or ～んですが in conversations:

(i) ちょっとペンをかりたいんですが。
I would like to borrow your pen, but ... (is it okay?)

(j) 帰(かえ)りたいんですが。
I want to go home, but (is it okay?)

(k) ちょっと休(やす)みたいんですが。
I would like to take a short break, but ... (is it okay?)

Note that ～たい can be used for expressing the desire of the first and the second person only, and may not be used for expressing the desire of the third person. (The desire of the third person requires another complex suffix, namely, ～がる. See Chapter Twenty-two.)

14 Working (はたらく and つとめる)

The English verb "to work" corresponds to either 働(はたら)く or 勤(つと)める in Japanese. 働(はたら)く emphasizes the physical act of working, but 勤(つと)める emphasizes the commitment that one makes by working. Accordingly, the choice of the particle used for the company or institution that one works at or one works for is different between the two:

(a) 会社(かいしゃ)で働(はたら)いています。
(I) work at a company.

(b) 会社に勤(つと)めています。
(I) work for a company.

15 それか: Or [Alternative idea]

The sentence connective word それか connects two sentences that express two alternative ideas.

(a) 今晩(こんばん)はカフェテリアで食(た)べます。それか、レストランで食べます。
I will eat at a cafeteria tonight. Or, I will eat at a restaurant.

(b) 将来(しょうらい)は社長(しゃちょう)になりたいです。それか、弁護士(べんごし)になりたいです。
In the future, I want to be a company president. Or, I want to be a lawyer.

For connecting two alternative questions, use それとも instead of それか.

(c) 今晩(こんばん)はカフェテリアで食べましょうか。それとも、レストランで食べましょうか。
Shall we eat at a cafeteria tonight? Or, shall we eat at a restaurant?

(d) 将来(しょうらい)は社長(しゃちょう)になりたいですか。それとも、弁護士(べんごし)になりたいですか。
In the future, do you want to be a company president? Or, do you want to be a lawyer?

– Writing –

ⓐ くにがまえ

口	くにがまえ *enclosure*
	Example: 国(くに) *country,* 困(こま)る *to be in trouble,* 囲(かこ)む *to surround,* 囚人(しゅうじん) *prisoner,* 固(かた)い *hard*

ⓑ しめすへん

ネ	しめすへん *rite, alter*
	Example: 会社(かいしゃ) *company,* 神(かみ) *god,* 福(ふく) *good fortune*

– Kanji List –

口・目・耳・足・手・背・長い・短い・多い・少ない・少し・国・中国・かん国・来月・食べもの・読書・好き・大好き・上手・下手・名前・運転・教える・お金・休む・社長・会社・社会学・会社いん・働く

Kanji	Readings / Meaning	Strokes	Example
口	くち・ぐち・コウ *mouth*	[3]	口(くち) *mouth*; 川口(かわぐち) *surname*
目	め・モク *eye, item*	[5]	目(め) *eye*
耳	みみ・ジ *ear*	[6]	耳(みみ) *ear*
足	あし・た-りる・ソク *leg, pair, suffice*	[7]	足(あし) *leg, foot*
手	て・シュ *hand*	[4]	手(て) *hand*; 上手(じょうず)(な) *skillful*; 下手(へた)(な) *unskillful*
背	せい・せ・ハイ *back, height*	[9]	背(せ・せい) *(people's) height*
長	なが-い・チョウ *long, eldest, chief*	[8]	長(なが)い *long*
短	みじか-い・タン *short*	[12]	短(みじか)い *short*
多	おお-い・タ *many, much*	[6]	多(おお)い *many, much*
少	すく-ない・すこ-し・ショウ *few, little*	[4]	少(すく)ない *few, little*; 少(すこ)し *a little, a few*
国	くに・コク *country*	[8]	国(くに) *country*; 中国(ちゅうごく) *China*; 韓国(かんこく) *Korea*
中	なか・チュウ・ジュウ *middle, inside*	[4]	中(なか) *inside*; 中国(ちゅうごく) *China*
来	く-る・き-ます・こ-ない・ライ *come, next*	[7]	来(く)る *to come*; 来月(らいげつ) *next month*

月	つき・ゲツ・ガツ *moon, month*	ノ 刀 月 月 [4]	Example: 来月(らいげつ) *next month* 三月(さんがつ) *March*
食	た-べる・ショク *eat*	ノ 人 𠆢 今 今 今 食 食 食 [9]	Example: 食(た)べる *to eat* 食(た)べもの *food*
読	よ-む・ドク *read*	丶 亠 亠 言 言 言 言 訁 訁 読 読 読 読 読 [14]	Example: 読(よ)む *to read* 読書(どくしょ) *reading*
書	か-く・ショ *write, book, document*	フ ラ ヨ ヨ 聿 聿 書 書 書 書 [10]	Example: 書(か)く *to write* 読書(どくしょ) *reading*
好	す-きな・コウ *favorite*	く 女 女 女' 好 好 [6]	Example: 好(す)きです *to like*
大	おお-きい・ダイ・タイ *big, great*	一 ナ 大 [3]	Example: 大(おお)きい *big* 大好(だいす)き(な) *to like a lot*
上	うえ・あ-がる・ジョウ *above, on, up, superior*	丨 卜 上 [3]	Example: 上(うえ) *above, on* 上手(じょうず)(な) *skillful*
下	した・さ-がる・ゲ・カ *under, down, inferior*	一 丅 下 [3]	Example: 下(した) *under* 下手(へた)です *unskillful*
名	な・メイ・ミョウ *name, famous, members*	ノ ク タ タ 名 名 [6]	Example: 名前(なまえ) *name*

前	まえ・ゼン *before, front, previous*	丶 ソ 䒑 广 前 前 前 前 前 [9]	Example: 名前(なまえ) *name* ～の前(まえ) *in front of ～*
運	はこ-ぶ・ウン *carry, fate*	丶 冖 冖 冖 冐 冐 冐 冒 軍 軍 渾 運 [12]	Example: 運転(うんてん)する *to drive* 運動(うんどう) *exercise*
転	ころ-ぶ・テン *roll, turn*	一 丅 万 百 百 亘 車 車 車 転 転 [11]	Example: 運転(うんてん)する *to drive* 自転車(じてんしゃ) *bicycle*
教	おし-える・キョウ *teach*	一 十 土 耂 耂 孝 孝 孝 孝 教 教 [11]	Example: 教(おし)える *to teach*
金	かね・キン *gold, metal, money*	ノ 人 𠆢 今 全 全 金 金 [8]	Example: お金(かね) *money* 金曜日(きんようび) *Friday*
休	やす-む *rest*	ノ イ 亻 什 什 休 [6]	Example: 休(やす)む *to rest, to be absent*
社	シャ・ジャ *shrine, company, assembling*	丶 ラ ネ ネ ネ 社 社 [7]	Example: 会社(かいしゃ) *a company* 社長(しゃちょう) *company president*
会	あ-う・カイ *meeting, association*	ノ 人 𠆢 亼 会 会 [6]	Example: 会社(かいしゃ) *a company* 社会学(しゃかいがく) *sociology*
学	まな-ぶ・ガク・ガッ *study*	丶 丷 ⺍ ⺍ 𭕄 学 学 学 [8]	Example: 学生(がくせい) *a student* 社会学(しゃかいがく) *sociology*

<table>
<tr><td rowspan="2">働

はたら-く・
ドウ
work</td><td>ノイイ仁仁伯伯伯俥俥偅働働 [13]</td></tr>
<tr><td>Example: 働(はたら)く to work</td></tr>
</table>

– Review –

Q1. Write the pronounciation of the kanji characters in the following phrases and sentences.

1. 目と口と耳と足。
2. 上手ですか。下手ですか。
3. 好きです。大好きです。
4. 会社で働きます。それか、大学で教えます。

Q2. Fill in the blanks creatively, then translate the sentences.

1. 山田さんは背が ______________ 。
2. スーザンさんは ______________ がきれいです。
3. ジェフさんは ______________ がいいです。
4. 日本は ______________ がおいしいです。
5. とうきょうは ______________ がべんりです。

Q3. Make a sentence using all of the items in each set. You will have to add some items and conjugate some verbs and adjectives.

1. (食べる・好きです・日本の食べもの)
2. (私・ほしい・車)
3. (食べる・～たい・すし)
4. (べんごし・～たい)
5. (かんじ・名前・書ける)

Q4. Explain the difference between the two sentences in each set.

1. A. ジョンさんと、マリーさんが来ます。

   B. ジョンさんや、マリーさんが来ます。

2. A. 私はケーキが好きです。

   B. 私はケーキは好きです。

3. A. 私はりょうりが上手です。

   B. 私はりょうりがとくいです。

Q5. Choose the appropriate options in the parentheses.

1. 日本は山がきれいです。(それに・それか)、魚(さかな) *fish* がおいしいです。
2. 私はいしゃになりたいです。(それに・それか)、べんごしになりたいです。
3. 会社(に・で)働きます。
4. 兄はからて(を・が)できます。
5. 私はお金(を・が)ほしいです。

Q6. Fill in the blanks.

For example: かく → かける

1. よむ → ______________
2. たべる → ______________
3. つくる → ______________
4. かう → ______________
5. する → ______________
6. くる → ______________
7. べんきょうする → ______________

Q7. Look at the map and state what food is delicious in each of the specified places.

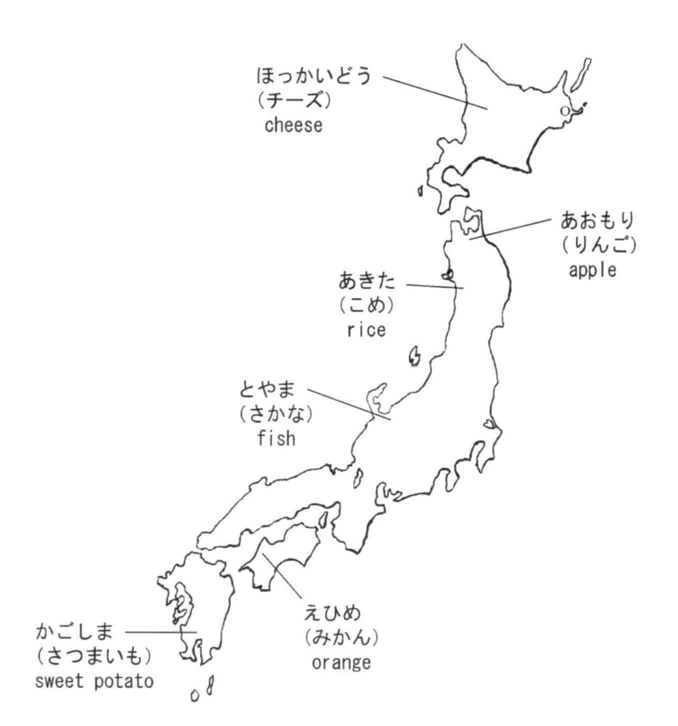

Tips and Additional Knowledge: Tongue Twisters

The following are some of the well-known Japanese Tongue Twisters. Try saying them as fast as you can. They may not be difficult for you although they are difficult for the Japanese. Let's see.

赤(あか)パジャマ黄(き)パジャマ茶(ちゃ)パジャマ
Red pajamas, yellow pajamas and brown pajamas.

スモモも桃(もも)も桃(もも)のうち
Plums and peaches are both in peach's family.

隣(となり)の客(きゃく)はよく柿(かき)食(く)う客(きゃく)だ
The guest at the next-door is the guest who often eats persimmons.

東京特許許可局(とうきょうとっきょきょかきょく)
Tokyo Patent Licensing Bureau.

生麦生米生卵(なまむぎなまごめなまたまご)
Raw wheat, raw rice and raw eggs.

庭(にわ)に二羽(にわ)鶏(にわとり)がいる
There are two roosters in the yard.

坊主(ぼうず)が屏風(びょうぶ)に上手(じょうず)に坊主(ぼうず)の絵(え)を書(か)いた
A Buddhist monk drew a picture of a Buddhist monk on a folding screen skillfully.

CHAPTER TWELVE

Talking About the Past

Lesson 50
夏休みはどこかへ行きましたか **Vacation** 184

Lesson 51
私のたんじょうびは12月24日です **Dates and Time** 186

Lesson 52
あのレストランはどうでしたか **Dining Experiences** 188

Lesson 53
兄弟とけんかしたことがありますか **Experiences** 190

Grammar and Usage 192

1. あう: To meet / to see 192
2. ～へ: To / toward～ [Direction] 192
3. ～で: Under the condition such as～ [Circumstantial condition] 192
4. Indefinite pronouns (なにか something, だれか someone, etc) 192
5. Negative pronouns (なにも nothing, だれも no one, etc) 193
6. いつ: When? [Question word for time] 193
7. ～ごろ: Approximately 193
8. Absolute time expressions 193
9. Relative time expressions 194
10. ～に: At, on, in [Absolute time of an event] 195
11. ～で: Due to [Cause / reason] 195
12. ～でした, ～かったです [Past tense of noun and adjective predicates] . . . 195
13. ～ど vs ～かい: ~times [The number of occasions] 196
14. Plain past affirmative forms of verbs (～た) 196
15. ～たことがある: I have ~ed [Experience] 196

Culture 197

- A ～ねん: The year～ [Expressing years] 197
- B National holidays 197

Writing 197

- a なつあし 197
- b ふゆがしら 197

Kanji List 198

Review 199

Tips and Additional Knowledge: Osaka Dialect 200

夏休みはどこかへ行きましたか Vacation

Notes Relating to This Lesson	
Grammar and Usage	
1 あう 192	5 Negative pronouns 193
2 ～へ 192	**Writing**
3 ～で 192	a なつあし 197
4 Indefinite pronouns 192	b ふゆがしら 197

Basic Vocabulary and Kanji

は˥る	春	*n. spring*
なつ˥	夏	*n. summer*
あ˥き	秋	*n. autumn, fall*
ふゆ˥	冬	*n. winter*
なつや˥すみ	夏休み	*n. summer vacation*
あ˥う	*w-u* 会う・会わない・会い・会って	*vi. to meet* 1
～へ		*prt. to, toward (pronunciation is "e")* 2

Newly introduced kanji:

春(はる)・夏(なつ) a・秋(あき)・冬(ふゆ) b・夏休(なつやす)み・
会(あ)う・会話(かいわ) (conversation)

春	一 = 三 夫 夫 表 春 春 春	夏	一 丆 丆 百 百 百 百 頁 夏 夏
秋	´ ˝ 千 千 禾 禾 禾´ 秒 秋	冬	ノ ク 夂 冬 冬

Dialog

Ben Lee asks Yoko Yamada about the summer vacation.

リー　：夏休みはどこかに行きましたか。

山田　：ええ。オーストラリアに行きました。

リー　：一人で行きましたか。

山田　：いいえ。姉と、兄と、三人で行きました。

リー　：ああ、そうですか。

山田　：リーさんは。

リー　：ぼくは中国へ行きました。そふに会いました。

山田　：ああ、そうですか。

Guess and Try 1

Circle the appropriate particle(s) in the parentheses.

1. 私は山田さん(を・と・に)会いました。1
2. 私は山田さん(を・に)見ました。1
3. オーストラリア(が・に・へ)行きました。2
4. 私は昨日(きのう)うちで母(はは)と二人(ふたり)(が・で)ワインを飲(の)みました。3

Guess and Try 2

Interpret the following sentences: 4 5

1. 明日(あした)はどこかへ行きます。

____

2. 明日はどこへも行きません。

____

Guess and Try 3

Look at the following sentences and state where the particles such as に, が and を are placed with respect to pronouns like だれか and だれも. 4 5

1. だれかに会いましたか。
— いいえ、だれにも会いませんでした。

2. どこかへ行きますか。
— いいえ、どこへも行きません。

3. だれか(が)来(き)ましたか。
— いいえ、だれも来ませんでした。

4. 何か(を)食(た)べましたか。
— いいえ、何も食べませんでした。

Drill 1: Mini-Conversation

だれかに言いましたか → だれにも言いませんでした

1. だれかと話しましたか
2. だれかに会いましたか
3. だれかから聞きましたか
4. どこかに行きましたか
5. どこかへ行きましたか

Drill 2: Mini-Conversation

だれか来ましたか → だれも来ませんでした

1. だれかいましたか
2. 何か食べましたか
3. 何かありましたか
4. 何かしましたか
5. 何か読みましたか

Task: Pair Work

Ask your partner whether he / she went anywhere during the last summer or winter vacation. If he / she did, ask additional questions to find out the details, for example, 何か買いましたか, 何か見ましたか, 何かしましたか, だれかに会いましたか. Take turns.

Vocabulary Collection (Traveling)	
友達(ともだち)に会(あ)う *to see one's friends*	
買物(かいもの)をする *to go shopping*	
おみやげを買(か)う *to buy a souvenir*	
美術館(びじゅつかん)に行(い)く *to visit an art museum*	
食事(しょくじ)をする *to dine*	スキーをする *to ski*
ショーを見(み)る *to see a show*	泳(およ)ぐ *to swim*

Short Reading

今年の夏休みはどこにも行きませんでした。毎日うちで勉強しました。でも、二年前の夏休みは友達とカナダに行きました。カナダには私の兄がいます。兄のうちの近くにはきれいな湖があります。それに、山も川もあります。兄のうちに二ヶ月泊(と)まりました。来年の夏休みは韓国(かんこく)にツアーで行くつもりです。

(今年(ことし) *this year,* 毎日(まいにち) *every day,* 二年前(にねんまえ) *two years ago,* 湖(みずうみ) *lake,* 川(かわ) *river,* 来年(らいねん) *next year,* ～ヶ月(かげつ) *~month(s),* 泊(と)まる *to stay,* ～にツアーで行く *to go on a tour to~*)

Writing

Write about your past summer vacations and your plan for the next summer vacation.

私のたんじょうびは12月24日です Dates and Time

Notes Relating to This Lesson	
Grammar and Usage	
6 いつ 193	10 ～に 195
7 ～ごろ 193	**Culture**
8 Absolute time expressions 193	Ⓐ ～ねん 197
9 Relative time expressions 194	Ⓑ National holidays 197

Basic Vocabulary and Kanji

ことし	今年	*n. this year*
きょ⌉ねん	去年	*n. last year*
らいねん	来年	*n. next year*
がっき	学期	*n. academic term*
たんじょ⌉うび	誕生日	*n. birthday*
う⌉そ	嘘	*n. lie, untruth (うそをつく to tell a lie)*
じょうだ⌉ん	冗談	*n. joke*
おそい	遅い・遅くない	*adj. late, slow*
おき⌉る	***i*-ru** 起きる・起きない・起き・起きて	*vi. to wake up*
い⌉つ		*q. when* 6
～ねん	～年	*c. ~years, ~th year* Ⓐ
～にち	～日	*c. ~th date*
～ごろ	～頃	*approximately (6時ごろ about 6 o'clock)* 7

Newly introduced kanji:

今年(ことし)・去年(きょねん)・来年(らいねん)・学期(がっき)・～日(にち)・～年(ねん)

去	一 十 土 去 去	期	一 ｢ ｻ 甘 甘 其 其 其 期 期 期 期

Dialog 1

Yoshio Tanaka and Mary Carter talk about their birthdays.

田中　：マリーさんのたんじょうびはいつですか。

カーター：私のたんじょうびは 12月(じゅうにがつ) 24日(にじゅうよっか)です。

田中　：ああ、クリスマス・イブですね。

カーター：はい。

田中　：ぼくの兄のたんじょうびは12月(じゅうにがつ) 25日(にじゅうごにち)ですよ。

カーター：ええ？

田中　：うそです。

Dialog 2

Yoshio Tanaka and Mary Carter talk about their daily schedule.

田中　：マリーさんはたいてい何時(なんじ)におきますか。

カーター：たいてい6時ごろにおきます。

田中　：はやいですね。何時にねますか。

カーター：12時です。

田中　：おそいですね。

Guess and Try 1

Fill in the blanks. 8 9

1.	昨日(きのう) *yesterday*	今日(きょう) *today*	明日(あした) *tomorrow*
2.	先週(せんしゅう) *last week*	今週(こんしゅう) *this week*	来週(らいしゅう) *next week*
3.	先月(せんげつ) *last month*	今月(こんげつ) ________	来月(らいげつ) ________
4.	去年 *last year*	今年 *this year*	来年 *next year*

5. 先(せん)学期　＿＿＿＿　今(こん)学期　＿＿＿＿　来(らい)学期 *next academic term*

6. 1990 年 5 月(がつ)21 日　月曜日(げつようび)　＿＿＿＿＿＿＿＿＿＿

Guess and Try 2

Look at the following sentences and state when the particle に is needed after a time phrase. [10]

1. 10 時(じ)にクラスに行(い)きます。
2. 月曜日(げつようび)にクラスに行きます。
3. 明日(あした)クラスに行きます。
4. 昨日(きのう)クラスに行きました。
5. 1 月(がつ)に日本に行きます
6. 1 月26 日に日本に行きます。
7. 来年日本に行きます。
8. 2003 年に日本に行きました。

Guess and Try 3

Fill in the blank. [6]

＿＿＿＿＿＿＿＿ 行きますか。

When will you go (there)?

Guess and Try 4

Underline the phrases that are not read as you would predict. [8]

ついたち (1 日)
ふつか (2 日)
みっか (3 日)
よっか (4 日)
いつか (5 日)
むいか (6 日)
なのか (7 日)
ようか (8 日)
ここのか (9 日)
とおか (10 日)
じゅういちにち (11 日)
じゅうににち (12 日)
じゅうさんにち (13 日)
じゅうよっか (14 日)
じゅうごにち (15 日)
じゅうろくにち (16 日)
じゅうしちにち (17 日)
じゅうはちにち (18 日)
じゅうくにち (19 日)
はつか (20 日)
にじゅういちにち (21 日)
にじゅうににち (22 日)
にじゅうさんにち (23 日)
にじゅうよっか (24 日)
にじゅうごにち (25 日)
にじゅうろくにち (26 日)
にじゅうしちにち (27 日)
にじゅうはちにち (28 日)
にじゅうくにち (29 日)
さんじゅうにち (30 日)
さんじゅういちにち (31 日)
なんにち (何日)

Drill: Reading

1. 1 日　2 日　3 日　4 日　5 日　6 日　7 日　8 日　9 日　10 日
2. 4 日　14 日　24 日
3. 7 日　17 日　27 日
4. 9 日　19 日　29 日

Task 1: Classroom Activity

Make a list of the major national holidays in your country and in Japan. Tell on which days they are in Japanese. B

Task 2: Classroom Activity

Using Dialog 1 as a model, ask the birthdays of your classmates. Find a person whose birthday is the same as yours or a family member's.

Short Reading

母の誕生日は、1 月 25 日です。今年はスペイン料理(りょうり)のレストランに行きました。私が払(はら)いました。父も兄も行きました。父の誕生日は、4 月 1 日です。去年はどこにも行きませんでした。うちで、すきやきを食べました。

(スペイン料理(りょうり) *Spanish cuisine,* 払(はら)う *to pay*)

Writing

Write about birthday events in your family.

あのレストランはどうでしたか Dining Experiences

Notes Relating to This Lesson	
Grammar and Usage	
11 ～で 195	12 ～でした, ～かったです 195

Basic Vocabulary and Kanji

か˥ぞく	家族	*n. family members*
このあいだ	この間	*the other day*
ま˥え	前	*n. the previous time, the front position*
し˥んせつ(な)	親切だ・親切じゃない	*adj. kind, thoughtful*
ゆうめい(な)	有名だ・有名じゃない	*adj. famous*
わる˥い	悪い・悪くない	*adj. bad*
いじわ˥る(な)	意地悪だ・意地悪じゃない	*adj. mean, nasty*

Newly introduced kanji: 前(まえ)

Dialog

Mary Carter is looking for a nice restaurant in the neighborhood and asks Yoshio Tanaka about it.

カーター：どこかいいレストランをしりませんか。
(～をしりませんか *Do you know~?*)

田中　：えきの近くの中華(ちゅうか)レストランはいいですよ。この間かぞくで行きました。
(中華(ちゅうか)レストラン *Chinese restaurant*)

カーター：どうでしたか。

田中　：とてもおいしかったです。

カーター：高かったですか。

田中　：いいえ、3人で4,000円でした。あそこはシュウマイでゆうめいなんですよ。
(シュウマイ *Chinese steam meat dumpling*)

カーター：ああ、そうですか。

Guess and Try 1

Fill in the blanks and interpret the sentences. 11

1. マンハッタンはかんこうきゃく ____ にぎやかです。
(かんこうきゃく *tourists*)

2. 兄はアルバイト ____ いそがしいです。
(いそがしい *busy*)

3. バスはゆき ____ 来ませんでした。
(ゆき *snow*)

Guess and Try 2

Fill in the blanks. 12

1. 今学期の文学の先生は日本人です。先学期の先生も日本人 __________ 。

2. この車は便利(べんり)です。前の車も便利 __________ 。

3. この車はエンジンがわるいです。前の車もエンジンが __________ 。

4. この車はいいです。前の車も __________ 。

Guess and Try 3

Fill in the blanks. 12

1. 今学期の文学の先生は日本人じゃありません。先学期の先生も日本人 __________ 。

2. この車は便利じゃありません。前の車も便利 ________。

3. 今学期の文学の先生はあまりやさしくありません。先学期の先生もあまり ________。

4. この車はよくありません。前の車も ________ ________。

Drill 1: Conjugation

高いです ⟶ 高かったです

1. わるいです
2. うるさいです
3. いいです
4. しずかです
5. にぎやかです
6. ゆうめいです
7. 日本人です

Drill 2: Formation

ねだん・高いです ⟶ ねだんが高かったです

1. サービス・わるいです
2. コーヒー・まずいです
3. ウエイター・いじわるです

Drill 3: Mini-Conversation

たべものは高かったですか ⟶ いいえ、高くありませんでした

1. レストランの中はきれいでしたか
2. レストランの中はしずかでしたか
3. ウエイターはしんせつでしたか
4. りょうりはおいしかったですか
5. サービスはよかったですか

Task: Classroom Activity

Collect the information about the restaurants in the neighborhood. Ask at least three classmates. Use the dialog as a model.

私(わたし)	
さん	
さん	
さん	
さん	

Short Reading

この間、家族で紅山(べにやま)レストランに行きました。シェフは長い包丁(ほうちょう)二本で海老(えび)や野菜(やさい)を目の前で切りました。それから、鉄板(てっぱん)の上で料理しました。とても、上手でした。シェフの話は、とてもおもしろかったです。料理はまあまあおいしかったです。でも、とても高かったです。

(包丁(ほうちょう) *knife,* 海老(えび) *shrimp,* 野菜(やさい) *vegetable,*
切(き)る *to cut; to chop,* 鉄板(てっぱん) *hot iron plate,*
話(はなし) *talking; story*)

Writing

Write about your experiences at some restaurants.

兄弟とけんかしたことがありますか Experiences

Notes Relating to This Lesson	
Grammar and Usage	
13 ～ど vs ～かい 196	15 ～たことがある 196
14 ～た 196	

Basic Vocabulary and Kanji

がいこく	外国	*n. foreign country*
けんか	喧嘩	*n. fight, quarrel* (弟とけんかをする *to have a fight with one's younger brother)*
とりあい	取り合い	*n. fight over taking something*
つまら˥ない	詰まらない・詰まらなくない	*adj. boring, unexciting, uninteresting*
はずかし˥い	恥ずかしい・恥ずかしくない	*adj. embarrassing, shameful*
おと˥す	*s*-**u** 落とす・落とさない・落とし・落として	*vt. to let something fall, to lose*
たと˥えば	例えば	*for example*
～とか		*etc*
～ど	～度	*c. ~times* 13

Newly introduced kanji:

外国(がいこく)・～度(ど)・今度(こんど)

外	ノ ク タ 夕 外	度	' 亠 广 户 庐 庐 府 度 度

Dialog

Yoshio Tanaka and Yoko Yamada talk about confrontations with other people.

田中　：山田さんは兄弟とけんかをしたことがありますか。

山田　：いいえ、ありません。田中さんは。

田中　：はずかしいんですが、よくします。

山田　：たとえば。

田中　：たとえば、テレビのとりあいとか。

山田　：ああ、そうですか。ともだちとけんかをしたことはありますか。

田中　：はい。大きいけんかは二度したことがあります。

Guess and Try 1

Look at the following table and state how the plain past affirmative forms are created. 14

Dictionary Form	Te-form	Plain Past Affirmative Form
たべる	たべて	たべた
みる	みて	みた
する	して	した
くる	きて	きた
いく	いって	いった
かく	かいて	かいた
およぐ	およいで	およいだ
のむ	のんで	のんだ

Guess and Try 2

What is the difference between the two sentences in each set? 15

1. A. 私は富士山(ふじさん)を見ました。
   (富士山(ふじさん) *Mt. Fuji*)

   B. 私は富士山を見たことがあります。

2. A. 私は富士山を見ませんでした。

   B. 私は富士山を見たことがありません。

3. A. 私は外国に行ったことがあります。

   B. 私は外国に行くことがあります。

Drill 1: Conjugation

食べる ⟶ 食べた

1. 書く
2. 働(はたら)く
3. 行く
4. およぐ
5. 言う
6. 買う
7. 休む
8. 飲む
9. 読む
10. 話す
11. ある
12. する
13. 来る

Drill 2: Formation

日本に行った ⟶ 日本に行ったことがありますか

1. うなぎを食べた
2. おさけを飲んだ
3. お父さんとけんかをした
4. クレジットカードをおとした
5. 日本のえいがを見た
6. ゆうめいな人とあくしゅをした
   (Shake hands with a famous person.)

Task: Small Group Work

Discuss your experiences about the following in the group.

1. 富士山(ふじさん)にのぼった *climbed Mt. Fuji*
2. 日本(にほん)のアニメーションを見(み)た
3. 日本人(にほんじん)のうちに行(い)った
4. Your choice!

Short Reading

この間はじめて日本人のうちに行きました。とても、小さかったです。台所は食器棚(しょっきだな)がたくさんありました。そして、小さいお皿(さら)がびっくりするほどたくさんありました。冷蔵庫(れいぞうこ)や、電子(でんし)レンジや、洗濯機(せんたくき)も小さかったです。でも、とてもきれいでした。畳(たたみ)の部屋で、床(ゆか)に座(すわ)りました。友達3人と、焼肉(やきにく)をしました。とても、楽しかったです。

(はじめて *for the first time,* 台所(だいどころ) *kitchen,*
食器棚(しょっきだな) *kitchen shelf; cabinet,* お皿(さら) *plates; dishes,*
びっくりするほど *surprisingly,*
電子(でんし)レンジ *microwave oven,*
洗濯機(せんたくき) *laundry machine,* 畳(たたみ) *straw mat,* 床(ゆか) *floor,*
焼肉(やきにく) *Korean-style barbecue*)

Writing

Write about one of your experiences related to Japanese culture.

– Grammar and Usage –

1 あう: To meet / to see

When you saw someone, you can either say 会いました or 見ました.

(a) 昨日山田さんに会いました。
I saw Ms. Yamada yesterday.

(b) 昨日山田さんを見ました。
I saw Ms. Yamada yesterday.

Sentence (a) means you met or ran into Ms. Yamada and she noticed you. By contrast, sentence (b) means you saw Ms. Yamada, but implies that she did not notice you when she was seen.

2 〜へ: To / toward〜 [Direction]

The direction of movement such as going, coming and returning is marked by 〜へ.

(a) 東京へ行きました。
I went to Tokyo.

(b) 東京へ来ました。
I came to Tokyo.

(c) 東京へ帰りました。
I returned to Tokyo.

The particle へ in the above sentences can be replaced by the particle に, as in the following sentences:

(d) 東京に行きました。
I went to Tokyo.

(e) 東京に来ました。
I came to Tokyo.

(f) 東京に帰りました。
I returned to Tokyo.

The sentences in (d), (e) and (f) give the impression that Tokyo is the final destination much more strongly than the sentences in (a), (b) and (c).

3 〜で: Under the condition such as 〜 [Circumstantial condition]

The particle 〜で can mark the "condition" or "circumstance" that underlies the given event or activity, showing "how" it is done.

(a) はだしで行きました。
(I) went (there) barefoot.

(b) 三人で行きました。
(I) went (there) in a group of three.

(c) きもので行きました。
(I) went (there) wearing a kimono.

(d) わりびきで買いました。
(I) bought (it) at a discounted price.

(e) なまで食べました。
(I) ate (it) raw.

(f) 私は昨日うちで母と二人でワインを飲みました。
I had wine with my mother at home yesterday.

4 Indefinite pronouns (なにか something, だれか someone, etc)

An indefinite pronoun such as "somewhere" and "anywhere" is composed of a question word and the particle か in Japanese. As you can see in the following examples, the particles が and を that follow an indefinite pronoun are usually deleted, although other particles (for example, で, と, へ and に) are not.

(a) 明日はモールへ行きます。
I will go to the mall tomorrow.

(b) 明日はどこへ行きますか。
Where are you going tomorrow?

(c) 明日はどこかへ行きますか。
Will you go to anywhere tomorrow?

(d) 明日はどこかへ行きます。
I will go to somewhere tomorrow.

(e) 何か(を)食べました。
(I) ate something.

(f) 何か(を)食べましたか。
Did (you) eat anything?

(g) だれか(が)来ました。
Someone came.

(h) 何か(が)あります。
There is something.

(i) どこかで食べます。
(I) will eat somewhere.

(j) だれかと食べます。
(I) will eat with someone.

(k) どこかへ行きます。
(I) will go somewhere.

(l) どこかに行きます。
(I) will go somewhere.

(m) だれかにてがみを書きます。
(I) will write a letter to someone.

5 Negative pronouns (なにも nothing, だれも no one, etc)

When a combination of a question word and the particle も occurs with a negative verb, they jointly form a negative pronoun like "nothing", "no one" or "nowhere" in English. For example, どこへも行きませんでした means *I went nowhere*. も follows the question word and its associated grammatical particle, but if the grammatical particle is が or を, it **must** be deleted (for example, だれも来ませんでした *No one came*.)

(a) だれかにてがみを書きましたか。
Did you write a letter to anyone?
— いいえ、だれにもてがみを書きませんでした。
— No, I didn't write a letter to anyone.

(b) どこかに行きましたか。
Did you go somewhere?
— いいえ、どこにも行きませんでした。
— No, I did not go anywhere.

(c) だれか来ましたか。
Did anyone come?
— いいえ、だれも来ませんでした。
— No, no one came.

(d) 何か食べましたか。
Did you eat anything?
— いいえ、何も食べませんでした。
— No, I ate nothing.

(e) 何もありません。
There is nothing.

(f) だれとも話しません。
I will not talk with anyone.

Negative pronouns such as だれも and なにも are unaccented pitch-wise. If they are pronounced with a wrong pitch, they may be interpreted differently.

6 いつ: When? [Question word for time]

The question word いつ can be used for asking the relative or absolute time of an event. You can also use a question phrase with a specific counter such as 何時に *at what o'clock*, 何曜日に *on what day*, 何日に *on what date*, 何月に *in what month* and 何年に *in what year*.

(a) いつ行きますか。
When are (you) going (there)?

(b) 何曜日に行きますか。
On what day are (you) going (there)?

7 ～ごろ: Approximately

ごろ means *approximately* or *about*, but unlike ぐらい, ごろ can follow only absolute time expressions.

(a) 2時ぐらいに行きました。
(I) went (there) approximately at two o'clock.

(b) 2時ごろに行きました。
(I) went (there) approximately at two o'clock.

(c) 2時間ぐらい勉強しました。
(I) studied for about two hours.

(d) 2時間ごろ勉強しました。 (✕)
(Ungrammatical)

(e) たばこを2本ぐらいすいました。
(I) smoked approximately two cigarettes.

(f) たばこを2本ごろすいました。 (✕)
(Ungrammatical)

8 Absolute time expressions

The following table summarizes the absolute time expressions.

Absolute Time Expressions			
Years	せんきゅうひゃくきゅうじゅうろくねん 1996年		にせんいちねん 2001年
	せんきゅうひゃくきゅうじゅうななねん 1997年		にせんにねん 2002年
	せんきゅうひゃくきゅうじゅうはちねん 1998年		にせんさんねん 2003年
	せんきゅうひゃくきゅうじゅうきゅうねん 1999年		にせんじゅうねん 2010年
	にせんねん 2000年		にせんじゅういちねん 2011年
Months	いちがつ 1月	ごがつ 5月	くがつ 9月
	にがつ 2月	ろくがつ 6月	じゅうがつ 10月
	さんがつ 3月	しちがつ 7月	じゅういちがつ 11月
	しがつ 4月	はちがつ 8月	じゅうにがつ 12月

Absolute Time Expressions

Dates	1日 (ついたち)	12日 (じゅうににち)	23日 (にじゅうさんにち)
	2日 (ふつか)	13日 (じゅうさんにち)	24日 (にじゅうよっか)
	3日 (みっか)	14日 (じゅうよっか)	25日 (にじゅうごにち)
	4日 (よっか)	15日 (じゅうごにち)	26日 (にじゅうろくにち)
	5日 (いつか)	16日 (じゅうろくにち)	27日 (にじゅうしちにち)
	6日 (むいか)	17日 (じゅうしちにち)	28日 (にじゅうはちにち)
	7日 (なのか)	18日 (じゅうはちにち)	29日 (にじゅうくにち)
	8日 (ようか)	19日 (じゅうくにち)	30日 (さんじゅうにち)
	9日 (ここのか)	20日 (はつか)	31日 (さんじゅういちにち)
	10日 (とおか)	21日 (にじゅういちにち)	
	11日 (じゅういちにち)	22日 (にじゅうににち)	
Days of the week	月曜日 (げつようび)	木曜日 (もくようび)	日曜日 (にちようび)
	火曜日 (かようび)	金曜日 (きんようび)	
	水曜日 (すいようび)	土曜日 (どようび)	
O'clock	1時 (いちじ)	5時 (ごじ)	9時 (くじ)
	2時 (にじ)	6時 (ろくじ)	10時 (じゅうじ)
	3時 (さんじ)	7時 (しちじ)	11時 (じゅういちじ)
	4時 (よじ)	8時 (はちじ)	12時 (じゅうにじ)
Minutes	1分 (いっぷん)	7分 (ななふん)	20分 (にじゅっぷん)
	2分 (にふん)	8分 / 8分 (はっぷん はちふん)	30分 (さんじゅっぷん)
	3分 (さんぷん)	9分 (きゅうふん)	40分 (よんじゅっぷん)
	4分 (よんぷん)	10分 (じゅっぷん)	50分 (ごじゅっぷん)
	5分 (ごふん)	11分 (じゅういっぷん)	60分 (ろくじゅっぷん)
	6分 (ろっぷん)	12分 (じゅうにふん)	

9 Relative time expressions

Relative time expressions specify the time relative to the time of the speech (for example, 明日 (あした) *tomorrow*) as opposed to the absolute time expressions that specify the time that you can point at on a calendar or on a clock (for example, 月曜日 (げつようび) *Monday*). The following are typical relative time expressions:

Relative Time Expressions

Past ← ● → Future

-2	-1	0	+1	+2
一昨日 (おととい) / 一昨日 (いっさくじつ) *the day before yesterday*	昨日 (きのう) / 昨日 (さくじつ) *yesterday*	今日 (きょう) *today*	明日 (あした) / 明日 (あす) *tomorrow*	明後日 (あさって) / 明後日 (みょうごにち) *the day after tomorrow*
先々週 (せんせんしゅう) *the week before the last*	先週 (せんしゅう) *last week*	今週 (こんしゅう) *this week*	来週 (らいしゅう) *next week*	再来週 (さらいしゅう) *the week after the next*
先々月 (せんせんげつ) *the month before the last*	先月 (せんげつ) *last month*	今月 (こんげつ) *this month*	来月 (らいげつ) *next month*	再来月 (さらいげつ) *the month after the next*
一昨年 (おととし) / 一昨年 (いっさくねん) *the year before the last*	去年 (きょねん) *last year*	今年 (ことし) *this year*	来年 (らいねん) *next year*	再来年 (さらいねん) *the year after the next*
	先学期 (せんがっき) *last semester*	今学期 (こんがっき) *this semester*	来学期 (らいがっき) *next semester*	
	前回 (ぜんかい) / 先回 (せんかい) *last time*	今回 (こんかい) *this time*	次回 (じかい) *next time*	

Relative time expressions do not have to be followed by any particle in a sentence.

10 ～に: At, on, in [Absolute time of an event]

The absolute time of an event such as 月曜日 *Monday* is followed by the particle ～に, although the relative time of an event such as 明日 *tomorrow* is not:

(a) 月曜日に行きます。
(I) will go (there) on Monday.

(b) 明日行きます。
(I) will go (there) tomorrow.

(c) 5時に行きます。
I will go (there) at five o'clock.

(d) 来週行きます。
I will go (there) next week.

(e) 1月に行きます。
I will go (there) in January.

(f) 1月26日に行きます。
I will go (there) on January 26th.

(g) 来年行きます。
I will go (there) next year.

This does not mean that relative time expressions may not be followed by any particle. In fact, they can be followed by a particle such as は, から and まで.

(h) 今年は働きません。
I will not work this year.

(i) 来年から日本に住みます。
I will live in Japan starting with next year.

11 ～で: Due to [Cause / reason]

The particle ～で can mark the reason for or the cause of some events or situations. For example, 私はスキーでけがをしました means *(I) got injured (due to) skiing.*

(a) マンハッタンは観光客でにぎやかです。
Manhattan is bustling with tourists.

(b) 兄はアルバイトでいそがしいです。
My brother is busy because he is working at a part-time job.

(c) バスは雪で来ませんでした。
The bus did not come due to the (heavy) snow.

(d) 秋田はおいしいお米で有名です。
Akita is famous for good rice.

(e) 私はかぜでクラスを休みました。
I missed the class because of my cold.

(f) 私は残業でつかれました。
I got tired because of the overtime work.

(g) かぜでまどが開きました。
The window opened because of the wind.

12 ～でした, ～かったです [Past tense of noun and adjective predicates]

The polite past tense forms of noun predicates and na-type adjectives are formed in the same way. If they are affirmative, just replace the ending です with でした, as in (a) and (b). If they are negative, just add でした at the end of the present form, as in (c) and (d).

(a) 今学期の文学の先生は日本人です。先学期の先生も日本人でした。
This semester's literature professor is a Japanese. The last semester's professor was also a Japanese.

(b) この車は便利です。前の車も便利でした。
This car is very convenient. The car I had before was also convenient.

(c) 今学期の文学の先生は日本人じゃありません。先学期の先生も日本人じゃありませんでした。
This semester's literature professor is not a Japanese. The last semester's professor was not a Japanese, either.

(d) この車は便利じゃありません。前の車も便利じゃありませんでした。
This car is not very convenient. The car I had before was also not very convenient.

An i-type adjective patterns differently. If it is affirmative, replace the inflection part い in the present forms with ～かった. If it is negative, just add でした at the end of the present form.

(e) 今学期の文学の先生はとてもやさしいです。先学期の先生もやさしかったです。
This semester's literature professor is very kind. The last semester's professor was also kind.

(f) 今学期の文学の先生はあまりやさしくありません。先学期の先生もあまりやさしくありませんでした。
This semester's literature professor is not very kind. The last semester's professor was not very kind, either.

いい *good* is an irregular adjective, whose stem alternates between い and よ (いいです・よかったです・よくありません・よくありませんでした).

The following table summarizes the polite forms of all the predicates:

The Polite Form of Predicates			
		Affirmative	**Negative**
Verb Predicate	present	食べます	食べません
	past	食べました	食べませんでした
Noun Predicate (Noun + Copula)	present	学生です	学生じゃありません
	past	学生でした	学生じゃありませんでした
Na-adjective Predicate	present	便利です	便利じゃありません
	past	便利でした	便利じゃありませんでした
I-Adjective Predicate	present	高いです	高くありません (高くないです)
	past	高かったです	高くありませんでした (高くなかったです)

13 ～ど vs ～かい: ～times [The number of occasions]

There are two counters for occasions or events: ～度 and ～回. The number of events in the past or in the future can be expressed by either one of them, although ～回 is preferred if the number is four or greater:

(a) 2度行きました。
(I) went (there) twice.

(b) 2度行ったことがあります。
(I) have been (there) twice.

(c) 2度行くつもりです。
(I) plan to go (there) twice.

(d) 2回行きました。
(I) went (there) twice.

(e) 2回行ったことがあります。
(I) have been (there) twice.

(f) 2回行くつもりです。
(I) plan to go (there) twice.

By contrast, the frequency of an event can be expressed by ～回, but not by ～度.

(g) 1週間に2回行きます。
(I) go (there) twice a week.

(h) 1週間に2度行きます。 (✕)
(Ungrammatical)

14 Plain past affirmative forms of verbs (～た)

The plain past affirmative form of a verb is created by replacing the final て or で in its te-form with た or だ, respectively. (See Chapter Ten for te-forms.) For example, the te-form of the verb たべる is たべて and its plain past affirmative form is たべた. Similarly, the て-form of the verb よむ is よんで and its plain past form is よんだ.

Dictionary Form	Te-form	Plain Past Affirmative Form
たべる *to eat*	たべて	たべた
みる *to watch*	みて	みた
かく *to write*	かいて	かいた
およぐ *to swim*	およいで	およいだ
はこぶ *to carry*	はこんで	はこんだ
よむ *to read*	よんで	よんだ
しぬ *to die*	しんで	しんだ
まつ *to wait*	まって	まった
はなす *to speak*	はなして	はなした
つくる *to make*	つくって	つくった
かう *to buy*	かって	かった
する *to do*	して	した
くる *to come*	きて	きた

15 ～たことがある: I have ～ed [Experience]

For expressing your experience, use the verb in the plain past tense form plus ～ことがある rather than just the verb in the past tense form. For example, 富士山を見たことがあります or 富士山を見たことがありません expresses what experience you have or you do not have, whereas 富士山を見ました or 富士山を見ませんでした just states what you did or you did not do at some specific time in the past.

If the verb before ことがある is in the present tense, this construction expresses one's habit or life style, rather than his / her experiences:

(a) 外国(がいこく)に行(い)ったことがあります。
(I) have the experience of being in a foreign country. /
(I) have been to a foreign country.

(b) 外国に行くことがあります。
(I) have occasions to go to a foreign country. /
(I) sometimes go to a foreign country.

– Culture –

Ⓐ ～ねん: The year～ [Expressing years]

There are two systems for expressing years in Japan: the Western system based on the Christian era and the Japanese system based on the reigns of emperors. When a new emperor ascends the throne, a new era name is created. For example, the year Emperor Heisei (平成天皇(へいせいてんのう)) ascended the throne (1989) was called 平成(へいせい)1年(ねん) in the Japanese system and 1989年 in the Western system. Accordingly, the following year was called 平成2年 in the Japanese system and 1990年 in the Western system. The same era name is used until a new emperor ascends the throne. The following are the last four era names and their periods:

明治(めいじ)：明治1年～明治45年 (1868–1912)
大正(たいしょう)：大正1年～大正15年 (1912–1926)
昭和(しょうわ)：昭和1年～昭和64年 (1926–1989)
平成(へいせい)：平成1年～ (1989–)

Ⓑ National holidays

The following are the national holidays in Japan:

1月1日	がんじつ (元日)	New Year's Day
Second Monday of January	せいじんのひ (成人の日)	Coming-of-age day
2月11日	けんこくきねんび (建国記念日)	National Founding Day
3月21日	しゅんぶんのひ (春分の日)	Vernal Equinox Day
4月29日	みどりのひ (緑の日)	Greenery Day
5月3日	けんぽうきねんび (憲法記念日)	Constitution Memorial Day
5月4日	こくみんのきゅうじつ (国民の休日)	National Holiday
5月5日	こどものひ (子供の日)	Children's Day
7月20日	うみのひ (海の日)	Marine Day
9月15日	けいろうのひ (敬老の日)	Respect-for-the-aged Day
9月23日	しゅうぶんのひ (秋分の日)	Autumnal Equinox Day
Second Monday of October	たいいくのひ (体育の日)	Health-sports Day
11月3日	ぶんかのひ (文化の日)	Culture Day
11月23日	きんろうかんしゃのひ (勤労感謝の日)	Labor Thanksgiving Day
12月23日	てんのうたんじょうび (天皇誕生日)	Emperor's Birthday (the current emperor)

– Writing –

ⓐ なつあし

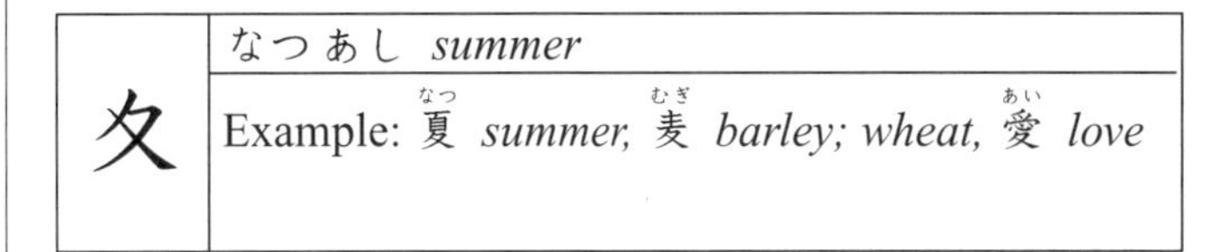

夂	なつあし *summer*
	Example: 夏(なつ) *summer,* 麦(むぎ) *barley; wheat,* 愛(あい) *love*

ⓑ ふゆがしら

夊	ふゆがしら *winter*
	Example: 冬(ふゆ) *winter,* 客(きゃく) *guest,* 各(かく) *each*

– Kanji List –

春・夏・秋・冬・夏休み・会う・会話・今年・去年・来年・学期・～日・～年・前・外国・～度・今度

Kanji	Readings / Meaning	Strokes	Examples
春	はる・シュン *spring*	[9]	Example: 春(はる) *spring*
夏	なつ・カ *summer*	[10]	Example: 夏(なつ) *summer*
秋	あき・シュウ *fall, autumn*	[9]	Example: 秋(あき) *autumn*
冬	ふゆ・トウ *winter*	[5]	Example: 冬(ふゆ) *winter*
休	やす-む・キュウ *rest*	[6]	Example: 休む(やすむ) *to rest* 夏休み(なつやすみ) *summer vacation*
会	あ-う・カイ *meeting, association*	[6]	Example: 会う(あう) *to meet* 会話(かいわ) *conversation* 会社(かいしゃ) *company*
話	はな-す・はなし・ワ *talk*	[13]	Example: 話す(はなす) *to speak* 会話(かいわ) *conversation* 電話(でんわ) *telephone*
今	いま・コン *now, present*	[4]	Example: 今(いま) *now* 今日(きょう) *today* 今年(ことし) *this year*
年	とし・ネン *year*	[6]	Example: 今年(ことし) *this year* 去年(きょねん) *last year* 三年(さんねん) *three years*
去	さ-る・キョ *leave*	[5]	Example: 去年(きょねん) *last year*
来	く-る・こ-ない・ライ *come, next*	[7]	Example: 来る(くる) *to come* 来年(らいねん) *next year*
学	まな-ぶ・ガク・ガッ *study*	[8]	Example: 来学期(らいがっき) *next academic term* 学生(がくせい) *students*
期	キ *term, period, expect*	[12]	Example: 今学期(こんがっき) *current academic term*
日	ひ・び・ニチ・ニ・ジツ *sun, day*	[4]	Example: 日本(にほん) *Japan* 3月(がつ)21日(にち) *March 21st*
前	まえ・ゼン *before, front, previous*	[9]	Example: 前(まえ)の先生(せんせい) *the previous teacher* 車(くるま)の前(まえ) *in front of the car* 名前(なまえ) *name*
外	そと・ガイ・ゲ *out, outer, other, foreign*	[5]	Example: 外(そと) *outside* 外国(がいこく) *foreign country*
国	くに・コク *country*	[8]	Example: 国(くに) *country* 中国(ちゅうごく) *China* 外国(がいこく) *foreign country*

度	' 亠 广 广 庐 庐 庐 度 度 [9]
ド *degree,* *frequency*	Example: 一度(いちど) *once* 今度(こんど) *next time*

– Review –

Q1. Write the reading of the following words and phrases.

1. 昨日　今日　明日
   去年　今年　来年

2. 1 日　2 日　3 日　4 日　5 日
   6 日　7 日　8 日　9 日　10 日

3. 1989 年 9 月 23 日

4. 2002 年 4 月 4 日

Q2. Conjugate the verbs following the example.

For example:

食べる → 食べた

1. およぐ → ____________
2. 話す → ____________
3. とる → ____________
4. 作る → ____________
5. ねる → ____________
6. 見る → ____________
7. 帰る → ____________
8. 来る → ____________
9. 行く → ____________
10. する → ____________

Q3. Answer the following questions in Japanese.

1. クリスマスはいつですか。
2. バレンタイン・デーはいつですか。
3. エイプリル・フールはいつですか。
4. 今月(こんげつ)は何月(なんがつ)ですか。
5. 先月(せんげつ)は何月でしたか。

Q4. Fill in the blanks and create sensible sentences.

1. 今日(きょう)はよく食べました。でも、昨日はぜんぜん
   ____________。
2. 昨日(きのう)の晩(ばん)はすしを ________。明日の晩も
   すしを ________。
3. 母のりょうりはいつもおいしいです。昨日の晩
   ごはんもとても ____________。
4. 昨日の晩ごはんはスパゲッティ ________。
   今日の晩ごはんもスパゲッティ ________。

Q5. Fill in the blanks appropriately.

1. 昨日(きのう)は ______ 行きましたか。
   Did you go anywhere yesterday?
   — いいえ、______ 行きませんでした。
   — No, I did not go anywhere.

2. 昨日は ______ 読(よ)みましたか。
   Did you read anything?
   — いいえ、______ 読みませんでした。
   — No, I did not read anything.

3. 昨日は ______ 勉強(べんきょう)しましたか。
   Did you study with anyone yesterday?
   — いいえ、______ 勉強しませんでした。
   — No, I didn't study with anyone.

4. 昨日は ______ 来ましたか。
   Did anyone come yesterday?
   — いいえ、______ 来ませんでした。
   — No, no one came yesterday.

Q6. Fill in the blanks with the particle に if necessary.

1. 私は昨日 ____ クラスに行きませんでした。
2. 私は水曜日 ____ しけんがあります。
3. 父はたいてい 7 時 ____ おきます。

4. 私は来年 ____ フランスに行きます。

5. あなたはいつ ____ アメリカに来ましたか。

6. あなたはたいてい何時 ____ ねますか。

Q7. Using the words in each set, make up a sentence and translate it.

1. 昨日・どこにも

2. いつ・中国(ちゅうごく)

3. 昨日・だれも

4. 今日・何も

5. だれとも

6. 月曜日

Tips and Additional Knowledge: Osaka Dialect

The Osaka dialect (大阪弁(おおさかべん)) is very distinct from the Tokyo dialect, which is considered to be the closest to the standard Japanese. The Osaka dialect has different pitch-accents, sentence intonations, sentence endings, suffixes and phrases. The following are some of the distinct daily-life phrases in the Osaka dialect.

	Osaka Dialect	**Tokyo Dialect**
Thank you	おおきに	ありがとう
Really?	ほんま?	ほんとう?
That's not good. You cannot do that.	あかん	いけない
That's wrong. That's different.	ちゃう	ちがう
To throw away	ほかす	すてる

CHAPTER THIRTEEN

Relating States and Events

Lesson 54
難しくて、たいへんです **College Courses** **202**

Lesson 55
昨日はテレビを見て、ねました **Listing Activities** **204**

Lesson 56
かぜをひいて、クラスを休みました **Causes and Results** **206**

Grammar and Usage **208**

1 Te-forms [Listing predicates] 208
2 〜に: For [The target of pros and cons] 208
3 のる: To ride, to take 209
4 〜に, 〜ために [Purpose] 209
5 それで: As a result [Resulting fact] 209
6 どうしたんですか: What happened? 209

Culture **209**

A はらじゅく 209
B New year holidays in Japan 210

Writing **210**

a ふるとり 210
b さんずいへん 210
c くさかんむり 210
d よつてん 210
e New year's cards (ねんがじょう) 210

Kanji List **211**

Review **211**

Tips and Additional Knowledge:
Abbreviated English Loan Words **212**

難しくて、たいへんです College Courses

Notes Relating to This Lesson	
Grammar and Usage	**Writing**
1 Te-forms 208	ⓐ ふるとり 210
2 〜に 208	

Basic Vocabulary and Kanji

れきし	歴史	*n. history*
ぶ˥つり	物理	*n. physics*
げんご˥がく	言語学	*n. linguistics*
しゅうしょく	就職	*n. employment*
らく˥(な)	楽だ・楽じゃない	*adj. easy (less labor intensive)*
と˥る	***r-u*** 取る・取らない・取り・取って	*vt. to take* (日本語を取る *to take a Japanese course)*
がんば˥る	***r-u*** 頑張る・頑張らない・頑張り・頑張って	*vt. to try one's best*

Newly introduced kanji:

言語学(げんごがく)・楽(たの)しい (fun)・楽(らく)です・
漢字(かんじ) (Chinese characters)・難(むずか)しい (difficult) ⓐ

楽	′ ľ ή ή ή 自 伯 泊 泊′ 泊″ 凃 率 楽 楽	字	′ ′′ 宀 宁 字 字
漢	` `` 氵 氵 氵 汁 汁 汁 浐 浐 渲 漢 漢		
難	一 十 廾 艹 艹 芒 苎 苎 草 莫 莫 莫 歎 歎 歎 歎 難 難		

Dialog

Yoshio Tanaka asks Mary Carter about the courses she is taking.

田中(たなか)　：マリーさんは今(いま)どのクラスをとっていますか。
(とっている *to be taking*)

カーター：コンピューターとれきしです。

田中　：コンピューターのクラスはどうですか。

カーター：先生(せんせい)がきびしくて、しゅくだいが多(おお)くて、たいへんです。

田中　：ああ、そうですか。
でも、コンピューターはしゅうしょくにいいですよ。

カーター：ええ、がんばります。

田中　：れきしのクラスはどうですか。

カーター：れきしのクラスは楽で、楽しいです。

田中　：ああ、そうですか。

Guess and Try 1

Fill in the blanks using the given adjectives after conjugating them appropriately. 1

1. 私の姉(あね)は ________________ です。
(やさしいです・明(あか)るいです・きれいです)

2. 私の姉は ________________ です。
(明るいです・きれいです・やさしいです)

3. 私の姉は ________________ 人です。
(やさしいです・明るいです・きれいです)

4. 私の姉は ________________ 人です。
(明るいです・きれいです・やさしいです)

5. 私の姉は ________________ 人です。
(あたまがいいです・やさしいです)

Guess and Try 2

Fill in the blanks with appropriate particles. [2]

1. ビタミンAは目(め) ____ いいです。
   Vitamin A is good for the eyes.

2. このかばんはりょこう ____ べんりです。
   This bag is convenient for traveling.

Drill 1: Conjugation

難しいです ⟶ 難しくて
まじめです ⟶ まじめで

1. きびしいです
2. 明るいです
3. 広いです
4. 安いです
5. べんりです
6. しずかです
7. きれいです
8. いいです

Drill 2: Formation

難しいです・たいへんです ⟶ 難しくて、たいへんです

1. まじめです・きびしいです
2. きびしいです・まじめです
3. 明るいです・きれいです
4. きれいです・明るいです
5. 安いです・いいです
6. あたまがいいです・ハンサムです
7. きれいです・広いです・べんりです

Task: Survey

Ask three of your classmates what courses they are taking and what the courses are like. (See Dialog.)

私(わたし)	
さん	
さん	
さん	

Vocabulary Collection (College Courses)	
化学(かがく) *chemistry*	経済学(けいざいがく) *economics*
言語学(げんごがく) *linguistics*	工学(こうがく) *engineering*
社会学(しゃかいがく) *sociology*	心理学(しんりがく) *psychology*
人類学(じんるいがく) *anthropology*	数学(すうがく) *mathematics*
生物学(せいぶつがく) *biology*	政治学(せいじがく) *political science*
物理(ぶつり) *physics*	文学(ぶんがく) *literature*
法学(ほうがく) *law*	歴史(れきし) *history*

Short Reading

私は今、物理と、日本語と、言語学のクラスをとっています。物理のクラスはテストが多くて、難しくて、大変です。日本語のクラスはとても楽しくて、好(す)きです。でも、宿題が多いです。言語学のクラスはちょっと難しいですが、とてもおもしろいです。よく友達といっしょに勉強します。来学期は、数学と、日本語と、歴史(れきし)をとるつもりです。

(〜をとっています *to be taking~*,
来学期(らいがっき) *next academic term*)

Writing

Write about the courses you are taking now and the ones you are going to take next term.

昨日はテレビを見て、ねました Listing Activities

Notes Relating to This Lesson	
Grammar and Usage	**Culture**
1 Te-forms 208	Ⓐ はらじゅく 209
3 のる 209	Ⓑ New year holidays in Japan 210
4 〜に, 〜ために 209	**Writing**
	ⓑ さんずいへん 210
	ⓔ New year's cards 210

Basic Vocabulary and Kanji

かいもの	買(い)物	*n. shopping* (買い物をする *to shop / to go shopping*)
そうじ	掃除	*n. cleaning* (掃除をする *to do cleaning*)
せんたく	洗濯	*n. laundry* (洗濯をする *to do the laundry*)
はらじゅく	原宿	*pn. Harajuku (name of a place)* Ⓐ
は˥	歯	*n. tooth* (歯をみがく *to brush one's teeth*)
かお	顔	*n. face*
あらう	*w*-**u** 洗う・洗わない・洗い・洗って	*vt. to wash*
きる	*i*-**ru** 着る・着ない・着・着て	*vt. to wear, to put on (one's clothes)*
のる	*r*-**u** 乗る・乗らない・乗り・乗って	*vi. to ride, to take (a form of transportation)* (バスに乗る *to take / get on a bus*) 3
みがく	*k*-**u** 磨く・磨かない・磨き・磨いて	*vt. to polish*
シャ˥ワーをあびる	シャワーを浴びる	*to take a shower*

Newly introduced kanji:

洗(あら)う・洗(せん)たく(洗濯(せんたく)) ⓑ・乗(の)る・買(か)いもの

洗	丶 丶 氵 氵 汁 汢 洴 涉 洗	乗	一 二 三 乒 乒 垂 垂 乗 乗

Dialog

Ben Lee asks Mary Carter what she did yesterday.

リー　　：昨日は何をしましたか。

カーター：昨日はちかてつに乗って、はらじゅくに行きました。

リー　　：ああ、よかったですね。今日は何をしますか。

カーター：今日は洗たくをして、買いものをして、りょうりをします。

リー　　：それは たいへんですね。

カーター：リーさんは。

リー　　：ぼくはえいがを見に行きます。

Guess and Try 1

Fill in the blanks with appropriate particles. 3

1. 私はバス ____ 大学に行(い)きました。
2. 私はバス ____ 乗(の)りました。

Guess and Try 2

Combine the two sentences into one sentence. 1

1. 昨日は勉強しました。それから、ねました。→
   昨日は ______________________
   ____
2. 今日は勉強します。それから、ねます。→
   今日は ______________________
   ____

Guess and Try 3

What is the difference between the following two sentences? 1

1. しゅくだいをして、テレビを見ました。
2. テレビを見て、しゅくだいをしました。

Guess and Try 4

Look at the following and state how the purpose of an action is expressed. [4]

1. 日本語を勉強しに日本に行きます。
   I will go to Japan to study Japanese.

2. 日本語を勉強するために日本に行きます。
   I will go to Japan to study Japanese.

3. 日本語を勉強しに本を買います。 (✕)
   (Ungrammatical)

4. 日本語を勉強するために本を買います。
   I will buy a dictionary to study Japanese.

Drill 1: Conjugation

食べる ⟶ 食べて

1. 見る
2. おきる
3. ねる
4. きる
5. 作る
6. 乗る
7. 洗う
8. みがく
9. 休む
10. 話す
11. する

Drill 2: Formation

うちに帰る・ねる ⟶ うちに帰って、ねました

1. 先生に会う・話す
2. はをみがく・かおを洗う
3. おきる・シャワーをあびる
4. パジャマをきる・ねる
5. そうじをする・洗たくをする
6. 休む・しゅくだいをする
7. しゅくだいをする・休む
8. バスに乗る・デパートに行く・買いものをする

Task: Survey

Ask three people what they did yesterday and what they are going to do today. (See Dialog.)

私	昨日	
	今日	
さん	昨日	
	今日	
さん	昨日	
	今日	
さん	昨日	
	今日	

Short Reading [B] [e]

昨日は元旦でした。朝、年賀状が届きました。父には200通、母には30通、私には25通来ました。9時ごろ神社に行きました。とても、にぎやかでした。おみくじをひきました。大吉でした。とても、うれしかったです。母のは小吉でした。うちに帰って、おせち料理を食べて、書きぞめをしました。弟と妹は羽根突きをしました。

(元旦 *New Year's Day,* 年賀状 *New Year's card,* 届く *to be delivered,* ～通 *a counter for letters,* 神社 *Shinto shrine,* おみくじ *fortune slips,* おみくじをひく *draw a fortune slip,* 大吉 *excellent luck,* うれしい *happy,* 小吉 *small luck,* おせち料理 *dishes for the New Year,* 書きぞめ *special New Year calligraphy,* 羽根突き *battledore and shuttlecock (or Japanese style badminton)*)

Writing

Write about what you did yesterday.

シャワーをあびる, シャワーあびる

かぜをひいて、クラスを休みました Causes and Results

Notes Relating to This Lesson	
Grammar and Usage	**Writing**
[1] Te-forms 208	ⓒ くさかんむり 210
[5] それで 209	ⓓ よつてん 210
[6] どうしたんですか ...209	

Basic Vocabulary and Kanji

くすり	薬	*n. medicine* (薬をのむ *to take medicine*)
きゅ⌉うりょう	給料	*n. salary, wages, pay*
いた⌉い	痛い・痛くない	*adj. painful* (あたまが痛い *to have a headache*)
いそがし⌉い	忙しい・忙しくない	*adj. busy*
つかれ⌉る	**e-ru** 疲れる・疲れない・疲れ・疲れて	*vi. to get tired*
おくれる	**e-ru** 遅れる・遅れない・遅れ・遅れて	*vi. to be late* (クラスに遅れる *to be late for class*)
やめる	**e-ru** 辞める・辞めない・辞め・辞めて	*vt. to quit, to resign*
ねぼうする	*irr.* 寝坊する	*vi. to oversleep*
かぜをひく	風邪を引く	*to catch a cold*
それで		*con. as a result* [5]
も⌉う		*adv. already* (もうだいじょうぶです *I'm already fine.*)
～てん	～点	*c. ~points*

Newly introduced kanji:

薬(くすり) ⓒ・～点(てん) ⓓ

薬	一 十 艹 艹 廾 苜 苜 苜 甘 菹 薬 薬 薬 薬 薬 薬
点	丨 卜 占 占 占 点 点 点 点

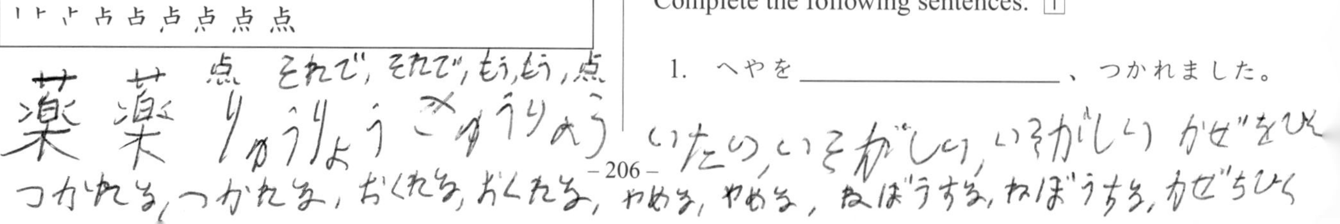

Dialog

A student who missed his Japanese class on the previous day comes to see his teacher at her office.

学生(がくせい)　：先生。

先生(せんせい)　：あっ、ジョンさん。どうぞ。

学生　：しつれいします。

先生　：昨日はクラスを休みましたね。

学生　：はい。

先生　：<u>どうしたんですか。</u>

学生　：かぜをひいたんです。それで、クラスを休んだんです。

先生　：ああ、かぜをひいて、休んだんですか。だいじょうぶですか。

学生　：ええ。今はもうだいじょうぶです。

先生　：ああ、よかったですね。

Guess and Try 1

Guess what the underlined part means. [6]

Guess and Try 2

The two sentences in each set are synonymous. Choose the appropriate options in the parentheses. [1] [5]

1. A. おきて、シャワーをあびました。

   B. おきました。(それから・それで)、シャワーをあびました。

2. A. きゅうりょうが安くて、会社をやめました。

   B. きゅうりょうが安かったです。(それから・それで)、会社をやめました。

Guess and Try 3

Complete the following sentences. [1]

1. へやを ______________ 、つかれました。

2. あたまが いたくて、＿＿＿＿＿＿＿＿＿＿。

3. ＿＿＿＿＿＿＿＿＿＿、クラスに おくれました。

Drill: Formation

ねぼうしました・クラスにおくれました ⟶ ねぼうして、クラスにおくれました

1. 勉強しました・100 点をとりました
2. かぜをひきました・クラスを休(やす)みました
3. あたまがいたかったです・薬をのみました
4. 5 時間勉強しました・つかれました
5. つかれました・ねました
6. いそがしかったです・しゅくだいをしませんでした
7. 難(むずか)しかったです・わかりませんでした
8. 勉強がたいへんでした・大学をやめました

Task: Roll Play / Skit

Variation 1:

S1:

You are a student of the Japanese language. You missed the exam that was given this morning and you decided to see the professor at his / her office.

S2:

You are a Japanese language teacher. One of your students, who missed today's exam, came to see you at your office.

Variation 2:

S1:

You are a student of the Japanese language. You missed ten classes all together this term (クラスを 10 回(かい)休(やす)む), and you are now very concerned about your grades. You decided to talk to the teacher.

S2:

You are a Japanese language teacher. One of your students, who missed ten classes this term, came to see you at your office.

Vocabulary Collection (Course Related Activities)

試験(しけん)をうける *to take an exam*

100 点(てん)をとる *to get 100 points*

クラスに出(で)る *to attend class*

クラスを休(やす)む *to miss class*

宿題(しゅくだい)を出(だ)す *to submit one's homework*

宿題(しゅくだい)を忘(わす)れる *to forget one's homework*

クラスに間(ま)に合(あ)う *to be in time for class*

クラスに遅(おく)れる / クラスに遅刻(ちこく)する *to be late for class*

単位(たんい)をもらう *to receive (academic) credits*

いい成績(せいせき)をもらう *to receive good grades*

Short Reading

僕(ぼく)は毎日うちから大学まで、バスと電車を使います。バスは 1 時間に 1 台です。電車は 2 時間に 1 本です。毎日 5 時のバスに乗って、電車の駅に行って、6 時 35 分の電車に乗ります。いつも 9 時ごろ、大学に着きます。昨日はバスが来なくて、6 時 35 分の電車に乗れませんでした。それで、8 時 35 分の電車に乗りました。大学には 11 時に着きました。9 時の日本語のクラスには間に合いませんでした。それで、先生の研究室に行って、謝(あやま)りました。

(毎日(まいにち) *every day,* 1 時間(いちじかん)に 1 台(だい) *one (bus) in an hour,* 2 時間に 1 本(いっぽん) *one (train) in two hours,* ～本(ほん・ぼん・ぽん) *counter for trains,* 着(つ)く *to arrive,* ～に間(ま)に合(あ)う *to be in time for~,* 研究室(けんきゅうしつ) *(research) office,* 謝(あやま)る *to apologize*)

Writing

Write about one of your bad experiences.

– Grammar and Usage –

1 Te-forms [Listing predicates]

For listing two or more verbs and adjectives in the same sentence, you need to convert them to te-forms except for the last verb or adjective in the sentence. (Remember that the particle と can list **only** nouns; it cannot list verbs and adjectives).

How to form the te-form of a verb is discussed in Chapter Ten. To form the te-form of a na-type-adjective, add で to its stem. To form the te-form of an i-type adjective, add くて to its stem.

(a) 山田さんのお兄さんはまじめで、やさしくて、ハンサムです。
Ms. Yamada's brother is studious, kind and handsome.

(b) あの人は日本人で、学生です。
That person is a Japanese and a student.

(c) テレビを見て、しゅくだいをして、ねました。
(I) watched TV, did (my) homework, and slept.

(d) しゅくだいをして、つかれました。
(I) did my homework, and got tired.

Depending on the context, the relationship between predicates varies. For example, the predicates listed in (a) and (b) have equal status, those listed in (c) express temporary ordered events, and those listed in (d) express events in a cause-and-result relationship.

The tense of the sentence is always expressed by the last verb or adjective as you can see in (e) and (f).

(e) テレビを見て、しゅくだいをして、ねます。
(I) will watch TV, do (my) homework, and sleep.

(f) テレビを見て、しゅくだいをして、ねました。
(I) watched TV, did (my) homework, and slept.

The te-form can also be used for listing adjectives that modify a noun. The last adjective must be in the pre-nominal form in this case.

(g) 山田さんのお姉さんはやさしくて、明るくて、きれいな人です。
Ms. Yamada's sister is a kind, cheerful and pretty person.

(h) 山田さんのお姉さんは明るくて、きれいで、やさしい人です。
Ms. Yamada's sister is a cheerful, pretty and kind person.

The te-forms of verbs and adjectives, both affirmative and negative, are summarized in the following table.

Te-forms		
	Affirmative	**Negative**
Verb	〜て (書いて)	〜なくて (書かなくて) 〜ないで (書かないで)
Copular verb (noun + copula)	〜で (学生で)	〜じゃなくて (学生じゃなくて)
Na-type adjective	〜で (便利で)	〜じゃなくて (便利じゃなくて)
I-type adjective	〜くて (高くて)	〜くなくて (高くなくて)

If the listed adjectives express contrasting properties, they should be listed in different clauses related by the connective particle が as below:

(i) 山田さんのお姉さんは明るくて、きれいですが、ちょっと意地悪です。
Ms. Yamada's sister is cheerful and pretty, but a bit mean.

2 〜に: For [The target of pros and cons]

The properties such as beneficial, harmful, suitable, necessary and useful can be understood only if we specify for what or for whom they hold. The latter is marked by the particle に.

(a) 日本語はビジネスにいいです。
Japanese is good (useful) for business.

(b) ビタミンAは目にいいです。
Vitamin A is good for the eyes.

(c) このかばんはりょこうに便利です。
This bag is convenient for traveling.

(d) バターは心臓によくありません。
Butter is not good for the heart.

(e) コンピューターは私にむいています。
Computers suit me. (I am suited for computers.)

(f) コンピュータは私の仕事に必要です。
Computers are necessary for my job.

(g) ファックスはビジネスに役立ちます。
Fax machines are useful for business.

3 のる: To ride, to take

The basic meaning of the verb 乗る is *to ride*, but it is used with any form of transportation such as airplanes, trains, ships and cars, as well as bicycles, motorcycles and horses. They are marked by the particle に.

(a) ひこうきに乗って下さい。
Please board the airplane.

(b) 自転車に乗って、大学に行きました。
I rode a bicycle, and went to the university.

4 〜に, 〜ために [Purpose]

The particle に follows a verb in the stem form and creates a phrase that expresses the purpose of going, coming and returning.

(a) カフェテリアに朝ごはんを食べに行きます。
I will go to the cafeteria to eat breakfast.

(b) ともだちに会いにサンフランシスコに行きます。
I will go to San Francisco to see my friend.

(c) ひるごはんを食べにうちに帰ります。
I will return home to eat lunch.

(d) 遊びに来て下さい。
Please come to play. / Please come to visit me.

Such a purpose phrase is exclusively used for indicating the purpose of coming, going and returning, and may not be used for indicating the purpose of other activities.

(e) 日本語を勉強しに日本に行きます。
I will go to Japan (in order) to study Japanese.

(f) 日本語を勉強しに本を買います。 (✕)
(Ungrammatical) Intended meaning: *I will buy a book in order to study Japanese.*

The purpose of doing something can be expressed by verbs in the plain form followed by ために, which is the combination of the noun ため *sake* and the particle 〜に. 〜ために can be used for the purpose of any activities including coming, going and returning.

(g) 日本語を勉強するために日本に行きます。
I will go to Japan (in order) to study Japanese.

(h) 日本語を勉強するために本を買います。
I will buy a book in order to study Japanese.

5 それで: As a result [Resulting fact]

それで connects two sentences that are in a "cause" and "result" relationship.

(a) よく勉強しました。それで、よくわかりました。
I studied hard. As a result, I understood very well.

The function of それで is very similar to that of ですから *therefore*, but they differ in that ですから can be used with a "command", "request" or "speculation", but それで cannot:

(b) 今日は雨がふります。ですから、かさをもっていってください。
It will rain today. So, bring an umbrella.

(c) 今日は雨がふります。それで、かさをもっていってください。 (✕)
(Ungrammatical)

(d) 今日は雨がふります。ですから、明日も雨がふるでしょう。
It will rain today. So, it will rain tomorrow, too.

(e) 今日は雨がふります。それで、明日も雨がふるでしょう。 (✕)
(Ungrammatical)

6 どうしたんですか: What happened?

When you notice that something is wrong with someone, you can ask the following questions to show your concern:

(a) どうしたんですか。
What is the matter with you? / What happened?

(b) どうしましたか。
What is the matter with you? / What happened?

(c) 何かあったんですか。
Did anything happen?

– Culture –

A はらじゅく

原宿 is a neighborhood in Tokyo where young people, especially teenagers, gather on weekends. They enjoy dancing, or just walking around wearing unusual costumes and make-up. You will be able to see performances and hear live music on the street.

Ⓑ New year holidays in Japan

The first week in January is a big holiday season called お正月休み *New Year holidays* in Japan. The Japanese are famous for being hardworking, but they relax and enjoy traditional customs during this week. They eat a variety of traditional foods called おせち料理. They often wear traditional Japanese clothes and visit Japanese shrines, and pray for good luck. Children get a gift of money called お年玉 from adults. They play traditional games such as 羽根突き *battledore and shuttlecock* or *Japanese style badminton* and たこあげ *kite-flying*. When they see people they know for the very first time in the new year, they say あけましておめでとうございます *A happy New Year* and 今年 (本年) もよろしくお願いします *I hope our relationship continues well this year*. They receive many New Year greeting cards called 年賀状 from their friends, relatives, students, business acquaintances and neighbors. They are delivered by the post office on January the 1st, all at once.

– Writing –

Ⓐ ふるとり

隹	ふるとり *bird*
	Example: 難しい *difficult,* 進む *to progress,* 雑誌 *magazine*

Ⓑ さんずいへん

氵	さんずいへん *water, liquid*
	Example: 泳ぐ *to swim,* 湖 *lake,* 海 *sea,* 酒 *rice wine,* 泣く *to cry,* 洗う *to wash,* 決める *to decide*

Ⓒ くさかんむり

艹	くさかんむり *plant*
	Example: 草 *grass,* 花 *flower,* 英語 *English,* 薬 *drug,* 苦しい *suffering,* 苦い *bitter*

Ⓓ よつてん

灬	よつてん *fire*
	Example: 点 *point; dot,* 黒 *black,* 熱 *fever; heat*

Ⓔ New year's cards (ねんがじょう)

If you use New Year's postcards from the post office or stationary stores or regular postcards written 年賀 in red right below the space for the stamp on the front, they will be delivered all at once right on New Year's day. You can write あけましておめでとうございます *A happy New Year* and 本年もよろしくお願いします *I hope our relationship continues well this year*. Or, you can write 謹賀新年 *A Happy New Year!*. If you buy New Year's lottery postcards, like the one below, you will see a number printed at the bottom of the front of the postcard. You can get a prize if you receive a postcard with a winning number.

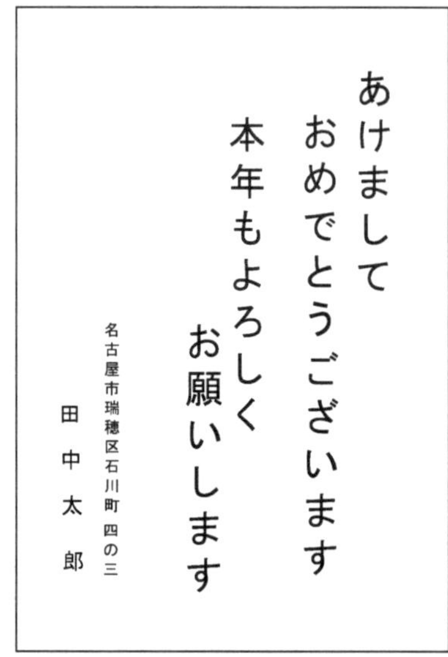

– Kanji List –

言語学・楽しい・楽です・漢字・難しい・洗う・洗たく・乗る・買いもの・薬・〜点

Kanji	Readings / Meaning	Strokes	Examples
言	い-う・ゲン・ゴン *say*	[7]	Example: 言う (い) *to say* 言語学 (げんごがく) *linguistics*
語	かた-る・ゴ *word, language*	[14]	Example: 日本語 (にほんご) *Japanese language* 言語学 (げんごがく) *linguistics*
学	まな-ぶ・ガク・ガッ *study*	[8]	Example: 学生 (がくせい) *a student* 大学 (だいがく) *a university* 言語学 (げんごがく) *linguistics*
楽	たの-しい・ガク・ラク *amuse, pleasant, music*	[13]	Example: 楽しい (たの) *enjoyable* 楽です (らく) *not difficult (easy)*
漢	カン *China*	[13]	Example: 漢字 (かんじ) *Chinese character*
字	ジ *letter, character*	[6]	Example: 漢字 (かんじ) *Chinese character*
難	むずか-しい・ナン *difficult*	[18]	Example: 難しい (むずか) *difficult*
洗	あら-う・セン *wash*	[9]	Example: 洗う (あら) *to wash*
乗	の-る・ジョウ *ride*	[9]	Example: 乗る (の) *to ride*
買	か-う・バイ *buy*	[12]	Example: 買う (か) *to buy* 買いもの (か) *shopping*
薬	くすり・ヤク *medicine*	[16]	Example: 薬 (くすり) *medicine*
点	テン *point, score*	[9]	Example: 100 点 (てん) *100 points*

– Review –

Q1. Fill in the blanks appropriately.

1. かぜを __________ ました。ですから、薬を __________ ました。
2. 7時にはを __________ ます。それから、シャワーを __________ ます。それから、ようふくを __________ ます。
3. 8時にバスに __________ ます。

Q2. Write the pronunciation of the kanji characters in the following sentences in hiragana.

1. かおを洗います。
2. このしごとは楽で、楽しいです。
3. 漢字は難しいです。
4. バスに乗ります。

Q3. Fill in the blanks with appropriate particles.

1. ジョンさん ____ 会いました。
2. ジョンさん ____ 見ました。
3. バス ____ 行きます。
4. バス ____ 乗ります。
5. ビタミンAは目 ____ いいです。
6. 私はあたま ____ いたいです。
7. クラス ____ 休みました。
8. クラス ____ おくれました。

Q4. Convert the verbs and adjectives to the te-form.

For example:

たべる → たべて

1. よむ → ________________
2. あそぶ → ________________
3. あう → ________________
4. おくれる → ________________
5. のる → ________________
6. むずかしい → ________________
7. らく(な) → ________________
8. いい → ________________

Q5. Combine the two sentences in each set to form one sentence.

1. 昨日はしゅくだいをしました。それから、テレビを見ました。
2. よく勉強しました。それで、100点をとりました。
3. 私のへやは新しいです。それに、広いです。
4. 私の兄はまじめです。それに、やさしいです。
5. 安かったです。それに、おいしかったです。

Q6. Choose the appropriate options in the parentheses.

1. ともだちに(会う・会い)に、日本に行きます。
2. 日本語を(勉強する・勉強し)ために、日本に行きます。
3. 晩ごはんを(食べる・食べ)に来て下さい。
4. えいがを(見る・見)に行きましょう。

Tips and Additional Knowledge: Abbreviated English Loan Words

Japanese has many English loan words that were abbreviated into four kana syllables.

アメフト *American football*	イタスパ *Italian spaghetti*
インテリ *intelligent*	エアコン *air conditioning*
コンビニ *convenience store*	デジカメ *digital camera*
パワステ *power steering*	ビフテキ *beef steak*
ファミコン *family computer*	プレステ *playstation*
ラジカセ *radio cassette tape recorder*	

CHAPTER FOURTEEN

Talking About Now

Lesson 57
なおきくんが わらっていますよ **Ongoing Events** 214

Lesson 58
父はびょういんでいしゃをしています **Occupation** 216

Lesson 59
うちの子供は遊んでばかりいます **Extreme Habit** 218

Lesson 60
おさけを飲んでいますね **Resulting State** 220

Lesson 61
ティーシャツを着ている人です **Clothing** 222

Grammar and Usage 224

1 Verbs for mental states (よろこぶ, etc) 224
2 いる: State 224
3 ～ている: To be in the middle of doing～ [Progressive state] 224
4 ～ている: To do～usually / always / often [Habitual state] 224
5 Occupation 224
6 あそぶ: To play 225
7 うちの～: Our～/ my～ 225
8 ～ばかり: To do nothing but～ [An extreme habit] . . 225
9 しる: To get to know 226
10 To live (すむ, せいかつする, いきる, etc) 226
11 ～ている: To have done～ [Resulting state] 226
12 To wear (きる, はく, かぶる, する, つける, etc) . . 227
13 ちがう: Wrong / different 227
14 Relative clauses 227

Culture 227

A Schools in Japan 227
B パチンコ 228

Kanji List 228

Review 229

Tips and Additional Knowledge: Musashi Miyamoto 230

なおきくんが わらっていますよ Ongoing Events

Notes Relating to This Lesson	
Grammar and Usage	
1 Verbs for mental states . . 224	
2 いる 224	
3 ～ている 224	

Basic Vocabulary and Kanji

おちゃ	お茶	*n. (Japanese) tea*
へ˥ん (な)	変だ・変じゃない	*adj. strange, weird, unusual*
わらう	*w*-**u** 笑う・笑わない・笑い・笑って	*vi. to laugh, to smile*
よろこ˥ぶ	*b*-**u** 喜ぶ・喜ばない・喜び・喜んで	*vi. to become pleased* 1
～くん	～君	*a friendly respectful-title for boys and young men or a formal respectful title for one's subordinates*

Newly introduced kanji:

お茶(ちゃ)

茶	一ー艹艾艾苓苓茶茶

Dialog

Yoko Yamada and John Smith notice that their classmate, Naoki Uchida, is smiling by himself in the classroom.

スミス　：ちょっと見て下さい。なおきくんがわらっていますよ。へんですね。

山田　：なおきくんはすう学(がく)のテストで 100 点をとったんです。

先生　：ああ、それでよろこんでいるんですね。

山田　：ええ。

Guess and Try 1

Interpret the following sentences. 2 3

1. 今朝ピザを食べました。
2. よくピザを食べます。
3. 今晩ピザを食べます。
4. 今ピザを食べています。

Guess and Try 2

Fill in the blanks. 2 3

1. 今、何をしていますか。
   — 今、お茶を ＿＿＿＿＿＿＿＿＿＿＿＿ 。
2. 今、何をしていますか。
   — 今、てがみを ＿＿＿＿＿＿＿＿＿ 。
3. 今、何をしていますか。
   — 今、おんがくを ＿＿＿＿＿＿＿＿＿＿ 。

Guess and Try 3

Explain the difference between the following two sentences. 2 3

1. 今(いま)ピザを食(た)べています。
2. 昨日(きのう)の 3 時(じ)にピザを食べていました。

Drill 1: Formation

食べる ⟶ 食べています

1. 見る
2. ねる
3. 作る
4. 書く
5. およぐ
6. 休む
7. わらう
8. 働く
9. 飲む
10. よろこぶ
11. 勉強する

Drill 2: Formation

食べる ⟶ 今、食べています

1. うちでねる
2. へやで休む
3. 会社で働く
4. 社長と話す
5. すう学を勉強する
6. ピアノをひく
7. お茶を飲む
8. たんごをふく習(しゅう)する

Task 1: Classroom Activity

Look at the picture and say what each person is doing using the words such as 何か *something*.

Task 2: Classroom Activity

One of the students makes a gesture of an activity very briefly, for about one or two seconds, and the rest of the students state what he / she is doing.

For example:

A ：(Makes a gesture of swimming)

B ：A さんは今ダンスをしています。

A ：いいえ。

C ：A さんはおよいでいます。

A ：はい、そうです。

Task 3: Classroom Activity

Ask some of your classmates what they were doing at 9 p.m. last night. Is there anyone who was doing exactly the same thing as you?

Short Reading

私は今一人で部屋にいます。母は今台所で晩御飯(ばんごはん)を作っています。兄は隣(となり)の部屋で勉強しています。弟と妹は一緒(いっしょ)にテレビを見ています。祖母は母の手伝いをしています。父は新聞を読んでいます。猫(ねこ)はこたつの中で寝ています。

(台所(だいどころ) *kitchen,* 祖母(そぼ) *grandmother,* 手伝(てつだ)い *assistance,* こたつ *a leg warmer (a low skirted table with a heater underneath)*)

Writing

Describe what the people at home or in your apartment are doing right now.

父はびょういんでいしゃをしています Occupation

Notes Relating to This Lesson	
Grammar and Usage	**Culture**
4 ～ている 224	A Schools in Japan 227
5 Occupation 224	

Basic Vocabulary and Kanji

しょく˥ぎょう・ごしょく˥ぎょう	職業・御職業	*n. occupation*
かんご˥し・かんご˥しさん	看護士・看護士さん	*n. nurse*
がくちょう・がくちょうさん	学長・学長さん	*n. school president*
こうちょう・こうちょうせんせ˥い	校長・校長先生	*n. school principal*
しょうが˥っこう	小学校	*n. elementary school* A
ちゅうが˥っこう	中学校	*n. junior high school* A
せんもんが˥っこう	専門学校	*n. special (vocational) school*
こうじょ˥う	工場	*n. factory*
よ˥る	夜	*n. night*

Newly introduced kanji:

学校(がっこう) (school)・学長(がくちょう)・校長(こうちょう)・小学校(しょうがっこう)・中学校(ちゅうがっこう)・高校(こうこう) (high school)・英語(えいご) (English)

校	一十才木木'木'木ᅩ木ᅮ杧校	英	一十廾廾芦苎英英

Dialog

Yoshio Tanaka talks with his teacher.

先生　：田中さん。ご兄弟(きょうだい)は。

田中　：兄と、姉と、妹と、弟がいます。

先生　：ああ、それはいいですね。お兄さんは何をしていらっしゃいますか。

田中　：兄は車のこうじょうで働いています。

先生　：ああ、そうですか。お姉さんは。

田中　：姉は小学校のきょうしです。妹はコンピューターの会社で働いています。よるはせんもん学校で英語を習っています。弟は高校に行っています。

先生　：ああ、そうですか。

Guess and Try 1

Explain the difference between the two underlined parts in the following sentences. 4

1. すみません。兄はうちにいません。今、<u>会社で働(はたら)いています。</u>5時(じ)に帰(かえ)ります。
2. 父(ちち)はぎんこうで働いています。母は高校でおしえています。兄はコンピューターの<u>会社で働いています。</u>

Guess and Try 2

What do the following sentences mean? 5

1. 父(ちち)はいしゃをしています。
2. 山田(やまだ)さんのお母(かあ)さんは大学(だいがく)の先生(せんせい)をしていらっしゃいます。

Drill 1: Formation

働く ⟶ 働きます・働いています

1. 書く
2. 行く
3. 習(なら)う
4. 教(おし)える
5. 作る

Drill 2: Formation

会社で働く ⟶ 会社で働いています

1. こうじょうで働く
2. びょういんで働く

3. 小学校に行く

4. 中学校に行く

5. 大学ですう学を教える

6. せんもん学校で英語を習う

Task 1: Pair Work

Pretend that you know the people below, state what their jobs are to your partner.

たかはしさん

よしかわさん

パークさんのお母さん

山田さんのお父さん

スミスさんのお父さん

田中さんのお姉さん

Task 2: Pair Work

Find out whether your partner has any siblings ((ご) 兄弟(きょうだい)), and if he / she does, ask what they do. Use the dialog as the model.

Vocabulary Collection (Occupation) 5

教師(きょうし) *teacher*	学生(がくせい) *student*
弁護士(べんごし) *lawyer*	店員(てんいん) *salesclerk*
店主(てんしゅ) *store owner*	秘書(ひしょ) *secretary*
主婦(しゅふ) *housewife*	床屋(とこや) *barber*
作業員(さぎょういん) *worker*	警察官(けいさつかん) *police officer*
ウエーター *waiter*	作家(さっか) *writer*
ウエートレス *waitress*	
社長(しゃちょう) *company president*	
会社員(かいしゃいん)(社員(しゃいん)) *company employee*	
ＯＬ(オー・エル) *female company employee (office lady)*	
コンピューター・プログラマー *computer programmer*	

Short Reading

私の父は大学の病院で医者をしています。母は主婦(しゅふ)ですが、英語や絵画を習っています。兄は高校で教師(きょうし)をしています。数学と物理を教えています。姉は会社で秘書(ひしょ)をしています。私は今高校に行っています。来年、卒業(そつぎょう)します。卒業して、コンピューターの会社で働くつもりです。

(主婦(しゅふ) *housewife,* 絵画(かいが) *painting,* 物理(ぶつり) *physics,* 秘書(ひしょ) *secretary,* 卒業(そつぎょう)する *to graduate*)

Writing

Write about the occupation of some of your family members.

CHAPTER FOURTEEN | Lesson 59

うちの子供は遊んでばかりいます Extreme Habit

Notes Relating to This Lesson	
Grammar and Usage	**Culture**
6 あそぶ 225	B パチンコ 228
7 うちの～ 225	
8 ～ばかり 225	

石	一ア不石石	林	一十才木木一村村林
子	了了子	供	ノイ仁什仕世供供
化	ノイ亻化	遊	丶亠方方方於斿斿游游遊

Basic Vocabulary and Kanji

か⌉がく	化学	*n. chemistry*
まんが	マンガ・漫画	*n. comic book*
むすこ・むすこさん	息子・息子さん	*n. son*
むすめ・むすめさん / おじょ⌉うさん	娘・娘さん / お嬢さん	*n. daughter*
パチンコ		*n. a Japanese pinball game* B
タバコ	煙草・タバコ	*n. tobacco, cigarette* (タバコをすう *to smoke*)
あそぶ	***b-u*** 遊ぶ・遊ばない・遊び・遊んで	*vi. to enjoy oneself, to play* 6
しゃべ⌉る	***r-u*** しゃべる・しゃべらない・しゃべり・しゃべって	*vi. to chat*
おこ⌉る	***r-u*** 怒る・怒らない・怒り・怒って	*vt. to get angry*
なく	***k-u*** 泣く・泣かない・泣き・泣いて	*vi. to cry*
なまけ⌉る	***e-ru*** 怠ける・怠けない・怠け・怠けて	*vi. to be lazy*
すう	***w-u*** 吸う・吸わない・吸い・吸って	*vi. to inhale* (タバコをすう *to smoke*)

Newly introduced kanji:

石田(いしだ) (surname)・林(はやし) (surname)・子供(こども) (child)・化学(かがく)・遊(あそ)ぶ

Dialog 1

A conversation between two housewives.

林　：石田さんの子供さんはよく勉強しますか。

石田：いいえ、うちの子供はぜんぜん勉強しませんよ。

林　：そうですか。

石田：ええ、いつも遊んでばかりいます。

Guess and Try 1

What does うちの in Dialog 1 mean? 7

Guess and Try 2

Explain the difference between the following two sentences. 8

1. 兄はマンガを読んでいます。
2. 兄はマンガを読んでばかりいます。

Dialog 2

A conversation between two housewives.

石田：林さんの子供さんはよく勉強しますか。

林　：ええ、まあまあします。

石田：いいですね。

林　：でも、うちの子供は英語ばかり勉強しているんですよ。それで、すう学もぶつりも化学もぜんぜん勉強しないんです。

Guess and Try 3

Explain the difference between the following two sentences. [8]

1. 兄はマンガを読(よ)んでばかりいます。
2. 兄はマンガばかり読んでいます。

Drill: Formation

食べる ⟶ 食べてばかりいます

1. ねる
2. しゃべる
3. おこる
4. なまける
5. 遊ぶ
6. なく
7. パチンコをする
8. タバコをすう

Task 1: Classroom Activity

Describe the people in the following picture using ばかり.

ルイーズさん

川口さんのお父さん

チャンイルさん

チェンさん

よし子さん

Task 2: Role-Play / Skit

A:

You are having a problem with the extreme behavior of someone near you (for example, family members, friends, roommates) or your pet, and you want to talk about him / her / it to your friend.

B:

Your friend talks about his / her problem. Give him / her some comments on it. If possible, give him / her some advice.

Vocabulary Collection (Habits)	
賭(か)け事(ごと)をする *to gamble*	
お酒(さけ)を飲(の)む *to drink (alcohol)*	
テレビを見(み)る *to watch TV*	
漫画(まんが)を読(よ)む *to read comic books*	
長電話(ながでんわ)をする *to talk on the phone for a long time*	
遊(あそ)ぶ *to play*	怠(なま)ける *to be lazy*
しゃべる *to chat*	タバコをすう *to smoke*

Vocabulary Collection (Responses for Complaints)
ひどいですね。 *That's terrible.*
困(こま)りましたね。 *You (we) are in trouble.*
それはよくありませんね。 *That's not good.*
大変(たいへん)ですね。 *That's a big deal.*
変(へん)ですね。 *That's strange.*
だいじょうぶですよ。 *That will be fine.*

Short Reading

私の弟は今大学生です。とてもいい大学に入りましたが、ぜんぜん勉強していません。インターネットを使って、他の人とゲームばかりしています。一日に12時間ぐらいします。ですから、大学の成績(せいせき)もよくありません。アルバイトもしません。うちの手伝いもしません。とても困(こま)っています。

(他(ほか)の人(ひと) *other people,* 成績(せいせき) *grades; performance,* 手伝(てつだ)い *help; assistance,* 困(こま)る *to be in trouble; to be concerned*)

Writing

Write about someone's extreme behavior.

おさけを飲んでいますね Resulting State

Notes Relating to This Lesson
Grammar and Usage

9 しる 226
10 To live 226
11 ～ている 226

Basic Vocabulary and Kanji

けいさつ˥かん	警察官	*n. police officer*
おり˥る	***i-ru*** 降りる・降りない・降り・降りて	*vt. to get off, to come down*
あく	***k-u*** 開く・開かない・開き・開いて	*vi. / vt. to open (cf.* 開(あ)ける *vt. to open)*
こ˥む	***m-u*** 混む・混まない・混み・混んで	*vi. to become crowded*
すく	***k-u*** すく・すかない・すき・すいて	*vi. to become less crowded* (おなかがすく *to become hungry)*
はじまる	***r-u*** 始まる・始まらない・始まり・始まって	*vi. to begin* (クラスが始まる *The class begins.)*
しる	***r-u*** 知る・知らない・知り・知って	*vt. to get to know* 9
す˥む	***m-u*** 住む・住まない・住み・住んで	*vi. to live (somewhere)* (日本に住む *to live in Japan)* 10
けっこんする	*irr.* 結婚する	*vi. to get married*
おなかがすいている		*hungry*
ま˥だ		*adv. (not～) yet* (まだ始(はじ)まっていない *(It) has not begun yet.)*

Newly introduced kanji:

住(す)む

住	ノイイ'仁什住住

Dialog

Yoshio Tanaka's brother is stopped by a police officer while driving.

けいさつかん：すみませんが、ちょっと車からおりてください。

田中の兄　：はい。

けいさつかん：ちょっとまっすぐ歩いて下さい。

(Mr. Tanaka's brother tries to walk straight, but he cannot.)

けいさつかん：おさけを<u>飲んでいます</u>ね。

田中の兄　：はい。どうもすみません。

Guess and Try 1

What does the underlined part in Dialog mean? 11

Guess and Try 2

What is the difference between the following two sentences? 11

1. 兄はけっこんしました。
2. 兄はけっこんしています

Guess and Try 3

Insert the given verbs into the blanks after changing them into te-forms: 11

(こむ・すく・あく・かりる・行く・住む・来る・しる)

1. ぎんこうはもう ____________ いますよ。
—じゃあ、行(い)きましょう。

2. このバスは ＿＿＿＿＿ いますね。
   — ええ。ひどいですね。(ひどい *terrible*)

3. あれっ。私のじしょがありません。
   — ああ、私が ＿＿＿＿＿ います。

4. 兄(あに)は今(いま)いません。今とうきょうに ＿＿＿＿＿ います。

5. 山田(やまだ)さんはまだ ＿＿＿＿＿ いません。

6. あの人を ＿＿＿＿＿ いますか。
   — いいえ、しりません。

7. 私は今(いま)とうきょうに ＿＿＿＿＿ います。でも、来年(らいねん)はおおさかに住むつもりです。

8. おなかが ＿＿＿＿＿ いるんです。早(はや)く食(た)べましょう。

Drill: Formation

私・けっこんする ⟶ 私は けっこんしています

1. ぎんこう・あく
2. クラス・はじまる
3. このバス・こむ
4. このでん車・すく
5. 兄・とうきょうに行く
6. 妹・うちに帰る
7. 母・ここに来る
8. 兄・ジョンさんの本をかりる
9. 山田さん・りょうに住む

Task 1: Pair Work

Look around the classroom. Report to your partner who is in the class and who is not.

For example:

スーザンさんは来(き)ています。
それから、パークさんも来ています。
でも、ジョンさんは来ていません。

Task 2: Small Group Work

Talk about the Japanese person you associate with most often.

For example:

A　：私は伊藤(いとう)さんとよく話(はな)します。伊藤さんはうちのとなりに住(す)んでいます。とてもやさしくて、いい人(ひと)です。

B　：伊藤さんは女の人ですか。

A　：はい。

C　：学生さんですか。

A　：…

Short Reading

私は外国人の友達がたくさんいます。一人はオーストラリア人のジャスティンさんです。ジャスティンさんは日本人と結婚(けっこん)していて、今東京に住んでいます。東京の大学で日本文学を勉強しています。ジャスティンさんは昼は大学で勉強して、夜は英語の専門学校で英語を教えています。

私は韓国人(かんこくじん)の友達もいます。キンさんです。キンさんのお父さんは貿易会社(ぼうえきがいしゃ)の社長さんです。キンさんは私のうちの近くに住んでいます。よくうちで一緒(いっしょ)にご飯(はん)を食べます。

(外国人(がいこくじん) *foreigner*)

Writing

Write about some of your friends from foreign countries.

ティーシャツを着ている人です Clothing

Notes Relating to This Lesson	
Grammar and Usage	
12 To wear 227	
13 ちがう 227	
14 Relative clauses 227	

Basic Vocabulary and Kanji

め[⌉]がね	眼鏡	*n. eyeglasses*
くつ⌉した	靴下	*n. socks*
ズ⌉ボン		*n. pants, trousers*
かっこい⌉い	かっこいい・かっこよくない	*adj. good looking (mainly for young men and boys)*
はく	***k*-u** はく・はかない・はき・はいて	*vt. to wear (items such as pants and shoes)* 12
かぶ⌉る	***r*-u** かぶる・かぶらない・かぶり・かぶって	*vt. to wear (items such as hats and caps)* 12
かけ⌉る	***e*-ru** 掛ける・掛けない・掛け・掛けて	*vi. to wear (eyeglasses), to hang* 12
ちがう	***w*-u** 違う・違わない・違い・違って	*vi. to be wrong, to be different* 13

Newly introduced kanji:

着(き)る (to wear)

着	丶 丷 䒑 䒑 羊 羊 𦍌 着 着 着 着 着

Dialog

Two young women are chatting at the cafeteria.

女の人1：ちょっと、見(み)てください。あそこにかっこいい人(ひと)がいますよ。

女の人2：あの人ですか。

女の人1：いいえ、ちがいますよ。あの人ですよ。

女の人2：あの人ですか。

女の人1：いいえ。あのジーンズをはいて、ティーシャツを着ている人ですよ。

女の人2：ああ、あの人ですか。あの人は私の兄です。

Guess and Try 1

Choose the appropriate option(s) in the parentheses. 12

1. セーターを(着て・はいて・して・かぶって・かけて)います。
2. スカートを(着て・はいて・して・かぶって・かけて)います。
3. スニーカーを(着て・はいて・して・かぶって・かけて)います。
4. スカーフを(着て・はいて・して・かぶって・かけて)います。
5. イヤリングを(着て・はいて・して・かぶって・かけて)います。
6. めがねを(着て・はいて・して・かぶって・かけて)います。
7. ぼうしを(着て・はいて・して・かぶって・かけて)います。

Guess and Try 2

Fill in the blanks. 14

1. あの人は私の兄です。
   That person is my brother.

2. あの ____________________ 人は私の兄です。
   That tall person is my brother.

3. あの ____________________ 人は私の兄です。
   That person, who is eating pizza, is my brother.

Drill: Formation

セーター ⟶ セーターを着ている人です

1. ブラウス
2. ジャケット
3. ドレス
4. スカート
5. ズボン
6. くつ
7. スニーカー
8. ネックレス
9. ネクタイ
10. めがね
11. ぼうし

Task 1: Pair Work

Describe what you are wearing to your partner.

Vocabulary Collection (Clothing)	
ジャケット *jacket*	ブラウス *blouse*
セーター *sweater*	ティーシャツ *T-shirt*
ズボン *trousers*	スカート *skirt*
ジーパン / ジーンズ *jeans*	スーツ *suit*
ワンピース / ドレス *dress*	手袋(てぶくろ) *gloves*
靴(くつ) *shoes*	靴下(くつした) *socks*
帽子(ぼうし) *hat, cap*	めがね *eyeglasses*
サングラス *sunglasses*	スカーフ *scarf*
ネックレス *necklace*	イヤリング *earring*

Task 2: Classroom Activity

You pick someone (any person) in your class, but do not reveal who he / she is. The rest of your classmates guess who you picked by asking questions. The following are the rules.

Rule 1: They can ask only yes / no questions, not content questions. They can ask about appearance, but cannot ask about nationality or sex. (For example, かみが長(なが)い人(ひと)ですか。ティーシャツを着ている人ですか。)

Rule 2: You can only answer "はい" or "いいえ" and cannot give any further information.

Rule 3: You cannot look at the person you are thinking of while answering questions.

Short Reading

私の母はいつもきれいな洋服(ようふく)を着ています。たいてい長いスカートをはいています。ズボンはあまりはきません。きれいなブラウスをたくさん持(も)っています。よくスカーフもします。でも、アクセサリーはあまりしません。姉はうちではティーシャツを着て、ジーンズをはいています。スカートはあまりはきません。でも、大学ではたいていブラウスを着て、スカートをはいています。いつも同(おな)じネックレスをしています。

(持(も)っている *to have,* 同(おな)じ *same*)

Writing

Write about what your family members usually wear.

– Grammar and Usage –

1 Verbs for mental states (よろこぶ, etc)

When the verbs such as よろこぶ *to get happy*, おこる *to get angry*, しんぱいする *to worry* and かなしむ *to get sad* are used to express one's mental states, they must be in the ～ている form.

(a) 兄(あに)はよろこんでいます。
My brother is happy.

(b) 父(ちち)はおこっています。
My father is angry.

(c) 母(はは)はしんぱいしています。
My mother is worried.

(d) 祖母(そぼ)はかなしんでいます。
My grandmother is sad.

2 いる: State

The verb いる means *to exist*. It is a verb, but it denotes a state rather than an action. いる can also function as an auxiliary verb, used after another verb in the te-form. As an auxiliary verb, it also expresses a state, which is a progressive, habitual, or resulting state. For example, ブラウンさんは日本語(にほんご)を勉強(べんきょう)しています has the following three possible interpretations:

(a) Progressive state:
Mr. Brown is studying Japanese (now).

(b) Habitual state:
Mr. Brown studies Japanese (regularly).

(c) Resulting state:
Mr. Brown has studied Japanese.

3 ～ている: To be in the middle of doing～ [Progressive state]

The construction ～ている can express a **progressive state**, where some activities progressively continue over a period of time. The tense of the verb いる specifies the time of the progressive state.

(a) ブラウンさんは今(いま)ピザを食(た)べています。
Mr. Brown is eating pizza now.

(b) ブラウンさんは昨日(きのう)3時(じ)にピザを食(た)べていました。
Mr. Brown was eating pizza at 3 o'clock yesterday.

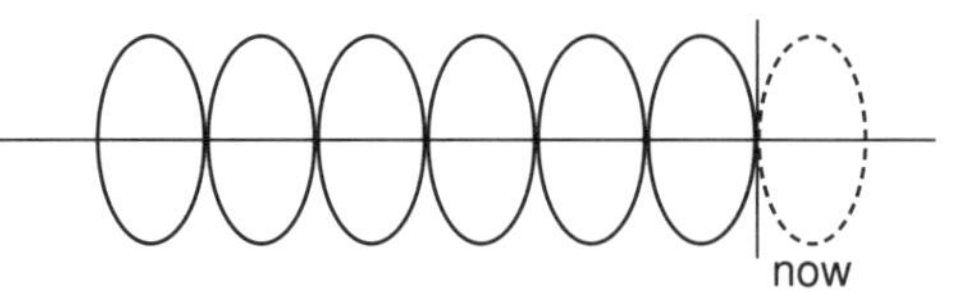

4 ～ている: To do～ usually / always / often [Habitual state]

The construction ～ている can also express a **habitual state**. For example, ブラウンさんは毎日(まいにち)ピザを食(た)べています means that Mr. Brown eats pizza every day as a habit, and he does not have to be eating pizza right now. ～ている can express one's regular activities, habits and occupations.

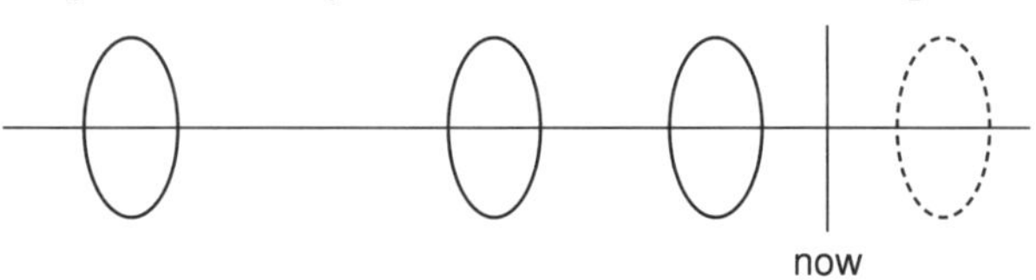

(a) 毎朝(まいあさ)テニスをしています。
(I) play tennis every morning.

(b) いつもマンガを読(よ)んでいます。
(I) am always reading a comic book.

(c) 週末(しゅうまつ)はたいてい本(ほん)を読(よ)んでいます。
(I) am usually reading a book on weekends.

(d) 兄(あに)はコンピューターの会社(かいしゃ)で働(はたら)いています。
My brother works at a computer company. /
My brother is a computer company employee.

(e) 母は大学(だいがく)で英語(えいご)を教(おし)えています。
My mother teaches English at a college. /
My mother is a college English teacher.

(f) 弟(おとうと)は高校(こうこう)に行(い)っています。
My brother goes to high school. /
My brother is a high school student.

5 Occupation

Most of the terms for occupation have two forms: humble form and respectful form. The following are some of the examples:

Occupations	Humble	Respectful
Teacher	きょうし 教師	せんせい 先生
Medical doctor	いしゃ 医者	おいしゃさん お医者さん
Nurse	かんごし 看護士	かんごしさん 看護士さん
Company president	しゃちょう 社長	しゃちょうさん 社長さん

Occupations	Humble	Respectful
Student	がくせい 学生	がくせいさん 学生さん
Secretary	ひしょ 秘書	ひしょのかた 秘書の方

Use the humble form for referring to your own occupation or your family members' occupation:

(a) 私はきょうしです。
I am a teacher.

(b) 母はきょうしです。
My mother is a teacher.

(c) ブラウンさんは先生です。
Mr. Brown is a teacher.

These occupation terms can be used with the verb する *to do* as below:

(d) 父はいしゃをしています。
My father is a doctor.

(e) 山田さんのお父さんは大学の先生をしていらっしゃいます。
Ms. Yamada's father is a college professor.

(f) 兄は学生をしています。
My brother is a student.

6 あそぶ: To play

The Japanese verb 遊ぶ is often translated as *to play* in English, but 遊ぶ can be used only as an intransitive verb, meaning *to play* or *to enjoy oneself*, but may not be used as a transitive verb with the particle を, meaning *to play* something such as sports, games and musical instruments.

(a) 子供がこうえんで遊んでいます。
A child is playing in the park.

(b) 子供とおりがみで遊びませんか。
Would you like to play origami with children?

(c) 奥さんとうちに遊びに来て下さい。
Please come to visit me with your wife.

(d) テニスを遊びました。それから、コンピューターゲームを遊びました。 (✕)
(Ungrammatical)

(e) テニスをしました。それから、コンピューターゲームをしました。
I played tennis. Then, I played a computer game.

7 うちの〜: Our〜 / my 〜

The Japanese often say うちの〜 instead of 私の〜 when talking about their own family members or items that belong to their houses. うちの〜 literally means *my house's*~, but it actually means *our*~ or *my*~.

(a) うちの子供は遊んでばかりいます。
Our child does nothing but play.

(b) うちの主人はお酒を飲まないんです。
My husband does not drink.

(c) うちの車は古いです。
Our car is old.

8 〜ばかり: To do nothing but〜 [An extreme habit]

When the particle 〜ばかり occurs in 〜ている construction, it expresses a habitual state that is very extreme. It is usually used to criticize someone's extreme habit. The particle 〜ばかり can occur in two different positions in a sentence. One is right after the verb in the te-form:

(a) 兄はいつもねてばかりいます。
My brother sleeps all the time.

(b) 兄はマンガを読んでばかりいます。
My brother does nothing but read comic books.

The other is after a noun phrase and a particle. Note that を and が must be deleted when they occur before ばかり:

(c) 兄はマンガばかり読んでいます。
My brother reads nothing but comic books.

(d) 兄ばかり食べています。
Only my brother (but no one else) is eating.

(e) ラスベガスにばかり行っています。
(He) goes nowhere but to Las Vegas.

Sentence (b) and sentence (c) are slightly different. Sentence (b) means that the frequency of his comic-book-reading activity is extremely high compared with the frequency of other activities he does. Sentence (c) means that the number of comic books he reads is extremely big compared with the number of other kinds of books that he reads. Such a subtle difference is often undetectable and these sentences are often used interchangeably.

9 しる: To get to know

The verb しる does not mean *to know*, but it means *to get to know*. For saying that you know something or someone, it must be in the ～ている construction (for example, 私は山田さんの電話番号をしっています。*I know Ms. Yamada's phone number.*). On the other hand, when you do not know something or someone, simply say しりません rather than しっていません.

10 To live (すむ, せいかつする, いきる, etc)

The verbs 住む, 生活する and 生きる all mean *to live*, but they are slightly different.

住む means *to have one's residential address at somewhere* (for example, 私はボストンに住んでいます *I live in Boston.*). It is a state and not an activity. The location is marked by the particle に when the verb is 住む.

生活する means *to live a daily life* (for example, ホワイトさんはボストンで生活しています *Mr. White lives in Boston.*). It is an activity. When the verb is 生活する, the location is marked by the particle で.

Finally, 生きる means *to stay alive* (for example, 祖父はまだ生きています。*My grandfather is still alive.*) or *to live one's life in a certain way* (for example, 楽しく生きます *(I) will live my life with fun.*).

11 ～ている: To have done～ [Resulting state]

The construction ～ている can express a current state that results from some action in the past. For example, sentence (a) and sentence (b) are similar in that John went to Tokyo at some point in the past, but only (b) means that *he is still in Tokyo* and (a) does not say anything about where he is now:

(a) ジョンさんは東京に行きました。
John went to Tokyo.

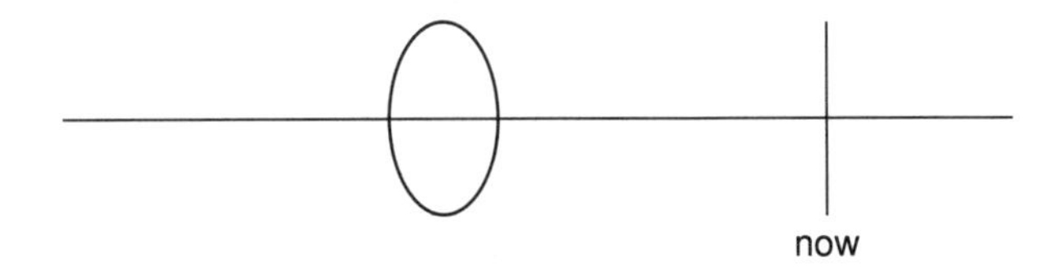

(b) ジョンさんは東京に行っています。
John has gone to Tokyo (and is still there).

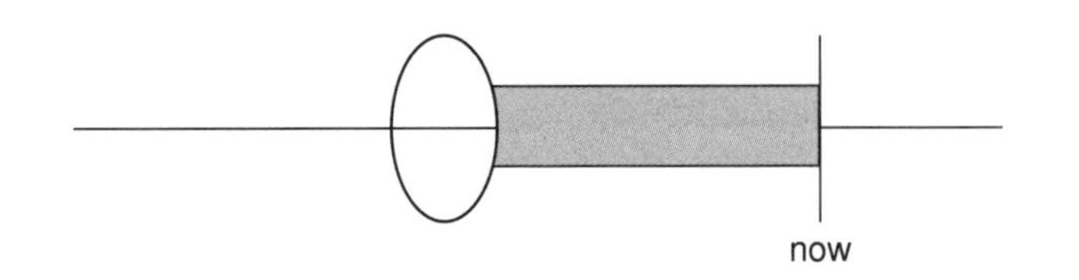

The following sentences all express the resulting state:

(c) お兄さんはもうけっこんしていますか。
Is your brother married?
— いいえ、まだけっこんしていません。
— *No, he is not married yet.*

(d) ぎんこうはもうあいていますよ。
The bank has already opened.
— じゃあ、行きましょう。
— *Then, let's go there.*

(e) このバスはこんでいますね。
This bus is crowded, isn't it?
— ええ。ひどいですね。
— *Yes, it is terrible.*

(f) あれっ。私のじしょがありませんね。
Oh, my dictionary is missing.
— ああ、私がかりています。
— *I have borrowed it.*

(g) あの人はたくさん本を読んでいます。ですから、たんごをたくさんしっています。
That person has read a lot of books. Therefore, he knows a lot of words.

(h) 私はおなかが すいています。
I am hungry.
— じゃあ、カフェテリアに行きませんか。
— *Then, shall we go to the cafeteria?*

(i) お兄さんはいらっしゃいますか。
Is your brother there?
— 今いません。兄は今とうきょうに行っています。
— *He is not in now. He has gone to Tokyo.*

(j) クラスはもうはじまっています。でも、山田さんはまだ来ていません。
The class has already begun. But Mr. Yamada has not come yet.

(k) 私は今とうきょうに住んでいます。でも、来年はおおさかに住むつもりです。
I live in Tokyo now. But I plan to live in Osaka next year.

If the verb expresses a change-of-state action such as *to get married*, *to open* and *to begin*, which one cannot keep doing over a period of time, the sentence only expresses the resulting state.

By contrast, if the verb expresses an action that one can keep doing progressively for some period of time, like *drinking*, *eating*, *studying* and *reading*, the sentence can be ambiguous between the progressive state reading and the resulting state reading. For example, お酒を飲んでいます is ambiguous: it means *someone is in the middle of drinking (progressive state)* or *someone is drunk (resulting state)*.

12 To wear (きる, はく, かぶる, する, つける, etc)

The English verb "to wear" can be used for almost all clothes and accessories, but there is no such convenient verb in Japanese. In Japanese, different verbs must be used depending on which part of the body the item is used. The verb 着る is for above-the-waste items such as shirts, blouses, jackets and sweaters. The verb はく is for waist-down items such as shoes, socks, pants, trousers and skirts. The verb かぶる is for items that you put on the top of your head, such as caps and hats. The verb する is used for accessories such as earrings, necklaces, scarves, watches, wigs, contact lenses, eyeglasses and sunglasses, and make-up. The verb つける can be used for fragrance and for some accessories and make-up. The verb かける, which literally means *to hang* is used for eyeglasses and sunglasses.

13 ちがう: Wrong / different

The verb ちがう means *to be different* or *to be wrong*. It makes sense because being wrong means being different from the correct answer or the fact.

(a) 日本のお米はアメリカのお米と違います。
Japanese rice is different from American rice.

(b) この2つのドレスはサイズが違います。
These two dresses differ in size.

(c) 答えが違いますよ。
(Your) answer is wrong.

(d) あの人は山田さんですか。
Is that person Ms. Yamada?
— いいえ、違います。
— *No, wrong.*

14 Relative clauses

In Japanese, modifiers of a noun always precede the modified noun. Modifiers can be adjective phrases (for example, 高い本 *expensive book*, きれいな人 *pretty person*, 読みたい本 *the book (I) want to read* and 会いたい人 *the person (I) want to see*), noun phrases plus の (for example, 日本語の本 *Japanese book* and 日本の人 *Japanese person*), or verb phrases (for example, 買う本 *the book (I) will buy* and 買った本 *the book (I) bought*). The modifiers can be very long and look like sentences. For example, in the following phrases, the entire string of words except the noun 本 is a modifier.

(a) 私が一番好きな本
the book that I like the best

(b) 父が昨日読んだ本
the book that my father read yesterday

(c) 父が昨日うちで読んだ本
the book that my father read at home yesterday

The modifiers that look like sentences are called **relative clauses**. In relative clauses, the verbs and adjectives must be in the plain form and the topic marker (〜は) may not be used. In addition, the noun phrase that corresponds to the modified noun must be absent in the relative clause. The following sentences are all ungrammatical because of these reasons:

(d) 父が昨日うちで読みました本 (**✕**)
(Ungrammatical) intended meaning: *the book that my father read at home yesterday*

(e) 父は昨日うちで読んだ本 (**✕**)
(Ungrammatical) intended meaning: *the book that my father read at home yesterday*

(f) 父が昨日うちで本を読んだ本 (**✕**)
(Ungrammatical) intended meaning: *the book that my father read at home yesterday*

– Culture –

A Schools in Japan

The Japanese education system is a 6-3-3-4 system and it consists of six years of 小学校 *elementary school*, three years of 中学校 *junior high school*, three years of 高校 high school and four years of 大学 *college*. The elementary school and junior high school are compulsory, but the high school and college are optional. 95% of students continue studying in the high school.

Ⓑ パチンコ

Pachinko is a Japanese pinball game originated in Nagoya after World War II. You can find a few pachinko halls in most Japanese cities and towns. Pachinko halls are easy to recognize, because they usually have big showy neon signs in front of the building and play loud music, usually marching songs, to attract and excite customers. You buy some small steel balls, sit in front of an upright glass-covered board full of nails and some holes, and start flipping the balls over the board to try to get them into the holes. If any ball gets into a winning hole, you win more balls. You can trade in the balls you won for the prize of your choice. Most of the prizes are daily-life items such as chocolates, cigarettes, soaps and umbrellas. And probably you can sell your prizes for money nearby. As pachinko is gambling, those who are under 18 years old are not allowed to play it.

– Kanji List –

お茶・学長・校長・学校・小学校・中学校・高校・英語・石田・林・子供・化学・遊ぶ・住む・着る

Kanji	Readings	Meaning	Strokes	Examples
茶	チャ・サ	*tea*	[9]	お茶 (ちゃ) *tea*
学	まな-ぶ・ガク・ガッ	*study*	[8]	学校 (がっこう) *school*; 学生 (がくせい) *student*
長	なが-い・チョウ	*long, eldest, chief*	[8]	学長 (がくちょう) *school president*; 社長 (しゃちょう) *company president*; 長い (なが) *long*
校	コウ	*school*	[10]	学校 (がっこう) *school*
小	ちい-さい・こ・お・ショウ	*small, little*	[3]	小さい (ちい) *small*; 小学校 (しょうがっこう) *elementary school*
中	なか・チュウ・ジュウ	*middle, inside*	[4]	中 (なか) *inside*; 中国 (ちゅうごく) *China*; 中学校 (ちゅうがっこう) *middle school*
高	たか-い・コウ	*high, expensive*	[10]	高い (たか) *expensive*; 高校 (こうこう) *high school*
英	エイ	*superb*	[8]	英語 (えいご) *English*
語	かた-る・ゴ	*word, language*	[14]	英語 (えいご) *English*; 日本語 (にほんご) *Japanese*
石	いし・セキ	*stone*	[5]	石田 (いしだ) *surname*
田	た・〜だ・デン	*rice field*	[5]	山田 (やまだ) *surname*
林	はやし・リン	*wood, grove*	[8]	林 (はやし) *surname*

子 こ・シ *child*	フ 了 子 [3] Example: 子供(こども) *child*
供 とも・ども・そな-える・キョウ・ク *offer*	ノ イ 仁 什 仕 件 供 供 [8] Example: 子供(こども) *child*
化 ば-ける・カ *change, -ization*	ノ イ 亻' 化 [4] Example: 化学(かがく) *chemistry*
遊 あそ-ぶ・ユウ *play, fun, wander*	丶 亠 方 方 方 方 方 斿 斿 游 游 遊 [12] Example: 遊(あそ)ぶ *to enjoy oneself* 遊(ゆう)えんち *amusement park*
住 す-む・ジュウ *dwell, inhabit*	ノ イ 亻' 亻 仁 仹 住 [7] Example: 住(す)む *to live, to reside* 住所(じゅうしょ) *an address*
着 つ-く・き-る・チャク *reach, arrive, wear*	丶 丷 䒑 ⺷ 羊 差 着 着 着 着 着 着 [12] Example: 着(つ)く *to arrive* 着(き)る *to wear*

– Review –

Q1. Circle the appropriate options in the parentheses.

1. ちょっと(ないて・なまけて)いますね。もう少(すこ)しよく勉強(べんきょう)して下(くだ)さい。

2. (ごしょくぎょう・しょくぎょう)は何ですか。
   — きょうしです。

3. 見(み)て下さい。山田さんが(ないています・わらっています)。
   — ええ、よろこんでいますね。

Q2. Write the pronounciation of the following kanji phrases, and state what is in common among the members of each set. It can be kanji characters, kanji components or meanings.

1. 使う・作る・休む・住む・働く・化学

2. 大学・学校・高校・小学校・中学校・学生

3. 社会学・化学・すう学・ぶん学

4. 学長・校長・社長

Q3. Following the example, conjugate the verbs.

For example:

たべる ➞ たべています

1. わらう ➞ ________________

2. よろこぶ ➞ ________________

3. きく ➞ ________________

4. はたらく ➞ ________________

5. ならう ➞ ________________

6. しゃべる ➞ ________________

7. なまける ➞ ________________

Q4. State the meaning of the underlined parts.

1. お姉(ねえ)さんは学生(がくせい)さんですか。
   — はい、姉(あね)は<u>大学(だいがく)に行(い)っています。</u>

2. テニスは好きですか。
   — はい、まいあさ弟と<u>テニスをしています。</u>
   (毎朝(まいあさ) *every morning*)

3. 弟さんは今(いま)いらっしゃいますか。
   — いいえ、今大学で<u>テニスをしています。</u>

4. 山田(やまだ)さんは、クラスに来(き)ていますか。
   — いいえ、<u>来ていません。</u>

5. ブラウンさんはどんな人ですか。
   — <u>ブラウンさんはめがねをかけています。</u>

6. ホワイトさんはちょっとへんですよ。
   — ええ。<u>おさけを飲(の)んでいるんです。</u>

7. 山田さんはたん語をよくしっていますね。
   — ええ、本をたくさん読んでいるんです。

Q5. Fill in the blanks with appropriate verbs that mean *to wear*.

兄はくつを ① ________ います。姉はネックレスを ② ________ います。父はめがねを ③ ________ います。母はきれいなセーター *sweater* を ④ ________ います。妹はかわいいスカートを ⑤ ________ います。弟はぼうしを ⑥ ________ います。

Q6. Fill in the blanks appropriately.

1. 山田さんのお父さんはおいしゃさんですか。
   — はい、父は ____________ です。
2. 山田さんのお兄さんは高校の先生ですか。
   — はい、兄は高校の ____________ です。
3. 田中さんの ____________ は学生さんですか。
   — はい、兄は ____________ です。

Q7. Insert ばかり in each of the sentences and make any necessary changes.

1. 兄はハンバーガーを食べています。
2. 弟はパチンコをしています。
3. 父は日曜日はねています。
4. 妹はともだちとしゃべっています。

Q8. Reorder the words in the parentheses appropriately and complete the sentences. Then, translate them into English.

1. 私の兄は(ジーンズ・人・です・はいている・を)
2. 兄は(人・食べる・よく・です)
3. 山田先生は(を・たくさん・だす・しゅくだい・先生・です)

Tips and Additional Knowledge: Musashi Miyamoto

宮元武蔵 (??–1645) was a great swordsman in the Edo period in Japan. The way he fought, with one sword in each hand, was very peculiar and was known as *nito-ryu* (two-weapon method). 武蔵 had fought in more than 60 duels by the age of 29 without losing in any one of them. 武蔵's last dual was with Sasaki Kojiro and it took place in 1612 on Ganryu Island. Later in his life, 武蔵 became a great artist. His paintings, sculptures and calligraphy are among the finest in Japanese history. He wrote the famous 五輪書 "The Book of Five Rings", which is a guide to strategy and swordsmanship.

CHALLENGE
(Chapter One to Chapter Fourteen)

Challenge 1

Read the following passage, which is written vertically from right to left, and answer the questions.

私の名前はエミー・チョーです。私はアメリカ人ですが、父と母は中国人です。うちはニューヨークのクイーンズにあります。そふとそぼもクイーンズにいます。クイーンズには中国やかん国の店やレストランがたくさんあります。

父と母とは中国語を話します。でも、兄や友達とは英語で話します。今、大学で日本語を勉強しています。ですから、日本語も少し話します。専攻はけいざい学です。しゅみはつりです。よくしゅうまつに父とつりをします。音楽も好きです。私のへやにはステレオがあります。CDもたくさんあります。日本のポップミュージックをよくききます。日本のテレビドラマやえいがもよく見ます。来年日本に留学するつもりです。大阪に友達がいます。でも、東京の大学で勉強するつもりです。

1. Is Amy a Chinese?
2. What languages does Amy speak?
3. What is Amy's major?
4. What does Amy like?
5. Is Amy planning to study in Osaka?

Challenge 2

Write an essay about yourself.

Challenge 3

Bill is on an airplane to Japan. He talks to the Japanese woman who is sitting next to him.

ビル　：東京までですか。

女の人　：いいえ、青森までです。

ビル　：青森はどこですか。

女の人　：本州の北です。北海道の近くです。

ビル　：いい所ですか。

女の人　：ええ。冬は寒いですが、きれいな所ですよ。

ビル　：お仕事ですか。

女の人　：いいえ。両親がいるんです。おたくはどちらまで。

ビル　：僕は名古屋までです。

女の人　：観光ですか。お仕事ですか。

ビル　：観光です。名古屋に友達がいるんです。

女の人　：ああ、いいですね。

ビル　：はい。ペンパルです。3年ぐらい手紙を交換しました。

女の人　：はじめて会うんですか。

ビル　：はい。

女の人　：それは楽しみですね。

1. Where is the woman going?
2. Where is Aomori located, and what kind of place is it?
3. What is the purpose of the woman's visit to Japan?
4. Where is Bill going?
5. What is the purpose of Bill's visit to Japan?

Challenge 4

Fill in the blanks with appropriate particles, if necessary. Do not use は nor も.

1. 7時にうち ____ かえります。
2. 母はうち ____ います。
3. 3時までうち ____ べんきょうします。
4. ねこはテーブル ____ 下 ____ ねています。
5. 本や ____ うち ____ 5分です。
6. すしは父 ____ 作ります。てんぷらは母 ____ 作ります。
7. 私は父 ____ ゴルフをします。
8. 私は山田さん ____ しょうたいします。
(しょうたいする *to invite*)
9. このネックレスは母 ____ あげます。
(あげる *to give*)
10. 私は学生 ____ です。
11. 姉 ____ 3人 ____ います。
12. 犬 ____ 2匹 ____ ねこ ____ 2匹 ____ います。
13. ペン ____ 書きます。
14. 車 ____ 大学に行きます。
15. 車 ____ 買います。
16. 兄はテニス ____ 大好きです。
17. 7時にテレビ ____ 見ます。
18. 私はお金 ____ ほしいです。
19. コンピューターはしゅうしょく ____ いいですよ。

Challenge 5

Conjugation: Complete the following tables. Do not worry about the meaning of the words.

Part I: Verbs whose dictionary forms end in a syllable other than る.

いく	いかない	いきます	いって
かく			かいて
およぐ			
つかう			
しぬ			
たのむ	たのまない		
のむ			のんで
あそぶ			
まつ			
はなす		はなします	
かす			かして

Part II: Verbs whose dictionary forms end in る.

はる	はらない		はって
とる			
うる			
つくる			
きる	きない	きます	きて
きる		きります	きって
ねる		ねます	ねて
ねる	ねらない	ねります	ねって
くる			
する			

Challenge 6

Kanji: Write the pronounciation of the kanji characters in the following sentences.

1. このじてん車は弟のです。この車は兄のです。
2. あの女の人と、あの男の人は日本人です。

3. 昨日の晩は、ピザを食べました。今晩はすきやきを食べます。私が作ります。

4. 今朝、山田さんと、田中さんと、川口さんが来ました。

5. すみません。今、何時ですか。
— 今、7時です。

6. 新しい本は高いです。古い本は安いです。ですから、古いのを買いました。

7. 大学で文学の勉強をするつもりです。

8. 姉のへやは広いです。でも、暗いです。妹のへやはせまいです。でも、明るいです。

9. 今日は、月曜日です。明日は火曜日です。

10. 漢字は難しいです。でも、日本語のクラスは楽しいです。

Challenge 7

Kanji: For each of the following characters, write words or compound words that include it.

For example:

人: 人・日本人・男の人

1. 日: ____________________
2. 今: ____________________
3. 月: ____________________
4. 生: ____________________
5. 学: ____________________
6. 大: ____________________
7. 本: ____________________
8. 曜: ____________________
9. 長: ____________________
10. 国: ____________________

APPENDIX ONE

Hiragana and Katakana

1. Basic syllabary

ん(ン) n	わ(ヮ) wa	ら(ラ) ra	や(ヤ) ya	ま(マ) ma	は(ハ) ha	な(ナ) na	た(タ) ta	さ(サ) sa	か(カ) ka	あ(ア) a
		り(リ) ri		み(ミ) mi	ひ(ヒ) hi	に(ニ) ni	ち(チ) chi	し(シ) shi	き(キ) ki	い(イ) i
		る(ル) ru	ゆ(ユ) yu	む(ム) mu	ふ(フ) fu	ぬ(ヌ) nu	つ(ツ) tsu	す(ス) su	く(ク) ku	う(ウ) u
		れ(レ) re		め(メ) me	へ(ヘ) he	ね(ネ) ne	て(テ) te	せ(セ) se	け(ケ) ke	え(エ) e
	を(ヲ) o	ろ(ロ) ro	よ(ヨ) yo	も(モ) mo	ほ(ホ) ho	の(ノ) no	と(ト) to	そ(ソ) so	こ(コ) ko	お(オ) o

*The characters in the parentheses are katakana.

2. Syllabary with voicing markers and plosive markers

ぱ(パ) pa	ば(バ) ba	だ(ダ) da	ざ(ザ) za	が(ガ) ga
ぴ(ピ) pi	び(ビ) bi	ぢ(ヂ) ji	じ(ジ) ji	ぎ(ギ) gi
ぷ(プ) pu	ぶ(ブ) bu	づ(ヅ) dzu	ず(ズ) dzu	ぐ(グ) gu
ぺ(ペ) pe	べ(ベ) be	で(デ) de	ぜ(ゼ) ze	げ(ゲ) ge
ぽ(ポ) po	ぼ(ボ) bo	ど(ド) do	ぞ(ゾ) zo	ご(ゴ) go

3. Syllabary for complex consonants

りゃ(リャ) rya	みゃ(ミャ) mya	ひゃ(ヒャ) ぴゃ(ピャ)・びゃ(ビャ) hya pya . bya	にゃ(ニャ) nya	ちゃ(チャ) ぢゃ(ヂャ) cha ja	しゃ(シャ) じゃ(ジャ) sha ja	きゃ(キャ) ぎゃ(ギャ) kya gya
りゅ(リュ) ryu	みゅ(ミュ) myu	ひゅ(ヒュ) ぴゅ(ピュ)・びゃ(ビュ) hyu pyu . byu	にゅ(ニュ) nyu	ちゅ(チュ) ぢゅ(ヂュ) chu ju	しゅ(シュ) じゅ(ジュ) shu ju	きゅ(キュ) ぎゅ(ギュ) kyu gyu
りょ(リョ) ryo	みょ(ミョ) myo	ひょ(ヒョ) ぴょ(ピョ)・びょ(ビョ) hyo pyo . byo	にょ(ニョ) nyo	ちょ(チョ) ぢょ(ヂョ) cho jo	しょ(ショ) じょ(ジョ) sho jo	きょ(キョ) ぎょ(ギョ) kyo gyo

4. Double consonants and long vowels

っ (ッ) pp, tt, kk, ss

ああ (アー) ā / aa	いい (イー) ī / ii	うう (ウー) ū / uu	えい / ええ (エー) ē / ee	おう / おお (オー) ō / oo

Basic Hiragana Stroke Order

a	あ
i	い
u	う
e	え
o	お
ka	か
ki	き
ku	く
ke	け
ko	こ
sa	さ
shi	し
su	す
se	せ
so	そ
ta	た
chi	ち
tsu	つ
te	て
to	と
na	な
ni	に
nu	ぬ
ne	ね
no	の
ha	は
hi	ひ
fu	ふ
he	へ
ho	ほ
ma	ま
mi	み
mu	む
me	め
mo	も
ya	や
yu	ゆ
yo	よ
ra	ら
ri	り
ru	る
re	れ
ro	ろ
wa	わ
o	を
n	ん

Basic Katakana Stroke Order

a	ア
i	イ
u	ウ
e	エ
o	オ
ka	カ
ki	キ
ku	ク
ke	ケ
ko	コ
sa	サ
shi	シ
su	ス
se	セ
so	ソ
ta	タ
chi	チ
tsu	ツ
te	テ
to	ト
na	ナ
ni	ニ
nu	ヌ
ne	ネ
no	ノ
ha	ハ
hi	ヒ
fu	フ
he	ヘ
ho	ホ
ma	マ
mi	ミ
mu	ム
me	メ
mo	モ
ya	ヤ
yu	ユ
yo	ヨ
ra	ラ
ri	リ
ru	ル
re	レ
ro	ロ
wa	ワ
o	ヲ
n	ン

Genko Yoshi (Composition paper)

You can write vertically or horizontally using genko yoshi, as shown in the examples, following the conventions below:

- Use one box for each character, even for small characters such as ゃ, ゅ, ょ and っ. Small characters are written in the right upper portion of a box when written vertically, but in the left bottom portion of a box when written horizontally.
- Use one box for each punctuation mark such as the comma "、", the period "。", the quotation marks "「 」" and parentheses "(　)". However, the comma (、) and the period (。) should not appear at the beginning of a line, but they can be placed outside the box, very near the preceding character or in the same box as the preceding character.
- The katakana elongation mark is a vertical line when writing vertically, but it is a horizontal line when writing horizontally.
- Write the title on the rightmost line when writing vertically, and on the topmost line when writing horizontally. Leave three or four boxes above the title.
- When writing vertically, the name of the writer is placed at the bottom of the line right next to the title line, but one box blank must be left after the name. When writing horizontally, the name is placed at the end of the line right below the title, but one box blank must be left after the name.
- Leave one box blank at the beginning of each paragraph.

Example of horizontal writing

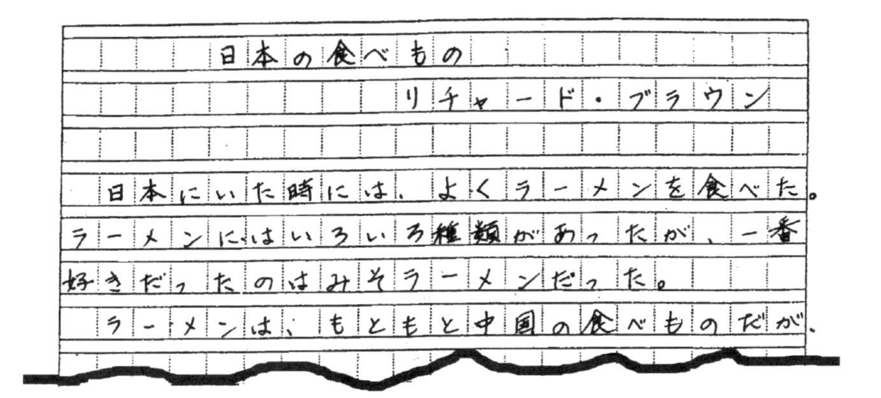

Example of vertical writing

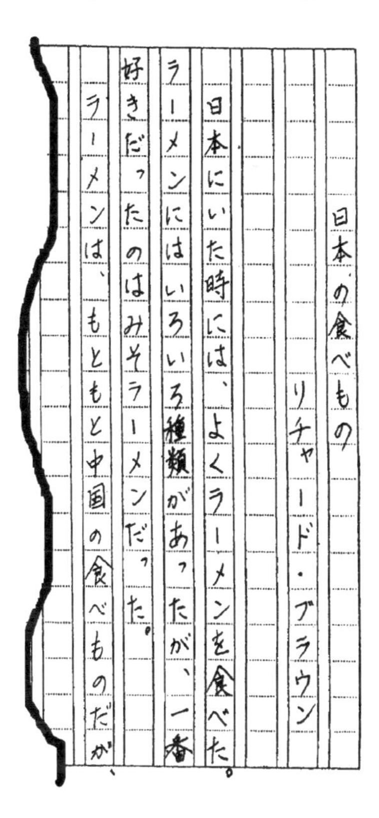

APPENDIX TWO

Verbs and Adjectives

Verb Forms

		Root Form	Plain Forms				Stem Form**	Te-form
			Present Affirmative	Present Negative	Past Affirmative	Past Negative		
Regular Verbs	Ru-verbs	たべ *eat* tabe	たべる	たべない	たべた	たべなかった	たべ	たべて
		み *see* mi	みる	みない	みた	みなかった	み	みて
	U-verbs	とr *take* tor	とる	とらない	とった	とらなかった	とり	とって
		かk *write* kak	かく	かかない	かいた	かかなかった	かき	かいて
		およg *swim* oyog	およぐ	およがない	およいだ	およがなかった	およぎ	およいで
		はなs *speak* hanas	はなす	はなさない	はなした	はなさなかった	はなし	はなして
		かw *buy* kaw	かう	かわない	かった	かわなかった	かい	かって
		かt *win* kat	かつ	かたない	かった	かたなかった	かち	かって
		のm *drink* nom	のむ	のまない	のんだ	のまなかった	のみ	のんで
		しn *die* shin	しぬ	しなない	しんだ	しななかった	しに	しんで
		あそb *play* asob	あそぶ	あそばない	あそんだ	あそばなかった	あそび	あそんで
Major Irregular Verbs		— do	する	しない	した	しなかった	し	して
		— come	くる	こない	きた	こなかった	き	きて
Slightly Irregular Verbs		あr *exist* ar	ある	ない	あった	なかった	あり	あって
		いk *go* ik	いく	いかない	いった	いかなかった	いき	いって
		いらっしゃr *exist* irasshar	いらっしゃる	いらっしゃらない	いらっしゃった	いらっしゃらなかった	いらっしゃい	いらっしゃって
		くださr *give* kudasar	くださる	くださらない	くださった	くださらなかった	ください	くださって
Copula (〜です)		—	〜だ	〜じゃない*	〜だった	〜じゃなかった*	—	〜で

* じゃ in the negative forms of the copular verb can be では (dewa).

** Polite forms of verbs are created by adding ます *present affirmative*, ません *present negative*, ました *past affirmative* or ませんでした *past negative* at the end of the stem forms of all the verbs except the copular verb.

Some Japanese Verbs

Ru-verbs	-る -e-ru	上げる・開ける・入れる・売れる・受ける・生まれる・得る・遅れる・教える・覚える・変える・掛ける・片付ける・考える・聞こえる・決める・加える・答える・下げる・閉める・調べる・捨てる・食べる・疲れる・出る・出かける・寝る・始める・離れる・晴れる・ほめる・負ける・間違える・見える・見せる・燃える・痩せる・辞める・汚れる・忘れる
	-る -i-ru	飽きる・生きる・いる・起きる・落ちる・降りる・借りる・感じる・着る・信じる・過ぎる・足りる・できる・閉じる・煮る・伸びる・見る・用いる
U-verbs	-る -r-u	余る・当たる・要る・移る・売る・送る・終わる・刈る・変わる・頑張る・曇る・困る・作る・叱る・通る・取る・直る・なる・残る・乗る・始まる・降る・曲がる・回る・やる・分かる
		***-iru / -eru** ending **u**-verbs: 帰る・切る・走る・しゃべる・練る・煎る・入る・散る・混じる・参る・知る・限る・減る・茂る・ける・照る・滑る
	-く -k-u	開く・歩く・頂く・動く・置く・驚く・書く・乾く・聞く・咲く・敷く・すく・たたく・着く・解く・掃く・働く・引く・吹く・開く・磨く・向く・沸く
	-ぐ -g-u	あおぐ・急ぐ・泳ぐ・かぐ・こぐ・騒ぐ・つなぐ・研ぐ・はぐ・はしゃぐ・防ぐ・脱ぐ
	-す -s-u	表わす・押す・おとす・移す・返す・隠す・貸す・乾かす・暮らす・消す・殺す・壊す・探す・指す・示す・倒す・足す・出す・だます・試す・とかす・通す・なくす・直す・残す・話す・離す・冷やす・干す・回す・許す・汚す・沸かす・渡す
	-う -w-u	会う・扱う・洗う・争う・言う・伺う・祝う・歌う・疑う・追う・行う・思う・買う・飼う・通う・従う・しまう・吸う・揃う・戦う・違う・使う・習う・縫う・匂う・願う・払う・拾う・間に合う・迷う・向かう・もらう・雇う・酔う
	-つ -t-u	打つ・勝つ・育つ・立つ・はなつ・待つ・持つ
	-む -w-u	産む・痛む・囲む・悲しむ・噛む・苦しむ・沈む・好む・拒む・混む・進む・住む・たたむ・楽しむ・頼む・つかむ・包む・積む・望む・飲む・挟む・含む・踏む・盗む・休む・止む・読む
	-ぬ -n-u	死ぬ
	-ぶ -b-u	遊ぶ・浮かぶ・選ぶ・転ぶ・叫ぶ・飛ぶ・並ぶ・運ぶ・ほころぶ・結ぶ・喜ぶ・呼ぶ
Irregular Verbs	Major irregular verbs: する・来る Slightly irregular verbs: ある・行く・いらっしゃる・くださる	
Copula	〜だ (〜です)	

Adjective and Copular Verb Forms

		I-type Adjectives	Na-type Adjectives	Noun + Copula
Stem		高	まじめ	車 (Noun part)
Pre-nominal Modifiers (Before a Noun)		高い	まじめな	車の
Plain Forms	Present Affirmative	高い	まじめだ	車だ
	Present Negative	高くない	まじめじゃない*	車じゃない*
	Past Affirmative	高かった	まじめだった	車だった
	Past Negative	高くなかった	まじめじゃなかった*	車じゃなかった*
Polite Forms	Present Affirmative	高いです	まじめです	車です
	Present Negative	高くありません 高くないです	まじめじゃありません* まじめじゃないです*	車じゃありません* 車じゃないです*
	Past Affirmative	高かったです	まじめでした	車でした
	Past Negative	高くありませんでした 高くなかったです	まじめじゃありませんでした* まじめじゃなかったです*	車じゃありませんでした* 車じゃなかったです*
Adverbs		高く	まじめに	—
Te-forms	Affirmative	高くて	まじめで	車で
	Negative	高くなくて	まじめじゃなくて*	車じゃなくて*

* じゃ in the negative forms can be では (dewa).

Some Japanese Adjectives

I-type Adjectives	明るい・新しい・うるさい・おいしい・多い・面白い・固い・可愛い・汚い・暗い・怖い・厳しい・少ない・ずるい・狭い・高い・楽しい・低い・ひどい・難しい・優しい・広い・古い・長い・悪い・つまらない・速い・早い・まずい・短い・安い・やわらかい
Na-type Adjectives	意地悪(な)・簡単(な)・嫌い(な)・きれい(な)・高価(な)・静か(な)・丈夫(な)・神経質(な)・スマート(な)・好き(な)・ハンサム(な)・便利(な)・不便(な)・まじめ(な)・立派(な)
Irregular / Indeterminacy	いい・大きい/大き(な)・小さい/小さ(な)

APPENDIX THREE

Counter List

～えん（～円）*~yen (~en)*

いちえん（一円）
にえん（二円）
さんえん（三円）
よえん（四円）
ごえん（五円）
ろくえん（六円）
ななえん（七円）
はちえん（八円）
きゅうえん（九円）
じゅうえん（十円）
なんえん（何円）

～か（～課）*Lesson~*

いっか（一課）
にか（二課）
さんか（三課）
よんか（四課）
ごか（五課）
ろっか（六課）
ななか（七課）
はちか（八課）
きゅうか（九課）
じゅっか（十課）
なんか（何課）

～かい（～階）*~th floor*

いっかい（一階）
にかい（二階）
さんかい（三階）
よんかい（四階）
ごかい（五階）
ろっかい（六階）
ななかい（七階）
はっかい / はちかい（八階）
きゅうかい（九階）
じゅっかい（十階）
なんかい（何階）

～かい（～回）*~times (Frequency)*

いっかい（一回）
にかい（二回）
さんかい（三回）
よんかい（四回）
ごかい（五回）
ろっかい（六回）
ななかい（七回）
はっかい / はちかい（八回）
きゅうかい（九回）
じゅっかい（十回）
なんかい（何回）

～かげつ（～ヶ月）*~month(s)*

いっかげつ（一ヶ月）
にかげつ（二ヶ月）
さんかげつ（三ヶ月）
よんかげつ（四ヶ月）
ごかげつ（五ヶ月）
ろっかげつ（六ヶ月）
ななかげつ（七ヶ月）
はちかげつ（八ヶ月）
きゅうかげつ（九ヶ月）
じゅっかげつ（十ヶ月）
なんかげつ（何ヶ月）

～がつ（～月）*Month*

いちがつ（一月）
にがつ（二月）
さんがつ（三月）
しがつ（四月）
ごがつ（五月）
ろくがつ（六月）
しちがつ（七月）
はちがつ（八月）
くがつ（九月）
じゅうがつ（十月）
なんがつ（何月）

～こ（～個）
(Inanimate objects such as apples and chairs)

いっこ（一個）
にこ（二個）
さんこ（三個）
よんこ（四個）
ごこ（五個）
ろっこ（六個）
ななこ（七個）
はちこ / はっこ（八個）
きゅうこ（九個）
じゅっこ（十個）
なんこ（何個）

～さい（～歳・～才）*~years old*
(Age of people and animals)

いっさい（一歳）
にさい（二歳）
さんさい（三歳）
よんさい（四歳）
ごさい（五歳）
ろくさい（六歳）
ななさい（七歳）
はっさい（八歳）
きゅうさい（九歳）
じゅっさい（十歳）
なんさい（何歳）

～さつ(～冊)
(Books and magazines)

いっさつ(一冊)
にさつ(二冊)
さんさつ(三冊)
よんさつ(四冊)
ごさつ(五冊)
ろくさつ(六冊)
ななさつ(七冊)
はっさつ(八冊)
きゅうさつ(九冊)
じゅっさつ(十冊)
なんさつ(何冊)

～しゅうかん(～週間) *~week(s)*

いっしゅうかん(一週間)
にしゅうかん(二週間)
さんしゅうかん(三週間)
よんしゅうかん(四週間)
ごしゅうかん(五週間)
ろくしゅうかん(六週間)
ななしゅうかん(七週間)
はっしゅうかん(八週間)
きゅうしゅうかん(九週間)
じゅっしゅうかん(十週間)
なんしゅうかん(何週間)

～じ(～時) *~o'clock*

いちじ(一時)
にじ(二時)
さんじ(三時)
よじ(四時)
ごじ(五時)
ろくじ(六時)
しちじ(七時)
はちじ(八時)
くじ(九時)
じゅうじ(十時)
なんじ(何時)

～じかん(～時間) *~hour(s)*

いちじかん(一時間)
にじかん(二時間)
さんじかん(三時間)
よじかん(四時間)
ごじかん(五時間)
ろくじかん(六時間)
しちじかん / ななじかん(七時間)
はちじかん(八時間)
くじかん(九時間)
じゅうじかん(十時間)
なんじかん(何時間)

～だい(～台)
(Mechanical objects)

いちだい(一台)
にだい(二台)
さんだい(三台)
よんだい(四台)
ごだい(五台)
ろくだい(六台)
ななだい(七台)
はちだい(八台)
きゅうだい(九台)
じゅうだい(十台)
なんだい(何台)

～つ(～つ)
(Inanimate objects such as apples and chairs)
*Available only up to ten. (Japanese native counter)

ひとつ(一つ)
ふたつ(二つ)
みっつ(三つ)
よっつ(四つ)
いつつ(五つ)
むっつ(六つ)
ななつ(七つ)
やっつ(八つ)
ここのつ(九つ)
とお(十)
いくつ(いくつ)

～つう(～通) *Letters*

For example: てがみを2通だしました。
I sent out two letters.

いっつう(一通)
につう(二通)
さんつう(三通)
よんつう(四通)
ごつう(五通)
ろくつう(六通)
ななつう(七通)
はっつう(八通)
きゅうつう(九通)
じゅっつう(十通)
なんつう(何通)

～てん(～点) *~point(s)*

いってん(一点)
にてん(二点)
さんてん(三点)
よんてん(四点)
ごてん(五点)
ろくてん(六点)
ななてん(七点)
はってん(八点)
きゅうてん(九点)
じゅってん(十点)
なんてん(何点)

～ど (～度) *~time(s) (Frequency)*

いちど (一度)
にど (二度)
さんど (三度)
よんど (四度)
ごど (五度)
ろくど (六度)
ななど (七度)
はちど (八度)
きゅうど (九度)
じゅうど (十度)
なんど (何度)

～ドル (～ドル) *~dollar(s)*

いちどる (一ドル)
にどる (二ドル)
さんどる (三ドル)
よんどる (四ドル)
ごどる (五ドル)
ろくどる (六ドル)
ななどる (七ドル)
はちどる (八ドル)
きゅうどる (九ドル)
じゅうどる (十ドル)
なんどる (何ドル)

～にち (～日)
(The days of the month)

ついたち (一日)
ふつか (二日)
みっか (三日)
よっか (四日)
いつか (五日)
むいか (六日)
なのか (七日)
ようか (八日)
ここのか (九日)
とおか (十日)
じゅういちにち (十一日)
じゅうににち (十二日)
じゅうさんにち (十三日)
じゅうよっか (十四日)
じゅうごにち (十五日)
じゅうろくにち (十六日)
じゅうしちにち (十七日)
じゅうはちにち (十八日)
じゅうくにち (十九日)
はつか (二十日)
にじゅういちにち (二十一日)
にじゅうににち (二十二日)
にじゅうさんにち (二十三日)
にじゅうよっか (二十四日)
にじゅうごにち (二十五日)
にじゅうろくにち (二十六日)
にじゅうしちにち (二十七日)
にじゅうはちにち (二十八日)
にじゅうくにち (二十九日)
さんじゅうにち (三十日)
さんじゅういちにち (三十一日)
なんにち (何日)

12月

月	火	水	木	金	土	日
	1	2	3	4	5	6
7	8	9	10	11	12	13
14	15	16	17	18	19	20
21	22	23	24	25	26	27
28	29	30	31			

～にち (かん) (～日 (間)) *~day(s)*

いちにちかん (一日間)
ふつかかん (二日間)
みっかかん (三日間)
よっかかん (四日間)
いつかかん (五日間)
むいかかん (六日間)
なのかかん (七日間)
ようかかん (八日間)
ここのかかん (九日間)
とおかかん (十日間)
なんにちかん (何日間)

～にん (～人) *~person(s), ~people*

ひとり (一人)
ふたり (二人)
さんにん (三人)
よにん (四人)
ごにん (五人)
ろくにん (六人)
ななにん / しちにん (七人)
はちにん (八人)
きゅうにん (九人)
じゅうにん (十人)
なんにん (何人)

～ねん (～年) *~year(s)*

いちねん (一年)
にねん (二年)
さんねん (三年)
よねん (四年)
ごねん (五年)
ろくねん (六年)
ななねん (七年)
はちねん (八年)
きゅうねん (九年)
じゅうねん (十年)
なんねん (何年)

~ねんせい(~年生) *~th grade*

いちねんせい(一年生)
にねんせい(二年生)
さんねんせい(三年生)
よねんせい(四年生)
ごねんせい(五年生)
ろくねんせい(六年生)
ななねんせい(七年生)
はちねんせい(八年生)
きゅうねんせい(九年生)
じゅうねんせい(十年生)
なんねんせい(何年生)

~はい(~杯) *~cups, ~glasses, ~spoonfuls*

いっぱい(一杯)
にはい(二杯)
さんばい(三杯)
よんはい(四杯)
ごはい(五杯)
ろくはい / ろっぱい(六杯)
ななはい(七杯)
はちはい / はっぱい(八杯)
きゅうはい(九杯)
じゅっぱい(十杯)
なんばい(何杯)

~ばん(~番) *Number ~, ~th*

いちばん(一番)
にばん(二番)
さんばん(三番)
よんばん(四番)
ごばん(五番)
ろくばん(六番)
ななばん(七番)
はちばん(八番)
きゅうばん(九番)
じゅうばん(十番)
なんばん(何番)

~ひき(~匹) Animals

いっぴき(一匹)
にひき(二匹)
さんびき(三匹)
よんひき(四匹)

ごひき(五匹)
ろくひき / ろっぴき(六匹)
ななひき(七匹)
はちひき / はっぴき(八匹)

きゅうひき(九匹)
じゅっぴき(十匹)
なんびき(何匹)

~ふん(~分) *~minutes*
(Identity of the minute)

いっぷん(一分)
にふん(二分)
さんぷん(三分)
よんぷん(四分)
ごふん(五分)
ろくふん / ろっぷん(六分)
ななふん(七分)
はちふん / はっぷん(八分)
きゅうふん(九分)
じゅっぷん(十分)
なんぷん(何分)

~ふん(かん)(~分(間)) *~minutes*
(Length of time in minutes)

いっぷんかん(一分間)
にふんかん(二分間)
さんぷんかん(三分間)
よんぷんかん(四分間)
ごふんかん(五分間)
ろくふんかん / ろっぷんかん(六分間)
ななふんかん(七分間)
はちふんかん / はっぷんかん(八分間)
きゅうふんかん(九分間)
じゅっぷんかん(十分間)
なんぷんかん(何分間)

~ほん(~本)
(Cylindrical shaped objects)

いっぽん(一本)
にほん(二本)
さんぼん(三本)
よんほん(四本)
ごほん(五本)
ろくほん / ろっぽん(六本)
ななほん(七本)
はちほん / はっぽん(八本)
きゅうほん(九本)
じゅっぽん(十本)
なんぼん(何本)

~まい(~枚)
(Flat shaped objects)

いちまい(一枚)
にまい(二枚)
さんまい(三枚)
よんまい(四枚)
ごまい(五枚)
ろくまい(六枚)
ななまい(七枚)
はちまい(八枚)
きゅうまい(九枚)
じゅうまい(十枚)
なんまい(何枚)

APPENDIX FOUR

Vocabulary Collection

1. Food

~ Food Category ~

くだもの（果物） *fruit*
にく（肉） *meat*
さかな（魚） *fish*
やさい（野菜） *vegetable*

~ Fruit ~

みかん *orange*
りんご *apple*
もも（桃） *peach*
バナナ *banana*

~ Meal ~

朝ご飯（あさごはん） *breakfast*
昼ご飯（ひるごはん） *lunch*
晩ご飯（ばんごはん） *supper*

~ Beverage ~

おさけ（お酒） *rice wine*
コーヒー *coffee*
おちゃ（お茶） *green tea*
ジュース *juice*
こうちゃ（紅茶） *black tea*
ビール *beer*
みず（水） *water*
ミルク *milk*
ウイスキー *whiskey*
ワイン *wine*

~ Japanese Food ~

うどん *white noodle*
うなぎ（鰻） *eel*
さしみ（刺身） *sashimi*
すきやき *sukiyaki*
すし（寿司） *sushi*

そば *buckwheat noodles*
てりやき *teriyaki*
てんぷら *tempura*
なっとう（納豆） *fermented soybean*
みそしる（味噌汁） *miso soup*
やきとり *barbecued chicken*
カレーライス *curry rice*
ラーメン *Chinese noodles*

~ Ethnic Variety ~

韓国料理（かんこくりょうり） *Korean cuisine*
中華料理（ちゅうかりょうり） *Chinese cuisine*
日本料理（にほんりょうり） *Japanese cuisine*
フランス料理（りょうり） *French cuisine*
メキシコ料理（りょうり） *Mexican cuisine*

~ Taste ~

かおり *aroma*
あまい（甘い） *sweet*
おいしい *delicious*
にがい（苦い） *bitter*
まずい *not delicious*
すっぱい（酸っぱい） *sour*
からい（辛い） *spicy*
しょっぱい *salty*

~ Western Food ~

アイスクリーム *ice cream*
ケーキ *cake*
サラダ *salad*
サンドイッチ *sandwich*
スープ *soup*
ステーキ *steak*
スパゲッティー *spaghetti*
ハンバーガー *hamburger*
ピザ *pizza*
ホットドッグ *hotdog*

2. Locations

~ Campus ~

学生会館 *student union*
体育館 *gymnasium*
カフェテリア *cafeteria*
図書館 *library*

~ In the Town ~

喫茶店 *coffee shop*
郵便局 *post office*
銀行 *bank*
デパート *department store*
病院 *hospital*
本屋 *bookstore*
スーパーマーケット
supermarket
レストラン *restaurant*

~ In the House ~

いま（居間） *living room*
おてあらい（お手洗い） *toilet*
おふろ（お風呂） *bathroom*
しょくどう（食堂） *dining room*
しんしつ（寝室） *bedroom*
だいどころ（台所） *kitchen*

うち *home*
アパート *apartment*
りょう（寮） *dormitory*
ホテル *hotel*

えき（駅） *station*
くうこう（空港） *airport*
ちゅうしゃじょう（駐車場）
parking lot

くに（国） *country*
まち（町） *town*
とし（都市） *city*
むら（村） *village*

~ Countries ~

かんこく（韓国） *Korea*
オーストラリア *Australia*
ちゅうごく（中国） *China*
カナダ *Canada*
にほん（日本） *Japan*
スペイン *Spain*
アメリカ *the U.S.A.*
ドイツ *Germany*
イギリス *England*
フランス *France*
イタリア *Italy*
ポーランド *Poland*

~ Cities ~

おおさか（大阪） *Osaka*
ソウル *Seoul*
きょうと（京都） *Kyoto*
ニューヨーク *New York*
とうきょう（東京） *Tokyo*
パリ *Paris*
シドニー *Sidney*
ボストン *Boston*
シャンハイ *Shanghai*
ロサンゼルス *Los Angeles*
サンフランシスコ *San Fransisco*

~ Fun Places ~

映画館 *movie theater*
動物園 *zoo*
公園 *park*
博物館 *museum*
水族館 *aquarium*
遊園地 *amusement park*

~ Landscape ~

うみ（海） *sea*
すなはま（砂浜） *beach*
かいがん（海岸） *seashore*
たいりく（大陸） *continent*
かざん（火山） *volcano*
みずうみ（湖） *lake*
かわ（川） *river*
やま（山） *mountain*
しま（島） *island*

~ Relative Location ~

あいだ（間） *between*
となり（隣） *next-door*
うえ（上） *top*
ひだり（左） *left*
うしろ（後） *behind*
まえ（前） *front*
した（下） *bottom*
みぎ（右） *right*
ちかく（近く） *vicinity*
よこ（横） *side*

~ Compass Direction ~

ひがし（東） *east*
みなみ（南） *south*
にし（西） *west*
きた（北） *north*

3. Things and Animals

~ In the Room ~

いす (椅子) *chair*
ようふく (洋服) *clothes*
しゃしん (写真) *photo*
カメラ *camera*
たんす *clothes chest*
ソファー *sofa*
つくえ (机) *desk*
テレビ *television*
ドア *door*
でんわ (電話) *telephone*
ヒーター *heater*
とけい (時計) *clock, watch*
ベッド *bed*

ほんばこ (本箱) *bookcase*
ラジオ *radio*
まど (窓) *window*
れいぞうこ (冷蔵庫) *refrigerator*

~ Reading ~

きじ (記事) *article*
てがみ (手紙) *letter*
ざっし (雑誌) *magazine*
ほん (本) *book*
し (詩) *poem*
レポート *report*
しょうせつ (小説) *novel*
ろんぶん (論文) *academic paper*
しんぶん (新聞) *newspaper*

~ Transportation ~

くるま (車) *car*
タクシー *taxi*
ふね (船) *ship*
バス *bus*
でんしゃ (電車) *train*
ちかてつ (地下鉄) *subway*
じてんしゃ (自転車) *bicycle*
ひこうき (飛行機) *airplane*

~ In Your Pocket ~

お金 *money*
財布 *purse*
かぎ *key*
ペン *pen*
クレジットカード *credit card*

~ Animals ~

いぬ (犬) *dog*
さる (猿) *monkey*
うし (牛) *cow*
ねこ (猫) *cat*
うま (馬) *horse*
ぶた (豚) *pig*

4. Things you wear

～をきる

コート *coat*
ジャケット *jacket*
セーター *sweater*
ティーシャツ *T-shirt*
ブラウス *blouse*
ベスト *vest*

～をかぶる

かつら *wig*
ぼうし (帽子) *hat / cap*

～をはく

くつ (靴) *shoes*
スカート *skirt*
くつした (靴下) *socks*
スニーカー *sneakers*
サンダル *sandals*
ズボン *pants*

～をする

とけい (時計) *watch*
スカーフ *scarf*
めがね (眼鏡) *glasses*
ネックレス *necklace*
イヤリング *earrings*
ブレスレット *bracelet*
サングラス *sunglasses*
ベルト *belt*

~ Adjectives for Things You Wear ~

かっこいい *cool*
かわいい *cute*
きれい (な) *beautiful*
下品 (な) *bad taste*
地味 (な) *conservative*
上品 (な) *elegant, good taste*
派手 (な) *showy*

5. School

~ がっこう School ~

こうこう（高校） *high school*
しょうがっこう（小学校）
elementary school
じゅく（塾） *cram school*
だいがく（大学） *university*
だいがくいん（大学院）
graduate school
ちゅうがっこう（中学校）
junior high school
ようちえん（幼稚園）
kindergarten

~ Class Related Terms ~

きょうしつ（教室） *classroom*
きょうかしょ（教科書） *textbook*
しけん（試験） *exam*
しゅくだい（宿題） *homework*
じゅぎょう（授業） *class*
クイズ *quiz*
テキスト *text*

~ Describing Classes ~

むずかしい（難しい） *difficult*
おもしろい（面白い） *interesting*
かんたん（な）（簡単（な）） *easy*
たのしい（楽しい） *amusing*
つまらない（詰まらない） *boring*

~ Academic Subjects ~

いがく（医学） *medical science*
えいご（英語） *English*
おんがく（音楽） *music*
かがく（化学） *chemistry*
きょういくがく（教育学）
education
けいえいがく（経営学）
business administration
けいざいがく（経済学）
economics
げんごがく（言語学） *linguistics*
しゃかいがく（社会学） *sociology*
しんりがく（心理学） *psychology*
じんるいがく（人類学）
anthropology
すうがく（数学） *mathematics*
せいじがく（政治学）
political science
せいぶつがく（生物学） *biology*
にほんご（日本語） *Japanese*
ぶつり（物理） *physics*
れきし（歴史） *history*
コンピューター・サイエンス
computer science

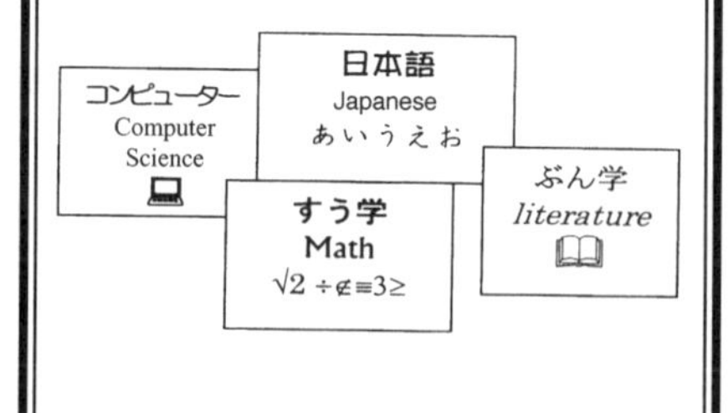

6. Time

げつようび (月曜日) *Monday*
かようび (火曜日) *Tuesday*
すいようび (水曜日) *Wednesday*
もくようび (木曜日) *Thursday*
きんようび (金曜日) *Friday*
どようび (土曜日) *Saturday*
にちようび (日曜日) *Sunday*

ついたち (1 日) *1st*
ふつか (2 日) *2nd*
みっか (3 日) *3rd*
よっか (4 日) *4th*
いつか (5 日) *5th*
むいか (6 日) *6th*
なのか (7 日) *7th*
ようか (8 日) *8th*
ここのか (9 日) *9th*
とおか (10 日) *10th*
じゅういちにち (11 日) *11th*
じゅうににち (12 日) *12th*
じゅうさんにち (13 日) *13th*
じゅうよっか (14 日) *14th*
じゅうごにち (15 日) *15th*
じゅうろくにち (16 日) *16th*
じゅうしちにち (17 日) *17th*
じゅうはちにち (18 日) *18th*
じゅうくにち (19 日) *19th*
はつか (20 日) *20th*
にじゅういちにち (21 日) *21th*
にじゅうににち (22 日) *22th*
にじゅうさんにち (23 日) *23th*
にじゅうよっか (24 日) *24th*
にじゅうごにち (25 日) *25th*
にじゅうろくにち (26 日) *26th*
にじゅうしちにち (27 日) *27th*
にじゅうはちにち (28 日) *28th*
にじゅうくにち (29 日) *29th*
さんじゅうにち (30 日) *30th*
さんじゅういちにち (31 日) *31th*

いちがつ (1 月) *January*
にがつ (2 月) *February*
さんがつ (3 月) *March*
しがつ (4 月) *April*
ごがつ (5 月) *May*
ろくがつ (6 月) *June*
しちがつ (7 月) *July*
はちがつ (8 月) *August*
くがつ (9 月) *September*
じゅうがつ (10 月) *October*
じゅういちがつ (11 月) *November*
じゅうにがつ (12 月) *December*

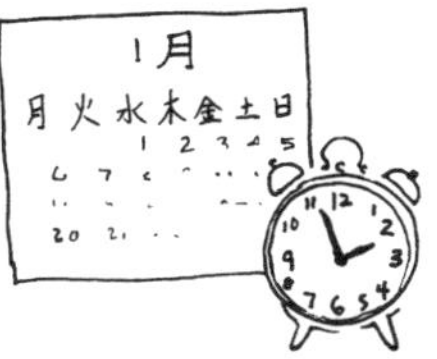

いちじ (1 時) *1 o'clock*
にじ (2 時) *2 o'clock*
さんじ (3 時) *3 o'clock*
よじ (4 時) *4 o'clock*
ごじ (5 時) *5 o'clock*
ろくじ (6 時) *6 o'clock*
しちじ (7 時) *7 o'clock*
はちじ (8 時) *8 o'clock*
くじ (9 時) *9 o'clock*
じゅうじ (10 時) *10 o'clock*
じゅういちじ (11 時) *11 o'clock*
じゅうにじ (12 時) *12 o'clock*

春(はる) *spring*
秋(あき) *fall*
夏(なつ) *summer*
冬(ふゆ) *winter*
春休み(はるやすみ) *spring vacation*
冬休み(ふゆやすみ) *winter vacation*
夏休み(なつやすみ) *summer vacation*

あさ (朝) *morning*
ごぜんちゅう (午前中) *morning*
ひる (昼) *noon*
ごご (午後) *afternoon*
ゆうがた (夕方) *evening*
ばん (晩) *night*
よる (夜) *night*

いま (今) *now*
けさ (今朝) *this morning*
こんばん (今晩) *this evening, tonight*
こんど (今度) *next time, sometime soon*

今月(こんげつ) *this month*
来月(らいげつ) *next month*
先月(せんげつ) *last month*

こんしゅう (今週) *this week*
せんしゅう (先週) *last week*
らいしゅう (来週) *next week*

今年(ことし) *this year*
来年(らいねん) *next year*
去年(きょねん) *last year*

きょう (今日) *today*
あした (明日) *tomorrow*
きのう (昨日) *yesterday*
おととい (一昨日) *the day before yesterday*
あさって (明後日) *the day after tomorrow*

7. People

~ Family ~

母・お母さん *mother*
父・お父さん *father*
兄・お兄さん *older brother*
姉・お姉さん *older sister*
妹 ・ 妹さん *younger sister*
弟 ・ 弟さん *younger brother*
祖母・おばあさん *grandmother*
祖父・おじいさん *grandfather*
兄弟 ・ご兄弟 *siblings*
両親 ・ご両親 *parents*
主人・ご主人 *husband*
家内・奥さん *wife*
子供・お子さん *child*
娘 ・お嬢さん *daughter*
息子・息子さん *son*
従兄弟 *cousin*

~ Gender / Age ~

女の人 *woman*
女性 *woman*
男の人 *man*
男性 *man*
子供 *child*
赤ちゃん *baby*
若い人 *young person*
お年よりの人 *old person*

~ Nationalities ~

韓国人 *Korean*
中国人 *Chinese*
日本人 *Japanese*

アメリカ人 *American*
オーストラリア人 *Australian*
イギリス人 *English*
スペイン人 *Spanish*
フランス人 *French*

~ Relationship ~

ガールフレンド *girlfriend*
ボーイフレンド *boyfriend*
ともだち(友達) *friend*

~ Personal Pronouns ~

わたし(私) *I, me*
ぼく(僕) *I, me (for male)*
わたしたち(私達) *we, us*
あなた *you*
あなたたち *you (plural)*
かれ(彼) *he, him*
かのじょ(彼女) *she, her*
かれら(彼ら) *they, them (male and mixed gender)*
かのじょら(彼女ら) *they, them (female)*

~ Occupation ~

弁護士・弁護士さん *lawyer*
教師・先生 *teacher*
医者・お医者さん *doctor*
看護士・看護士さん *nurse*
会社員・会社員さん *company employee*
店員・店員さん *salesclerk*
学生・学生さん *student*

~ Students ~

小学生 *elementary school student*
中学生 *middle school student*
高校生 *high school student*
大学生 *college student*
大学院生 *graduate student*
留学生 *exchange stude*

8. Actions

~ Sports ~

運動 *exercise*
空手 *karate*
剣道 *kendo*
柔道 *judo*
水泳 *swimming*
相撲 *sumo wrestling*

釣 *fishing*
野球 *baseball*
エアロビクス *aerobics*
ゴルフ *golf*
サッカー *soccer*
スキー *ski*
テニス *tennis*
バスケットボール *basketball*
フットボール *football*

~ Daily Routine ~

起きる *to wake up*
顔を洗う *to wash one's face*
歯をみがく *to brush one's teeth*
お風呂に入る *to take a bath*
シャワーをあびる *to take a shower*
お手洗いに行く *to go to the toilet*
ひげをそる *to shave oneself*
(お)化粧をする *to put on make-up*
髪をとかす *to comb one's hair*
洋服を着る *to get dressed*

~ Motion ~

いく(行く) *to go*
くる(来る) *to come*
かえる(帰る) *to return*
はいる(入る) *to enter*
すわる(座る) *to sit down*
たつ(立つ) *to stand up*
のる(乗る) *to ride*

~ Music Instruments ~

ピアノをひく *to play the piano*
バイオリンをひく *to play the violin*
ギターをひく *to play the guitar*
クラリネットをふく *to play the clarinet*
サクソフォンをふく *to play the saxophone*
フルートをふく *to play the flute*
ドラムをたたく *to play the drum*

~ Household Chores ~

そうじをする *to clean (rooms)*
料理をする *to cook*
買物をする *to go shopping*
ご飯を作る *to fix a meal*
洗濯をする *to do the laundry*

読む *to read*
書く *to write*
作る *to make*
勉強する *to study*
使う *to use*
見る *to watch*
買う *to buy*
食べる *to eat*
飲む *to drink*

~ Pastime Activities ~

映画をみる *to watch a movie*
絵をかく *to draw*
歌をうたう *to sing a song*

音楽をきく *to listen to music*
買物をする *to go shopping*
雑誌をよむ *to read a magazine*
写真をとる *to take pictures*
友達と遊ぶ *to hang around with one's friends*
友達に電話をする *to call one's friends*
手紙をかく *to write a letter*
旅行をする *to go on a trip*
しゃべる *to chat*
のんびりする *to relax*
カラオケをする *to do (sing) karaoke*
ドライブをする *to drive around*
パーティーをする *to throw a party*
パチンコをする *to play a pachinko game*
コンピューター・ゲームをする *to play a computer game*

9. Properties and States

~ Room Temperature ~

さむい(寒い) *cold*
すずしい(涼しい) *cool*
あつい(暑い) *hot*
あたたかい(暖かい) *warm*

~ Rooms / Buildings ~

明(あか)るい *bright*
低(ひく)い *low*
新(あたら)しい *new*
広(ひろ)い *spacious*
きれい(な) *beautiful*
不便(ふべん)(な) *inconvenient*
暗(くら)い *dark*
古(ふる)い *old*
せまい *not spacious*
便利(べんり)(な) *convenient*
高(たか)い *tall*
立派(りっぱ)(な) *splendid*

~ Person ~

やさしい(優しい) *kind*
きびしい(厳しい) *strict*
きれい(な) *pretty, beautiful*
ハンサム(な) *handsome*
わかい(若い) *young*
まじめ(な)(真面目(な)) *serious*

~ Color ~

あか(赤) *red*
ちゃいろ(茶色) *brown*
あお(青) *blue*
きいろ(黄色) *yellow*
しろ(白) *white*
みどり(緑) *green*
くろ(黒) *black*

~ Mental State ~

いたい(痛い) *painful*
いそがしい(忙しい) *busy*
うれしい(嬉しい) *happy*
さびしい(寂しい) *lonely*
かなしい(悲しい) *sad*
くるしい(苦しい) *suffering*
うらやましい *to be envious*
こわい(怖い) *to be scared*
はずかしい *ashamed*

10. Health

~ Symptoms of Illnesses ~

風邪(かぜ)をひく *to catch a cold*
せきをする *to cough*
くしゃみをする *to sneeze*
熱(ねつ)がある *to have a fever*
吐(は)く *to vomit*
吐気(はきけ)がする *to have nausea*
寒気(さむけ)がする *to have a chill*
下痢(げり)をする *to have diarrhea*
頭(あたま)が痛(いた)い *to have a headache*
関節(かんせつ)が痛い *to have joint pain*
鼻水(はなみず)が出(で)る *to have a runny nose*
鼻(はな)が詰(つ)まっている *to have a stuffy nose*

~ Medical Specialties ~

げか(外科) *surgery*
しか(歯科) *dentistry*
がんか(眼科) *ophthalmology*
さんふじんか(産婦人科) *obstetric / gynecology*
ないか(内科) *internal medicine*
ひふか(皮膚科) *dermatology*

~ Treatment ~

薬(くすり)をのむ *to take medicine*
注射(ちゅうしゃ)をする *to give a shot*

~ Diagnosis ~

かぜ(風邪) *cold*
ぜんそく(喘息) *asthma*
ねんざ(捻挫) *sprain*
がん *cancer*
かふんしょう(花粉症) *hay fever*
もうちょう(盲腸) *appendicitis*
しょくちゅうどく(食中毒) *food poisoning*
こっせつ(骨折) *bone fracture*
はいえん(肺炎) *pneumonia*

~ Body Parts ~

め(目) *eye*
あたま(頭) *head*
くち(口) *mouth*
かお(顔) *face*
みみ(耳) *ear*
は(歯) *tooth*
せ(背) *height*
おなか(お腹) *belly, stomach*
あし(足) *foot, leg*
のど(喉) *throat*
て(手) *hand, arm*
ゆび(指) *finger*
かみ(髪) *hair*
こし(腰) *lower back, hip*

APPENDIX FIVE

Kanji List

	New Kanji Words and Compounds	New Kanji Characters	Writing Notes Related to Kanji
Chapter Two	私(わたし)・～人(じん)・日本人(にほんじん)・何(なん)・ぶん学(がく)・すう学(がく)・本(ほん)・山田(やまだ)・川口(かわぐち)・人(ひと)・犬(いぬ)・学生(がくせい)・先生(せんせい)・車(くるま)	私 人 日 本 何 学 山 田 川 口 犬 生 先 車	Kanji strokes Kanji readings
Chapter Three	母(はは)・お母(かあ)さん・父(ちち)・お父(とう)さん・兄(あに)・お兄(にい)さん・大学(だいがく)・大学(だいがく)いん・男(おとこ)の人(ひと)・女(おんな)の人(ひと)	母 父 兄 大 男 女	Kanji components ひとあし：儿 ちから：力
Chapter Four	一(いち)・二(に)・三(さん)・四(よん・し)・五(ご)・六(ろく)・七(なな・しち)・八(はち)・九(きゅう)・十(じゅう)・～月(がつ)・～月(がつ)生(う)まれ・～年生(ねんせい)・～時(じ)・何時(なんじ)・～分(ふん・ぷん)・高(たか)い・安(やす)い・百(ひゃく)・千(せん)・万(まん)・～円(えん)	一 二 三 四 五 六 七 八 九 十 今 月 年 時 分 高 安 百 千 万 円	Conjugational endings ひとがしらら：𠆢 なべぶた：亠 うかんむり：宀
Chapter Five	今日(きょう)・明日(あした)・行(い)く・来(く)る・来(き)ます・来(こ)ない・帰(かえ)る・山(やま)・安田(やすだ)・田中(たなか)	明 行 来 帰 中	ひへん：日
Chapter Six	でん車(しゃ)・じてん車(しゃ)・歩(ある)いて・～時間(じかん)・～分(ふん)(間(かん))・食(た)べる・飲(の)む・書(か)く・朝(あさ)・昼(ひる)・晩(ばん)・昨日(きのう)・今朝(けさ)・今晩(こんばん)・作(つく)る・使(つか)う・買(か)う・見(み)る	歩 間 食 飲 書 朝 昼 晩 昨 作 使 買 見	もんがまえ：門 しょくへん：飠 にんべん：亻
Chapter Seven	木(き)・間(あいだ)・近(ちか)く・上(うえ)・下(した)・中(なか)・右(みぎ)・左(ひだり)・月曜日(げつようび)・火曜日(かようび)・水曜日(すいようび)・木曜日(もくようび)・金曜日(きんようび)・土曜日(どようび)・日曜日(にちようび)	木 近 上 下 右 左 水 金 土	しんにょう：辶 おのづくり：斤
Chapter Eight	～本(ほん)・～枚(まい)・～冊(さつ)・～台(だい)・姉(あね)・お姉(ねえ)さん・妹(いもうと)・兄弟(きょうだい)・弟(おとうと)・～匹(ひき)・～人(にん)・勉強(べんきょう)する	枚 冊 台 姉 妹 弟 匹 勉 強	きへん：木 ぼくづくり：攵 おんなへん：女 ゆみへん：弓

	New Kanji Words and Compounds	New Kanji Characters	Writing Notes Related to Kanji
Chapter Nine	大(おお)きい・小(ちい)さい・新(あたら)しい・古(ふる)い・ 明(あか)るい・暗(くら)い・広(ひろ)い・近(ちか)い・ 日本語(にほんご)・文(ぶん)ぽう・文学(ぶんがく)	小 新 古 暗 広 語 文 勉 強	まだれ: 广 ごんべん: 言
Chapter Ten	言(い)う・話(はな)す・読(よ)む・聞(き)く・下(くだ)さい・ 立(た)つ・出(だ)す・入(はい)る・見(み)せる・早(はや)い・ 速(はや)い・習(なら)う・れん習(しゅう)・ふく習(しゅう)・ 道(みち)・曲(ま)がる・東(ひがし)・西(にし)・南(みなみ)・北(きた)	言 話 読 聞 立 出 入 早 速 習 道 曲 東 西 南 北	
Chapter Eleven	口(くち)・目(め)・耳(みみ)・足(あし)・手(て)・背(せ)・長(なが)い・ 短(みじか)い・多(おお)い・少(すく)ない・少(すこ)し・国(くに)・ 中国(ちゅうごく)・かん国(こく)・来月(らいげつ)・食(た)べもの・ 読書(どくしょ)・好(す)き・大好(だいす)き・上手(じょうず)・ 下手(へた)・名前(なまえ)・運転(うんてん)・教(おし)える・ お金(かね)・休(やす)む・社長(しゃちょう)・会社(かいしゃ)・ 社会学(しゃかいがく)・会社(かいしゃ)いん・働(はたら)く	目 耳 足 手 背 長 短 多 少 国 好 名 前 運 転 教 休 社 会 働	くにがまえ: 口 しめすへん: 礻
Chapter Twelve	春(はる)・夏(なつ)・秋(あき)・冬(ふゆ)・夏休(なつやす)み・会(あ)う・ 会話(かいわ)・今年(ことし)・去年(きょねん)・来年(らいねん)・学期(がっき)・ 〜日(にち)・〜年(ねん)・前(まえ)・外国(がいこく)・〜度(ど)・今度(こんど)	春 夏 秋 冬 去 期 外 度	なつあし: 夂 ふゆがしら: 夂
Chapter Thirteen	言語学(げんごがく)・楽(たの)しい・楽(らく)です・漢字(かんじ)・ 難(むずか)しい・洗(あら)う・洗(せん)たく・乗(の)る・ 買(か)いもの・薬(くすり)・〜点(てん)	楽 漢 字 難 洗 乗 薬 点	ふるとり: 隹 さんずいへん: 氵 くさかんむり: 艹 よつてん: 灬
Chapter Fourteen	お茶(ちゃ)・学校(がっこう)・学長(がくちょう)・校長(こうちょう)・ 小学校(しょうがっこう)・中学校(ちゅうがっこう)・高校(こうこう)・英語(えいご)・ 石田(いしだ)・林(はやし)・子供(こども)・化学(かがく)・遊(あそ)ぶ・ 住(す)む・着(き)る	茶 校 英 石 林 子 供 化 遊 住 着	

APPENDIX SIX

Basic Vocabulary List

adj.	: adjective	**n.**	: noun
adv.	: adverb	**pn.**	: proper noun
aux.	: auxiliary	**pron.**	: pronoun
c.	: counter	**prt.**	: particle
con.	: conjunction	**q.**	: question word
cop.	: copula	**vi.**	: intransitive verb
interj.	: Interjection	**vt.**	: transitive verb

No category mark: phrases, suffixes or prefixes

あ

あいだ	**n.**	間 *the position between (two items)* 3	CH 7
あう	**vi.**	***w*-u** 会う・会わない・会い・会って *to meet* (田中さんに会う *to meet Mr. Tanaka*) 1	CH 12
あお	**n.**	青 *blue color* 1	CH 8
あか	**n.**	赤 *red color* 1	CH 8
あかるい	**adj.**	明るい・明るくない *bright, cheerful*	CH 9
あき	**n.**	秋 *autumn, fall*	CH 12
あく	**vi.**	***k*-u** 開く・開かない・開き・開いて *to open* (ドアが開く *The door opens.*) (*cf.* 開ける *vt. to open*)	CH 14
あさ	**n.**	朝 *morning* 7	CH 6
あさごはん	**n.**	朝御飯 *breakfast*	CH 6
あさって	**n.**	明後日 *the day after tomorrow*	CH 8
あし	**n.**	足 *foot, leg*	CH 1
あした	**n.**	明日 *tomorrow* 5	CH 5
あそこ	**pron.**	*over there* 10	CH 5
あそびにいく		遊びに行く *to visit somewhere or someone for fun*	CH 11
あそびにくる		遊びに来る *to be visited by someone*	CH 11
あそぶ	**vi.**	***b*-u** 遊ぶ・遊ばない・遊び・遊んで *to enjoy oneself, to play* (子供が公園で遊んでいる *Children are playing in the park.*) 6	CH 14
あたま	**n.**	頭 *head*	CH 11
あたらしい	**adj.**	新しい・新しくない *new*	CH 9
あつめる	**vt.**	***e*-u** 集める・集めない・集め・集めて *vt. to collect* (*cf.* 集まる *vi.*)	CH 10
あなた	**pron.**	貴方 *you (2nd person pronoun)* 2	CH 2
あに・おにいさん	**n.**	兄・お兄さん *older brother* 1	CH 3
あね・おねえさん	**n.**	姉・お姉さん *older sister* 1	CH 3
あの〜		*that ~over there* 11	CH 2
アパート	**n.**	*apartment*	CH 6
あまり (〜ない)	**adv.**	*(not) often, (not) much* 14 15	CH 5
アメリカ	**n.**	*the United States of America*	CH 2
あらう	**vt.**	***w*-u** 洗う・洗わない・洗い・洗って *to wash*	CH 13
ある	**vi.**	***r*-u** ある・ない*・あり・あって *to exist* 1	CH 7
あるいて		歩いて *on foot, by walking*	CH 6
あるく	**vi.**	***k*-u** 歩く・歩かない・歩き・歩いて *to walk*	CH 6
アルバイト	**n.**	*part-time job (the German word, Arbeit)*	CH 8
あれ	**pron.**	*that one (over there)* 11	CH 2

い

いい	**adj.**	*irr.* いい・よくない *fine, good*	CH 4
いいえ		*no, wrong* 3	CH 2
いう	**vt.**	***w*-u** 言う・言わない・言い・言って *to say* (こたえを言う *to say the answer*)	CH 10
いえ	**n.**	家 *house*	CH 9
いく	**vi.**	***k*-u** 行く・行かない・行き・行って *to go* (東京に行く *to go to Tokyo*) 6	CH 5
いくら	**q.**	*how much* 4	CH 4
いざかや	**n.**	居酒屋 *izakaya bar (casual Japanese-style bar)* E	CH 5
いしゃ・おいしゃさん	**n.**	医者・お医者さん *medical doctor*	CH 11
いじわる(な)	**adj.**	意地悪だ・意地悪じゃない *mean, nasty*	CH 12
いす	**n.**	椅子 *chair*	CH 2
いそがしい	**adj.**	忙しい・忙しくない *busy*	CH 13
いたい	**adj.**	痛い・痛くない *painful* (あたまが痛い *to have a headache*)	CH 13

いち	**n.**	一 *one*	CH 1
いちばん	**adv.**	一番 *the most, the best*	CH 11
い⌉つ	**q.**	*when* [6]	CH 12
いっしょに	**adv.**	一緒に *together*	CH 1
いってください		言って下さい *Please say (it).*	CH 1
いつも	**adv.**	*always, all the time* [1]	CH 6
いとこ	**n.**	従兄弟 *cousin*	CH 8
いぬ	**n.**	犬 *dog*	CH 2
いま	**n.**	今 *now*	CH 4
いもうと・いもうとさん	**n.**	妹・妹さん *younger sister* [1]	CH 3
いらっしゃる	**vi.**	*r-***u** いらっしゃる・いらっしゃらない・いらっしゃい*・いらっしゃって *to exist (honorific)* [1]	CH 7
いる	**vi.**	*i-***ru** いる・いない・い・いて *to exist* [1]	CH 7
いろ	**n.**	色 *color*	CH 8

う

うえ	**n.**	上 *top part, above* [3]	CH 7
うしろ	**n.**	後 *behind* [3]	CH 7
うそ	**n.**	嘘 *lie, untruth* (うそをつく *to tell a lie)*	CH 12
うた	**n.**	歌 *song*	CH 11
うたう	**vt.**	*w-***u** 歌う・歌わない・歌い・歌って *to sing*	CH 5
うち	**n.**	家 *house, home*	CH 5
うなぎ	**n.**	鰻 *eel* Ⓒ	CH 1
うみ	**n.**	海 *sea, ocean*	CH 5
うるさい	**adj.**	うるさい・うるさくない *noisy*	CH 8
うんてんする	**vt.**	*irr.* 運転する *to drive* (車を運転する *to drive a car)*	CH 11

え

えいが	**n.**	映画 *movie, film*	CH 6
えいがかん	**n.**	映画館 *movie theater*	CH 5
えいご	**n.**	英語 *English language*	CH 2
えいわじてん	**n.**	英和辞典 *English-Japanese dictionary*	CH 2
えき	**n.**	駅 *railway station*	CH 7
〜えん	**c.**	〜円 *~yen (¥)* Ⓓ	CH 4
えんぴつ	**n.**	鉛筆 *pencil*	CH 2

お

おいしい	**adj.**	美味しい・美味しくない *delicious, tasty*	CH 11
おおい	**adj.**	多い・多くない *many, a lot* [1]	CH 11
おおきい	**adj.**	*irr.* 大きい・大きくない *big* (大きな *variation)*	CH 9
おおさか	**pn.**	大阪 *Osaka (name of a place)*	CH 1
おかあさん	**n.**	お母さん *mother*	CH 1
おかね	**n.**	お金 *money*	CH 11
おきる	**vi.**	*i-***ru** 起きる・起きない・起き・起きて *to wake up*	CH 12
おくれる	**vi.**	*e-***ru** 遅れる・遅れない・遅れ・遅れて *to be late* (クラスに遅れる *to be late for class)*	CH 13
おこる	**vi.**	*r-***u** 怒る・怒らない・怒り・怒って *to get angry*	CH 14
おしえる	**vt.**	*e-***ru** 教える・教えない・教え・教えて *to teach* (子供に日本語を教える *to teach children Japanese)*	CH 11
おじゃまします		お邪魔します *I'll come in (lit. I am going to disturb you)* [7]	CH 9
おそい	**adj.**	遅い・遅くない *late, slow*	CH 12
おちゃ	**n.**	お茶 *(Japanese) tea*	CH 14
おと	**n.**	音 *sound, volume*	CH 10
おとうさん	**n.**	お父さん *father*	CH 1
おとうと・おとうとさん	**n.**	弟・弟さん *younger brother* [1]	CH 3
おとこのひと	**n.**	男の人 *man* [5]	CH 3
おとす	**vt.**	*s-***u** 落とす・落とさない・落とし・落として *to let something fall, to lose*	CH 12
おどる	**vi.**	*r-***u** 踊る・踊らない・踊り・踊って *to dance*	CH 11
おなかがすいている		*hungry*	CH 14
おにいさん	**n.**	お兄さん *older brother*	CH 1
おねえさん	**n.**	お姉さん *older sister*	CH 1
おねがいする	**vt.**	*irr.* お願いする *to ask a favor of someone*	CH 10
おみやげ	**n.**	お土産 *souvenir*	CH 11
おもしろい	**adj.**	面白い・面白くない *funny, interesting, amusing*	CH 8
およぐ	**vi.**	*g-***u** 泳ぐ・泳がない・泳ぎ・泳いで *to swim*	CH 6
おりがみ	**n.**	折り紙 *origami*	CH 1
おりる	**vi. / vt.**	*i-***ru** 降りる・降りない・降り・降りて *to get off, to come down* (バスをおりる *to get off a bus)*	CH 14

おんがく	n.	音楽 *music*	CH 11
おんなのひと	n.	女の人 *woman* [5]	CH 3

か

〜か	prt.	*or* (A か B *A or B*) [4]	CH 11
〜か	prt.	*sentence-final question particle* [7]	CH 2
〜が	con.	*but* [7]	CH 11
〜が	prt.	*subject marker* [11]	CH 6
カメラ	n.	*camera*	CH 4
〜かい	c.	〜階 *~th floor*	CH 7
がいこく	n.	外国 *foreign country*	CH 12
がいこくご	n.	外国語 *foreign language*	CH 9
かいしゃ	n.	会社 *company*	CH 11
かいしゃいん・かいしゃいんさん	n.	会社員・会社員さん *company employee*	CH 11
かいもの	n.	買(い)物 *shopping* (買い物をする *to shop / to go shopping*)	CH 13
かいわ	n.	会話 *conversation*	CH 9
かう	vt.	***w-u*** 買う・買わない・買い・買って *to buy* (くつを買う *to buy shoes*)	CH 6
かえる	vi.	***r-u*** 帰る・帰らない・帰り・帰って *to return to one's home, country or base* [6]	CH 5
かお	n.	顔 *face*	CH 13
かがく	n.	化学 *chemistry*	CH 14
かかる	vi.	***r-u*** かかる・かからない・かかり・かかって *to cost, to take*	CH 6
かぎ	n.	鍵 *key*	CH 3
かく	vt.	***k-u*** 書く・書かない・書き・書いて *to write* (手紙を書く *to write a letter*)	CH 6
がくせい	n.	学生 *student*	CH 1
がくちょう・がくちょうさん	n.	学長・学長さん *school president*	CH 14
かける	vi.	***e-ru*** 掛ける・掛けない・掛け・掛けて *to wear (eyeglasses), to hang* [12]	CH 14
かさ	n.	傘 *umbrella*	CH 3
かす	vt.	***s-u*** 貸す・貸さない・貸し・貸して *to loan, to lend* (弟に本をかした *(I) loaned a book to my brother.*)	CH 10
かぜをひく		風邪を引く *to catch a cold*	CH 13
かぞく	n.	家族 *family members*	CH 12
〜かた	n.	〜方 *person (polite) (cf.* 人*)*	CH 2
〜がつ	c.	〜月 *months of the year* (一月 *January*)	CH 4
〜がつうまれ		〜月生まれ *a person born in the month of~*	CH 4
がっき	n.	学期 *academic term*	CH 12
かっこいい	adj.	かっこいい・かっこよくない *good looking (mainly for young men and boys)*	CH 14
がっこう	n.	学校 *school*	CH 1
かど	n.	角 *corner*	CH 10
かのじょ	pron.	彼女 *her, she*	CH 11
かばん	n.	鞄 *bag*	CH 2
カフェテリア	n.	*cafeteria*	CH 2
かぶる	vt.	***r-u*** かぶる・かぶらない・かぶり・かぶって *to wear (items such as hats and caps)* [12]	CH 14
かみ	n.	髪 *hair of the head*	CH 11
かようび	n.	火曜日 *Tuesday* [6]	CH 7
〜から	prt.	*from~*	CH 2
カラオケ	n.	*karaoke* Ⓓ	CH 5
からて	n.	空手 *karate* Ⓐ	CH 1
かりる	vt.	***i-ru*** 借りる・借りない・借り・借りて *to borrow* (弟にかばんをかりた *(I) borrowed a bag from my brother.*)	CH 11
かれ	pron.	彼 *he, him*	CH 11
かわいい	adj.	可愛い・可愛くない *cute*	CH 3
かんこく	n.	韓国 *Korea*	CH 2
かんごし・かんごしさん	n.	看護士・看護士さん *nurse*	CH 14
かんたん(な)	adj.	簡単だ・簡単じゃない *easy*	CH 2
がんばる	vt.	***r-u*** 頑張る・頑張らない・頑張り・頑張って *to try one's best*	CH 13

き

き	n.	木 *tree*	CH 7
ききとり	n.	聞き取り *listening comprehension*	CH 9
きく	vt.	***k-u*** 聞く・聞かない・聞き・聞いて *to listen, to inquire, to ask* (おんがくをきく *to listen to the music*) (先生にきく *to ask the teacher*)	CH 10
きた	n.	北 *north* [3]	CH 7
きたない	adj.	汚い・汚くない *dirty*	CH 9

きって	n.	切手 *stamp*	CH 8
きのう	n.	昨日 *yesterday*	CH 6
きびしい	adj.	厳しい・厳しくない *strict*	CH 10
きもの	n.	着物 *kimono*	CH 1
きゃく	n.	客 *customer, guest*	CH 4
きゅう/く	n.	九 *nine*	CH 1
きゅうりょう	n.	給料 *salary, wages, pay*	CH 13
きょう	n.	今日 *today* [5]	CH 5
きょうし・せんせい	n.	教師・先生 *teacher*	CH 11
きょうだい・ごきょうだい	n.	兄弟・御兄弟 *siblings*	CH 8
きょうと	pn.	京都 *Kyoto (name of a place)*	CH 1
きょねん	n.	去年 *last year*	CH 12
きらい(な)	adj.	嫌いだ・嫌いじゃない *hating (to hate~)*	CH 11
きる	vt.	***i-ru*** 着る・着ない・着・着て *to wear, to put on (one's clothes)*	CH 13
きれい(な)	adj.	綺麗だ・綺麗じゃない *pretty, beautiful* [2]	CH 3
ぎんこう	n.	銀行 *bank*	CH 5
きんようび	n.	金曜日 *Friday* [6]	CH 7

く

くすり	n.	薬 *medicine* (薬をのむ *to take medicine)*	CH 13
(〜て)ください		〜て下さい *please do~* [4]	CH 10
くださ˥い		下さい *give me~* (〜を下さい *give me~)* [6]	CH 4
くち	n.	口 *mouth*	CH 1
くつ	n.	靴 *shoes*	CH 2
くつした	n.	靴下 *socks*	CH 14
くに	n.	国 *country, home country*	CH 11
くらい	adj.	暗い・暗くない *dark, gloomy*	CH 9
〜ぐらい/〜くらい		*approximately* (10分ぐらいかかる *It takes about 10 minutes.)* [4]	CH 6
クラス	n.	*class*	CH 5
くる	vi.	*irr.* 来(く)る・来(こ)ない・来(き)・来(き)て *to come* [6]	CH 5
くるま	n.	車 *car*	CH 2
くろ	n.	黒 *black color* [1]	CH 8
〜くん		〜君 *a friendly respectful title for boys and young men or a formal respectful title for ones subordinates*	CH 14

け

けいえいする	vt.	*irr.* 経営する *to run (a business)* (レストランを経営する *to run a restaurant)*	CH 11
けいざいがく	n.	経済学 *economics*	CH 8
けいさつかん	n.	警察官 *police officer*	CH 14
けいたいでんわ	n.	携帯電話 *cellular phone*	CH 3
けさ	n.	今朝 *this morning*	CH 6
けしゴム	n.	消しゴム *eraser*	CH 8
けっこんする	vi.	*irr.* 結婚する *to get married* (田中さんと結婚する *to get married to Mr. Tanaka)*	CH 14
げつようび	n.	月曜日 *Monday* [6]	CH 7
けんか	n.	喧嘩 *fight, quarrel* (弟とけんかをする *to have a fight with one's younger brother)*	CH 12
げんごがく	n.	言語学 *linguistics*	CH 13
けんどう	n.	剣道 *kendo (Japanese fencing)* Ⓐ	CH 1

こ

ご	n.	五 *five*	CH 1
〜ご		〜語 *~language* (日本語 *Japanese language)*	CH 2
こうえん	n.	公園 *park*	CH 5
こうこう	n.	高校 *high school*	CH 3
こうさてん	n.	交差点 *intersection*	CH 7
こうじょう	n.	工場 *factory*	CH 14
こうちょう・こうちょうせんせ˥い	n.	校長・校長先生 *school principal*	CH 14
ここ	pron.	*here* [10]	CH 5
ごご	n.	午後 *p.m., afternoon* [3]	CH 4
ごぜん	n.	午前 *a.m.* [3]	CH 4
ごぜんちゅう	n.	午前中 *after dawn before noon (morning) (c.f.* ごぜん *a.m.)*	CH 8
こちら	pron.	*this way, this side, this person* [1]	CH 2
ことし	n.	今年 *this year*	CH 12
こども・こどもさん/おこさん	n.	子供・子供さん/お子さん *child* [1]	CH 3
この〜		*this~* [11]	CH 2
このあいだ		この間 *the other day*	CH 12
ごはん	n.	ご飯 *cooked rice, meal* Ⓑ	CH 6
こむ	vi.	***m-u*** 混む・混まない・混み・混んで *to become crowded*	CH 14
これ	pron.	*this one* [11]	CH 2

～ごろ		～頃 *approximately* (6時ごろ *about 6 o'clock*) [7]	CH 12
こんど	**n.**	今度 *next time, this time* [5]	CH 11
こんばん	**n.**	今晩 *this evening, tonight*	CH 5

さ

～さい	**c.**	～才・～歳 *a counter for age, ~years old*	CH 4
さいふ	**n.**	財布 *wallet*	CH 3
さくぶん	**n.**	作文 *composition*	CH 9
さくら	**n.**	桜 *cherry tree, cherry blossom*	CH 7
さけ・おさけ	**n.**	酒・お酒 *rice wine, alcoholic beverage in general*	CH 11
さしみ	**n.**	刺身 *sliced raw fish* Ⓒ	CH 1
～さつ	**c.**	～冊 *a counter for bound objects such as books and magazines*	CH 8
ざっし	**n.**	雑誌 *magazine*	CH 6
さびしい	**adj.**	寂しい・寂しくない *lonely*	CH 8
さん	**n.**	三 *three*	CH 1

し

～じ	**c.**	～時 *~o'clock*	CH 4
じかん	**n.**	時間 *time*	CH 11
～じかん	**c.**	～時間 *~hours* [3]	CH 6
しけん	**n.**	試験 *exam, test* (試験をうける *to take an exam*)	CH 8
しごと	**n.**	仕事 *job* (仕事をする *to work*)	CH 8
じしょ	**n.**	辞書 *dictionary*	CH 7
しずか(な)	**adj.**	静かだ・静かじゃない *quiet*	CH 9
した	**n.**	下 *bottom part, below, under* [3]	CH 7
じつは	**adv.**	実は *as a matter of fact*	CH 11
しつもん	**n.**	質問 *question*	CH 1
しつれいします		失礼します *I'll come in / I'll leave (Lit. I will be rude.)* [3]	CH 10
じてんしゃ	**n.**	自転車 *bicycle*	CH 6
じゃあ	**interj.**	*then* [12]	CH 2
～じゃありません／～ではありません	**cop.**	*not to be (polite / neutral present negative form of ～だ)* [6]	CH 2
しゃかいがく	**n.**	社会学 *sociology*	CH 8
しゃしん	**n.**	写真 *photograph*	CH 7
しゃちょう・しゃちょうさん	**n.**	社長・社長さん *company president*	CH 11
しゃべる	**vi.**	***r-u*** しゃべる・しゃべらない・しゃべり・しゃべって *to chat*	CH 14
シャワーをあびる		シャワーを浴びる *to take a shower*	CH 13
じゅう	**n.**	十 *ten*	CH 1
しゅうしょく	**n.**	就職 *employment*	CH 13
じゅうどう	**n.**	柔道 *judo (Japanese wrestling)* Ⓐ	CH 1
しゅうまつ	**n.**	週末 *weekend*	CH 5
しゅくだい	**n.**	宿題 *homework*	CH 1
しょうがっこう	**n.**	小学校 *elementary school* Ⓐ	CH 14
じょうず(な)	**adj.**	上手だ・上手じゃない *skillful (to be good at~)* [6]	CH 11
じょうだん	**n.**	冗談 *joke*	CH 12
しょうらい	**n.**	将来 *future*	CH 11
しょくぎょう・ごしょくぎょう	**n.**	職業・御職業 *occupation*	CH 14
しる	**vt.**	***r-u*** 知る・知らない・知り・知って *to get to know* [9]	CH 14
～じん		～人 *~person (nationality)* (日本人 *Japanese person*) [4]	CH 2
しんせつ(な)	**adj.**	親切だ・親切じゃない *kind, thoughtful*	CH 12
しんぶん	**n.**	新聞 *newspaper*	CH 6

す

すいようび	**n.**	水曜日 *Wednesday* [6]	CH 7
すう	**vt.**	***w-u*** 吸う・吸わない・吸い・吸って *to inhale* (タバコをすう *to smoke*)	CH 14
すうがく	**n.**	数学 *mathematics*	CH 2
すき(な)	**adj.**	好きだ・好きじゃない *to be fond of~ (to like~)*	CH 11
すきやき	**n.**	すき焼き *sukiyaki* Ⓒ	CH 1
すぎる	**vt.**	***i-ru*** 過ぎる・過ぎない・過ぎ・過ぎて *to pass*	CH 10
すく	**vi.**	***k-u*** すく・すかない・すき・すいて *to become less crowded* (おなかがすく *to become hungry*)	CH 14
すくない	**adj.**	少ない・少なくない *scarce, little, few* [1]	CH 11
すこし	**adv.**	少し *a little, a few, slightly* [5]	CH 8
すし	**n.**	鮨・寿司 *sushi* Ⓒ	CH 1
スプーン	**n.**	*spoon*	CH 6
ズボン	**n.**	*pants, trousers*	CH 14
すむ	**vi.**	***m-u*** 住む・住まない・住み・住んで *to live (somewhere)* (日本に住む *to live in Japan*) [10]	CH 14

する	vt.	*irr.* する・しない・し・して *to do* 14	CH 6
すわる	vi.	*r-u* 座る・座らない・座り・座って *to sit* (いすにすわる *sit on the chair*)	CH 10

せ

ぜんぶで		全部で *all together*	CH 4
せ / せい	n.	背 *height of people and animals*	CH 11
せまい	adj.	狭い・狭くない *non-spacious, narrow* (狭いへや *a small room*)	CH 9
～せん / ぜん	n.	～千 *one thousand*	CH 4
せんこう	n.	専攻 *academic major*	CH 2
せんせい	n.	先生 *teacher*	CH 1
ぜんぜん (～ない)	adv.	*(not) at all* 14 15	CH 5
せんたく	n.	洗濯 *laundry* (洗濯をする *to do the laundry*)	CH 13
せんもん	n.	専門 *specialty (cf.* 専攻*)*	CH 2
せんもんがっこう	n.	専門学校 *special (vocational) school*	CH 14

そ

そうじ	n.	掃除 *cleaning* (掃除をする *to do cleaning*)	CH 13
そうすると		*if (you do) so, in that case* 11	CH 10
そうですか		*Oh, I see. / Really?* A	CH 2
そこ	pron.	*there (near you)* 10	CH 5
その～		*that~ (near you)* 11	CH 2
そば	n.	*vicinity (cf.* ちかく*)* 3	CH 7
そふ・おじいさん	n.	祖父・おじいさん *grandfather*	CH 8
そぼ・おばあさん	n.	祖母・おばあさん *grandmother*	CH 8
それ	pron.	*that one (near you)* 11	CH 2
それか	con.	*or (cf.* それとも*)* 15	CH 11
それから	con.	*and then, in addition* 2	CH 6
それで	con.	*as a result* 5	CH 13
それに	con.	*furthermore, moreover* 6	CH 9

た

～たい	aux.	～たい・～たくない *to want to do something* (食べたい *to want to eat*) 13	CH 11
～だい	c.	～台 *a counter for mechanical objects*	CH 8
たいいくかん	n.	体育館 *gym*	CH 2
だいがく	n.	大学 *university*	CH 3
だいがくいん	n.	大学院 *graduate school*	CH 3
だいすき(な)	adj.	大好きだ・大好きじゃない *to be extremely fond of~*	CH 11
たいてい	adv.	*usually, in general* 1	CH 6
たいへん(な)	adj.	大変だ・大変じゃない *a lot of trouble, difficult task*	CH 6
たかい	adj.	高い・高くない *expensive, tall, high*	CH 4
たくさん	adv.	沢山 *a lot*	CH 8
だす	vt.	*s-u* 出す・出さない・出し・出して *to hand in, to take out* (しゅくだいを出す *to hand in one's homework*)	CH 10
たつ	vi.	*t-u* 立つ・立たない・立ち・立って *to stand up*	CH 10
たてもの	n.	建物 *building*	CH 2
たと˥えば		例えば *for example*	CH 12
たのしい	adj.	楽しい・楽しくない *fun, entertaining, amusing*	CH 9
タバコ	n.	煙草・タバコ *tobacco, cigarette* (タバコをすう *to smoke*)	CH 14
たべもの	n.	食べ物 *food*	CH 11
たべる	vt.	*e-ru* 食べる・食べない・食べ・食べて *to eat*	CH 6
だれ	q.	誰 *who* 14	CH 2
たんご	n.	単語 *word, vocabulary*	CH 9
たんじょうび	n.	誕生日 *birthday*	CH 12
たんす	n.	箪笥 *clothes chest*	CH 7

ち

ちいさい	adj.	*irr.* 小さい・小さくない *small* (小さな *variation*)	CH 9
ちか	n.	地下 *basement*	CH 7
ちかい	adj.	近い・近くない *near (c.f.* 近く *vicinity)*	CH 9
ちがう	vi.	*w-u* 違う・違わない・違い・違って *to be wrong, to be different* 13	CH 14
ちかく	n.	近く *vicinity* 3	CH 7
ちかてつ	n.	地下鉄 *subway*	CH 6
ちち・おとうさん	n.	父・お父さん *father* 1	CH 3
ちゅうがっこう	n.	中学校 *junior high school* A	CH 14

ちゅうごく	**n.**	中国 *China*	CH 2
ちゅうしゃじょう	**n.**	駐車場 *parking lot, parking garage*	CH 7
ちょっと	**adv.**	*slightly, a little* 9	CH 2

つ

〜つ	**c.**	*a native counter for a variety of objects*	CH 8
つかう	**vt.**	*w*-**u** 使う・使わない・使い・使って *to use* (ペンを使う *to use a pen*)	CH 6
つかれる	**vi.**	*e*-**ru** 疲れる・疲れない・疲れ・疲れて *to get tired*	CH 13
つきあたり	**n.**	突き当たり *dead-end*	CH 10
つくえ	**n.**	机 *desk*	CH 2
つくる	**vt.**	*r*-**u** 作る・作らない・作り・作って *to make* (すしを作る *to make sushi*)	CH 6
つまらない	**adj.**	詰まらない・詰まらなくない *boring, uninteresting, unexciting*	CH 12
〜つもりです		*I plan to do~* 12	CH 6

て

て	**n.**	手 *hand, arm*	CH 1
〜で	**prt.**	*by~, in~, at~, with~* 5	CH 6
テレビ	**n.**	*television*	CH 4
ていしょく	**n.**	定食 *set menu*	CH 6
デート	**n.**	*date*	CH 8
てがみ	**n.**	手紙 *letter*	CH 6
〜です	**cop.**	*to be (polite / neutral present affirmative form of* 〜だ*)* 6	CH 2
ですから	**con.**	*therefore, so* 4	CH 8
デパート	**n.**	*department store* Ⓐ	CH 5
でも	**con.**	*but, however* 16	CH 5
〜てん	**c.**	〜点 *~points*	CH 13
てんいん	**n.**	店員 *salesclerk*	CH 4
でんき	**n.**	電気 *electric light, electricity*	CH 7
でんしゃ	**n.**	電車 *(electric) train*	CH 6
てんぷら	**n.**	天麩羅 *tempura* Ⓒ	CH 1
でんわ	**n.**	電話 *telephone*	CH 4
でんわばんごう	**n.**	電話番号 *telephone number*	CH 4

と

〜ど	**c.**	〜度 *times* 13	CH 12
〜と	**prt.**	*and* (ラジオとカメラ *a radio and a camera)* 5	CH 4
〜という		*called~* 12	CH 10
どう	**q.**	*how* 5	CH 9
とうきょう	**pn.**	東京 *Tokyo (name of a place)*	CH 1
どうぶつ	**n.**	動物 *animal*	CH 2
どうぶつえん	**n.**	動物園 *zoo*	CH 5
とおい	**adj.**	遠い・遠くない *far*	CH 9
とおり	**n.**	通り *street*	CH 7
〜どおり		〜通り *~street* (三番どおり(さんばんどおり) *3rd street)*	CH 7
〜とか		*etc*	CH 12
ときどき	**adv.**	時々 *sometimes* 14	CH 5
とくい(な)	**adj.**	得意だ・得意じゃない *skillful* 6	CH 11
どくしょ	**n.**	読書 *reading*	CH 11
とけい	**n.**	時計 *watch, clock*	CH 2
どこ	**q.**	*where*	CH 5
ところ	**n.**	所 *place*	CH 11
としょかん	**n.**	図書館 *library*	CH 2
どちら	**q.**	*which way, which direction*	CH 2
とても	**adv.**	*very much* 9	CH 2
どなた	**q.**	*who (polite) (cf.* だれ*)* 14	CH 2
となり	**n.**	隣 *next door, next position* 3	CH 7
どの〜	**q.**	*which ~* 11	CH 2
ともだち	**n.**	友達 *friend*	CH 3
どようび	**n.**	土曜日 *Saturday* 6	CH 7
とりあい	**n.**	取り合い *fight over taking something*	CH 12
とる	**vt.**	*r*-**u** 取る・取らない・取り・取って *to take* (日本語をとる *to take a Japanese course)*	CH 13
〜ドル	**c.**	*~dollars ($)*	CH 4
どれ	**q.**	*which one* 11	CH 2
どれぐらい		*approximately how long / much / many*	CH 6
どんな	**q.**	*what kind of* 2	CH 9

な

なか	**n.**	中 *inside, middle* 3	CH 7
ながい	**adj.**	長い・長くない *long (length)*	CH 11
なく	**vi.**	*k*-**u** 泣く・泣かない・泣き・泣いて *to cry*	CH 14
なくす	**vt.**	*s*-**u** なくす・なくさない・なくし・なくして *to lose* (さいふをなくす *to lose one's purse)*	CH 10

なつ	n.	夏 *summer*	CH 12
なつやすみ	n.	夏休み *summer vacation*	CH 12
なな / しち	n.	七 *seven*	CH 1
なまえ・おなまえ	n.	名前・お名前 *name*	CH 1
なまける	vi.	*e-***ru** 怠ける・怠けない・怠け・怠けて *to be lazy*	CH 14
ならう	vt.	*w-***u** 習う・習わない・習い・習って *to learn* 7	CH 10
なりた	pn.	成田 *Narita (name of a place)*	CH 1
なる	vt.	*r-***u** なる・ならない・なり・なって *to become* (学生になる *to become a student)*	CH 11
なん / なに	q.	何 *what* 8	CH 2

に

に	n.	二 *two*	CH 1
～に	prt.	*to~* 8	CH 5
にがて(な)	adj.	苦手だ・苦手じゃない *unskillful* 6	CH 11
にぎやか(な)	adj.	にぎやかだ・にぎやかじゃない *bustling, cheerful, lively, crowded*	CH 11
にし	n.	西 *west* 3	CH 7
～にち	c.	～日 *~th date*	CH 12
にちようび	n.	日曜日 *Sunday* 6	CH 7
にほん	n.	日本 *Japan*	CH 1
にほんご	n.	日本語 *Japanese language*	CH 1
にほんじん	n.	日本人 *Japanese people*	CH 2
～にん / り	c.	～人 *a counter for people*	CH 8

ぬ

ね

～ね	prt.	*~, isn't it* (きれいですね *It's beautiful, isn't it?)* 3	CH 3
ねこ	n.	猫 *cat*	CH 2
ねだん	n.	値段 *price*	CH 10
ねぼうする	vi.	*irr.* 寝坊する *to oversleep*	CH 13
ねる	vi.	*e-***ru** 寝る・寝ない・寝・寝て *to go to bed, to sleep*	CH 6
～ねん	c.	～年 *~years, ~th year* Ⓐ	CH 12
～ねんせい	c.	～年生 *a counter for an academic year or grade* (一年生 *first grade, freshman)*	CH 4

の

～の	prt.	*~'s, of~* (私の兄 *my brother)* 4	CH 3
ノート	n.	*notebook*	CH 8
のむ	vt.	*m-***u** 飲む・飲まない・飲み・飲んで *to drink*	CH 6
のる	vi.	*r-***u** (乗る・乗らない・乗り・乗って *to ride, to take (a form of transportation)* (バスに乗る *to take / get on a bus* 3	CH 13

は

は	n.	歯 *tooth* (歯をみがく *to brush one's teeth)*	CH 13
～は	prt.	*as for~ (topic marker) Exceptional pronunciation (wa)* 5	CH 2
ハンサム(な)	adj.	ハンサムだ・ハンサムじゃない *handsome*	CH 3
はい		*yes, right* 3	CH 2
はいる	vi.	*r-***u** 入る・入らない・入り・入って *to enter* (へやに入る *to enter the room)*	CH 10
はく	vt.	*k-***u** はく・はかない・はき・はいて *to wear (items such as pants and shoes)* 12	CH 14
はし	n.	橋 *bridge*	CH 10
はし・おはし	n.	箸・お箸 *chopsticks*	CH 6
はじまる	vi.	*r-***u** 始まる・始まらない・始まり・始まって *to begin* (クラスが 始まる *The class begins.)*	CH 14
はずかしい	adj.	恥ずかしい・恥ずかしくない *embarrassing, shameful*	CH 12
はたらく	vi.	*k-***u** 働く・働かない・働き・働いて *to work* (レストランで働く *to work at a restaurant)* 14	CH 11
はち	n.	八 *eight*	CH 1
パチンコ	n.	*a Japanese pinball game* Ⓑ	CH 14
はつおん	n.	発音 *pronunciation*	CH 9
はな	n.	鼻 *nose*	CH 1
はなす	vt.	*s-***u** 話す・話さない・話し・話して *to tell, to talk* (ともだちと話す *to talk with one's friend)*	CH 10
はは・おかあさん	n.	母・お母さん *mother* 1	CH 3
はやい	adj.	早い・早くない *early* 6	CH 10
はやい	adj.	速い・速くない *fast, speed* 6	CH 10

はらじゅく	pn.	原宿 *Harajuku (name of a place)* A	CH 13
はる	n.	春 *spring*	CH 12
～はん	n.	～半 *half*	CH 4
ばん	n.	晩 *evening, nigh* 7	CH 6
ばんごはん	n.	晩御飯 *supper, dinner*	CH 6

ひ

ひがし	n.	東 *east* 3	CH 7
～ひき / びき / ぴき	c.	～匹 *a counter for animals*	CH 8
ひきだし	n.	引き出し *drawer*	CH 7
ひく	vt.	*k*-**u** 弾く・弾かない・弾き・弾いて *to play string instruments and keyboards* (ピアノをひく *to play the piano)* 14	CH 6
ひくい	adj.	低い・低くない *low, not tall*	CH 9
ひこうき	n.	飛行機 *airplane*	CH 6
ひだり	n.	左 *left* 3	CH 7
ひと	n.	人 *person (cf.* ～かた*)*	CH 2
ひとつ		一つ *one (piece)*	CH 6
ひとりっこ	n.	一人っ子 *only one child*	CH 8
ひま(な)	adj.	暇だ・暇じゃない *not busy, free*	CH 5
～ひゃく/びゃく/ぴゃく	n.	～百 *one hundred*	CH 4
びょういん	n.	病院 *hospital*	CH 5
ひる	n.	昼 *noon, daytime* 7	CH 6
ひるごはん	n.	昼御飯 *lunch*	CH 6
ひろい	adj.	広い・広くない *spacious, wide*	CH 9

ふ

プール	n.	*swimming pool*	CH 6
ふく	vt.	*k*-**u** 吹く・吹かない・吹き・吹いて *to blow, to play (wind instruments)* (トランペットを吹く *to play the trumpet)* 14	CH 6
ふくしゅう(を)する	vt. / vi.	*irr.* 復習(を)する *to review*	CH 10
ふたつ		二つ *two (pieces)*	CH 6
ぶつり	n.	物理 *physics*	CH 13
ふとん	n.	布団 *futon mattress* A	CH 8
ふべん(な)	adj.	不便だ・不便じゃない *inconvenient*	CH 9
ふゆ	n.	冬 *winter*	CH 12
ふるい	adj.	古い・古くない *old (for non-animate items)* 1	CH 9
ぶん	n.	文 *sentence*	CH 9
～ふん(かん) / ぷん(かん)	c.	～分(間) *~minutes (the duration of time)* 3	CH 6
～ふん / ぷん	c.	～分 *minutes*	CH 4
ぶんがく	n.	文学 *literature*	CH 2
ぶんぽう	n.	文法 *grammar*	CH 9

へ

～へ	prt.	*to, toward (pronunciation is "e")* 2	CH 12
へた(な)	adj.	下手だ・下手じゃない *unskillful (to be not good at~)* 6	CH 11
ベッド	n.	*bed*	CH 8
べつに	adv.	別に *(not) particularly*	CH 11
へや	n.	部屋 *room*	CH 7
へん(な)	adj.	変だ・変じゃない *strange, weird, unusual*	CH 14
べんきょう(を)する	vt. / vi.	*irr.* 勉強(を)する *to study* 8	CH 6
べんごし・べんごしさん	n.	弁護士・弁護士さん *lawyer*	CH 11
べんり(な)	adj.	便利だ・便利じゃない *convenient* (便利なじしょ *a convenient dictionary)*	CH 9

ほ

ぼうえき	n.	貿易 *trading* (貿易会社 *trading company)*	CH 11
ぼうし	n.	帽子 *cap, hat*	CH 2
ぼく	pron.	僕 *I, me (the first person pronoun for male)*	CH 8
ほしい	adj.	欲しい・欲しくない *to want (some items)* 12	CH 11
ほん	n.	本 *book*	CH 2
～ほん / ぼん / ぽん	c.	～本 *a counter for cylindrical objects*	CH 8
ほんばこ	n.	本箱 *bookcase*	CH 7
ほんや	n.	本屋 *bookstore* 9	CH 5

ま

まあまあ	adv.	*more or less* 9	CH 2
～まい	c.	～枚 *a counter for flat objects*	CH 8
まえ	n.	前 *the previous time, the front position*	CH 12

まえ	n.	前 *front, front position* 3	CH 7
まがる	vt.	*r-u* 曲がる・曲がらない・曲がり・曲がって *to make a turn*	CH 10
〜ました		*polite past affirmative suffix for verbs* 10	CH 6
まじめ(な)	adj.	真面目だ・真面目じゃない *studious, serious, honest*	CH 10
〜ます		*polite present affirmative suffix for verbs* 3	CH 5
まずい	adj.	まずい・まずくない *not delicious*	CH 11
〜ません		*polite present negative suffix for verb* 3	CH 5
〜ませんでした		*polite past negative suffix for verb verb* 10	CH 6
まだ	adv.	*(not~) yet* (まだ始まっていない *(It) has not begun yet.)*	CH 14
まっすぐ	adv.	*straight*	CH 10
〜まで	prt.	*up to, until* 5	CH 7
まど	n.	窓 *window*	CH 2
〜まん	n.	〜万 *ten thousand*	CH 4
まんが	n.	マンガ・漫画 *comic book*	CH 14

み

みがく	vt.	*k-u* 磨く・磨かない・磨き・磨いて *to polish*	CH 13
みぎ	n.	右 *right*	CH 7
みじかい	adj.	短い・短くない *short (length)*	CH 11
みせる	vt.	*e-ru* 見せる・見せない・見せ・見せて *to show*	CH 10
みそしる	n.	味噌汁 *miso soup*	CH 6
みち	n.	道 *street, road*	CH 10
みなみ	n.	南 *south* 3	CH 7
みみ	n.	耳 *ear*	CH 1
みる	vt.	*i-ru* 見る・見ない・見・見て *to watch, to look* (テレビを見る *to watch TV)*	CH 6

む

むずかしい	adj.	難しい・難しくない *difficult*	CH 2
むすこ・むすこさん	n.	息子・息子さん *son*	CH 14
むすめ・むすめさん / おじょ˥うさん	n.	娘・娘さん / お嬢さん *daughter*	CH 14

め

め	n.	目 *eye*	CH 1
〜め	c.	〜目 *a counter for ordinal numbers* (一つ目 *the first)* 13	CH 10
めがね	n.	眼鏡 *eyeglasses*	CH 14
めんせつ	n.	面接 *interview*	CH 8

も

〜も	prt.	*also* 13	CH 2
もう	adv.	*already* (もうだいじょうぶです *I am already fine)*	CH 13
もういちど		もう一度 *once more*	CH 1
もうすこし	adv.	もう少し *a little more*	CH 10
もくようび	n.	木曜日 *Thursday* 6	CH 7
もしもし		*Hello! (on the phone)*	CH 7
もちろん	adv.	勿論 *surely, certainly*	CH 11
もっていく		持って行く *to take (something) (there)* 2	CH 10
もってくる		持って来る *to bring (something) (here)* 2	CH 10
もの	n	物 *thing, item, object*	CH 11

や

〜や	prt.	*and so on, etc* 3	CH 11
やさしい	adj.	優しい・優しくない *kind, nice*	CH 10
やすい	adj.	安い・安くない *cheap, inexpensive*	CH 4
やすむ	vt. / vi.	*m-u* 休む・休まない・休み・休んで *to rest, to take a day off, to be absent from~*	CH 11
やちん	n.	家賃 *rent for houses and apartments*	CH 9
やま	n.	山 *mountain*	CH 5
やめる	vt.	*e-ru* 辞める・辞めない・辞め・辞めて *to quit, to resign*	CH 13

ゆ

ゆうがた	n.	夕方 *early evening, dusk*	CH 5
ゆうびんきょく	n.	郵便局 *post office*	CH 5
ゆうめい(な)	adj.	有名だ・有名じゃない *famous*	CH 12
ゆっくり	adv.	*slowly*	CH 1

よ

～よ	**prt.**	*sentence-final emphasis marker* [10]	CH 2
ようふく	**n.**	洋服 *clothes*	CH 6
よく	**adv.**	*often, well* [14]	CH 5
よこ	**n.**	横 *side* [3]	CH 7
よむ	**vt.**	*m*-**u** 読む・読まない・読み・読んで *to read* (本を読む *to read a book*)	CH 6
よる	**n.**	夜 *night*	CH 14
よろぶ	**vi.**	*b*-**u** 喜ぶ・喜ばない・喜び・喜んで *to become pleased* [1]	CH 14
よん / し	**n.**	四 *four*	CH 1

ら

ラジオ	**n.**	*radio*	CH 4
らいげつ	**n.**	来月 *next month*	CH 11
らいねん	**n.**	来年 *next year*	CH 12
らく(な)	**adj.**	楽だ・楽じゃない *easy (less labor intensive)*	CH 13

り

りっぱ(な)	**adj.**	立派だ・立派じゃない *splendid, elegant, gorgeous, great*	CH 9
りょう	**n.**	寮 *dormitory*	CH 2
りょうしん・ごりょうしん	**n.**	両親・御両親 *parents*	CH 8
りょうり	**n.**	料理 *cooking*	CH 11
りょこう	**n.**	旅行 *traveling*	CH 11

る
れ

れい / ゼロ	**n.**	零・ゼロ・0 *zero*	CH 4
れいぞうこ	**n.**	冷蔵庫 *refrigerator*	CH 8
れきし	**n.**	歴史 *history*	CH 13
レストラン	**n.**	*restaurant*	CH 5
れんしゅう(を)する	**vt. / vi.**	*irr.* 練習(を)する *to practice*	CH 10

ろ

ろく	**n.**	六 *six*	CH 1

わ

わえいじてん	**n.**	和英辞典 *Japanese-English dictionary*	CH 2
わかる	**vi.**	*r*-**u** 分かる・分からない・分かり・分かって *to know, to understand* [7]	CH 5
わたし	**pron.**	私 *I, me (1st person pronoun)* [2]	CH 2
わたる	**vt.**	*r*-**u** 渡る・渡らない・渡り・渡って *to cross, to cross over*	CH 10
わらう	**vi.**	*w*-**u** 笑う・笑わない・笑い・笑って *to laugh, to smile*	CH 14
わるい	**adj.**	悪い・悪くない *bad*	CH 12

を

～を	**prt.**	*direct object marker* [9]	CH 6

ん

～んです		*it is the case that~* [6]	CH 6

APPENDIX SEVEN

Note List

Grammar and Usage

Topic	Note	Chapter
Absolute time expressions	8	CH 12
Adjectives (高い, 高価な, etc)	3	CH 9
Adverbs derived from adjectives (〜く and 〜に)	8	CH 10
An overview of verb conjugation	1	CH 5
Basic Japanese sounds	1	CH 1
Counters	2	CH 4
Degree adverbs (とても, ぜんぜん, まあまあ, etc)	8	CH 9
Demonstrative pronouns for location	10	CH 5
Demonstratives (あれ, あの〜, etc)	11	CH 2
Gratitude (ありがとうございます, etc)	3	CH 1
Greetings (こんにちは, おはようございます, etc)	7	CH 1
Imitating words (ワンワン, ネバネバ, etc)	6	CH 8
Indefinite pronouns (なにか something, だれか someone, etc)	4	CH 12
Introduction (はじめまして, よろしく, etc)	5	CH 1
Negative adverbs (あまり, ぜんぜん, etc)	15	CH 5
Negative pronouns (なにも nothing, だれも no one, etc)	5	CH 12
Number phrases [Numeral + counter]	3	CH 8
Numbers	1	CH 4
Particle combination (〜には, 〜にも, etc)	17	CH 5
Parting (さようなら, etc)	8	CH 1
Personal pronouns (私, あなた, etc)	2	CH 2
Plain forms of verbs (食べる, 食べない, etc)	2	CH 5
Plain past affirmative forms of verbs (〜た)	14	CH 12
Polite prefix (お〜 and ご〜)	16	CH 1
Present tense	4	CH 5
Relative clauses	14	CH 14
Relative time (明日, 昨日, etc)	5	CH 5
Relative time expressions	9	CH 12
Respectful titles (〜さん, 〜くん, etc)	6	CH 1
Syllable structure in Japanese	7	CH 4
Te-forms [Listing predicates]	1	CH 13
Colors	1	CH 8
Daily time frame (あさ, ばん, etc)	7	CH 6
Family members (母, お母さん, etc)	1	CH 3
Frequency (よく, ときどき, etc)	14	CH 5
Genders (男の人, 女の人, etc)	5	CH 3
Occupation	5	CH 14
Proportional frequency (たいてい, いつも, etc)	1	CH 6
Relative location	3	CH 7
Skills (とくい(な), にがて(な), etc)	6	CH 11
Working (はたらく and つとめる)	14	CH 11
The te-form of verbs (〜て / で)	1	CH 10
The verbs that mean "to play"	14	CH 6
To live (すむ, せいかつする, いきる, etc)	10	CH 14
To wear (きる, はく, かぶる, する, つける, etc)	12	CH 14
Verbs for learning (ならう, まなぶ, べんきょうする, etc)	7	CH 10
Verbs for mental states (よろこぶ, etc)	1	CH 14
Verbs of existence (ある, いる and いらっしゃる)	1	CH 7
Verbs of going and coming (行く, 来る and 帰る)	6	CH 5
X という Y: Y called X [Introducing a new item with its proper name]	12	CH 10
〜かん [The duration of time]	3	CH 6
あう: To meet / to see	1	CH 12
あそぶ: To play	6	CH 14
あっ: Oops! / oh! [Shock]	11	CH 1
あのう: Ahhh, ... [Initiating talk]	13	CH 1
いいです: Good / no, thank you	10	CH 10
いくら: How much? [Question word for price]	4	CH 4
いつ: When? [Question word for time]	6	CH 12
いる: State	2	CH 14
うちの〜: Our〜 / my〜	7	CH 14
おおい, すくない: Numerous, scarce	1	CH 11
おげんきですか: How are you?	15	CH 1
おじゃまします [When entering someone else's residence]	7	CH 9
おねがいします: Please〜 [Favor]	10	CH 1
〜か [Sentence final question particle]	7	CH 2
〜か: Or [Disjunctive listing]	4	CH 11
〜から: From〜 [Starting point]	4	CH 7
〜が [Subject marker]	11	CH 6
〜が: But [Conflict / contrast]	7	CH 11
きれい(な): Beautiful, pretty, clean and neat	2	CH 3
〜くする, 〜にする: To make something〜 / to make oneself〜 [Change]	9	CH 10
〜ください: Please do〜 [Requesting]	9	CH 1
〜ぐらい: Approximately〜	4	CH 6
こちら: This person	1	CH 2
〜ことができる: Can do〜 [Potential]	11	CH 11
こんど: This time / next time	5	CH 11
ございます: To have, to be	7	CH 7
ごぜん, ごご: a.m., p.m.	3	CH 4
〜ごろ: Approximately	7	CH 12
しつれいします [Entering and leaving someone else's office]	3	CH 10
しる: To get to know	9	CH 14
じゃあ: Then, in that case [Transition]	12	CH 2
〜じん [Nationality / citizenship / ethnic background of people]	4	CH 2

Note	No.	Chapter
すこし: A few / a little / slightly [Quantity / amount / degree]	5	CH 8
すみません: Excuse me / I am sorry [Apology / attention catching]	12	CH 1
～する [Verb formative]	8	CH 6
そうすると: Then [Subsequent fact]	11	CH 10
それか: Or [Alternative idea]	15	CH 11
それから: And then / in addition [Multiple events]	2	CH 6
それで: As a result [Resulting fact]	5	CH 13
それに: Furthermore [Additional fact]	6	CH 9
～たい: To want to do～ [Desire for action]	13	CH 11
～たことがある: I have ～ed [Experience]	15	CH 12
だれ, どなた: Who [Question word for people]	14	CH 2
ちがう: Wrong / different	13	CH 14
ちょっと, まあまあ: Slightly, more or less	9	CH 2
ちょっと: It's a little... [Declination]	13	CH 5
ちょっと: A little bit [Expression softener]	14	CH 1
～つもりです: It is planned that～ [Plan]	12	CH 6
～ている: To be in the middle of doing～ [Progressive state]	3	CH 14
～ている: To do～ usually / always / often [Habitual state]	4	CH 14
～ている: To have done～ [Resulting state]	11	CH 14
～てください(ませんか): Please do～, could you do～ [Requesting]	4	CH 10
～で: Under the condition such as～ [Circumstantial condition]	3	CH 12
～で: Due to [Cause / reason]	11	CH 12
～で: By, with, in, at [How the action takes place]	5	CH 6
～でした, ～かったです [Past tense of noun and adjective predicates]	12	CH 12
～です(だ): To be [Copula]	6	CH 2
ですから: Therefore [Consequence]	4	CH 8
でも: But [Conflict / contrast]	16	CH 5
～と: And [Listing marker for nouns]	5	CH 4
～と: With～ [Accompaniment]	7	CH 8
～ど vs ～かい: ～times [The number of occasions]	13	CH 12
どう: How [Question word for a property (predicate)]	5	CH 9
どうしたんですか: What happened?	6	CH 13
どうぞ: Go ahead (and do～), please (do～) [Offering]	2	CH 1
どうも: Indeed [Gratitude / apology-intensifier]	4	CH 1
どんな: What kind of～ [Question word for a property (prenominal)]	2	CH 9
なに, なん: What [Question word for non-human items]	8	CH 2
～に: At, on, in [Absolute time of an event]	10	CH 12
～に: For [The target of pros and cons]	2	CH 13
～に: To～ [Target, destination]	8	CH 5
～に, ～ために [Purpose]	4	CH 13
～には... がある: There is an... in～, I have an... in～ [Existence]	2	CH 8
～ね: ～, Isn't it? [Sentence final confirmation marker]	3	CH 3
～の [Noun-maker]	8	CH 11
～の: One [Pronominal element]	4	CH 9
～の: ～'s [Modifier marker]	4	CH 3
のる: To ride, to take	3	CH 13
～は [Contrast]	9	CH 11
～は: As for～, speaking of～ [Topic marker]	5	CH 2
～は～が～です: As for ～, ～is ～	2	CH 11
～は... にある: ～is at / in... [The location of things and people]	2	CH 7
はい, いいえ: Yes / no [Agreement / disagreement]	3	CH 2
はやい: Early / fast	6	CH 10
～ばかり: To do nothing but～ [An extreme habit]	8	CH 14
ふるい: Old	1	CH 9
～へ: To / toward～ [Direction]	2	CH 12
ほしい: To want something [Desire for items]	12	CH 11
～ました, ～ませんでした [Polite suffixes in the past tense]	10	CH 6
～ましょう: Let's do～	12	CH 5
～ましょうか: Shall we～?, shall I～? [Making a suggestion / offering help]	5	CH 10
～ます, ～ません [Polite suffixes in the present tense]	3	CH 5
～ませんか: How about ～ing? [Suggesting]	11	CH 5
～まで: Up to～, until～ [Ending point]	5	CH 7
～め: ～th [Creating ordinal numbers]	13	CH 10
～も: Too, also [Addition]	13	CH 2
もっていく, もってくる: To take / to bring	2	CH 10
～や(屋): ～store / ～shop	9	CH 5
～や: And so on, etc [Example-listing]	3	CH 11
～よ: I tell you [Sentence final emphasis particle]	10	CH 2
～ようび [The days of the week]	6	CH 7
～(ら)れ: Can do～ [Potential]	10	CH 11
わかる: To understand / to know	7	CH 5
～を [Direct object marker]	9	CH 6
～を [Direct object marker: the domain of movement]	14	CH 10
～をください: Please give me～ [Purchasing]	6	CH 4
～んです: It is the case that～	6	CH 6
～んですか: Is it the case that～? [Confirming]	13	CH 6

Culture

Acknowledging and responding	A	CH 2
Asking others their age	B	CH 4
Bowing	B	CH 1
Describing family members	A	CH 3
Japanese currency	D	CH 4
Japanese food	C	CH 1
Japanese islands	E	CH 1
Japanese names	D	CH 1
Lucky and unlucky numbers	A	CH 4
Modesty	F	CH 1
National holidays	B	CH 12
New year holidays in Japan	B	CH 13
Polite high pitch	A	CH 7
Rejecting	C	CH 5
Repeating	B	CH 5
Rice	B	CH 6
Salesclerks and customers	C	CH 4
Schools in Japan	A	CH 14
Table manners	A	CH 6
Traditional martial arts	A	CH 1
いざかや: Izakaya bar	E	CH 5
カラオケ: Karaoke	D	CH 5
こうばん: Police boxes	A	CH 10
デパート: Department store	A	CH 5
〜ねん: The year〜 [Expressing years]	A	CH 12
はらじゅく	A	CH 13
パチンコ	B	CH 14
ふとん: Futon mattress	A	CH 8
ファーストフード・レストラン	C	CH 6
めいし: Name cards (Business cards)	E	CH 4

Writing

Hiragana	a	CH 1
Kanji components	a	CH 3
Kanji strokes	a	CH 2
New year's cards (ねんがじょう)	e	CH 13
Punctuation and format	b	CH 1
Reading kanji	b	CH 2
うかんむり	d	CH 4
おくりがな	a	CH 4
おのづくり	b	CH 7
おんなへん	c	CH 8
カタカナ	e	CH 4
きへん	a	CH 8
くさかんむり	c	CH 13
くにがまえ	a	CH 11
ごんべん	b	CH 9
さんずいへん	b	CH 13
しめすへん	b	CH 11
しょくへん	b	CH 6
しんにょう	a	CH 7
ちから	c	CH 3
なつあし	a	CH 12
なべぶた	c	CH 4
にんべん	c	CH 6
ひとあし	b	CH 3
ひとがしら	b	CH 4
ひへん	a	CH 5
ふゆがしら	b	CH 12
ふるとり	a	CH 13
ぼくづくり	b	CH 8
まだれ	a	CH 9
もんがまえ	a	CH 6
ゆみへん	d	CH 8
よつてん	d	CH 13